LAKOTA NOON

The Indian Narrative of Custer's Defeat

GREGORY F. MICHNO

Mountain Press Publishing Company
Missoula, Montana

Time-segment maps by Jennifer Hamelman

Cover art courtesy of the Southwest Museum, Los Angeles
Photo CT.1: Kicking Bear muslin

Library of Congress Cataloging in Publication Data

Michno, Gregory, 1948–
    Lakota noon : the Indian narrative of Custer's defeat / Gregory F. Michno.
        p.   cm.
    Includes bibliographical references and index.
    ISBN 0-87842-349-4 (alk. paper). — ISBN 0-87842-356-7 (alk. cloth)
    1. Little Bighorn, Battle of the, Mont., 1876—Personal narratives.
2. Cheyenne Indians—Wars, 1876—Personal narratives.   3. Dakota Indians—
Wars, 1876—Personal narratives.   I. Title.
E83.876.M5   1997
973.8'2—dc21   97-13581
                                                                                    CIP

PRINTED IN U.S.A.

Mountain Press Publishing Company
P.O. Box 2399 • Missoula, MT 59806
Phone 406-728-1900

CONTENTS

Figures

Time-segment Maps

ACKNOWLEDGMENTS

I would like to thank a number of people for helping me with the manuscript, first of all, those who read it and gave their comments and helpful suggestions: Tom Bookwalter, Bruce Trinque, Jim Schneider, and Don Horn. Thanks to Robert Utley, who gave me some suggestions, plus loaned me his computer disks of interviews he had painstakingly extracted from the Walter Campbell Collection. Thanks to Phyllis Davis and Elden Davis for the use of the microfilm reader to sift through countless Walter Camp notes. Thanks to the Montana Historical Society, the Nebraska State Historical Society, the State Historical Society of North Dakota, and the Little Bighorn Battlefield for providing many useful photographs. I appreciate the assistance of those folks at the University of Oklahoma, Western History Collections, for locating and copying many of Walter S. Campbell's notes; to those at the Denver Public Library, for Walter Camp's letters; to those at the Harold B. Lee Library at Brigham Young University, for the microfilm reels of Walter Camp's notes; and to the Braun Research Library of the Southwest Museum, Los Angeles, for the many photocopies from the George B. Grinnell Collection.

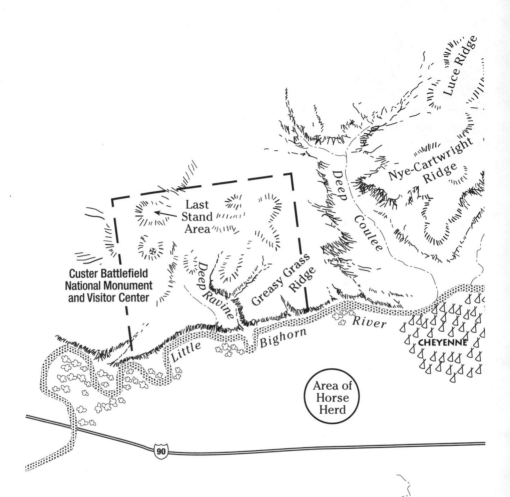

Luce Ridge

Nye-Cartwright Ridge

Deep Coulee

Last
Stand
Area

Greasy Grass Ridge

Deep Ravine

Custer Battlefield
National Monument
and Visitor Center

Little Bighorn River

CHEYENNE

Area of
Horse
Herd

90

Squaw Creek

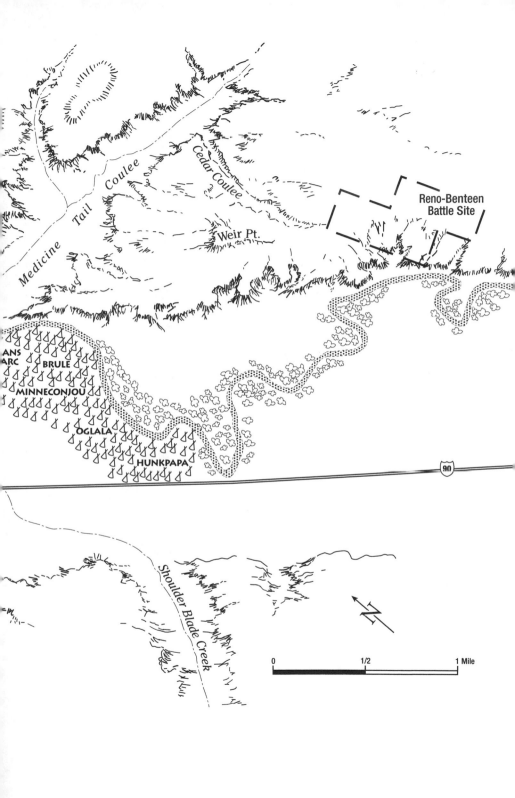

Reno-Benteen
Battle Site

Cedar Coulee

Medicine Tail Coulee

Weir Pt.

ANS
ARC   BRULE

MINNECONJOU

OGLALA

HUNKPAPA

90

Shoulder Blade Creek

N

0   1/2   1 Mile

CHEYENNE	OGLALA	MINNECONJOU
AH American Horse	BE Black Elk	B Beard
A Antelope	CH Crazy Horse	FE Feather Earring
BB Big Beaver	EE Eagle Elk	FB Flying By
BF Big Foot	FN Fears Nothing	H Hump
BH Bobtail Horse	FH Flying Hawk	IT Iron Thunder
BW Brave Wolf	FE Foolish Elk	L Lights
CB Cut Belly	HD He Dog	OB One Bull
I Ice	LB Lone Bear	RH Red Horse
LW Lame White Man	LD Low Dog	SB Standing Bear
LH Little Hawk	RF Red Feather	TR Turtle Rib
NW Noisy Walking	RH Red Hawk	WB White Bull
SW Soldier Wolf	SE Shave Elk	
TB Tall Bull	SB Short Bull	HUNKPAPA
TM Two Moon	WC White Cow Bull	BM Black Moon
WS White Shield		CK Crow King
WT Wolf Tooth	BRULÉ	G Gall
WL Wooden Leg	TE Two Eagles	IC Iron Cedar
YN Yellow Nose	HH Hollow Horn Bear	IH Iron Hawk
YT Young Two Moon		MR Moving Robe
	ARAPAHO	PW Pretty White Buffalo
TWO KETTLE	LH Left Hand	RF Rain In The Face
RE Runs The Enemy	W Waterman	SB Sitting Bull

Individual and Tribal Symbols Key.

PREFACE

With the possible exception of the Battle of Gettysburg, the Battle of the Little Bighorn may be the most written about fight in American history. Even though it has been covered so extensively, it still might be our most misinterpreted, misconstrued conflict. After the almost limitless verbiage expended on the matter, how can we justify another book on the subject? In plain fact, we still have not adequately explained what ought to be the first priority in writing the history of this battle: what happened?

The perceived problem with the Little Bighorn fight, of course, stems from the fact that there were no white survivors of Custer's battalion. Granted, hundreds of soldiers walked the field of death a few days after the fight, and many left records of their impressions of how the battle appeared to have been fought. But it was all secondary guesswork, ranging from the fairly accurate to the absurd. The white chroniclers cannot tell us what happened.

It seems simple enough, then, to turn to the only ones who witnessed the entire battle. The Indian accounts, however, have their own peculiar set of problems. Historian William A. Graham commented about them in his sourcebook of Custeriana, in an introductory chapter he titled "A Word to the Wise." The Indians, Graham said, were an alien race. They differed in point of view, in approach, in mental attitude, and in psychology, and just because one could speak their language did not necessarily mean one could understand the native who used it. Graham decided he could not use Indian accounts in his narratives because they "contradicted each other to such an extent that I found them irreconcilable."[1]

Regardless of the difficulties involved in using eyewitness Indian narratives, they are still of much greater value than secondary speculation. Therefore, if we are ever going to find out what happened in that battle, we must use both white and Indians sources; further, we must realize that the Indian sources are more important and should take precedence whenever any apparent conflict arises between the two.

While some authors would eliminate Indian accounts altogether, there have been a number of chroniclers who have attempted to tell the story from the Indian point of view, with varying degrees of success. Author Wayne Sarf has characterized some of them rather succinctly: Dee Brown's *Bury My Heart at Wounded Knee* (1970) was "mendacious" while David H. Miller's *Custer's Fall* (1957) was "absurd." As for a couple of books utilizing both points of view, Sarf thought Mari Sandoz's *Battle of the Little Bighorn* (1966) was "novelistic" and Evan Connell's *Son of the Morning Star* (1984) was "incoherent."[2] In keeping with Sarf's one-word review mode, we might add Robert Kammen's, Frederick Lefthand's, and Joe Marshall's *Soldiers Falling Into Camp* (1992) as amusing.

In short, previous attempts to utilize Indian sources to depict battle events have been less than auspicious. The biggest drawback to their success lies in chronologi-

---

1. William A. Graham, *The Custer Myth: A Source Book of Custeriana* (Harrisburg, PA: The Stackpole Company, 1953; reprint, Lincoln: University of Nebraska, 1986), 3.
2. Wayne Michael Sarf, *The Little Bighorn Campaign: March–September 1876* (Conshohocken, PA: Combined Books, 1993), 301.

cal considerations. The Indians gave us plenty of details; what we seem to have the most trouble with is their chronology. In one sentence, an Indian might describe how he caught a horse on Custer's field; in the next, he might tell how he shot at a retreating trooper during the valley fight, completely reversing the time sequence. Miller's book suffers because of the Indian tendency to forgo the white man's chronology. There is an amorphous quality to it, a feeling that events are placed too early or too late, or that they float in space as a series of anecdotes unsecured to either time or terrain. On the other hand, Kammen, Lefthand, and Marshall proved that lax scholarship is not the provenance of any race. The authors relied much on Indian oral tradition, and thus persisted in repeating traditional errors, such as depicting George Custer dying at the river and Rain In The Face slicing open Tom Custer. They also added some gems of their own, such as the anachronistic error that the Lakotas at the battle used the term "Medicine Tail Creek," and that Curly secretly warned the Lakotas of Custer's approach. In addition, their treatment of Custer and the 7th Cavalry was truly egregious.[3]

At the time of this writing, the latest book to make its appearance with the intention of telling the Indian side of the story is James Welch's *Killing Custer*. The author, a self-acknowledged fiction writer and poet, said the book "certainly will not provide any startling revelations from a historical and military standpoint." Then what is the point? It appears to be another fashionable denigration of nineteenth-century Americans, with particular venom for the frontier U.S. Army.

Welch states that "whites wrote the history" of the Indian conflicts, and it has been "carefully distorted throughout the years to justify the invasion and subjugation of the indigenous people."[4] As a remedy, Welch intends to tell his own version of the Indian side of the story. To accomplish this, we might expect him to rely almost exclusively on primary Indian sources, but such is not the case in *Killing Custer*. In the chapter dealing specifically with the Little Bighorn fight, a cursory review shows only about seven of the twenty-six sources he cites could be considered primary Indian narratives.[5] How can an author purport to tell the Indian side of the story by relying so heavily on secondary white source material, the very history he condemns as "carefully distorted" in the first place?

Lakota Noon does not tell the Indian side of the story—it lets the Indians tell it. There is a great difference. Indians recalling the battle in 1886 or 1926 were not concerned with political correctness or how they might conspire to lay a guilt trip on a future generation. They told us what happened. That is all we wish to know. *Lakota Noon* uses their words to tell what happened and leaves the sermons to novelists and ideologues.[6]

---

3. Robert Kammen, Joe Marshall, and Frederick Lefthand, *Soldiers Falling Into Camp: The Battles at the Rosebud and the Little Bighorn* (Encampment, WY: Affiliated Writers of America, 1992). From pages 25 to 36, where Custer and his regiment make their first appearance, this writer, with a limited knowledge of the topic, counts almost two dozen errors or misrepresentations.

4. James Welch with Paul Stekler, *Killing Custer: The Battle of the Little Bighorn and the Fate of the Plains Indians* (New York: W. W. Norton & Company, 1994), 17–22, 46–47.

5. Ibid., 303–7.

6. Patricia Nelson Limerick, *The Legacy of Conflict: The Unbroken Past of the American West* (New York: W. W. Norton & Company, 1987), 216, 232, 349. Limerick argues that there can be no monolithic "Indian side" to any story, just as there is no single white, black, Asian, or Hispanic side. Agreed.

Heretofore, I had assumed that seeking to find out what happened in our past was a noble endeavor. However, numerous students of the Little Bighorn battle have been treated by some professional historians as less than serious because their main interest *is* to seek out what happened. They have been pejoratively labeled "Custer buffs" and have been called bigots, buffoons, and worse. It seems their desire to know *what happened* lacks a higher purpose and apparently is not as socially redeeming as moralizing between right and wrong.[7] Regardless of the labels attached, and barbs hurled at the "buffs," the necessity of knowing what happened must precede any attempt at intelligent interpretation.

Admittedly there are problems with relying on Indian testimony and oral tradition to grasp the sequence of events at the Little Bighorn. Yet, if we could overcome the chronological inconsistencies inherent in the Indian accounts, we might be on our way to getting a fairly accurate rendition of the battle. The first steps toward accomplishing this are to determine the size and location of the village and to place its inhabitants at their various positions when the battle began. This work freezes the action six times per hour, framing different people's movements within a time-terrain and time-event structure. By trying to determine Indian activity at ten-minute intervals, we can more easily connect them to the physical landscape and separate the possible from the impossible.[8] Most of the Indian accounts begin making sense when we consider their very personal and specific nature. They tell us just what went on in their limited field of vision, which is exactly what we desire from eyewitnesses. From a number of specific accounts, we can reconstruct the general battle. The Indian accounts do interlock. They stitch together like Aunt Martha's old patchwork quilt. They are not irreconcilable when placed in a proper framework.

Question might be raised as to why I start the clock at 3 P.M. Certainly there is evidence that suggests the correct starting time might be nearer to 1 P.M. Yet, the exact time is not as important as the relative time. If we show that the entire sequence took three hours, it is not so important when the battle starts. I chose 3 P.M. to correspond with John Gray's exhaustive time-motion study of the soldier movements at the Little Bighorn, allowing for ready-made comparisons and reference points between my work and his.[9]

---

7. Ibid., 100, 298; Brian W. Dippie, *Custer's Last Stand: The Anatomy of an American Myth* (Lincoln: University of Nebraska Press, 1976), xi, xiii, from an introduction to the 1994 edition; Brian W. Dippie, "Of Bullets, Blunders, and Custer Buffs," *Montana The Magazine of Western History* 41, no. 1 (winter 1991): 77–80.

8. While constructing a stop-motion framework, I thought of physicist Werner Heisenberg's "uncertainty principle," in which he argued of the impossibility of ever pinpointing the exact location or velocity of subatomic particles. He argued that when testing for location we lose the ability to measure the speed, or, while testing for speed we will be unable to pinpoint location. The very act of measurement destroys our ability to predict either quantity with accuracy. Popular science writer Timothy Ferris suggests that the Heisenberg limitation does not depend on the inadequacies of any particular technology but is fundamental to every act of observation. I hope that plotting men across a battlefield proves less trying than delving into quantum physics. Those interested in further pursuing the "uncertainty" topic might read Richard Rhodes, *The Making of the Atomic Bomb* (New York: Simon & Schuster, 1986), 129–31; Peter Coveney and Roger Highfield, *The Arrow of Time* (New York: Ballantine Books, 1990), 125–26; Timothy Ferris, *The Mind's Sky: Human Intelligence in a Cosmic Context* (New York: Bantam Books, 1993), 204–5.

9. John S. Gray, *Custer's Last Campaign: Mitch Boyer and the Little Bighorn Reconstructed* (Lincoln: University of Nebraska Press, 1991).

The choice of ten-minute intervals developed from a trial and error process. It seemed a bit brash, if nigh impossible, to attempt, as Gray did, to pinpoint moves to the minute and second. This over-preciseness of his otherwise fine study presses the issue and appears too contrived. I wrote the initial draft of *Lakota Noon* in fifteen-minute segments, but that left too much latitude. Adjusting the intervals to ten minutes left room for six analyses per hour and kept close enough track of individual moves without the tight constraints of monitoring every minute. It also allows us to use circumstance and event to correlate times. Time-motion may say Indian X could have ridden from the village to the Little Bighorn River; but time-motion framed by time-event raises doubt about that possibility if Indian Y saw Indian X fighting at Medicine Tail Ford.

While running the battle in a stop-action mode with a short assessment after each segment may alleviate some chronology problems, we still face the question of how to present the Indian narratives. Do we treat their stories in a literary or historical sense? Historian Robert M. Utley commented on this dilemma. On the one hand we have Walter S. Campbell, writing under the pen name Stanley Vestal and presenting himself as a historian while telling us stories about Sitting Bull and White Bull in a literary fashion. Other scholars of the genre include Mari Sandoz, in her biography of Crazy Horse, and John G. Neihardt, in his books about Black Elk. Utley says such books are good literature but bad history.[10] On the other hand we have books of first-hand accounts: Kenneth Hammer's *Custer in '76* and Richard Hardorff's *Lakota Recollections* immediately come to mind. Although these books are tremendous source collections for scholars, all but hard-core students of the Little Bighorn would probably find them rather dry and tedious.

My hope, then, would be to blend these techniques, producing a work that is neither too literary and novelized nor overly repetitive and bland. Recapitulation is unavoidable, however, for the story must be repeated through the eyes of each observer who saw only minor variations of the same theme. The participants tell their own story. Their words as recorded by their interpreters appear in quotation marks, while the remainder is paraphrased from their accounts or inferred from corroborating narratives. The expressions are simple. The Indians spoke in unsophisticated terms or used sign language, and their interpreters and interviewers transcribed their accounts in a similarly economical fashion. The narratives likewise are couched in easy terms, which may appear uninspiring at times. You will encounter such phrases as "I got my pony," "the women fled," "the soldiers ran," "the Indians shot," or "we crossed the river" time and again. This is not for want of an adequate thesaurus. I have tried to remain as close to the actual wording as possible without reprinting the accounts verbatim and without cosmetically touching up so much that it becomes a work of historical fiction.

The individual Indian narratives can be read either vertically or horizontally. That is, you can read them in the conventional, page-by-page chronological manner, in which the participants tell what they did during a ten-minute segment, and

---

10. Robert M. Utley, *The Lance and the Shield: The Life and Times of Sitting Bull* (New York: Henry Holt & Company, 1993), xvi.

then move on to the next time period. Or, you may choose to follow the exploits of one particular character throughout the battle. As an example, the heading "5:50–6:00, **White Bull** [last 5:40, next 6:10]" means you are currently reading of White Bull's activities from 5:50 to 6:00; his narrative last appeared in the 5:40 time slot and will next appear at 6:10.

Some readers may find that my "discussion" following each ten-minute segment breaks up the flow of the battle. It does, but it also offers an opportunity to examine my rationale and interpretations. To me, the discussion segments are an integral part of the story, besides offering some fascinating insights into Little Bighorn historiography.

In the course of reading this book, it will become obvious that I did not concern myself with the causes of the battle, the marching done by the soldiers prior to the fight, the paths taken by the Indians to get to the valley of the Little Bighorn, or even the fate of Major Reno's and Captain Benteen's men after the Indians bypassed them to deal with Custer. Those stories are adequately told elsewhere. What drove my effort was an overwhelming, irresistible desire to find out *what happened*—explained primarily through the actions and movements of the Indians—on the field that day to cause the destruction of five companies of United States Cavalry. Thus, *Lakota Noon* dives right into the battle, and when the smoke clears and the hot barrels of the guns cool down, the story of the main action on the Little Bighorn is over.

Although this is chiefly an Indian story, an evaluation of Lt. Col. George A. Custer is unavoidable. Essentially harboring neutral feeling about the man, I find that many past accounts have been colored by their authors' particular prejudices about him as a person. Here we find that Custer is not at all the inept egomaniac that some have depicted; to the contrary, he proves to be a very competent field commander.

I did not set out to prove anything in this work. I am not concerned with assessing blame or debating the morality of war. As history professor William Savage Jr. so aptly stated: "I do believe I have heard quite enough from both sides [the New Left and the Old Right]. I do not care to be . . . subjected to the cacophony of their respective rantings. I have no interest in the commentaries of thoroughly politicized historians."[11]

In summary, I was not content with prior explanations about the Battle of the Little Bighorn, and this study developed as a consequence of constructing a framework to learn for myself, to my own satisfaction, what happened. It has been an educational experience that confirmed some of my preconceptions while exposing the need to alter others. I am at ease with the results—at least until the next new evidence appears.

The first chapter considers the size of the village, a necessary introduction that allows us to better understand subsequent events. The three central chapters cover

---

11. William W. Savage Jr., "A Manifesto," *Journal of the West* 33, no. 4 (October 1994): 3–4.

approximately three hours on the afternoon of June 25, 1876. The first hour deals with Reno's fight in the valley. The second hour takes us into the coulees and ridges above the Little Bighorn River where Reno is stymied and Custer is first confronted. The third hour follows the Custer fight to its denouement. Maps at the beginning of each ten-minute segment locate the action in these three areas— south, central, and north. The maps are coded A, B, or C, with their legends corresponding to the areas identified in figure 2. Individual Indians and their tribal affiliations are symbolized on the maps, allowing us to correlate the "where" and "when" of their paths with the "what" of their narratives. The key to these symbols (fig. 14) is located at the end of the book, following the index, for ready reference.

The process of using the Indians as a vehicle to uncover the mysteries of the Little Bighorn has made me more attached to them as individuals and as a people, sharing vicariously in their trials and tribulations. Thus, the final chapter traces out a few remaining lifelines of a handful of survivors who futilely gave so much that they and their families might live. In their struggle for survival, they unknowingly reached the apex of their existence as a people.

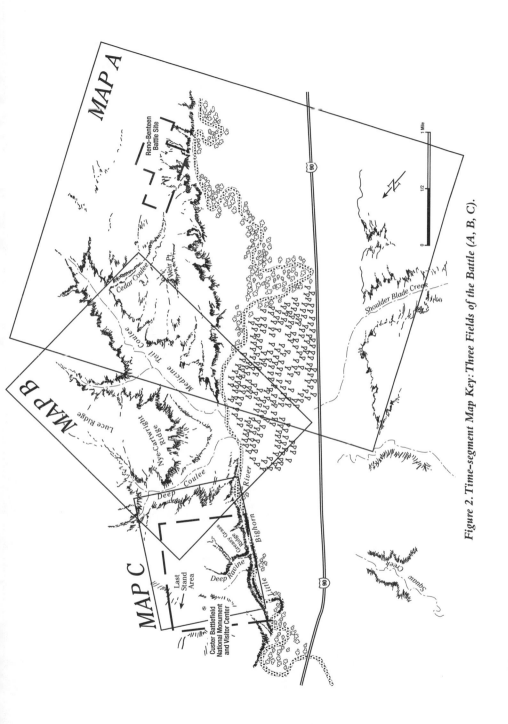

Figure 2. Time-segment Map Key: Three Fields of the Battle (A, B, C).

I

Village

JUNE 25. MORNING

The scene was reminiscent of a thousand similar mornings. The east-facing lodge openings admitted arrows of light from the red-orange sun making its appearance over the bluffs. A few wandering dogs yipped here and there, rummaging for scraps of food. Ponies grazed on the luxuriant grasses, watched over by a few sleepy boys. Early risers began to cook their breakfasts. The curling smoke drifted lazily above the tipis, caught by a slight northerly breeze and carried up the valley. A haze enveloped the bottomlands, the start of another hot day.

There would be nothing extraordinary about this image were it not for the fact that this was an unusually large combined village of Lakota and Cheyenne, mostly, currently engaged in a struggle for the continued existence of their way of life. Although such was the case, the villagers had no inclination that today would be their Armageddon, their Götterdämmerung. Realization comes only long afterwards, with the benefit of hindsight, when chroniclers peer through the elegiacal mists to ascribe hours and minutes of universal import to events that participants could only view as just another day. As they carried on with routine decisions—whether to sleep a little while longer, to go fishing, to round up the ponies, to dig for some wild turnips—an entire way of life was about to come to balance on the fulcrum of this one day.

In the white man's ledger books the scene has been played many times, but from an obviously different perspective. What began as another routine day in the participants' lives has become an epic. We read it in our literature and see it in our movies. George Armstrong Custer and his gallant band of defenders are overwhelmed by hordes of swarming, savage Indians. The troopers go down, one by one, to the last man, overcome by sheer weight of numbers. It is part of the "epic of defeat," a cherished Western tradition that has been with us for hundreds, even thousands, of years, from Thermopylae and Masada to Roncesvalles, the Alamo, and Isandhlwana. Similar to others of its genre, the Little Bighorn battle is usually rendered in an accepted "heroic" way. To ease the pain of defeat, a glorious fight is imagined, surpassing even the loss itself. The battle becomes an epic for the edification of the living.[12]

Although none of us today experienced the formulation of the myth first-hand, we absorb it vicariously as it is passed on through our media and literature. In his book *Fatal Environment*, Richard Slotkin tells us we are the promulgators of our own legends. He does not believe the "archetypal" myth accounts for the tenacious grip that "last stand" stories have on our psyches. Our myths, he argues, do not come from a collective historical consciousness.[13] Nevertheless, whether myth appears as a facet of traditional Western culture, or as an invented product of the media, the last stand image has exerted a hold on us that has defied the years.

12. Bruce A. Rosenberg, *Custer and the Epic of Defeat* (University Park: Pennsylvania State University Press, 1974), 216, 218, 235–38.
13. Richard Slotkin, *Fatal Environment: The Myth of the Frontier in the Age of Industrialization 1800–1890* (New York: HarperCollins, 1994), 26–28.

We find no shame, we place no onus on a heroic band of defenders succumbing to overwhelming odds. As inheritors of the Western military tradition, Americans in particular have a hard time accepting the fact that they may be beaten in a fair fight. When Americans fail, justifications and excuses follow, and the notion that one can ease a conscience by portraying the defeated as a victim of some foul conspiracy has become even more pronounced in modern society.[14] If we lost a battle, the deck must have been stacked against us. The enemy fought in some uncivilized manner, a mindless horde, with no regard for their own lives.

If there were not overwhelming numbers involved, then there must have been dirty tactics, a back-stab, a sell-out, a traitor, a conspiracy. In America's own Civil War, battles were fought in which the larger Union army was put to flight. The men in the ranks knew the answer for their humiliation: "We are sold! Sold again!" they cried.[15]

If not numbers or conspiracy, then a grand blunder must have been committed by someone, and the search for a scapegoat commences. At the Little Bighorn we can find at least two good excuses to satisfy our need to point the finger of blame. First, the number of Indians was so great that an entire regiment of cavalry could not have hoped to stand against them. Second, the fact that an attack was even attempted proves that the commander, Lieutenant Colonel Custer, must have been contemptuous of the Indians, power and glory hungry, or outright insane. Overwhelming enemies, combined with a villain, are the stuff of epics, and of tragedies.

Both excuses are symbiotic in that they live and feed off each other. Was Custer a glory hunter? The village he attacked was so large it was unconquerable, and only an insane glory hunter would have attempted to attack it. Custer attacked it. Therefore, Custer must have been a glory hunter. And since this glory hunter chose to attack, it must have been a very large village. Such unregimented reasoning spans the line between circular fallacies and Catch-22s.[16]

In fact, the village and the number of warriors may not have been as large as historically depicted and, as a consequence, Custer may not have been crazy for attacking it. Just how big was the village?

The eyewitnesses indicated sizes in such disparate terms that it is sometimes difficult to believe they were describing the same camp. Blackfoot Lakota Chief Kill Eagle estimated the camp to be six miles long by one mile wide, packed with tipis "just as thick as they could be put up." The Minneconjou Beard stated that there were six great camp circles stretching four miles along the river. White Bull said there were three miles of tipis. Sitting Bull said the camp was nearly three miles

---

14. Charles J. Sykes, *A Nation of Victims: The Decay of the American Character* (New York: St. Martin's Press, 1992), xiii.

15. Byron Farwell, *Ball's Bluff: A Small Battle and Its Long Shadow* (McLean, VA: EPM Publications, 1990), 177–95; Shelby Foote, *The Civil War: A Narrative Fredericksburg to Meridian* (New York: Random House, 1963), 87.

16. David H. Fischer, *Historians' Fallacies* (New York: Harper & Row, 1970), 49. A counterweight to some of these far-fetched accusations comes from Gregory J. W. Urwin in "Was the Past Prologue?: Meditations on Custer's Tactics at the Little Bighorn," 7th Annual Symposium, Custer Battlefield Historical & Museum Association (Hardin, MT: CBH&MA, 1993): 24, 31–34. Urwin shows that many of Custer's actions were simply morale boosters. He was much less impetuous than some writers would have us believe. He was tactically skillful, thought out his options, did not engage in theatrics, and remained true to character.

long. Crow King estimated it was closer to two and a half miles long. The Minneconjou Hump said the camp was strung along the river for more than two miles. The Hunkpapa Gall said the camp was more than two miles long, valley-wide, and in places a long way from the water. The Oglala Flying Hawk said the extreme length of the village was about one and one-half miles. Another Oglala, Fears Nothing, said all the Indians were encamped on one square mile of land.[17] The estimates range from one to six miles in length.

However, the Indians were notably unreliable when it came to using the white man's measurements. They measured distance not in miles but by the time it took to travel. Ten miles might be described as one-fourth of a day of medium walking. Historian George E. Hyde wrote that Indians "knew the size of a four-point blanket" but not the size of an acre. Inspector James M. Walsh, of the North West Mounted Police, said one could not depend on any Indian's statement in regard to time or numbers.[18]

When the Indians spoke of the camp size without regard to mile measurements, their assessments were much more uniform. Pretty White Buffalo said the Cheyenne and Sans Arc camps were at the lower (north) end of the village, across from the easy (Medicine Tail) crossing of the river. The Minneconjou Standing Bear said the mouth of Muskrat (Medicine Tail) Creek was north of the Santee camp, which was the northernmost of the circles. Two Moon, a Northern Cheyenne, said the village stretched from Sitting Bull's Hunkpapa camp at Big Shoulder's allotment (Shoulder Blade Creek) to the Cheyenne camp at Medicine Tail's place. Wooden Leg stated that the Cheyenne camp was just a little upstream and across from Medicine Tail Coulee, and at the other end were the Hunkpapas, just northeast of the present Garryowen station, with all the camps east of the road, which today is the modern highway, I-90. The Oglala Red Hawk drew a map showing the camps centered at the mouth of Medicine Tail Coulee. The Cheyenne Soldier Wolf assisted interviewer George B. Grinnell by drawing a map that depicted the camp conforming to the course of the river, with its northernmost limits across from Dry (Medicine Tail) Creek. The map Fears Nothing drew showed the entire camp between Water Rat (Medicine Tail) Creek to just north of Box Elder (Shoulder Blade) Creek. Standing Bear and Flying Hawk both produced maps that showed the northernmost limit of the camp to be south of Medicine Tail Creek.[19]

17. Graham, *The Custer Myth*, 55, 69, 77, 79; Usher L. Burdick, *David F. Barry's Indian Notes on the Custer Battle* (Baltimore: The Proof Press, 1937), 9–10; David Humphreys Miller, "Echoes of the Little Bighorn," *American Heritage* 22, no. 4 (June 1971): 37; Stanley Vestal, *Warpath: The True Story of the Fighting Sioux Told in a Biography of Chief White Bull* (Boston: Houghton-Mifflin Company, 1934; reprint, Lincoln: University of Nebraska Press, 1987), 191; Richard G. Hardorff, *Lakota Recollections of the Custer Fight: New Sources of Indian-Military History* (Spokane, WA: Arthur H. Clark Company, 1991), 25, 50.
18. Edward Kadlacek and Mabell Kadlacek, *To Kill an Eagle: Indian Views on the Last Days of Crazy Horse* (Boulder, CO: Johnson Publishing Company, 1981), 138; George E. Hyde, *A Sioux Chronicle* (Norman: University of Oklahoma Press, 1993), 204; Graham, *The Custer Myth*, 72.
19. James McLaughlin, *My Friend the Indian* (Seattle: Superior Publishing Company, 1970), 45; Raymond J. DeMallie, ed., *The Sixth Grandfather: Black Elk's Teachings Given to John G. Neihardt* (Lincoln: University of Nebraska Press, 1985), 185; Hardorff, *Lakota Recollections*, 134; Thomas B. Marquis, *Wooden Leg: A Warrior Who Fought Custer* (Lincoln: University of Nebraska Press, 1931), 206–9; Richard Allan Fox Jr., *Archaeology, History, and Custer's Last Battle: The Little Bighorn Reexamined* (Norman: University of Oklahoma Press, 1993), 217, 300–303.

Looking south up the valley where the village stood. —courtesy of Don Schwarck, South Lyon, Michigan

When identifying the bounds of the village by references to the terrain, the Indian estimates of its size are much more uniform than when they tried to measure it in miles. Invariably, the Indians indicated the camp's upper (southern) end began at the Hunkpapa circle near Shoulder Blade Creek and the westernmost loop of the Little Bighorn River. A number of Maj. Marcus A. Reno's men also indicated the southern end of the camp was just around that bend beyond their skirmish line, the distance estimates ranging from seventy-five to several hundred yards. We can fix the camp's southern terminus with reasonable accuracy. Likewise, the Indians fixed the northern limits of the Cheyenne and Santee lodges at the camp's lower end, just across from the mouth of Medicine Tail Coulee (see fig. 1).[20] Using terrain as a framework, the camp is only one and one-half miles long.

The Indians had a good excuse for mileage discrepancies. How did the white eyewitnesses compare? In Reno's battalion, Lt. George Wallace thought the camp was more than three miles long and up to one-half mile wide, containing maybe

---

20. The southern creek flowing out of the western bluffs to the Little Bighorn was called Box Elder or Shoulder Blade Creek by the Indians; it is labeled Shoulder Blade Creek on modern geological survey maps. The creek flowing from the eastern hills to the river, across from the northern end of the camp, is shown as Medicine Tail Coulee on modern maps; it was called Dry, Water Rat, or Muskrat Creek by battle participants. The northern creek running out of the western hills to the Little Bighorn, north of the village where many of the women and children fled, was called Chasing Creek or Squaw Creek; it is labeled Squaw Creek on modern maps.

1,800 lodges and 9,000 warriors. Capt. Myles Moylan said it was certainly three miles or more long and 200 to 300 yards wide with 1,800 lodges and 3,600 warriors. Lt. Charles DeRudio testified that the village was three or four miles long and up to one and one-half miles wide in places. Capt. Frederick Benteen said there were maybe 1,800 tipis in a village three to four miles long. Lt. Winfield S. Edgerly stated the village was three miles long and one-half to three-fourths of a mile wide, containing maybe 4,000 warriors. The soldiers crossing the field a few days after the fight gave similar estimates. Sgt. Hugh A. Hynds of the 20th Infantry said the remains of the Indian camp stretched for four miles. Scout Billy Jackson said the camp was four miles long. Lt. Alfred B. Johnson of the 7th Infantry said the camp was fully four miles long and three-quarters of a mile wide. Second Cavalry Lt. Charles Roe said the village was an enormous circle three miles across. Brig. Gen. Alfred H. Terry wrote in his diary that the village was three miles long and one mile wide.[21]

The soldiers consistently described a larger village than did the Indians, but their estimations did not stem from lack of familiarity with English measurements. First, Reno's men could not see the full extent of the camp when they were closest to it in the valley. By viewing it end-on, they might have gotten a fair notion of its width, but its length would have been impossible to determine from the valley position. Later, while entrenched on the bluffs to the southeast, with the advantage of a higher elevation, they could get a glimpse of the far northern end. But then they peered across extra miles of intervening valley, river, and woods, with the smoke and dust hanging heavily in the bottoms and a slight northern breeze blowing toward them.

Second, as previously mentioned, there was reluctance on the part of these inheritors of Western military tradition to countenance the possibility of being defeated by a foe without the unfair advantage of astronomical numbers. The astronomical numbers must have come from an immense village.

Third, as a result of battle shock syndrome, soldiers under combat stress are likely to distort and exaggerate the events and terrain around them. Men's perceptions under those conditions are more than a passive analysis. Memory is a practiced re-creation of events rather than a faithful replay of what our senses recorded. A supposedly well-remembered event has dredged-up details filled in with general knowledge. We "paint in" our own details with educated guesses. Memory is a creative process based on predilections. What a person remembers is strongly slanted toward his needs. The fear Reno's men experienced shaped their perceptions and dampened their disposition to scrutinize the situation for inconsistencies and gaps in logic. Recent studies of post-traumatic stress disorder even point to the possibility that the white survivors, experiencing "psychic numbing" and "emotional anesthesia," simply could *not* give an accurate rendering of the

21. Ronald H. Nichols, ed., *Reno Court of Inquiry: Proceedings of a Court of Inquiry in the Case of Major Marcus A. Reno* (Crow Agency, MT: Custer Battlefield Historical & Museum Association, 1992), 22, 63, 81, 234, 237, 320, 409, 419, 452; A. A. Hynds, "Sergeant Hynds' Reminiscences," *Research Review* 6, no. 4 (winter 1972): 67; Alfred B. Johnson, "Custer's Battlefield," *Bighorn Yellowstone Journal* 2, no. 4 (autumn 1993): 7, 18; John M. Carroll, ed., *The Two Battles of the Little Bighorn* (New York: Liveright, 1974), 205; *The Field Diary of General Alfred H. Terry: The Yellowstone Expedition—1876* (Ft. Collins, CO: The Old Army Press, 1978), 9.

objects and terrain.[22] To the beaten, exhausted, hungry, frightened survivors of the 7th Cavalry, the village and its remains must have appeared truly monstrous.

A fourth factor influencing the men's perception of the camp was not a product of their psychological state of mind. The remains of the village after it was abandoned late June 26 *were* larger than the actual occupied village as it stood on the morning of June 25. A portion of the camp had packed up and moved northwest down the valley during that day and a half. Plans had been made to move downstream to search for game, and some had already started to move when Reno struck. Some lodges were hurriedly pulled down to move out of harm's way; others, following Lakota custom, moved their lodges to a new location upon the death of a family member. Remnants of the post-battle village gave the impression of a camp perhaps twice its actual size.[23]

The troops under General Terry and Col. John Gibbon, approaching from the north on June 27, passed through the far northern end of the secondary campsite and made their way beyond the southern limits of the June 25 camp before reaching Reno's command on the bluffs. Two days later, when the united commands headed north, it was Reno's turn to cross the entire length of both day's camps. Almost all the men involved interpreted the campsites as one large village perhaps three or four miles long. The "evidence" had played tricks on them, now indicating a much larger camp than had actually existed four days earlier.[24]

This situation prefaced the story that would later develop. There was an immense village. Custer was swamped by untold numbers of savages. Why in the world would he have attacked such a large camp? Again, he must have been a deranged glory hunter. The cycle lives and grows off itself—replicating, multiplying, and mutating.[25]

Twentieth-century secondary reconstructions of the battle echoed much of the white eyewitness accounts concerning the size of the camp. In 1904, Cyrus T. Brady wrote and used illustrations in a book that showed the Indian camps stretched along the river for "several miles." Custer's defeat was primarily caused by his disobedience of orders and "a vastly greater number of Indians" than anyone

---

22. John McCrone, *The Ape That Spoke: Language and the Evolution of the Human Mind* (New York: William Morrow & Company, 1991), 68–69, 72–74, 114–16; Rosenberg, *Epic of Defeat*, 260–61; Greg Michno, "Space Warp: The Effects of Combat Stress at the Little Bighorn," *Research Review* 8, no. 1 (January 1994): 28; Kathleen Hall Jamieson, *Dirty Politics: Deception, Distraction, and Democracy* (New York: Oxford University Press, 1993), 16–17, 41–42; American Psychiatric Association, eds., *Diagnostic and Statistical Manual of Mental Disorders DSM III-R* (Washington, D.C.: American Psychiatric Association, 1987), 236–37, 248–50.

23. Edgar I. Stewart, *Custer's Luck* (Norman: University of Oklahoma Press, 1955), 312; Thomas B. Marquis, *Keep the Last Bullet for Yourself: The True Story of Custer's Last Stand* (Algonac, MI: Reference Publications, 1976), 80, 82; Graham, *The Custer Myth*, 55; John S. Gray, *Centennial Campaign: The Sioux War of 1876* (Ft. Collins, CO: The Old Army Press, 1976), 354; Marquis, *Wooden Leg*, 376.

24. Jamieson, *Dirty Politics*, 60; Anthony R. Pratkanis and Elliot Aronson, *Age of Propaganda: The Everyday Use and Abuse of Persuasion* (New York: W. H. Freeman & Company, 1992), 27–28. Apparently there are two modes of cognitive processing, central and peripheral. The first is analytic, the second less conscious and more accepting of visual cues. The visuals are processed peripherally and critical acuity does not come into play. Fear increasingly deflects the testing of information for validity. It could be that our battle survivors not only *wanted* to "remember" a large village, they very likely *had* to.

25. Robert M. Utley, *Custer and the Great Controversy: The Origin and Development of a Legend* (Pasadena, CA: Westernlore Press, 1960); Paul A. Hutton, "From Little Big Horn to Little Big Man: The Changing Image

expected. In 1926, Col. William A. Graham wrote a comparatively objective account of the fight. In it, he concluded that the village was four miles long by one-half mile wide, containing 1,500 lodges and 4,000 warriors. The primary reason for Custer's defeat was that he lacked knowledge of the great number of Indians he would face.[26]

The 1930s were dominated by a style of biography known as debunking. One-time heroes were in for a mud bath, and Custer was a chief target. In 1934 Frederic Van de Water epitomized this fashion. Custer was insubordinate, callous, sadistic, and egotistical. He was defeated because of ineptitude, disobedience of orders, and a headlong pursuit of glory. The village was more than three miles long and the number of warriors he faced must have been at least 4,000. Other Custerphobes of the decade included Earl A. Brininstool and C. E. DeLand. A 1939 publication by Fred Dustin spread a similar venom. The "real" reason for the defeat, Dustin wrote, was because of factionalism, vicious habits (drinking and gambling), jealousy, vanity, and conceit. Custer, who was no Indian fighter, with only one battle at a sleeping village and two skirmishes to his credit, foolishly took on a camp three miles long that may have contained 10,000 to 12,000 people and 3,000 to 3,500 warriors.[27]

In 1951 the tarnished Custer legend received a slight reprieve with the appearance of Dr. Charles Kuhlman's study. He thought Custer faced a village about two miles long, containing 3,000 warriors—a "swirling mass of enemies." But, unlike Dustin, Kuhlman alleged that Custer had simply been taking a calculated risk. A once "outstandingly successful" commander in the Civil and Indian Wars did not suddenly become incompetent. In 1955, Edgar I. Stewart produced a well-balanced study that has since become one of the fairest standard references of the battle. Yet, Stewart also thought Custer faced perhaps the largest gathering of Indians ever on the North American continent—3,000 warriors in a village that extended several miles along the river. Custer knew that enormous numbers of Sioux were there, but he thought the 7th could handle the situation and disobeyed the spirit of his orders by attacking. In 1957, David H. Miller wrote of the battle from the Indian point of view. He claimed to have interviewed 71 participants between 1935 and 1955, and from them he deduced that the valley contained seven camp circles, each one-half mile in diameter—12,000 people, with more than 4,000 warriors—stretching almost four miles along the river. Many of these Indians were interviewed in the 1920s by Dr. Thomas B. Marquis. Though he thought there were perhaps 12,000 men, women, and children in the camp, he understood from

of a Western Hero in Popular Culture," *Western Historical Quarterly* 7, no. 1 (January 1976); Paul A. Hutton, "'Correct in Every Detail': General Custer in Hollywood," *Montana The Magazine of Western History* 41, no. 1 (winter 1991).

26. Cyrus T. Brady, *Indian Fights and Fighters* (McClure, Philips & Company, 1904; reprint, Lincoln: University of Nebraksa Press, 1971), 234, 238, 259; William A. Graham, *The Story of the Little Bighorn: Custer's Last Fight* (New York: Century Company, 1926; reprint, Lincoln: University of Nebraska Press, 1988), 34, 75, 93.

27. Frederic F. Van de Water, *Glory Hunter: A Life of General Custer* (Indianapolis: Bobbs-Merrill Company, 1934; reprint, Lincoln: University of Nebraska Press, 1988), 345, 361–70; Hutton, "Big Horn to Big Man," 33–34; Dustin, *Custer Tragedy*, 105–6, 209.

their terrain descriptions that the camp ran less than two miles, from the Garryowen loop of the river to the mouth of Medicine Tail Coulee.[28]

The decade of the 1960s saw the publication of Thomas Berger's *Little Big Man*, in which Custer was again depicted as vain, cruel, bordering on the insane, and hunting for the glorious victory that would lead him to the presidency of the United States. This theme, written as "history," was also presented by Mari Sandoz in 1966. Custer should have known that there were six to eight warriors for every one of his troopers, 3,000 to 4,000 of them, ready to fight for their homes and families. The camp consisted of five great circles in tight order along three miles of river. Custer foolishly divided his forces and attacked on worn-out horses, mindful of his "desperate destiny," aware that "no one voted against a national hero."[29]

For the most part, the 1970s saw a continuation of a tradition begun with the debunkers of the 1930s and enhanced by a new "consciousness" that reacted negatively against anything to do with the military-industrial complex. Stephen Ambrose wrote in 1975 that Custer faced more than 3,000 warriors, and he produced a map that showed the village to be longer than three miles. Ambrose said Custer told his officers he would attack "the largest Indian camp on the North American continent," while inconsistently affirming that Custer severely underestimated his enemy. He was defeated because he attacked too soon, he lost the element of surprise, and he refused to take along extra troops because "he wanted all the glory for the 7th Cavalry." As a counterweight to the Ambrose train of thought, John Gray's 1976 work was a study in moderation. Gray said the camp contained 1,000 lodges that extended for miles along the bottoms (three miles, according to the map in his 1991 book). There were 1,700 to 2,000 warriors. Custer lost because he divided his forces, which were beaten in detail. He attempted it simply because of inadequate enemy intelligence, underestimating the strength and temper of his foe. He was not disobedient, rash, or stupid.[30]

In 1985 a local Little Bighorn rancher, Henry Weibert, concluded from his lifelong study of the battle that Custer faced 10,000 Indians with 3,000 warriors. They issued from a camp three miles long that extended one mile north of Medicine Tail Coulee. Over the years, historian Robert Utley adjusted his assessment of Indian numbers. In 1960 he said there were 15,000 people with more than 3,000 fighting warriors. In 1973 he thought the warriors could have numbered anywhere between 1,500 and 6,000, depending on the source. In his 1988 biography of Custer, Utley decided there were 1,000 lodges containing 7,000 people and 2,000 warriors. In his 1993 biography of Sitting Bull, he said there were 1,800 fighting men. In all of his publications, Utley said the camp stretched about three miles along the valley. Douglas D. Scott, in a 1989 book highlighting the

28. Charles Kuhlman, *Legend Into History: The Custer Mystery* (Harrisburg, PA: The Stackpole Company, 1951), 153–58; Stewart, *Custer's Luck*, 308, 312, 493–94. David Humphreys Miller, *Custer's Fall: The Indian Side of the Story* (Lincoln: University of Nebraska Press, 1957), x, 46, 48; Thomas B. Marquis, *Custer on the Little Big Horn* (Algonac, MI: Reference Publications, 1967), 14, 20; Marquis, *Last Bullet*, 81.

29. Mari Sandoz, *The Battle of the Little Bighorn* (New York: J. B. Lippincott Company, 1966), 108–9, 175–82; Mari Sandoz, *Crazy Horse: Strange Man of the Oglalas* (Lincoln: University of Nebraska Press, 1961), 324.

30. Stephen E. Ambrose, *Crazy Horse and Custer: The Parallel Lives of Two American Warriors* (New York: Doubleday & Company, 1975), 429, 431, 444–45; Gray, *Centennial Campaign*, 176, 182–83, 357; Gray, *Custer's Last Campaign*, 268.

archaeological discoveries on the battlefield, said the Indians numbered about 10,000, including 2,000 to 3,000 warriors, in a camp that stretched three and one-half miles long.[31]

Recently there have been studies that question earlier assumptions of a large camp with an overwhelming number of warriors. In 1984, Robert Marshall traced the growth of the camp as additional lodges attached themselves, from their separate villages in the winter of 1876, through the formation of the "Great Camp," and to the final concentration of June 25. He concluded that there were only 600 to 640 lodges, with a strength of 800 to 1,200 warriors—no more than Custer expected. In 1993, Richard Fox Jr. also attempted to place the village in a more proper perspective, indicating a maximum of 2,000 warriors in a village of perhaps 6,000. The camp, however, is shown to extend only one mile, from a loop of the river north of Garryowen to Medicine Tail Coulee.[32] Fox's map, along with that of Marquis, are the two that come closest to matching the Indian estimations of the camp size in terms of terrain.

Works by Gray, Fox, and Marshall offer us better balance in their depictions of the camp size and Custer's role in the outcome. As Fox noted, the more sensational and inaccurate the story, the greater the number of Indians that appear.[33] I might add, also, that the greater the number of Indians, the more Custer is made out to be a buffoon for attacking them.

The tradition, however, dies hard. In 1994 James Welch passed on the story that there were 8,000 Indians in a village three miles long, and Custer did almost everything wrong in attacking. In 1995 Charles M. Robinson argued that Custer was disjointed, thoughtless, unimaginitive, used poor judgment, and disobeyed orders in attacking a village that stretched three miles along the river and two miles out into the plain.[34]

In 1990 and 1992 two studies by Roger Darling appeared. In the spirit of the debunkers, we were once again presented with a village in terms similar to the fear-induced, exaggerated proportions expressed by Reno's men. The village was three miles long, one mile wide, and contained more than 1,900 lodges. The number of Indians was termed "an unprecedented massing." We find that Custer's decision to attack was a departure, an aberration, a fundamental behavioral transformation. Custer should receive no credit for astute tactics. His "obsession" to attack was so great, "that even confronted with this incredible Indian force before him, the spell was not broken." Custer deluded himself into

---

31. Henry Weibert and Don Weibert, *Sixty-Six Years in Custer's Shadow* (Billings, MT: Falcon Press Publishing Company, 1985), 18, 22, 24, 57; Robert M. Utley, "The Battle of the Little Bighorn," in *Great Western Indian Fights*, ed. B. W. Allred (Lincoln: University of Nebraska Press, 1960), 241, 248; Robert M. Utley, *Frontier Regulars: The United States Army and the Indian 1866–1891* (New York: Macmillan Publishing Company, 1973), 266; Robert M. Utley, *Cavalier in Buckskin: George Armstrong Custer and the Western Military Frontier* (Norman: University of Oklahoma Press, 1988), 179, 184; Utley, *Lance and the Shield*, 142; Douglas D. Scott, Richard A. Fox Jr., Melissa A. Connor, and Dick Harmon, *Archaeological Perspectives on the Battle of the Little Bighorn* (Norman: University of Oklahoma Press, 1989), 13, 16.
32. Robert A. Marshall, "How Many Indians Were There?" in *Custer and His Times, Book Two*, ed. John M. Carroll (Little Bighorn Associates, 1984), 219; Fox, *Archaeology, History*, 255–56, 282–83, 306.
33. Ibid., 255.
34. Welch, *Killing Custer*, 50, 166; Charles M. Robinson III, *A Good Year to Die: The Story of the Great Sioux War* (New York: Random House, 1995), 34–35, 154, 163.

invincibility, he was not rational, and he defeated himself through poor generalship in a series of self-reinforcing blunders.[35]

Enough. It is high time we wipe our slates clean from these distorted conceptions of events at the Battle of the Little Bighorn. Since argument from a purely historical standpoint has not worked well in the past, we might try looking at the problem through physical and spatial considerations. First, we must realize that "large" or "many" are relative adjectives interpreted individually. The Arikara scout Red Star accompanied the expedition up the valley of the Rosebud. He considered the abandoned Dakota camps that he saw "large"—one-third to one-half mile across. The Brulé Lakota Little Day remembered her childhood in the 1870s, when a large encampment consisted of thirty tipis. Beard said there were thousands of Lakotas at the fight. "How many thousands?" he was asked. He dismissed the question with a wave of his hand. "In that long-ago time none of my people knew more than a thousand numbers," he said. "We believed no honest man needed to know more than that many."[36]

What was the configuration of this "large" camp on the Little Bighorn? We cannot know exactly, but chances are it was not set up, according to David Miller, in seven circles one-half mile or more in diameter. Seven of these would overflow the valley. They would not fit into the one-and-one-half-mile stretch of valley east of the modern highway depicted by the Indians.

Were the camps, in fact, circular? It may be that a circle is just a convenient word, analogous to a gathering of lodges set in no particular configuration, not unlike the Indian use of kinship terms such as "father" or "grandmother," when there may have been no actual kinship involved, or when aunts and uncles can be considered as mothers and fathers, or cousins considered as brothers and sisters.[37] Certainly there was no necessity for setting up camps in large circles on the Little Bighorn. The people moved in an established order, the Cheyennes in front and the Hunkpapas trailing. Tipis were usually set up with the portals facing east to welcome the morning sun and because of the prevailing west winds common to these latitudes. It was not good to set up directly under trees because of danger from lightning and high winds; yet, the site was chosen for ample supplies of water and wood, good grazing and forage for the horses, and security. Level, wooded bottomlands cradled by bluffs were ideal. Once a year, at the annual sun dance, higher, open areas were generally sought so the village could be arranged strictly circular. At other times, the tipis were set up in an informal assemblage determined by family relationships and geographical considerations. Relatives sought to camp near each other, often with tipis of young married couples close to one of their parents' lodges. The trees, the streams, and the configuration of the land made formal camp

35. Roger Darling, *A Sad and Terrible Blunder: Generals Terry and Custer at the Little Bighorn: New Discoveries* (Vienna, VA: Potomac-Western Press, 1990), 204, 209–12; Roger Darling, *General Custer's Final Hours: Correcting a Century of Misconceived History* (Vienna, VA: Potomac-Western Press, 1992), 4, 9, 17–20, 24, 26.

36. Orin G. Libby, ed., *The Arikara Narrative of the Campaign Against the Hostile Dakotas—June 1876* (Glorieta, NM: Rio Grande Press, 1976), 82; Royal B. Hassrick, *The Sioux: Life and Customs of a Warrior Society* (Norman: University of Oklahoma Press, 1964), 13; Miller, "Echoes," 37.

37. Reginald and Gladys Laubin, *The Indian Tipi: Its History, Construction, and Use* (Norman: University of Oklahoma Press, 1957), 110; Thomas B. Marquis, *The Cheyennes of Montana* (Algonac, MI: Reference Publications, 1978), 180–81.

A Lakota camp on the Laramie River, set up conforming to the course of the stream.
—Nebraska State Historical Society

circles impossible.[38] The sun dance of 1876 had been held on the Rosebud, in a valley barely one-half mile wide on each side of the creek, about three weeks earlier. At the Little Bighorn, there was no need to set up the camp in regulated circles. Marching order, and familial and geographical considerations, dictated tipi placement.

How large an area did the Indian camp encompass? Using the inhabitants' terrain descriptions, we can draw a trapezoid with its long base running along the line of the modern interstate highway and its parallel, shorter base running along the river. The connecting lines run from the river south of Medicine Tail to the Garryowen loop, and from the river north of Medicine Tail west to the highway (see fig. 1). One square mile equals 640 acres. The area of our trapezoid is a bit more than one and one-fourth square miles, or about 877 acres. The Indians said the village fit within these geographical confines.

How large is a tipi? Prior to the nineteenth century and the widespread use of horses, ancient tipi rings averaged twelve to seventeen feet across. With the introduction of the horse, enabling the Indians to transport heavier loads, they could build larger lodges. Hunting parties typically used smaller tipis, about twelve feet in diameter. Family lodges were larger; one source claims eighteen feet was average, while another states twenty-two feet as the norm.[39]

38. Laubin, *Tipi*, 36–37, 293–95; Hassrick, *The Sioux*, 173–74; George E. Hyde, *Life of George Bent Written From His Letters* (Norman: University of Oklahoma Press, 1968), 200. The "accepted" story that Indians always set their lodges in a circle with openings and portals facing east is amply debunked by the half-Cheyenne George Bent. He indicates that once there was a twenty-five-year hiatus between times when Cheyennes camped together in a great circle. Also, he avers that openings in the circle were always in the direction the camp was moving, and he tells of instances when lodges were simply pitched in groups strung out along riverbanks.

39. Hassrick, *The Sioux*, 211–13; Laubin, *Tipi*, 6, 13, 27–28, 282.

For our purpose, we will construct a tipi a bit larger than average, 23.4 feet across. Its area is about 48 square yards. How many 48-square-yard tipis could we fit into an acre of land? An acre contains 4,840 square yards. If the tipis were packed in with their sides touching, we could fit one hundred 48-square-yard tipis almost perfectly into our acre (see fig. 3).[40]

By now readers may be realizing the impossibility of some of the historic village-size and mileage estimates. Let us take a closer look at one of the most recent estimates—Roger Darling's enormous village of 1,900 tipis packed into a three-mile-by-one-mile area. There are 640 acres in a square mile. Packed to the limit, we could fit 64,000 tipis in that space—192,000 of them in three square miles. The

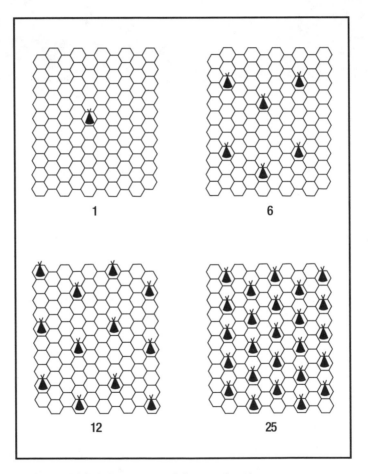

Figure 3. Tipis Per Acre. *Each honeycomb grid represents one acre (4,840 square yards) divided into one hundred 48-square-yard hexagons.*

40. An acre may be difficult for some readers to visualize. It is an area almost 70 yards square. If we reshape it into a rectangle, the area would be about the size of a 90-yard football field (53.33 yards wide and nearly 91 yards long)—a much more concrete visual for many of us.

An 1879 photo of Spotted Eagle's Lakota village on the Tongue River. Tipis appear clustered at approximately 18 to 20 per acre. —Little Bighorn Battlefield National Monument

number of people per lodge has been variously estimated at three to seven. At five per lodge, this village could contain 960,000 people—almost one million souls in three square miles of Montana valley—a ridiculous notion, of course. We must subtract some tipis, for obviously they would not be packed like sardines in a can, 100 per acre. Let's start by removing half of them, so we have 50 tipis per acre. Now there are 32,000 tipis per square mile. Still too many. Cut the density in half again and there are 16,000 tipis. Too many. Let's make it 12 tipis per acre. This sounds reasonable, but it still leaves us with 7,680 tipis in one square mile and 23,040 in a three-mile-square village. What next? How about only six tipis per acre? Now we have 3,840 tipis per square mile—11,520 in three square miles. But Darling said this was an enormous village, three square miles of Indian lodges—1,900 tipis! Back to the cutting board. How about two tipis per acre? With only two tipis per acre—per 90-yard football field—we still have 1,280 lodges in a square mile and 3,840 in the three-mile-square village. What do we do next? There had to be *some* tipis there. The fact is, we need to construct only one tipi per acre in order to satisfy Darling's figures—1,920 tipis in a three-square-mile village.

This configuration is nonsense. Custer could have driven an armored division down the valley and scarcely touched a buffalo hide. The Indians did not separate as far as one tipi per acre. Families could not have camped together, there would have been no mutual protection in numbers, no benefits of village life—there would have been no village.

In this context, Gray's observation that, because there were nearly one thousand lodges extending along the bottom for miles, the first view of the village "must have given Custer a shock," is nothing short of ludicrous.[41] This is one tipi about every two acres! If Custer saw a "village" of such a configuration, he probably would have cursed his bad luck for the Indians having already fled.

Obviously, the Indians camped closer together than in Gray's or Darling's depictions. To make any sense of the numbers we must implode the size of the village. Two tipis per acre—or 1,280 lodges in a square mile—exceeds Gray's estimate of 1,000 without allowing for the extra two square miles. Three tipis per acre equals 1,920 in a square mile, which exceeds Darling's estimate of 1,900 without counting the extra two square miles. But would a village have dispersed so far apart as to contain only three tipis per acre? By consulting any number of photographs of village sites taken in the last half of the nineteenth century, we can see tipis clustered according to the geographical, familial, and security considerations previously noted.

Conservatively, we can place a dozen tipis in an acre, but this gives us 7,680 tipis in one square mile—still 5,000 lodges more than our highest estimates, and with absolutely no need for two additional square miles. The truth is that the area needed for the village does not even amount to one square mile.

Figure 4 considers the area required for different levels of tipi density. By cross-referencing the number of tipis per acre (12, for example) with the number of tipis (2,000), we find the area required (in this case, 167 acres, or .26 of a square mile). For a village of 2,000 tipis to cover three square miles, the lodges would have to be dispersed to about one per acre. On the other hand, a village of 2,500 lodges at a density of six tipis per acre would require only about three-fifths (.65) of a square mile.

A Lakota camp on the open prairie with tipis clustered at perhaps one dozen per acre.
—Little Bighorn Battlefield National Monument

41. Gray, *Centennial Campaign*, 176.

Number of Tipis	Tipis per Acre				
	1	6	12	25	
500	**500** .78	**83** .13	**42** .07	**20** .03	**Acres** Sq. Miles
1,000	**1,000** 1.56	**167** .26	**83** .13	**40** .06	
1,200	**1,200** 1.87	**200** .31	**100** .16	**48** .07	
1,500	**1,500** 2.34	**250** .39	**125** .19	**60** .09	
1,800	**1,800** 2.81	**300** .47	**150** .23	**72** .11	
2,000	**2,000** 3.12	**333** .52	**167** .26	**80** .13	
2,500	**2,500** 3.90	**416** .65	**208** .33	**100** .16	

Figure 4. *Tipi Density*

What was the camp's configuration? If we allow one and one-half miles (2,640 yards) of river frontage from the Garryowen loop to the mouth of Medicine Tail, and extend back from the river only 300 yards, we have an area of 792,000 square yards, or 163 acres. Placing only 12 tipis per acre, we have reached our upper estimates of camp size with 1,956 tipis. It appears that even the one-and-one-fourth-square-mile trapezoid we constructed to encompass the maximum dimensions as depicted by the Indians is too large. Wooden Leg said the camp rested entirely east of where the modern highway runs, but this does not mean it extended from the river all the way to the highway. For all practical purposes, perhaps excepting an isolated lodge or two, the camp extended back from the river only a few hundred yards, generally conforming to the course of the stream (see fig. 1).

Only Captain Moylan estimated the village width at 200 to 300 yards. Whether this was the result of close observation and calculation or serendipity, we cannot know. The fact is, the picture of this "enormous" village that has been presented to us for more than a century was a product of the factors discussed above: an inability to see the entire camp; spatial distortion induced by combat stress; reluctance to admit defeat by a "savage" foe without the advantage of overwhelming numbers; and being deceived by the camp's secondary extension. The camp ran one and one-half miles along the river and three hundred yards back from it. The area covered by the main bulk of the village on June 25 amounted to only *one-quarter square mile.*

Impossible, you say? Fine. Double the area and disperse the tipis from twelve per acre down to six. The village still takes up only *one-half square mile.* And remember, we are dealing with Darling's 1,900 lodges. When using other scholar's estimations of 1,000 lodges, the village shrinks even further. There is no getting around it. The village on the Little Bighorn was enormous only in the imagination of the participants and chroniclers who, consciously or subconsciously, wanted to or had to see it that way.

It may be that the villages Custer faced in November 1868 on the Washita River were larger than the Little Bighorn camps. Black Kettle's Cheyenne village at the upper end of the Washita complex was analogous to Sitting Bull's Hunkpapa camp at the upper end on the Little Bighorn. From Sitting Bull's camp, white eyewitnesses said the village stretched three or four miles. Custer himself said that from Black Kettle's camp, a continuous Indian village stretched for a distance of twelve miles—Cheyennes, Arapahos, Kiowas, Comanches, and Apaches. De Benneville Randolph Keim, war correspondent for the *New York Herald,* went through the abandoned campsites after the fight, much as had Colonel Gibbon's men after the Little Bighorn battle. Keim found the debris of an enormous village. The goods they burned left a trail of fire and smoke along the Washita for six or seven miles.[42]

If the estimates of three or four miles on the Little Bighorn were exaggerated by a factor of two, and the village was really one and one-half to two miles in length, Custer's estimate at the Washita might also be adjusted down to six miles. Regardless, a six-mile-long village on the Washita was too large to attack. Custer hit Black Kettle on the upper end, feinted toward the rest, and withdrew. A one-and-one-half-mile village on the Little Bighorn was within Custer's power to defeat. He attempted to attack the entire complex.

The village Custer saw from the bluffs did not produce any monstrous shock to his system. It was big, certainly, and that is what his last message read: "Come on. Big village. Be quick. Bring Packs." But seeing tipis covering a quarter or even a half square mile of ground was not enough to stop him as if he had run headfirst into a brick wall. Nor was he transformed into a medieval berserker, bent only on the destruction of his foe, regardless of the cost. He retained all of the faculties that

---

42. George Armstrong Custer, *My Life on the Plains or, Personal Experiences with Indians* (Norman: University of Oklahoma Press, 1962), 246, 289; De B. Randolph Keim, *Sheridan's Troopers on the Borders: A Winter Campaign on the Plains* (Lincoln: University of Nebraska Press, 1985), 148–49.

brought him through many a tight spot in the past. It was another calculated gamble, like many others that Custer had waged throughout the Civil War and the Indian Wars.

Accurately estimating the camp's true dimensions eliminates some of the distortions exploited by the debunkers of the past. There is no longer any need for conspiracy theories or for placing the blame on the field commander of the 7th Cavalry. Custer was not an insane glory hunter. Knowing the village's true porportions enables us to interpret some events in a different perspective. Medicine Tail Coulee did not lead directly into the center of the Indian camp. Custer *could have* crossed at Medicine Tail and hit the northern end of the camp, but a number of factors ruled against it: the noncombatants had already fled to the north; the majority of warriors were fighting in the south; and Reno's force was no longer holding as the "anvil" for Custer to strike against. As we shall see in more detail in a later chapter, Custer may have feinted down Medicine Tail toward the camp to draw off the warriors who had just routed Reno out of the valley and were pursuing him in the hills. His move to the river was calculated to draw attention away from Reno by threatening the lower camp. It worked admirably, and Custer may have lost his life, not as a result of glory hunting but because he felt a responsibility to pull his subordinate out of harm's way.

Visualizing the camp in its proper proportions also allows us to trace Indian movements across the battlefield with a greater degree of accuracy. For example, we will find that a proper conception of the village size changes the fallacious depiction of Crazy Horse leading warriors in a far sweep down the valley and circling north of Custer's battalion. Crazy Horse did leave the camp and travel north. But the north end of the camp was at Medicine Tail Coulee, not two miles farther down the valley. An enhanced understanding of Indian accounts that heretofore may have seemed confusing or contradictory is possible when operating within the parameters of a smaller village.

One lesson to be gained from this is that we must seriously study the Indian testimony. We cannot dismiss it as contradictory and therefore useless. Colonel Graham would not use Indian accounts in his story of the battle. Gen. Hugh Scott "threw up his hands" with the conflicting testimony. Earl Brininstool said their stories were not dependable. Fred Dustin preferred to rely on the white officers because of "the traditional truthfulness of their class,"[43] showing an ethnocentric reluctance to give proper weight to Indian testimony.

Corollary to this is the problem that stems from an overreliance on secondary evidence: an incorrect premise can be sustained and perpetuated to the forfeiture of accuracy. Placing faith in primary Indian testimony will avoid some of these predicaments. It should be no surprise that the Indian accounts were closest to reality. It was their village. They knew the area before, during, and after the battle. When they discussed the camp size in terms of the terrain, they told us its true proportions.

---

43. Graham, *Story of the Little Bighorn*, 86.

As long ago as 1900, Dr. Charles A. Eastman, a Santee Dakota, wrote that the number of Indian warriors had always been overestimated; there were only about 1,000 of them in the fight.[44] The Indians did not crush Custer with overwhelming numbers. He attacked a village he could have defeated. But the Indians that day did not flee. They stood to defend their homes and families. Custer lost his life in a fair fight.

The morning sun rose relentlessly. Some of the haze burned out of the valley of the Little Bighorn. The horses would need watering. Children would go swimming in the river to escape the increasing heat. Some of the men would just be rolling out of their buffalo robes while the women began preparations to take down the lodges. A large herd of antelope was reported to the north. The village would head downriver in search of game and fresh grass. For the approaching soldiers, with their watches set on Chicago time, it may have been about three o'clock in the afternoon. For the Lakotas, it was high noon.

---

44. Graham, *The Custer Myth*, 97.

II

Valley

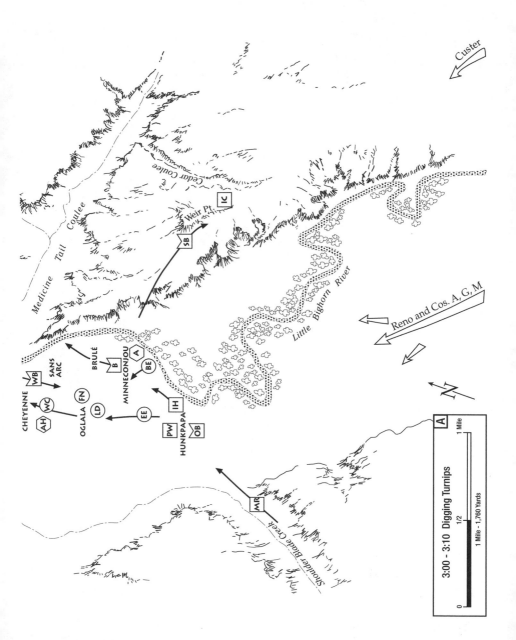

Custer

Reno and Cos. A, G, M

Little Bighorn River

Medicine Tail Coulee

Cedar Coulee

Weir Pt.

SB

IC

BRULÉ

SANS ARC

WB

CHEYENNE

AH WC

OGLALA FN

LD

EE

MINNECONJOU

B

BE

A

IH

PW OB

HUNKPAPA

MR

Shoulder Blade Creek

N

3:00 - 3:10 Digging Turnips

A

0   1/2   1 Mile

1 Mile = 1,760 Yards

Digging Turnips, 3:00–3:10

PW 3:00–3:10, **Pretty White Buffalo** (Pte San Waste Win) [next 3:10]. The wife of the Hunkpapa warrior Spotted Horn Bull had been up late the night before preparing for the march they would be making this morning. She was awakened by her brother, White Eyebrows, who had been out dancing with the other young people all night. He was hungry and had come to her tipi looking for food.

Pretty White Buffalo unpacked some of her bundles to prepare him a breakfast of buffalo meat stewed with turnips. The Lakota men would probably head northwest today, toward the Yellowstone. The women would be there to assist them, for it was their duty and their pleasure to do so. Continuing her chores, Pretty White Buffalo had no thought of a fight that day with the white man. No one expected an attack, the young men were not even out watching for soldiers.

As the women packed, preparing to break camp, some Indians had been east of the Greasy Grass where they had shot a buffalo. Some women and children had been nearby digging turnips when they first saw the soldiers coming from the east. They ran to warn the camp. Pretty White Buffalo heard the alarm and quickened her pace, but the tipis were not yet down. The men told the women to hurry, for the village was not made for a fight and they must move as fast as possible. "I have seen my people prepare for battle many times," said Pretty White Buffalo, "and this I know: that the Sioux that morning had no thought of fighting."[45]

MR 3:00–3:10, **Moving Robe** (She Walks With Her Shawl—Tasinamani Win, or Tashenamani) [next 3:10]. The daughter of the Hunkpapa Crawler was about twenty-three years old during the fight against General Custer (Pehin Hanska). Moving Robe was digging wild prairie turnips (*ti' psinla*) with other girls several miles from camp when she saw a cloud of dust rise beyond the bluffs in the east. Peering into the distance toward the camp on what was already turning out to be a hot and sultry day, she saw a warrior riding swiftly, shouting that soldiers were only a few miles away and that the women, children, and old men should run for the hills in the other direction.

Moving Robe did nothing of the kind. She threw down the pointed ash stick she had been using to root up turnips and ran for her tipi.[46]

A 3:00–3:10, **Antelope** (Kate Bighead) [next 3:10]. Associated with the Southern Cheyennes during most of her childhood, Antelope joined the Northern Cheyennes with her brothers White Bull and White Moon and lived in the Black Hills country in the days before the Battle of the Little Bighorn. Their band of about forty lodges had been attacked on the Powder River in March 1876, and they left the Cheyenne camp and spent the subsequent months traveling with the Lakotas, with some of Crazy Horse's Oglalas.

---

45. James McLaughlin, *My Friend the Indian* (Seattle: Superior Publishing Company, 1970), 43–44.
46. Hardorff, *Lakota Recollections*, 91–92.

As summer approached, the traveling bands grew larger with additions from the reservations. By the time they had moved down Reno Creek to the Greasy Grass, there were six main camp circles, with more Indians than Antelope had ever seen together at one time. Only a few Northern Cheyennes were absent, and there were even a few families of Southern Cheyennes present. They had just moved to the west side of the river and would stay there but one night, preparing to go down the valley the next day in search of large antelope herds reported to the north. On the morning of June 25, Antelope went with an Oglala woman to visit some friends among the Minneconjou, up the valley from them. She found her friends bathing in the river and joined them. Other groups of men, women, and children were playing or fishing all along the stream. Everyone was having a good time and no one was thinking about battle. A few women began taking down their lodges, getting ready for the upcoming move down the valley. It was sometime past the middle of the forenoon when two Lakota boys came running toward Antelope and her friends, shouting, "Soldiers are coming!"[47]

BE 3:00–3:10, **Black Elk** (Hehaka Sapa) [next 3:10]. The thirteen-year-old Oglala, born on the Little Powder River in what is now Wyoming, had been up since daybreak. Accompanied by a cousin, he had gone to take several families' horses out to graze. His father had cautioned him to keep his eyes open and to keep a long rope on at least one horse so it would be easy to catch. As the sun climbed higher, they turned the horses loose and went back to camp for breakfast.

Black Elk did not feel right. He had already experienced several great spiritual visions that would eventually lead him to become a respected Oglala holy man as an adult. This morning he had a funny feeling, believing that in an hour or so something terrible might happen. People were already swimming down at the river. He did not feel much like participating, but decided to go anyway. He greased up his body.

At the river near the Hunkpapa camp Black Elk heard criers yelling that the chargers were coming. They said soldiers had been spotted back at the old campsite where the lone tipi with the dead warriors had been left. The criers then ran to the Oglala camp. Black Elk could hear the alarm being given from one camp to the next. He headed for his tipi.[48]

LD 3:00–3:10, **Low Dog** [next 4:50]. The sun was about at noon the day of June 25, and the Oglala Low Dog slept in his lodge until a commotion in the camp brought him sluggishly to his senses. It was a warning that white warriors were coming after them. Apparently some horses had been lost and Indians went back on the trail to look for them. White scouts saw the Indians and tried to kill them, but one Indian outran the pursuers and brought word to the camp.

Low Dog thought it was a false alarm, but he lost no time in getting ready, just in case. "I did not think it possible that any white men would attack us, so strong as we were," Low Dog said. When he got his gun and emerged from his lodge, he

47. Marquis, *Custer on the Little Big Horn*, 82–84.
48. Raymond J. DeMallie, ed., *The Sixth Grandfather: Black Elk's Teachings Given to John G. Neihardt* (Lincoln: University of Nebraska Press, 1985), 180–81.

realized the warnings must have been correct. It sounded like an attack had begun somewhere beyond the end of the village where Sitting Bull and the Hunkpapas were camped.[49]

EE 3:00–3:10, **Eagle Elk** [next 3:30]. A warrior in full manhood at age twenty-five and a cousin of Crazy Horse, the Oglala Eagle Elk was contemplating walking back to his tipi the morning of June 25. He had been out dancing and socializing the entire night at the various affairs that were held in many of the village circles. He thought it must have been after eight in the morning when the people stopped dancing and began to go home to get something to eat.

Eagle Elk was still talking with his friends when a Hunkpapa woman called to him that she had been told that attackers were approaching fast. Another Indian took the warning lightly, joking that there was no need to rush off, for no one was going to kill them all at once. A second call from the same woman repeated the admonition.

There was something to that warning, Eagle Elk said. He was going home. He picked up his blanket and started walking when he was joined by his friend Red Feather. They started across the Hunkpapa camp circle when they heard shooting towards the river.[50]

WB 3:00–3:10, **White Bull** (Lazy White Buffalo—Pte San Hunka) [next 3:10]. White Bull, a Minneconjou Lakota, was the son of Makes Room and Good Feather Woman and a nephew of the Hunkpapa Sitting Bull. He had two brothers, One Bull and Kills Standing, and three sisters, Uses Her Own Words, Shell Woman, and Four Times Woman. As was customary, White Bull stayed in the tipi of his wife, Holy Lodge, a member of the Sans Arc tribe. At twenty-six years of age, White Bull was already a famous warrior who had partaken in numerous fights, counted many coups, and stolen many horses since the Fetterman battle ten years earlier.

At daybreak, White Bull stepped out of his wife's lodge on the northern side of the Sans Arc camp. Holy Lodge's father, Iron White Man, was camped next to them. White Bull loosened the picket ropes of his family's horses and drove them north to the breaks by the river. Eighteen or twenty of the forty animals—five running horses, four mares, one mule, and some geldings—were his. Owning so many animals made him wealthy. Sitting Bull owned twenty, and the richest Indian might own forty to sixty. White Bull led the animals along the Greasy Grass, one-half mile from camp, and watched as they drank their fill. When they finished, he drove them farther north of the camp to a place with good grass and left them to graze. About eight in the morning he went home for breakfast.

With his belly full, ready for a day's work, White Bull took his Winchester rifle and two cartridge belts and headed back to the horses. It was turning out to be a hot, lazy, almost windless day, and the trails were dusty. White Bull was herding his horses north of the camp on the west side of the river, about 125 yards from the bank.

---

49. Graham, *The Custer Myth*, 75.
50. Hardorff, *Lakota Recollections*, 99–100.

It was not quite time for the midday watering. White Bull had no thoughts of any approaching danger when suddenly he heard a man yelling an alarm. He climbed a slight hill; across the long flat to the south he could see the soldiers approaching. He jumped on his best running horse, a fast bay mare, and began driving the ponies back to camp.[51]

The Minneconjou White Bull was a nephew of Sitting Bull and was destined to count many coups in the battle. —Little Bighorn Battlefield National Monument

---

51. Ibid., 107–8; Vestal, *Warpath*, 191–92; White Bull, Box 105, Notebooks 23, 24; White Bull, Box 106, Notebook 48, Walter S. Campbell Collection, Western History Collections, University of Oklahoma Library. Notebook 23 places White Bull on the flat west of the river, while Notebook 24 indicates he was on the north side. Hardorff, in *Lakota Recollections*, 109, says the names of only two of Makes Room's sons are known. However, White Bull, in Box 106, Notebook 48 of Campbell's notes, indicates the third son's name was Kills Standing.

OB 3:00–3:10, **One Bull** (Lone Bull—Tatanka Winjila) [next 3:10]. Born at Bear Butte in what is now South Dakota, White Bull's younger brother was adopted at the age of four by his uncle, Sitting Bull. He married the Hunkpapa Red Whirlwind Woman (Scarlet Whirlwind), and their lodge was next to Sitting Bull's. Twenty-two years old that summer, One Bull was one of Sitting Bull's bodyguards. He and the Hunkpapa Gray Eagle, Sitting Bull's brother-in-law, protected him, looked after his property, and saw that his orders were carried out.

One Bull had taken the family horses to the river that morning. At midday he and Gray Eagle went back to the pony herd and again drove them to the Greasy Grass for the noon watering. After they drank their fill of cool water, he picketed them and returned to his tipi.

One Bull was inside combing his hair when he heard a commotion. He thought it must have been about two o'clock, according to the white man's time. He stepped outside. An Indian named Brown Back had reached camp and was spreading the alarm. He passed the word to Fat Bear, who in turn brought the word to One Bull. Camped in one of the southernmost lodges, One Bull was among the first to find out what was happening. The soldiers were coming, Fat Bear cried. They had already killed a boy named Deeds, who had gone out to picket a horse. One Bull quickly turned back toward Sitting Bull's tipi.[52]

IH 3:00–3:10, **Iron Hawk** [next 3:10]. A large boy at fourteen years of age, Iron Hawk had already participated in raids and battles, including the fight with General Crook on the Rosebud eight days earlier. He had slept late that Sunday morning, and the sun was overhead as he finished up his breakfast.

What seemed to have the makings of another warm, lazy day, was interrupted by criers riding through the camp, spreading the word that "chargers are coming." Iron Hawk jumped up and rushed out of his tipi to get his horse. He learned that some Indians had been out east hunting and looking for ponies when they discovered the troops coming. Deeds, one of the boys with the party, had been killed. Others rode quickly back to the camp to give the alarm.

Iron Hawk ran for the horses that were grazing near the camp. He was able to rope one, but the others began to stampede. His older brother had already caught his horse and began to head them off. Iron Hawk could see the children running up from the river where they had been swimming. The women, the children, and the horses of Iron Hawk's family all headed downstream.[53]

FN 3:00–3:10, **Fears Nothing** [next 3:30]. Fears Nothing and his wife, White Cow Robe, camped with the Oglalas in the middle of a one-square-mile section of land between Water Rat (Medicine Tail) Creek and Box Elder (Shoulder

---

52. Hardorff, *Lakota Recollections*, 109; One Bull, Box 105, Notebooks 19, 41; One Bull, Box 104, Folder 6, Walter S. Campbell Collection, Western History Collections, University of Oklahoma Library; Jerome A. Greene, *Lakota and Cheyenne: Indian Views of the Great Sioux War, 1876–1877* (Norman: University of Oklahoma Press, 1994), 54. David Miller, in "Echoes," 30, says that One Bull was out with the horses when the firing began, and he could see the dust rising and hear the pounding of the iron-shod hoofs of the soldier horses. For reasons that will become apparent later, I choose not to use this rendition.

53. John G. Neihardt, *Black Elk Speaks: Being the Life Story of a Holy Man of the Oglala Sioux* (Lincoln: University of Nebraska Press, 1979), 119–20; Hardorff, *Lakota Recollections*, 63–64.

Blade) Creek. He understood that the warning of Custer's advance was given by an Oglala. There had been a party of Indians going to Red Cloud Agency, and one was late in starting, following behind the others, when he saw the dust from the approaching soldiers. He rushed back to notify the camps.

The Oglala who returned to warn the village had a watch taken from one of General Crook's dead soldiers at the battle on the Rosebud. According to it, Custer began his attack at one o'clock in the afternoon. There was no expectation that more soldiers would come after them. Scouts had reported that Crook's men, who the Indians had battled the week before, had fallen back and they did not expect any further fighting.

Fears Nothing's horses were down below, north of the Indian camps, and he waited for his mounts to be brought in. Already he could see some of the women fleeing, leaving their lodges standing, heading toward the mouth of Chasing (Squaw) Creek.[54]

SB 3:00–3:10, **Standing Bear** (Mato Najun) [next 3:10]. The Minneconjou Standing Bear was sixteen years old in the summer of 1876. He awoke late the morning of the fight. The women were already out digging turnips and two of his uncles were gone hunting. Another uncle and his old and feeble grandmother were all that remained in their tipi. When the sun was overhead, Standing Bear decided to go down to the river to swim.

Upon returning from the river, he threw on a shirt and braided his hair. Grandmother fried some meat on the ashes of the fire to feed them. While they ate, Standing Bear's uncle said, "After you are through eating you had better go and get the horses, because something might happen all at once, we never can tell."

Before they finished their meal, there was a commotion outside. A crier announced that chargers were coming and that one of two men out looking for horses had already been killed. Standing Bear also learned that an Oglala named Black Bear had been east of the river and up near the divide looking for horses. He had spotted soldiers approaching and came back to warn the camps. "I told you before, that this would happen," admonished his uncle. "You'd better go right away and get the horses."

Standing Bear ran downstream. On the way he remembered that his older brother Iron Hail (Beard) and another man were already out herding the horses on Muskrat (Medicine Tail) Creek below the Santee camp. He cut directly to the river, waded the breast-deep waters, and climbed up a prominent hilltop called Black Butte. Nearly breathless, he reached the top and peered to the south, upstream.

There he saw soldiers. They were spread out, coming down the slope to the Greasy Grass. Standing Bear stood and watched for a time, catching his breath. The soldiers crossed the river and were coming down the flat toward the Hunkpapa camp. He would have to get back, but suddenly he realized the folly of running off without his moccasins. Stuck in the midst of a large cactus bed, he could only pick

---

54. Ibid., 25–26, 28, 32. One might question if the message-bearing Oglala knew about the operational workings of a watch.

his way through with extreme caution. When Standing Bear next looked upstream, he saw more soldiers to the south and east, on the same side of the river as he.[55]

B 3:00–3:10, **Beard** (Iron Hail—Wasu Maza) [next 3:10]. Standing Bear's seventeen-year-old older brother, Beard, remembered their camp as being the largest he had ever known. There were thousands of Lakota fighting men and their families, a number larger, Beard affirmed, than any honest man needed to know.

Beard's Minneconjous were led by Hump, Fast Bull, and High Backbone. Crazy Horse led the Oglalas, Inkpaduta led the Santees, and Lame White Man and Ice led the Cheyennes. Yet, when they were camped together, all acknowledged the Hunkpapa Sitting Bull as the leader. The Indians rallied around him because he stood for freedom and the old way of life.

The Minneconjou Beard, seventeen years old in 1876, would live the longest of any Indian participant in the fight on the Greasy Grass River. —Little Bighorn Battlefield National Monument

55. Ibid., 57–58; DeMallie, *Sixth Grandfather*, 184–85; Neihardt, *Black Elk*, 113–14; Kenneth Hammer, ed., *Custer in '76: Walter Camp's Notes on the Custer Fight* (Provo: Brigham Young University Press, 1976; reprint, Norman: University of Oklahoma Press, 1990), 214.

Like so many others, Beard had slept late the morning of the fight. He had been hunting buffalo the day before, but had to ride far to find them because the large number of people in the valley had driven the herds away. He brought some meat home but was very tired after all the work.

When Beard awoke to stretch and rub the sleep from his eyes, the women were already up and two of his uncles had gone on another hunt. The sun was high overhead. Beard walked to the river for a swim, but soon became hungry and returned to the tipi for dinner.

His grandmother and a third uncle were there. While eating, Beard's uncle told him that when he finished he ought to tend to the horses. "Something might happen today. I feel it in the air."

Beard hurried down to Muskrat Creek where he joined his younger brother, who was herding the horses. By the time he got there, he heard yelling back in the village. People were shouting about white soldiers riding toward the camp. Beard left the family ponies and decided to climb the bluffs along the east bank of the river for a better look.[56]

AH 3:00–3:10, **American Horse** [next 3:50]. The Northern Cheyennes American Horse and Magpie Eagle were among the last to bring in their people to the combined village. Magpie Eagle's scouts had seen more soldiers moving up the Rosebud after Three Stars (Crook) had been driven away. They had been camped on Reno Creek when the scouts brought word. The next morning they moved into the big bottomland and joined the Ohmeseheso (Cheyenne) village.

The day after, more scouts were back on the Rosebud, watching to see what the soldiers were going to do. Crook's men were going away, but the second group (Custer's) was heading toward the village. A Cheyenne scout returned and reported this news. In the meantime, four or five lodges of Lakotas that had set out for Red Cloud Agency also discovered Custer's troops. They were frightened and turned back. When they reached the main camp, their report caused great alarm.

American Horse was in the Cheyenne camp at the lower end of the village. An old man crier rode around the circle shouting that soldiers were coming. As American Horse heard it, the warning stated that soldiers were about to charge the upper and lower ends of the village.

The soldiers struck first at the upper end. American Horse quickly dressed for war and, since he kept his horse picketed close by his lodge, he would get there early. He was the only Cheyenne council chief to take part in the fighting on that part of the field.[57]

56. Miller, "Echoes," 37–38.
57. Father Peter John Powell, *People of the Sacred Mountain: A History of the Cheyenne Chiefs and Warrior Societies 1830–1879*, vol. 2 (San Francisco: Harper & Row, 1981), 1006, 1011–12; Greene, *Lakota and Cheyenne*, 48–49; Dan L. Thrapp, *Encyclopedia of Frontier Biography*, vol. 1, (Lincoln: University of Nebraska Press, 1988), 21–22. There were several individuals named American Horse. One Oglala, aka Iron Shirt, was killed in September 1876, at Slim Buttes. Another was at Red Cloud Agency and missed the battle. The American Horse of our narrative was one of George B. Grinnell's numerous Northern Cheyenne informants. Greene has incorrectly identified him as an Oglala Lakota.

WC   3:00–3:10, **White Cow Bull** (Ptebloka Ska) [next 3:10]. As had other Oglala tribesmen, White Cow Bull slept late on the morning of the battle. Dances through the night had celebrated the victory over Gray Fox (Crook) the week before. Waking up hungry, White Cow Bull dressed and went to a nearby tipi to ask an old woman for food. Benefiting from customary Lakota hospitality, he was filling his stomach when the woman suddenly ventured, "Today attackers are coming."

White Cow Bull asked the old woman how she knew, but she said no more. When he finished eating he caught his best pony, an iron-gray gelding, and rode to the Cheyenne camp. He felt hale and hearty.

In his twenty-eighth year of manhood, White Cow Bull had been with many women but had never taken a wife. Yet, there was a pretty young Cheyenne woman named Meotzi (Monahsetah) who had caught his eye. His Cheyenne friends said she was originally from the southern branch of the tribe, but no Cheyenne man could marry her because she had a seven-year-old son born out of wedlock. In addition, the boy's father was said to be the white soldier chief called Long Hair. He had taken Meotzi to his tent after his soldiers killed her father, Little Rock, eight years ago during the fight on the Washita River. Meotzi, in her twenties and still unmarried, now lived with the Northern Cheyennes with her son, Yellow Bird. He had light streaks in his hair and always seemed to be with his mother in the daytime. White Cow Bull could never get a minute alone with Meotzi. At night he would come calling. Meotzi knew he wanted to walk with her under the courting blanket, but she would only talk to him through the tipi and would never consent to come outside.[58]

Perhaps this would finally be White Cow Bull's lucky day. Riding for a time around the Cheyenne circle, he saw Meotzi carrying firewood up from the river. Yellow Bird was with her. White Cow Bull just smiled and said nothing.

Riding on, White Cow Bull decided to visit his Cheyenne friend Roan Bear. One of the Fox Warrior Society, Roan Bear was on guard duty that day at the medicine lodge where the sacred buffalo hat was kept. Roan Bear had to remain at his post, for the buffalo hat, *Issiwun* (*Esevone*), had the power to control the abundance of game animals, and with it the people would never go hungry. The two men were soon joined by the Cheyenne Bobtail Horse, and the three of them spent the morning and early afternoon telling stories of their past brave deeds. It was after midday when they heard shooting far to the south of the Hunkpapa circle.[59]

---

58. Although I have included the Yellow Bird (or Yellow Swallow, or Yellow Tail) story because it is part of White Cow Bull's narrative, there is much evidence against the child being Custer's, regardless of its popularizing by Mari Sandoz. Meotzi was already seven months pregnant when she met Custer, and the child was born a full-blood Indian. There is conjecture of a second child, but no evidence or documentation has been found. See Barbara Zimmerman, "Mo-nah-se-tah: Fact or Fiction?" 4th Annual Symposium, Custer Battlefield Historical & Museum Association (Hardin, MT: CBH&MA, 1990), 1–8.

59. Ibid., 32–33; George Bird Grinnell, *The Cheyenne Indians: Their History and Ways of Life*, vol. 1 (Lincoln: University of Nebraska Press, 1972), 2–3; Richard Erdos and Alfonso Ortiz, eds., *American Indian Myths and Legends* (New York: Pantheon Books, 1984), 34–36; Marquis, *Cheyennes of Montana*, 138. The other great medicine object of the Cheyennes, the sacred arrows (*Mahotse*), were usually kept by the southern branch of the tribe.

❧ DISCUSSION. It is apparent from the Indian reactions during the first ten minutes of the battle, and it will become increasingly evident, that Custer had surprised the camp. Their words and deeds belie any assertion that Custer walked into a well-prepared ambush. The Indians had fought Brig. Gen. George Crook on the Rosebud on the 17th of June in an action they initiated twenty miles from their camp. They did not want soldiers approaching their village. They would not have allowed Custer to get so near had they known he was in the area. As at the Rosebud, they would have preferred to challenge him miles away so that, if they lost, the women and children would still have time to break camp and run.[60]

It is true that there were warnings given by isolated Indians who had happened upon the approaching soldiers earlier that morning. Two Indians, perhaps hunting stray horses, had seen the troops near the Rosebud–Little Bighorn divide. Nearby, another group of about seven Indians on their way to Red Cloud Agency in Nebraska had also spotted Custer's bivouac fires. A third group of Cheyennes under Little Wolf, on their way from the agency to the camp, came upon the troops before they left the valley of the Rosebud. Scouts from the latter group, possibly Medicine Bull and Red Cherries, discovered items dropped or left behind by the troops during their night halt and were subsequently chased away by troopers returning for that lost baggage in the morning. A fourth group of Indians, which included Brown Back and the boy Deeds, was confronted by Custer's Indian scouts near the site of Reno's initial crossing to the west bank of the Little Bighorn. Deeds died in this encounter, and Brown Back may have brought the warning to the camp just ahead of the soldiers.[61]

A number of other Indians who discovered Custer's approach may have also raced back to warn the camp shortly before Reno struck. Their presence and their warning were commented on by the villagers, including Low Dog, Fears Nothing, and Iron Hawk (who specifically mentioned Deeds), or by Indians returning from a horse hunt or from an attempt to go to the agency. Standing Bear named Black Bear as one of the Indians who returned to warn the village. Although the Oglala Black Bear indicated he was with the party heading for the agency, he did not admit he came back to sound the alarm, possibly because he still feared retaliation.[62] In the next time segment we will see that the Oglala He Dog thought it was Fast Horn who returned from the agency group to warn the others. The Cheyenne Little Hawk said the soldiers' presence on the Rosebud was reported, "but Custer must have traveled as fast as the man who brought the news."[63]

Whoever the actual Indians were, the warning they brought came on such short notice that no effective countermeasures could have been implemented before Reno's men were upon them. The situation was not unlike hearing a tornado siren sounding, then peering out the window to see the vortex only a few blocks away and moving closer. Where to go or what to do? Practically, the solution would be

60. Jay Smith, "What Did Not Happen at the Battle of the Little Bighorn," *Research Review* 6, no. 2 (June 1992): 12.
61. Richard G. Hardorff, *Hokahey! A Good Day to Die! The Indian Casualties of the Custer Fight* (Spokane: The Arthur H. Clark Company, 1993), 21–30; Powell, *Sacred Mountain*, 1032.
62. Hammer, *Custer in '76*, 203.
63. Greene, *Lakota and Cheyenne*, 62.

to head for the cellar and hope for the best. The Indian villagers were faced with a similar dilemma. That they were able to respond as well as they did is to their credit.

There were premonitions of an upcoming attack. One of the most often repeated was Sitting Bull's vision resulting from his day and night participation in the sun dance on June 4–5, back on the Rosebud. The vision, said to have originated from the pain of the dance, the swirl of color and sound, and the domain from beyond the earth, resulted in a picture of bluecoat soldiers falling headfirst into the Lakota camp circle. His vision convinced the people that soon a great battle would be fought and won. Also, two nights before the battle, the Cheyenne holy man Box Elder had a dream. When he awoke he sent a crier through the village, cautioning people to keep their horses tied up nearby their lodges. "In my dream I saw soldiers coming," he warned.[64]

In the village on the morning of June 25, Black Elk, who later became a renowned Oglala holy man, claimed to have a premonition, a "funny feeling" that a great battle was in the offing. A hungry White Cow Bull, eating a breakfast provided by an unnamed Oglala woman, was told "today attackers are coming." Standing Bear and Beard both recorded that their uncle warned them to collect their horses because he felt something might happen that day.

The soldiers also wrote of premonitions and omens. In a late-night council on June 22, Custer was said to have unbosomed himself to the officers, being conciliatory and subdued and showing a lack of confidence. The marked change from his usual brusque and aggressive manner led Lieutenant Wallace to tell Lt. Edward S. Godfrey that he thought Custer would be killed soon; he had never heard him talk that way before. Two days later, as the 7th Cavalry came across the abandoned sun dance camp, Custer's headquarters flag was blown down, falling toward the rear. Godfrey picked it up and stuck the staff back in the ground, only to see it fall again to the rear. Godfrey said the incident made no impression on him at the time, but Wallace later reminded him of the occurrence and felt sure it was an omen of defeat. Apparently even the scout Charley Reynolds had a strong prescience of disaster and twice tried to get Brig. Gen. Alfred Terry to release him from the expedition. On the morning of the battle, the Arikara scout Bloody Knife also predicted he would not see the next setting of the sun.[65]

Scientifically, not much stock can be placed in premonitions. It takes but little imagination to look back on an event and intuit some insignificant, minor occurrence as an omen. So-called premonitions or dreams occur daily, and, given the sheer number of daydreamers, the likelihood of a thought actually becoming reality is statistically quite probable.[66] This is particularly true in battle, where virtually 100 percent of the men about to face the fire would naturally have thoughts concerning their own mortality. That some of them would die is less a proof of premonitory powers than it is an illustration that all men share similar thoughts of survival.

---

64. Gray, *Centennial Campaign*, 331; Kammen, Marshall, and Lefthand, *Soldiers Falling*, 46–47; Powell, *Sacred Mountain*, 1008.

65. Edward S. Godfrey, "Custer's Last Battle 1876," *Century Magazine* (January 1892; reprint, Golden, CO: Outbooks, Inc., 1986), 17–18; Edgar I. Stewart, *Custer's Luck* (Norman: University of Oklahoma Press, 1955), 248, 263; Fred Dustin, *The Custer Tragedy: Events Leading up to and Following the Little Big Horn Campaign of 1876* (Ann Arbor, MI: Edwards Brothers, 1939; reprint, El Segundo, CA: Upton & Sons, 1987), 101.

66. Richard Dawkins, *The Blind Watchmaker* (New York: W. W. Norton & Company, 1986), 159, 163.

What a person "remembers" about a battle is determined exclusively by his subsequent feelings about the fight and his particular role in it. Our memory of such events is an imaginative construction based on our attitudes and beliefs.[67] Had no great battle occurred, or had the cavalry fought and won, no one would have recalled premonitions of death. (How many harbingers of disaster were recorded about the Battle of the Washita?) The omens would have been as insignificant and insubstantial as the gust of wind that blew down Custer's flag, dissipating to nothingness as it eddied among the cottonwoods and sweet grass along the Rosebud on a forgotten day in June.

Yet, speculations of premonitions, though they make good copy, are not so important to our understanding of the battle. The intuition of Standing Bear's and Beard's uncle is secondary to the discrepancies in the two accounts, which the observant reader has assuredly noted.

Standing Bear told his story to interviewer Eli S. Ricker in 1907, to Walter M. Camp in 1910, and to John G. Neihardt in 1931. He said he went for a swim, came back to his tipi to eat, and heard his uncle give the warning. His brother, Beard, was at the creek herding the horses. Beard told his story to David H. Miller in 1936. He said he went to the river to swim, came back to the tipi to eat, and heard his uncle give the warning. He then hurried to the creek where his brother Standing Bear was herding the horses. Each brother remembered being in the tipi while the other was out with the horses.

The stories are very similar, with the exception of a key reversal. Both cannot be correct. The Standing Bear interviews were earlier, one of them by nearly three decades, thus his chroniclers could not have been influenced by Miller's portrayal. The likelihood of a *correct* remembrance is enhanced the closer in time one is to the event being described. On these counts, the Standing Bear rendition would appear to be the more reliable. At seventy-eight years of age, perhaps Beard was plagued by a faulty memory. Perhaps Miller innocently recorded the sequence wrong. Yet, the question has been raised as to why Miller waited nearly twenty years after his interviews, and after all the participants were dead, to publish his findings. And, as historian Richard G. Hardorff noted, information exists that places doubts on Miller's research methods. To prove his point, he cited Walter S. Campbell's (Stanley Vestal's) accusations that Miller appropriated Campbell's research data to publish as his own.[68]

Regardless of the caution flags that may make me wary of Miller's interviews, we cannot discard the testimony. To do so would invite a charge of using evidence selectively. There are enough conflicting accounts of the Battle of the Little Bighorn to enable anyone to prove or disprove almost any imaginable scenario by using only those accounts that support one's particular argument. My attempt here is to use all the coherent Indian accounts available, pausing only to point out some of the apparent inconsistencies.

---

67. Rosenberg, *Epic of Defeat*, 263.
68. Hardorff, *Hokahey!*, 24. It is interesting to note that Campbell also waited over twenty years after his interviews with White Bull to publish the "truth" that the old warrior was Custer's slayer. Campbell waited until White Bull was dead because, he said, "I feared that if his story were published . . . some hothead might harm the old man." See Stanley Vestal, "The Man Who Killed Custer," *American Heritage* 8 (February 1957): 91.

RUDE AWAKENINGS, 3:10–3:20

WL 3:10–3:20, **Wooden Leg** (Kum mok quiv vi ok ta) [next 3:40]. The Northern Cheyenne Eats From His Hand was born on the Cheyenne River near the Black Hills in 1858. His name changed to Wooden Leg when he proved he could walk all day without tiring. By his eighteenth year, he had grown near to his adult size of six feet two inches tall and 235 pounds.

The seven people living in Wooden Leg's family lodge included his father, White Buffalo Shaking Off The Dust (Many Bullet Wounds), his mother, Eagle Feather On The Forehead, his older brother, Yellow Hair, his older sister, Crooked Nose, his younger brother, Twin, and his sister Fingers Woman. Wooden Leg owned two

The eighteen-year-old Cheyenne Wooden Leg received his name when he proved he could walk all day long without tiring. —Little Bighorn Battlefield National Monument

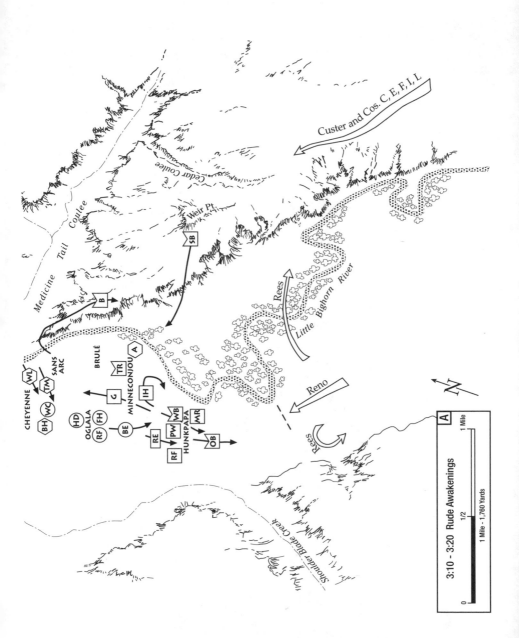

Custer and Cos. C, E, F, I, L

Cedar Coulee

Weir Pt.

Medicine Tail Coulee

Rees

Little Bighorn River

Reno

Rees

SB

B

BRULÉ

SANS ARC

CHEYENNE

WI

TM

WC

BH

OGLALA

HD

RF

FH

MINNECONJOU

TR

A

G

IH

BE

RE

RF

PW

WB

MR

OB

HUNKPAPA

Shoulder Blade Creek

N

A

3:10 - 3:20 Rude Awakenings

0   1/2   1 Mile

1 Mile - 1,760 Yards

of the family's nine horses. He once owned a muzzleloader, but lost it the previous March when soldiers attacked their village on the Powder River. He still had a cap-and-ball six-shooter.

The night before there had been a dance, a social affair for the young people. Wooden Leg participated for awhile, then a friend suggested that they go to the festivities in another camp. They spent the rest of the night dancing in the next village with the Sans Arc girls. The first signs of dawn had started to appear when the dance ended, and Wooden Leg walked wearily back to his lodge. He did not enter it, but dropped down outside to sleep for a few hours.

When he awoke, he went inside the lodge and his mother prepared his break-fast. "You must go for a bath in the river," she told him. Accompanied by Yellow Hair, he went to the Greasy Grass and found Indians of all ages splashing in the water. The sun was high and the weather was hot. After washing and cooling off, the brothers found a shade tree to doze under. In his sleep, Wooden Leg dreamed of a great crowd of people and much noise. Startled, he awoke to find it was no dream. There was a commotion in the camps. He and Yellow Hair hurried out from the trees and saw people running.

Wooden Leg had no thought of fighting, for his people had just driven away the soldiers on the Rosebud last week. But he heard shooting somewhere above the upper camp circles. Women began screaming. An old man was calling, "Soldiers are here! Young men, go out and fight them."

Wooden Leg ran to his lodge. Some women were already packing up for the flight. Some were heading north, some across the river. Wooden Leg grabbed his lariat and six-shooter and headed for the herd. The Cheyenne horses were grazing down in the valley below the camp. Boys from each tribe guarded their band's horses and kept them separated. He found some Cheyenne herder boys and told them what was going on. Wooden Leg caught his breath while the horses were being driven in. He could walk all day, but he was not very good at running. He walked back to his lodge, where his father had roped his favorite horse from the herd just driven in. Wooden Leg prepared for battle.[69]

G 3:10–3:20, **Gall** (Pizi, or Co kam i ya ya) [next 3:20]. Born on the Moreau River in South Dakota in either 1838 or 1840 and orphaned as a child, the Hunkpapa known as Pizi, Man Who Goes In The Middle, or Comes In Center was a chief of a warrior society, even though he was near the customary maximum age (thirty-seven) for continued warrior activity. He had fought Custer before, in August of 1873, in battles along the Yellowstone River.[70]

Like almost everyone else that day, Gall was caught unprepared by the attack. He did indicate that buffalo scouts brought word that soldiers were camped east of the divide on the previous night. That was surprising because, as far as Gall knew,

69. Marquis, *Wooden Leg*, 1, 210–18.
70. Marquis, *Custer on the Little Big Horn*, 106–7; White Bull, Box 105, Notebook 24, Campbell Collection; Steven W. Myers, "Roster of Known Hostile Indians at the Battle of the Little Bighorn," *Research Review: The Journal of the Little Bighorn Associates* 5, no. 2 (June 1991): 16; James Patrick Dowd, *Custer Lives!* (Fairfield, WA: Ye Galleon Press, 1982), 37, 40; Dan L. Thrapp, *Encyclopedia of Frontier Biography*, vol. 2 (Lincoln: University of Nebraska Press, 1988), 527. Though most sources show Gall to be thirty-six to thirty-eight years old at the time of the battle, Marquis indicates he was only twenty-nine.

the only soldiers in the country were still in the south with General Crook. He was sitting in his lodge going about his business. "I can't say that I or anyone else was in command," he admitted. When he heard the shout, "They are coming," evidently first raised by some boys running from the southeast and into the Blackfoot camp, everyone rushed for their guns and horses.

Some of the Hunkpapa horse herd was located down the valley. Gall headed north.[71]

WC 3:10–3:20, **White Cow Bull** [last 3:00, next 4:00]. While passing time with Roan Bear and Bobtail Horse and hoping Meotzi might walk by, White Cow Bull had heard shooting to the south. Just then an Oglala rode into the circle at a gallop, shouting, "Soldiers are coming! Many white men are attacking!"

White Cow Bull translated the warning into *Shahiyela* (Cheyenne), and soon the Cheyenne camp was caught up in the excitement. As a Fox warrior on guard that day, Roan Bear could not abandon his post at the lodge of the *Issiwun*. While they talked about what course of action to take, White Cow Bull saw Two Moon run into camp from the river with three or four horses.

"*Nutskaveho!*" Two Moon called out. "White soldiers are coming! Everybody run for your horses." When some of the braves began to gather, White Cow Bull heard Two Moon exhort the Cheyennes not to run away, but to stand and fight. It was a good brave-up talk to make them strong.[72]

TM 3:10–3:20, **Two Moon** (Ish hayu Nishus) [next 3:40]. Two Moon was born in 1842 in the Shoshone territory of western Wyoming. His father, Carries the Otter, was an Arikara captive who married into the Northern Cheyenne tribe. Two Moon had been an active warrior since the age of thirteen, when he was a government scout for a short while. At the time of the Little Bighorn fight, he was a minor chief of the Kit Fox Society.

The Cheyenne camp was located across from the mouth of Medicine Tail's coulee. In the village that morning, there was talk of holding another dance and the people began to paint themselves, cook, cut tobacco, and get ready. They thought the white men were far away and they did not expect to fight that morning. Two Moon went to the ponies, which were kept east of the river and north of the camp. Back in the hills he looked up the valley and saw a great dust cloud. Puzzled as to its meaning, he continued to drive his family's forty horses to the river and washed them down with cool water.

Finally nearing his camp, Two Moon again looked up the valley where the dust now looked like a whirlwind. Lakota horsemen came running into camp shouting, "Soldiers come! Plenty white soldiers." He ran to his tipi to call to his brother-in-law to get his horses. Up the valley came the sounds of many guns being fired, along with the Cheyenne battle cry of "Hay-ay, hay-ay!"

Outside the tipi, Two Moon could not see any Indians. The men were out gathering up the ponies and the women were hurriedly packing for flight. Soon,

---

71. Burdick, *Barry's Notes*, 9–11; Marquis, *Custer on the Little Big Horn*, 110; Graham, *The Custer Myth*, 92.
72. Miller, "Echoes," 33.

the old men, women, and children began to appear, running through the camp, and then came the young men, rushing to prepare for battle.

Two Moon gathered his weapons, caught a white horse, and rode out into the village circle. He called out: "I am Two Moon, your chief. Don't run away. Stay here and fight. You must stay and fight the white soldiers. I shall stay even if I am to be killed."[73]

IH 3:10–3:20, **Iron Hawk** [last 3:00, next 3:20]. A number of Iron Hawk's family's horses had stampeded down toward the Minneconjou tipis. He managed to bridle one and joined in the chase. "I fled with the horses among the Minneconjous," he recalled. Then, perhaps not satisfied with the implications of his statement, he added, "That is, I tried to get them out of the danger zone. I headed them off and brought them back."

Returning from his quick roundup, Iron Hawk joined other Hunkpapas in the camp to hear Sitting Bull admonish, "Boys, take courage, would you see these little children be taken away from me as dogs?" The Hunkpapas began to rally.[74]

OB 3:10–3:20, **One Bull** [last 3:00, next 3:30]. Chaos was spreading through the camp. Warriors rushed to catch their ponies. Women and children screamed and cried. Old men shouted out advice. The people began to flee to the west without striking the tipis or carrying off their belongings.

One Bull reached Sitting Bull's tipi and grabbed his muzzleloader. Just then his uncle entered the lodge and took the old gun from him. Sitting Bull handed him a *pogamoggan*, a stone-headed war club. From a buckskin case he took out his own rawhide shield, a beautiful piece of work made by Sitting Bull's father and decorated with a blue-green sky, a red man, four feathers, horns, and a yellow border. Sitting Bull hung it over One Bull's shoulder. The shield was for protection and to be used as a symbol of the chief's authority.

"You will take my place and go out and meet the soldiers that are attacking us," Sitting Bull ordered. "Parley with them, if you can. If they are willing, tell them I will talk peace with them."

Sitting Bull buckled his cartridge belt as they hurried outside. His deaf-mute adopted son, Blue Mountain, brought him his black stallion. Iron Elk, another bodyguard, handed him a Winchester carbine and a revolver. The chief hopped on the stallion's back to look for his old mother and get her to safety. As many young warriors gathered around One Bull, he gave a slight shudder, thinking of the responsibility he had been given. Without a word, he raised his uncle's shield high in the air so all could see it. Then he led them out to meet the soldiers.

One Bull quickly discovered that any peace talk would be impossible. Even as he approached the line of white horsemen, the firing had been going on fairly

---

73. Frazier Hunt and Robert Hunt, *I Fought with Custer: The Story of Sergeant Windolph, Last Survivor of the Battle of the Little Big Horn* (New York: Scribner's, 1954; reprint, Lincoln: University of Nebraska Press, 1987), 211–12; Hardorff, *Lakota Recollections*, 129–31, 134–35, 138; Dale T. Schoenberger, *The End of Custer: The Death of an American Military Legend* (British Columbia, Canada: Hancock House Publishers, 1995), 282. There has been much ado about how to spell Two Moon's name. Schoenberger insists that it should be Two Moons, from a 1917 death certificate for "Thomas Two Moons." Fine. Except his name wasn't "Thomas" either.

74. Neihardt, *Black Elk*, 120; DeMallie, *Sixth Grandfather*, 190.

heavily. He could see the soldiers' Arikara scouts trying to capture the Indian ponies off to the west of the camp. One Bull rode up to some Lakotas, raised his war club and shield high, and suggested they all charge at once. Even with this display of courage, One Bull lifted his head to pray, "Wakontonka help me so I do not sin but fight my battle."[75]

Likewise, Sitting Bull was soon disillusioned about the possibility of a parley. Gray Whirlwind reported that Sitting Bull had said he did not want his children to fight until he told them to, because the army might have been bringing rations or

Gray Whirlwind claimed that when Sitting Bull's best gray horse was shot, he was finally convinced to attack the soldiers. —State Historical Society of North Dakota

---

75. Miller, "Echoes," 30–31; One Bull, Box 105, Notebooks 19, 41, Campbell Collection; Greene, *Lakota and Cheyenne*, 54–56. Campbell's notes render One Bull's plea to the Great Spirit as, "Have mercy on me God that [I?] have no sin."

coming to make peace. Soon after, Sitting Bull's horse, which Gray Whirlwind described as a gray, was shot in two places, and Sitting Bull changed his tune. "Now my best horse is shot," he said. "It is like they have shot me. Attack them."[76]

B 3:10–3:20, **Beard** [last 3:00, next 3:20]. Although he went to the horses after hearing his uncle's premonition of trouble, Beard hesitated near Muskrat Creek when he heard the shouting in the village. Climbing Black Butte on the river's eastern bluffs, he soon reached a good vantage point to look at the surrounding countryside.

"I saw a long column of soldiers coming and a large party of Hunkpapa warriors, led by Sitting Bull's nephew, One Bull, riding out to meet them," said Beard. "I could see One Bull's hand raised in the peace sign," he added.

The conciliatory sign was unsuccessful, however, for all at once the soldiers spread out and began to fire. The fight was on. Beard ran back down to Muskrat Creek to look for his horse.[77]

SB 3:10–3:20, **Standing Bear** [last 3:00, next 3:40]. While wending his way through the cactus as fast as his bare feet would allow him, Standing Bear peered over his shoulder. In addition to the soldiers now beginning the attack in the valley, the ominous dust cloud farther down the bluffs got closer and closer.

Suddenly, a second group of soldiers, which Standing Bear later learned were Custer's men, made their appearance on a high hill to the south of him. They pulled up and halted. By then, Standing Bear had made his way down to clearer ground. He ran barefooted as fast as he could. Beard could take care of the horses. He would head straight back to his tipi.[78]

HD 3:10–3:20, **He Dog** (Sunka Bloka) [next 3:40]. This son of the Oglalas Black Rock and Blue Day Woman was born in 1840 near Bear Butte, South Dakota. He Dog was a warrior and a leader, displaying his martial abilities in March 1876 at the Powder River fight and the previous week in the battle with Crook. The move to the Little Bighorn was made with the thought that there would be no more fighting for a time. There were wives and children to protect and buffalo to be hunted. The Indians wished to be left alone.

Some scouts had been back east on the Rosebud–Little Bighorn divide, near a place called the Crow's Nest, when they discovered Custer coming. Of the scouts, which included Fast Horn, Black Bear, and Dirt Kettle, only Fast Horn rode quickly back to the camp to give the warning. The others went on to the agencies.

As Fast Horn spread the alarm in the Oglala camp, soldiers were already making their appearance to the south of the Hunkpapa circle. The Hunkpapas were the first Indians to confront them, and many of them were on foot, for the unexpected attack did not give them time to round up their mounts. In the Oglala camp, with

76. Gray Whirlwind, Box 105, Notebook 14, Campbell Collection. Gray Whirlwind, a.k.a. Sunken Ass, later saw Sitting Bull at the river on a sorrel, apparently after exchanging his wounded gray. Also, Little Soldier, in Box 104, Folder 6, claims that Sitting Bull liked white and gray horses best. He probably rode a gray, then a sorrel, not a black, during the battle.

77. Miller, "Echoes," 38.

78. DeMallie, *Sixth Grandfather*, 185.

many other tipis buffering the assault, He Dog had more time to get himself and his horse ready for battle.[79]

(A) 3:10–3:20, **Antelope** [last 3:00, next 3:50].Very soon after the two Lakota boys shouting their warning of approaching soldiers had run past the women, Antelope heard the shooting begin. She went to hide in the brush along the river with some other women. While waiting there, the popping sounds of gunfire increased.

Antelope could hear women and children screaming and old men calling the young warriors out to battle. As she peered out of the bushes, she could see the noncombatants hurrying afoot to the benchlands west of the villages while throngs of mounted men raced toward the skirt of timber south of the Hunkpapa camp circle. The guns down there were clattering now.[80]

(TR) 3:10–3:20, **Turtle Rib** [next 4:30]. The twenty-eight-year-old Minneconjou had not expected a fight that day. Three days before he had been with Lame Deer's band when they had engaged a considerable number of Crows. After that, they rode toward the village following the Indian trail from the Rosebud. They may have been the last Indians to use that trail before the soldiers followed behind them.

Turtle Rib had just joined the main camp one day before the battle and was still tired. On a day remarkable for its number of late-sleeping Indians, Turtle Rib partook of one of the most protracted siestas. Slumbering when Reno's soldiers were reported coming down the valley, he awoke to the noise and commotion of a battle nearly upon him. Already he could see enemy Ree (Arikara) Indians getting away with a drove of Lakota ponies. He would have to move fast if he wanted to get into this fight.[81]

(RF) 3:10–3:20, **Red Feather** [next 3:20]. Red Feather was a member of Big Road's band of Northern Oglalas. Like many others in his tribe, he had been up very late the night before, dancing and chasing after the girls. He was sleeping hard. He awoke to hear a woman say that it was time to take the horses out to pasture.

Red Feather rolled off of his robe and sat up to rub his eyes. He heard someone else call out, "Go get horses—buffaloes are stampeding!" He had not yet fully registered the information when other Indians began dashing into the camp with the ponies. One, known as Magpie, shouted, "Get away as fast as you can, don't wait for anything, the white men are charging!"

The shooting began. Red Feather could see soldiers firing into Sitting Bull's camp. Hunkpapas ran to the Oglala camp, and some Oglalas, also caught up in the early panic, ran with them. Red Feather got his pony and began to prepare for battle.[82]

---

79. Hammer, *Custer in '76*, 205–6; Hardorff, *Lakota Recollections*, 73.
80. Marquis, *Custer on the Little Big Horn*, 84.
81. Hammer, *Custer in '76*, 201.
82. Hardorff, *Lakota Recollections*, 81–82.

RE   3:10–3:20, **Runs The Enemy** (Tok kahin hpe ya) [next 3:20]. As a young warrior of fifteen, Runs The Enemy acquired his adult name by chasing an Assiniboine right into the midst of his own village and emerging without a scratch. Now thirty years old, he was a veteran of many battles with the Assiniboines, the Arikaras, and white soldiers, most recently against Crook just eight days earlier. This summer, as a warrior chief, Runs The Enemy led upwards of 130 Two Kettle Lakotas. They had been in the valley camp for two days.

On the morning of the battle, Runs The Enemy was up earlier than most. All was quiet. The horses were loose and feeding in the hills to the north, west, and south. He walked over to the main lodge, where several leading men were talking and smoking. It looked to be a lazy, restful day.

About two hours before noon, a band of Lakotas that had visited Runs The Enemy earlier that morning came rushing back with the alarming news that soldiers were coming. He did not believe it. Crook's soldiers had been chased away and were not near enough to attack. In addition, soldiers had never before attacked one of their Lakota camps in the daytime. Runs The Enemy sat back down with the men and continued smoking.

The reverie was cut short, however, by the report of rifles. Bullets began whizzing into the camp from the other side of the river. Runs The Enemy dropped his pipe and ran as fast as he could to his tipi. He heard screams throughout the camp, "The soldiers are here! The soldiers are here!"

The herders brought the horses down from the hills and into camp, and the dust grew as thick as smoke. Runs The Enemy grabbed his gun and cartridge belt. In the noise and confusion, the Indians did not know what to do. People rushed about. Women ran for the hills. Runs The Enemy was angry. Guns were still firing in the upper part of the camp. He did not have time to put on his war bonnet or prepare for battle. He jumped on his horse and pulled its head toward the sound of the firing.[83]

RF   3:10–3:20, **Rain In The Face** [next 5:00]. A Hunkpapa Lakota, Rain In The Face was born about 1835 near the forks of the Cheyenne River in what is now South Dakota. Neither his father nor grandfather had been chiefs, and he and his five brothers struggled for all they had. His mother's family included some noted ancestors; however, Rain In The Face said, "they left me no chieftanship. I had to work for my reputation."

The village had recently crossed from the Tongue River to the Little Bighorn because game was scarce. Crook had just retreated to Goose Creek, a move Rain In The Face thought was "more wise than brave." Here on the Greasy Grass he did not anticipate any more trouble. In fact, some warriors were making preparations to go on a raid against the Crows. Rain In The Face decided he would join them.

Although he was over forty years old, the rigors of the warpath did not deter him. Rain In The Face had been a belligerent sort ever since he was a boy. At ten

---

83. Joseph K. Dixon, *The Vanishing Race: The Last Great Indian Council* (Garden City, NY: Doubleday, Page & Company, 1913), 1, 63–65, 170–72.

years of age he got into a fight with a "friendly" Cheyenne, who bloodied his face, leaving a mixture of paint and blood striking enough to prompt other Lakota boys to give him his lifelong name. As a young man, during an all-day fight against the Gros Ventres, a shower had partly washed away and streaked the red and black paint on his face. Again, he was christened Rain In The Face.

That was many years ago. This morning, Rain In The Face had been invited to a feast at one of the young men's warrior lodges, where they discussed plans for the

Rain In The Face was a tested warrior who received his name as an obstreperous young man when he got into a fight with a Cheyenne who bloodied his face.
—Little Bighorn Battlefield National Monument

sortie against the Crows. "While I was eating my meat we heard the war-cry," Rain In The Face said. They all rushed out of the lodge and saw a warrior riding at top speed from the Hunkpapa camp, giving the warning. The "Long-Haired Chief" (Custer) appeared very suddenly, Rain In The Face declared. "It was a surprise."

In the distance, they could hear the reports of the soldier guns, which sounded differently from the guns of his people. Rain In The Face dropped his dinner and ran to his tipi.[84]

FH 3:10–3:20, **Flying Hawk** [next 3:50]. Flying Hawk, one of Sitting Bull's numerous nephews, was born in 1852 to the Oglala Black Fox and Iron Cedar Woman near the Black Hills. That Sunday morning he was in his lodge in the village, of which the Oglalas, Hunkpapas, Minneconjous, and Cheyennes comprised the main camps. The extreme length of all the camps was about one and one-half miles, with the heaviest concentration in the upper part of the valley.

It was in the day and just before dinner, which may have been as early as nine in the morning in Flying Hawk's estimation, when he first heard warning of the attack. Looking to the south, he could see a dust cloud, but he did not know what caused it. Some said it was caused by soldiers approaching. One chief said he saw a flag waving from a pole high up on the hill.

The answer came soon enough, when the soldiers began firing into the tipis among the women and children. It was the first Flying Hawk knew that there was serious trouble. Now the women grabbed their children by the hand, caught up their babies, and ran in every direction. Flying Hawk and his brother Kicking Bear prepared for action. Together they would look to Crazy Horse to lead them into battle.[85]

PW 3:10–3:20, **Pretty White Buffalo** [last 3:00, next 3:20]. While she busily worked at taking down her tipi, Pretty White Buffalo anxiously looked to the bluffs across the Greasy Grass. It was true. Soldiers were coming, riding parallel with, and about a rifle shot back from, the river. She could see metal flashing in the sun and thought it must be from their sabers. Still, she felt comparatively secure, for their downstream course would lead them away from the Hunkpapa circle.

With her attention diverted to the enemy moving along the ridges, she had no inkling of the nearer danger approaching up the valley. Just south of the Hunkpapa circle was a small camp of Blackfeet Lakota, and a bit south of it was a bend in the river and a fringe of trees. The broken character of the bluffs, the strip of timber on the west bank of the river, and the way the camp was situated had hidden the advance of the soldiers from the south.

Reno's carbines opened up on them almost without warning. "Like that, the soldiers were upon us," Pretty White Buffalo declared. The bullets rattled through the tipi poles of the Hunkpapa and Blackfeet, coming from the strip of trees extending out from the west bank of the Greasy Grass.

They had been taken by surprise, attacked from a direction they did not expect.

84. Charles A. Eastman (Ohiyesa), "Rain-In-The-Face: The Story of a Sioux Warrior," *Bighorn Yellowstone Journal* 2, no. 3 (summer 1993): 13, 17–18; Thrapp, *Frontier Biography*, vol. 3, 1188.

85. M. I. McCreight, *Firewater and Forked Tongues: A Sioux Chief Interprets U.S. History* (Pasadena, CA: Trail's End Publishing Company, 1947), 111–12; Hardorff, *Lakota Recollections*, 49–50, 53.

Through the wailing of the women and children, Pretty White Buffalo watched the men mount up, sing their battle songs, and race for the fight beyond the Blackfeet lodges. She likened the scene to that of a fire driven by a great wind, sweeping through the heavy grasslands of the buffalo range. Thus did the warriors rush through the village toward the timber, where the soldiers of the white chief had stopped to fight.[86]

BE 3:10–3:20, **Black Elk** [last 3:00, next 3:30]. After the criers had rushed by with the alarm, Black Elk made his way back to his father's lodge, where he was lucky enough to find his cousin just arriving with the horses he had been watering. Black Elk's older brother had already bridled up his sorrel and was off. His father said, "Your brother has gone to the Hunkpapas. You had better take this gun over to him."

Black Elk readied his buckskin mare and rode in the direction of the dust. Nearing the conflict, the smoke cleared enough for him to see the soldiers. Even at a distance, they looked tall and husky—a formidable foe. Just then they began to fire and the Hunkpapas fell back on foot. Along the river, Black Elk noticed naked children running for their lodges. As he searched, he learned from another Indian that a boy had already been killed. Black Elk only wanted to find his brother and get to a place of safety.

Black Elk's hunt was cut short when his brother found him. He took the gun Black Elk had brought and told him to go back. Then his brother spun on his horse and headed for the woods beyond the Hunkpapa camp.

Black Elk thought for a moment. He watched the receding dust kicked up from his brother's sorrel. Men gathered in front of the timber on the opposite side of the soldiers. His brother and his father had told him to go right back home. But he did have his own six-shooter—one that his sister had given him. Black Elk glanced down the valley in the direction of his father's lodge, then upstream to the quickening battle. He kicked his pony in the sides and headed toward the brush after his brother.[87]

WB 3:10–3:20, **White Bull** [last 3:00, next 3:20]. White Bull drove his ponies south to the Minneconjou camp. After seeing his own family off to safety, he rode his bay to the Hunkpapa lodges. There was great confusion as the people abandoned their tipis and streamed north. White Bull noticed young girls with shawls clutched over their heads, fat matrons puffing and perspiring, and old women hobbling along with their sticks.

On the north side of the Hunkpapa circle he passed the lodge of his father, Makes Room. On the south side of the circle at his uncle's lodge he found his brother One Bull and saw his aunt and young cousins running away. Warriors were gathering and Sitting Bull was haranguing them, "Get busy and do something," and, "Brave up. Boys, it will be a hard time—brave up!" Just then, White Bull heard the noise of soldier carbines and the first shots began coming through the tipis.[88]

86. McLaughlin, *My Friend the Indian*, 44.
87. Neihardt, *Black Elk*, 109–10; DeMallie, *Sixth Grandfather*, 181–82.
88. Hardorff, *Lakota Recollections*, 108–9; Vestal, *Warpath*, 192–93; White Bull, Box 105, Notebook 24, Campbell Collection.

MR 3:10–3:20, **Moving Robe** [last 3:00, next 3:40]. Winded from her long run after she stopped digging turnips, Moving Robe reached camp to find her father, Crawler, bringing in the horses. When she burst inside the tipi, she found her mother hurriedly preparing for the flight. There she heard the news that her young brother, One Hawk (Deeds), had been killed.

Holding back a tear, Moving Robe went outside to see soldiers on the bluffs across the Greasy Grass. She heard some scattered shots and heard the Hunkpapa Hawk Man calling for the Indians to charge. As her father prepared for battle, Moving Robe sang a death song for her brother.

Her heart was bad. "Revenge!" she cried, "for my brother's death." When she was only seventeen, she had accompanied a Lakota war party on a raid against the Crows. Today she would fight to defend her village and avenge her brother. Moving Robe quickly braided her hair, painted her face crimson, and rushed to get her

The old Hunkpapa Crawler was the father of Moving Robe.
—State Historical Society of North Dakota

horse tied to a nearby thicket. "I was mourning," she declared. "I was a woman, but I was not afraid."

By this time the soldiers had formed a battle line in the valley about one-half mile from her tipi. The next moment, there was a terrific crash of carbines and bullets shattered the tipi poles. Some women were killed right in their own camp. Men cried out and women wailed. The enchanting tremolo of the death songs Moving Robe heard during the brief lulls in the firing inspired her.

Moving Robe mounted her black horse. She saw a warrior adjust his quiver, grab his tomahawk, and run to his horse, when, suddenly, he recoiled and dropped to the ground, shot down next to his tipi. She heard Hawk Man shouting out orders to mount up. She and her father followed a group of Hunkpapas along the fringe of the woods moving toward the soldiers.[89]

❧ DISCUSSION. In this segment, Reno's Companies A, G, and M reached their northernmost mounted advance, after which they dismounted and moved forward perhaps another hundred yards on foot. Guidons were set up. Indian auxiliaries on the right flank had entered the timber to steal Lakota horses while others crossed the river to the flats on the east bank to capture more of the pony herd. The Arikaras and Crows on the left sought Lakota ponies on the western hills, but they were repulsed before completing their mission. The firing became heavy, with soldier volleys registering in the southern camps. During this time, Custer traveled north along the bluffs and had passed the spot where Reno would later entrench.

The Indian accounts reviewed in this early segment of the battle further cement the assertion that the village was surprised. After an all-night dance, Wooden Leg was caught sleeping under a shade tree near the river. Turtle Rib was still stretched out on his buffalo robes in his tipi when Reno arrived. Runs The Enemy arose early but was casually engaged with some other men when the first warning came and refused to believe it even as the attack commenced. Rain In The Face was caught at dinner with a mouthful of meat. Flying Hawk said bullets smacking into the tipis was the first he knew of any trouble. In Sitting Bull's own lodge there was confusion. His tipi that day was occupied by eight people: Sitting Bull; his two wives (sisters Four Robes and Seen By The Nation); the latter's two boys from a previous marriage, Little Soldier and Blue Mountain; the former's newborn twin daughters; and the wives' brother, Gray Eagle. When Reno attacked, Four Robes was so frightened that she grabbed only one of the infant twins. In the hills, when she was asked where the other one was, she realized what she had done, passed the child in her arms to a neighbor, and ran back to the tipi to retrieve the other. Later, the one she left behind was called Fled And Abandoned, or Abandoned One.[90] Obviously, this was not the household of a man who supposedly knew soldiers were coming and set a trap for them.

It follows that those critics who condemn Lt. Col. George A. Custer for foolishly attacking a prepared village in the middle of the day do not have much of an

89. Wayne Wells, "Little Big Horn Notes: Stanley Vestal's Indian Insights," *Greasy Grass* 5 (May 1989): 11; Hardorff, *Lakota Recollections*, 92–94.

90. White Bull, Box 105, Notebook 24, Campbell Collection; Utley, *Lance and Shield*, 150; Hardorff, *Lakota Recollections*, 119.

argument.[91] His approach worked. His opponent was surprised. One major tactical condition for a successful battle was satisfied.[92]

There have been questions raised concerning the likelihood of troopers near enough to the village to have fired into it, killing six to ten women and children. Certainly the firepower potential was there. Reno's 131 men each carried a .45 Springfield carbine with one hundred rounds of ammunition and a .45 Colt revolver with twenty-four rounds.[93] If a hundred of the men fired only half of their carbine ammunition, upwards of 5,000 bullets could have been sent in the direction of the village. Surely there was the possibility of a dozen noncombatant casualties.

Several Indians commented about the tipis being hit. Runs The Enemy noted that bullets came into the camp from across the river. Pretty White Buffalo said the bullets "rattled" into the Hunkpapa and Blackfeet tipis. White Bull said the soldiers' first shots came through the tipis. Moving Robe mentioned the bullets shattering the tipi poles and people being shot down next to their lodges. The Hunkpapa Crow King told of a woman who was shot in the shoulder while standing near him.[94]

Reno got close enough to place his carbines well within killing range. A trained trooper could fire a Springfield up to seventeen times per minute, projecting a slug farther than 1,000 yards, with accuracy at 250 yards. Lieutenant Wallace testified that the troops got within 75 to 100 yards of the tipis, while Pvt. James Wilber of Company M stated that about ten troopers, including himself, Sgt. John Ryan, Pvt. Roman Rutten, and Pvt. John H. Meier, actually got among the Hunkpapa tipis before turning back.[95] Nevertheless, a factor contributing to the low number of noncombatant casualties may have been the result of the southernmost tipis being set up on a flat just a bit lower in elevation than the point from which the troops were firing. This may account for the stories of bullets hitting the tipi tops.[96]

Another cause of the high fire may have stemmed from inadequate training and the nature of the Springfield carbine itself. The relatively slow muzzle velocity of 1,150 feet per second required a steep trajectory if the carbines were set to hit

91. Stewart, *Custer's Luck*, 278–79; Graham, *The Custer Myth*, 313; Robert P. Hughes, "The Campaign Against the Sioux in 1876," *Journal of the Military Service Institution of the United States* 18, no. 79 (January 1896): passim.

92. Smith, "What Did Not Happen," 8–10.

93. Kenneth M. Hammer, *The Glory March* (Monroe, MI: Monroe County Library System, 1980).

94. Hardorff, *Hokahey!*, 35.

95. Ronald H. Nichols, "The Springfield Carbine at the Little Big Horn," 2nd Annual Symposium, Custer Battlefield Historical & Museum Association (CBH&MA, 1988), 59; Nichols, *Reno Court*, 25; Hammer, *Custer in '76*, 148; J. W. Vaughn, *Indian Fights: New Facts on Seven Encounters* (Norman: University of Oklahoma Press, 1966), 153. In the last account, Vaughn indicates that a number of U.S. Army artifacts were found north of the Garryowen river bend and in the bottomlands at the southern edge of the village. He surmised that these came from Arikara scouts who charged ahead of the main line.

One author, Robert Nightengale, believes these cartridges found around the Garryowen loop are too far north to have come from Reno's battalion. He states there are no accounts from Reno's men that indicated they were in the tipis. (Wilber's account belies that assessment.) The result is that Nightengale believes the destruction caused to the lodges and people in the southern end of the village must have come from Custer's battalion attacking from the north. For this unfathomable assertion and more, see Robert Nightengale, *Little Big Horn* (Edina, MN: DocuPro Services, 1996), 111–13, 115.

96. Hardorff, *Hokahey!*, 35.

Indians issuing from the village at 500 yards and the sights were not changed; at 300 yards, the bullets would be more than twelve feet over the Indians' heads. Poor marksmanship and haste may have been important factors in the hail of bullets that hit the tipi tops.[97]

However, the issue of high fire had been a concern of riflemen since at least the Civil War. Well aware of the problem, Confederate Gen. Thomas C. Hindman, at the Battle of Prairie Grove in 1862, ordered his men to take deliberate aim and fire as low as the knee. Likewise, Union Gen. William S. Rosecrans at Stones River called to his men to shoot low and give the enemy a blizzard at their knees. Brig. Gen. Gouverneur K. Warren, at the Battle of Weldon Railroad in 1864, shouted to his men, "Fire low! Low! Low!" There are many references to officers telling their men that they must aim low, simply to counteract the natural inclination of a flinching rifleman to shoot too high.[98] The low number of Indian casualties may have been chiefly the result of untrained, undisciplined fire.

The bottomland in the middle distance was where the southernmost Hunkpapa tipis were hit by fire from Reno's battalion.

---

97. Lynn H. Wilke, "A Sight Picture: Paint & Feathers," *Newsletter*, Little Bighorn Associates 28, no. 5 (July 1994): 5–6. Wilke compares the Springfield's muzzle velocity with the modern M-16, which, at 3,250 feet per second and a flat trajectory, means that a bullet will hit just about where it is aimed without sight adjustments.

98. Paddy Griffith, *Rally Once Again: Battle Tactics of the American Civil War* (Wiltshire, England: Crowood Press, 1987), 88–89; James Lee McDonough, *Stones River—Bloody Winter in Tennessee* (Knoxville: University of Tennessee Press, 1980), 116; Noah Andre Trudeau, *The Last Citadel: Petersburg, Virginia, June 1864–April 1865* (Little, Brown & Company, 1991), 171.

Although the troopers' aim might have been the cause of the noncombatant casualties, they insisted that they did not make it a policy to shoot women and children. Though the possibility of accidental killings is quite likely, some among Reno's force did not share the scruples that supposedly restricted the soldiers. About the time Reno made his farthest advance down the valley, head Arikara scout Bloody Knife and other Rees had been in the timber, cutting out some Lakota horses. The Rees, explained scout Little Sioux, saw three women and two children running across the flats from the bluffs toward the river about at the spot where they were to cross later. He and Red Star fired at them. They were joined by Boy Chief and Strikes Two and they all rode through the timber to kill them. Though Little Sioux said the subsequent sight of two hundred horses east of the river terminated their pursuit of the women, guide George Herendeen said that the Ree scouts did kill some women, for the bodies of at least six squaws were found in a little ravine.[99]

Whether the deaths were caused by random shooting or deliberate perpetration, the fact is that women and children did die. Their bodies were found by Indians and by whites in the southern camps and upstream in the timber and along the river.

Returning to the Indian accounts, a minor difficulty arises with David H. Miller's rendition of the One Bull and Beard narratives. The story that One Bull rode south of the village as Sitting Bull's emissary seems reasonable enough. However, somewhere on the bluffs upriver from the junction of Medicine Tail Creek and the Little Bighorn, Beard is said to have seen One Bull riding out to meet the soldiers. Not only did he recognize One Bull from almost one and one-half miles away, but he saw him raise his hand in a peace gesture. This would be quite an extraordinary feat, even for one with exceptional eyesight. In fact, recognizing any individual at that distance amid smoke, dust, and hundreds of horses and men in motion would be nigh impossible. In addition, those of us with an acuity for visualizing line of sight over uneven terrain, or those of us who may have played any number of combat board games know that one cannot have direct sight of an object even when the observer is elevated a few hundred feet, when the distance between them is over one mile and the object lies directly behind intervening terrain such as hundreds of tipis or a copse of trees.[100] Counsel Lyman Gilbert at the Reno Court of Inquiry had difficulty believing Lieutenant DeRudio when the latter claimed he could recognize Custer and his party from a thousand yards away by their particular mode of dress, even while silhouetted on the edge of a bluff. Gen. Hugh L. Scott also doubted the authenticity of DeRudio's sighting.[101]

Certainly Beard could not have recognized One Bull, given the distance of their positions, the poor visibility, and the intervening terrain. Yet Miller transcribed Beard's narrative into a direct statement that he saw One Bull. It is possible that Beard later learned One Bull was somewhere out there with the vanguard of Indians, and Miller can be accused of nothing more than a little poetic license in

---

99. Libby, *The Arikara Narrative*, 150–51; Graham, *The Custer Myth*, 260; Hardorff, *Hokahey!*, 32–34.
100. "Squad Leader," (Baltimore: The Avalon Hill Game Company, 1977), 3, 14–15; "A Gleam of Bayonets," (New York: Simulations Publications, 1980), 7–8, 16.
101. Nichols, *Reno Court*, 343; Stewart, *Custer's Luck*, 358.

attempting to present us with one of those edifying corroborations that makes historical writing ring true. Then again, later we will see that other Miller accounts prove troublesome as well.

Other account discrepancies you may have noted can be found in the Eagle Elk and Red Feather narratives. In the 3:00–3:10 segment, Eagle Elk said he had stayed out all night long and was just making the sleepy trip back home when he was joined by Red Feather. In the 3:10–3:20 segment, however, Red Feather, still asleep on his robes in his tipi, is rudely awakened by shouts about white men attacking. Eagle Elk could not have been walking with Red Feather from the Hunkpapa camp when the shooting started, since Red Feather claimed to have been sound asleep at the time.

Red Feather was interviewed by Gen. Hugh L. Scott in 1919. Eagle Elk told his story to John G. Neihardt in 1944. The simple fact that Red Feather's story came twenty-five years earlier would tend to give it more weight. At ninety-three years of age, Eagle Elk may have mistaken a few details. It is possible that he walked home with someone other than Red Feather. Then again, it is also possible that there was more than one Red Feather.[102]

---

102. Hardorff, *Lakota Recollections*, 81, 99, 100.

First Confrontation, 3:20–3:30

PW 3:20–3:30, **Pretty White Buffalo** [last 3:10, next 4:00]. As the warriors streamed south to confront Reno's men, Pretty White Buffalo began to take heart, putting aside her thoughts of flight. Though other women loaded their travois and fled or milled about, waiting to determine the fate of their husbands and sons, Pretty White Buffalo saw that the men were not afraid, and she decided to wait and see what would happen.

She thought she could divine the soldier plans. Long Hair, she guessed, had gone along the bluffs to give battle from the front of the village on the river, while cunningly sending Reno to attack from the rear. But, Pretty White Buffalo believed, the Great Spirit had been watching over his red children that day and caused Reno to attack too soon. Long Hair was still three miles away when the Indians had almost finished with the soldiers attacking her end of the village.

Even then, had Reno's men charged their horses right into the Indian camp, the power of the Lakota might have been broken that day. The ground from the river to the tipis was open and level, but the soldiers dismounted and came in on foot, giving the Indians a chance to rally. The braves ran over the soldiers, Pretty White Buffalo said, "and beat them down as corn before the hail."[103]

IH 3:20–3:30, **Iron Hawk** [last 3:10, next 3:40]. While listening to Sitting Bull shouting words of courage to the rallying Hunkpapas, Iron Hawk looked beyond the edge of the tipis toward the soldier battle line. He could not see them directly, but their position from the smoke of their firing was plain. They were just beyond the point of timber.

Iron Hawk got back to the business at hand, helping to rouse the warriors to do their duty. He assisted in gathering weapons and helped them mount their horses. The braves nearest him collected along the flank of the soldiers close to the high bank that bordered the river bottom on the west. The unmounted Hunkpapa warriors raced into the brush that ran along that bank.

While caught up in the excitement, Iron Hawk suddenly realized that the battle was about to swirl on without him. He had not even begun to prepare himself.[104]

B 3:20–3:30, **Beard** [last 3:10, next 3:40]. After watching the soldiers in the valley firing at the advancing Hunkpapas, Beard ran back down the butte for the horses grazing near the mouth of Muskrat Creek. His brother Standing Bear, who he thought was tending the horses, was nowhere to be seen.

Looking around, Beard located and caught his favorite war pony, a small buckskin mustang called Little Yellow Horse (Sunkawakan Zi Chischila). He mounted him and raced back to his tipi to get ready for battle.[105]

---

103. McLaughlin, *My Friend the Indian*, 44–45.
104. DeMallie, *Sixth Grandfather*, 190; Hardorff, *Lakota Recollections*, 64.
105. Miller, "Echoes," 38.

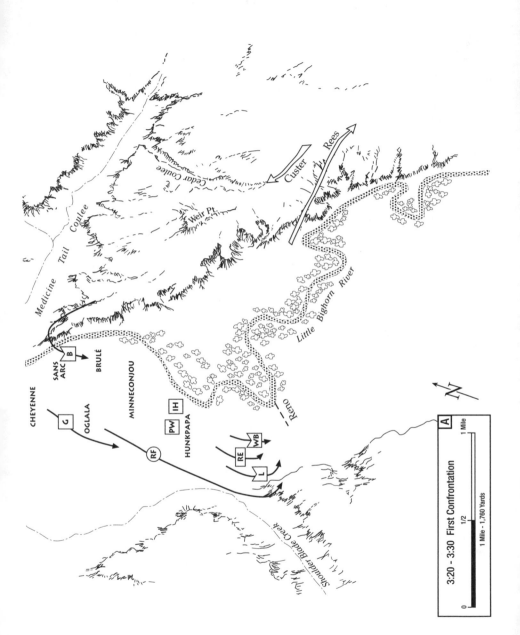

3:20 - 3:30 First Confrontation

RF 3:20–3:30, **Red Feather** [last 3:10, next 3:30]. While some Oglalas had been caught up in the minor panic that had begun in the Hunkpapa camp, Red Feather stoically bridled up the pony that he had kept tied up near his tipi. As he made ready he noticed many other Indians catching their horses and running to the bluffs in the west.

Almost finished, Red Feather saw Crazy Horse come out of his lodge with his bridle and rifle. The two Oglalas were good friends. Six years earlier, his sister, Black Shawl Woman, had married Crazy Horse. Since then, they had shared many adventures.

Crazy Horse was concerned that his horses were not in yet. "Take any horse," Red Feather suggested, for there was little time to waste. He swung up on his pony's back. Crazy Horse was not yet ready. Red Feather turned to follow the other warriors west to the hills.

Reaching the bluff above a little creek to the west of the soldier line, Red Feather noticed that many other warriors, Oglala and Hunkpapa, had the same idea. Quite a congregation was forming. Below him, he could see the camps in a great commotion. The sun was well up. It would be a good day for battle.[106]

WB 3:20–3:30, **White Bull** [last 3:10, next 3:30]. After watching the soldier bullets crash into the tipis, White Bull left Sitting Bull and One Bull and continued to the village outskirts, where he saw a lively fight going on in the open valley.

The soldiers shot from the saddle and advanced, moving the Indians back and getting close to the camp. Everything was smothered in dust and smoke as Indians on both sides dashed about, fighting for the horses. White Bull thought he could see Rees getting away with about ten head of Lakota horses, but the Indians gathered in such numbers that the Rees retreated, leaving their captured ponies once again in Lakota hands. The soldiers then dismounted and formed a line facing north, where they set up a flag.[107]

L 3:20–3:30, **Lights** (Cragre, or Chases Red Clouds—Mahpiyah luwa isaye) [next 4:10]. The young Minneconjou nicknamed Lights was twenty-three years old at the time of the battle. The coming of the soldiers was a surprise to him. Indians had just arrived in camp telling of seeing dust clouds to the east when Custer and his men appeared, though at that time no one knew whose soldiers they were.

Lights remembered the time as being about 9:30 in the morning when the fight broke out above the Hunkpapa camp. There was considerable confusion and intense excitement. The women and children were scattering down the stream and up in the hills.

Of the two main Minneconjou chiefs, Lame Deer and Spotted Elk, Lights chose to fight under the latter. Lights was among the first to get ready for battle. He and a comrade exposed themselves to the firing in front of Reno's skirmish line, making their way south and west toward the bluffs and around the soldiers' left flank.

---

106. Hardorff, *Lakota Recollections*, 82.
107. Ibid., 109–11; Vestal, *Warpath*, 193; White Bull, Box 105, Notebook 23, Campbell Collection.

Lights went ahead of a gathering group of Indians on the bluff. He was well out in front and south of the ridge when suddenly his friend crumpled to the ground with a gunshot wound to the head. The other Indians were braving up for a charge, but Lights would go no further in this attack. He knelt down to take care of his wounded friend.[108]

RE 3:20–3:30, **Runs the Enemy** [last 3:10, next 3:50]. Since he had not gone through his normal battle preparations, Runs The Enemy thought he would be one of the first to reach the fight. However, by the time he got to the battle line he found many Indians were there ahead of him. And there were casualties. The first thing Runs The Enemy found was a horse, bridled up, reins hanging loose, and a dead Indian on the ground next to it.

Lakotas were rushing up the hills to the west, nearly all of them virtually naked. Runs The Enemy peered toward the soldier line. Their uniforms, pack saddles, and black horses made them look like great buffalo. Looking to the bluffs, Runs The Enemy saw a lone Indian going downhill toward the soldiers and the river. It seemed as if all the soldiers focused their attention on him. Smoke enveloped his horse and billowed all along the line. "When we saw that the smoke was all going toward the soldiers," Runs The Enemy said, "that gave us a chance to charge from this side, and we all made a rush."[109]

G 3:20–3:30, **Gall** [last 3:10, next 3:30]. The fight had opened up at the edge of the timber south of Gall's lodge. He anxiously listened to the gunfire and wondered what was taking place up there. Rounding up his horses beyond the Cheyenne lodges, it didn't appear that he would get back in time to participate.

As soon as he brought his ponies together, his plan was to try and head off the soldiers from the creek. Gall headed south, circling on the outside of the village for that purpose.[110]

◄ DISCUSSION. In this segment we find the troopers holding their skirmish line position, with Company M on the left, A in the center, and G on the right. This line was a very tentative formation. From its right near the edge of the timber by an old dry channel of the river, it extended left only a short way into the valley. According to Lieutenant Wallace, about seventy-five men manned the line. With the normal five-yard interval between files, the line would have stretched about 375 yards. Sgt. Ferdinand A. Culbertson of Company A thought the line extended only 200 to 250 yards. When Company G was withdrawn to secure the horses being held in the woods, the files had to spread even thinner to maintain the position's integrity. Wallace was critical of the skirmish line as drawn by Lt. Edward Maguire for the Reno Court of Inquiry. As depicted, it extended nearly across the valley to the bluffs in the west. Wallace testified that had he drawn it, he would have cut off three-fourths of it. Indeed, interpreter Fred Gerard believed that the foot-

108. Hardorff, *Lakota Recollections*, 163–65, 172.
109. Dixon, *Vanishing Race*, 172.
110. Marquis, *Custer on the Little Big Horn*, 110; Graham, *The Custer Myth*, 92.

hills were at least 1,000 to 1,200 yards beyond the left of the line.[111] As such, the line was nearly useless in preventing passage around its flank. An army of clay pigeons could have trundled by with little molestation from Reno's gunfire. The Indians had no trouble bypassing it. We need to visualize this line in much more modest terms than it has been shown in the past.

From the rear of the skirmish line, Lt. Charles A. Varnum caught a glimpse of Company E, the Gray Horse Company, riding on the bluffs. Within a few minutes, in the woods to the east of the right flank, Lieutenant DeRudio saw Custer, Lt. William W. Cooke, and another man waving their hats on the highest bluffs.[112] To the west, the Ree auxiliaries abandoned their attempt to cut out Lakota ponies in the foothills. To the east, other Rees, after possibly killing some women, captured a number of ponies and made their way up the bluffs. Near the top, they passed the rear of Custer's column, which was beginning its journey down Cedar Coulee.

In the Indian village there was turmoil and excitement. Questions have been raised as to the whereabouts of Sitting Bull during the action. It has been suggested that the great medicine man had perhaps vacated the scene as soon as the bullets began to fly. The Oglala Low Dog did not put much stock in Sitting Bull's prowess as a warrior. "If some one would lend him a heart he would fight," Low Dog sneered. Gall indicated Sitting Bull was in his tipi during the battle, making medicine, but doing no fighting. Years later, Gall was said to have denounced Sitting Bull as a coward and a fraud.[113]

In fact, Sitting Bull was doing what any older warrior of his standing would be expected to do—seeing to the safety of his family and rallying the young braves. The forty-two-year-old medicine man ordered One Bull and Good Bear Boy to attempt a parley with the soldiers as he tried to send his mother off to a place of refuge. In the camp circle Iron Hawk later heard him admonishing the warriors to fight to protect the children. White Bull said Sitting Bull was not off making medicine, because he saw and heard him on the south side of the Hunkpapa circle rallying the warriors. He had been shot in the foot recently, White Bull said, and it had not healed right, "so S[itting] B[ull] couldn't run."

There were no grounds for Gall to say Sitting Bull stayed away from the fight because of cowardice. As author Thomas B. Marquis attested, one could as well believe that Grant denounced Lincoln, or Pershing denounced Wilson, for cowardice in not taking a gun and going to the front line. With the exception of firing a long-range bullet or two from near the camp, Sitting Bull did not fight, but neither did he shirk his duties as an inspirational leader.[114]

There is some question as to whether Sitting Bull and One Bull moved family members to the hills or remained in the village and let the old men help remove the women and children. As long ago as 1881, Judson Elliott Walker concluded that Sitting Bull did not accompany the women and children away from the village at the outset of Reno's attack. Robert Utley, 112 years later in his 1993 biography of Sitting Bull, opted for the evidence that states both Sitting Bull and One Bull took

111. Nichols, *Reno Court*, 23, 48, 93, 216, 367.
112. Ibid., 174–75, 338.
113. Graham, *The Custer Myth*, 76, 92; Marquis, *Custer on the Little Big Horn*, 106–7.
114. Marquis, *Custer on the Little Big Horn*, 107; White Bull, Box 105, Notebook 24, Campbell Collection.

The Hunkpapa medicine man Sitting Bull did not take part in the fighting, but remained near the camp to rally the warriors. —Little Bighorn Battlefield National Monument

their mothers to the hills before returning to the camp to organize the defense.[115] Although a case can be made for either interpretation, our time-event-terrain framework is a bit too restrictive to allow that much latitude of movement. The time is insufficient for Sitting Bull and One Bull to gather up their mothers, ride them to the bluffs, and return to their tipis to accomplish the other actions reported of them. Preparation for, and a round-trip to, even the nearest bluff—about one mile distant—would have taken a bare minimum of fifteen minutes. But the women and children were said to have congregated at Chasing (Squaw) Creek, about two

115. Judson Elliott Walker, *Campaigns of General Custer in the Northwest, and the Final Surrender of Sitting Bull* (New York: Promontory Press, 1881), 95–96; Utley, *Lance and Shield*, 150, 361.

miles northwest of the Hunkpapa camp. Had Sitting Bull and One Bull gone on that four-mile jaunt, they would have missed most of the Reno fight. White Bull passed by his parents' lodge on the way to Sitting Bull's tipi.[116] At his uncle's lodge he found both Sitting Bull and One Bull. Campbell recorded White Bull's words: "When I got to SB camp—his wife, child & everyone ran away & every man who could fite got on a horse & stood ground—SB with latter & had gun."[117]

Sitting Bull did not first take his family to safety. One Bull was his bodyguard and he did not run off to look after his mother. He met his uncle at his lodge and was given a shield, weapons, and instructions to attempt to parley with the soldiers. Thus, One Bull was one of the first warriors to ride south while Sitting Bull remained in camp, where a number of participants heard him giving "brave-up" talks. Neither had the time nor the wherewithal for the familial amenities of riding their mothers to safety.

By the time Reno was forced into the timber, the Indians had made a hasty dash to round up their ponies. The number and location of the pony herd need to be assessed. The earliest indication that there was a tremendous number of Indian horses came from the Crow scouts as they peered from the hill known as the Crow's Nest, just about dawn on June 25. They claimed there was a large pony herd near the sleeping village almost fifteen miles away. Standing nearby was the chief of scouts, Lieutenant Varnum. "Look for worms on the grass," they said, but Varnum's untrained eye could see nothing. Later, with the sun a little higher, guides Mitch Bouyer and George Herendeen said they could see the village, and interpreter Fred Gerard described a large moving black mass, but Lieutenant Colonel Custer could not see it.[118]

After the soldiers got to the village there was surprisingly little, if any, mention about the great horse herd. Not until the encampment was packed up and moving south on June 26 did the sight stimulate comment by some of Reno's men on the hill. Their statements were recorded at Reno's Court of Inquiry in 1879. Lieutenant Varnum testified that the village must have contained 15,000 Indians, and to move it would have required "an immense herd" of about 20,000 ponies. George Herendeen called the pony herd "a dark, moving mass" and estimated its size at 20,000 to 25,000 head. Captain McDougall said the moving village contained a massive pony herd two or three miles long and very broad, with 3,000 to 4,000 of them carrying riders. Lieutenant Edgerly testified that the mass was from two to three and one-half miles long and from one-half to one mile wide. The moving ponies looked to him "like a lot of brown underbrush," or "as if someone was moving a heavy carpet over the ground." There must have been 20,000 horses and they "were being driven just as dense as they could drive them."[119]

The court recorder (akin to a prosecutor) at the inquiry, Lt. Jesse M. Lee, waited until his closing statement to comment on the ludicrousness of such varied

116. At least Makes Room stayed there. His wife, Good Feather, seems to have spent much of her time living in her brother Sitting Bull's tipi, at least when One Bull was young.

117. White Bull, Box 105, Notebook 24, Campbell Collection.

118. John M. Carroll, ed., *Custer's Chief of Scouts: The Reminiscences of Charles A. Varnum* (Lincoln: University of Nebraska Press, 1987), 87; Gray, *Centennial Campaign*, 167–68.

119. Nichols, *Reno Court*, 186, 298, 451–52, 534.

testimony. He drew the court's attention to the diverse opinions given for the numbers of Indian warriors, which ranged from 1,500 to 9,000. Also, from the witnesses he understood that the moving village must have been about two and one-half miles long and one-half mile wide—a dense mass, as closely packed as it could be. If we allow 54 square feet per pony—a space 9 feet long by 6 feet wide— the herd could have contained 1,134,220 ponies! By giving each pony four times the space, 216 square feet, there would still be 283,555 ponies. Taking a different tack, Lee illustrated that if there were about 28,000 ponies, still more than the usual estimates of 20,000, then each animal would have had a grazing space of 2,160 square feet, which was hardly a dense mass. In fact, they would have appeared somewhat scattered.[120]

Although we might question some of Lee's math, his attempt to inject some common sense into the proceedings was commendable, albeit in vain. Densely packed ponies, even 20,000 or more of them, just do not take up the great area that the soldiers claimed. If we accept these estimates and pack them like a "brown underbrush" or "heavy carpet" at six square yards per horse, we have filled about 25 acres out of the 640 acres in one square mile. This is only about *4 percent of one square mile*. Referring back to figure 1, such an "immense" herd falls within the circle shown in the valley north of the camp. Even spread at much greater intervals, it is hardly a mass of "worms" that would cover the benchlands.

One study indicated that three horses were needed to haul an average-sized tipi plus belongings.[121] Were there perhaps 1,500 tipis? Then the Indians needed 4,500 horses. Were there 1,500 warriors owning an average of perhaps five ponies each? Then add another 7,500 head, totaling only about 12,000 horses. Even if each warrior owned five to ten ponies, the totals are still much less than the 20,000 to 28,000 estimated by the soldiers.

Where were these horses located before the fight commenced? Some may have been on the bluffs above the floodplain of the Little Bighorn. Runs The Enemy said the horses were feeding on the hills to the north, west, and south, but many others explained that the animals were in the valley, much closer to the camp and river. The Minneconjou ponies were north of the camp, in the valley just west and east of the river. White Bull said they were only about one-half mile north of the village and a little more than one hundred yards west of the river. Beard placed them approximately in the same area, north of the camp and by the mouth of Muskrat Creek, while Standing Bear said they were below the Santee camp and between the two branches of Muskrat Creek (Deep Coulee and Medicine Tail Coulee). Campbell helped One Bull draw a map (fig. 5) that showed the "horses ranging on flat."

Some of the Hunkpapa horses were near the village and river. Iron Hawk said some horses were right near the tipis, while the others were a bit to the north and east, along the river toward the Minneconjou tipis. To retrieve his horses, Gall went in the valley north of the Cheyenne camps.

---

120. Ibid., 626.
121. Laubin, *Tipi*, 282.

The Oglala Fears Nothing said the horses were north, below the camps, while Red Feather had his horses near his tipi. Numerous others must have been nearby, for Red Feather's words to Crazy Horse were, "Take any horse." The Cheyenne Two Moon said their horses were north of the camp and east of the river.

Given the reality of a village that probably covered about one-half square mile of the valley floor, there was no need to move the horses miles away up in the hills. They could have been more economically placed close at hand—easier for the boys to watch and feeding on the more luxuriant grasses of the bottomlands. This

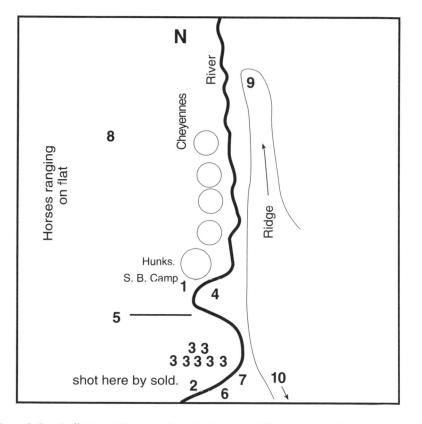

Figure 5. One Bull Map. 1. Horseman from s[outh] reports sold[iers] coming. *2.* Deeds—bro[ther] of Hona. *3.* Ind[ians] could see dust. *4.* Sold[iers]—sold[iers] leave horses at 4 on flat in bend of river. *5.* Ind[ian] line skirmish on horseback. *6.* From S[itting] B[ull's] camp to 6 where sold[iers] recrossed—5 miles or maybe less. *7.* Only 4 sold[iers] alive across R[iver] at 7. *8.* Many at 8 near S[itting] B[ull] & not in fite. *9.* Fite on hill 9—about 1 hour. *10.* Whites at 10, on hill stay several days? Leave 2nd nite.
—Based on a map One Bull drew with Walter Campbell's help (W. S. Campbell Collections, University of Oklahoma).

is not only where the majority of Indians said the horses were kept but also where the Ree scouts with Reno later captured a number of them—in the valley and near the camp. An "immense" Indian pony herd did not cover the benchlands surrounding a "gigantic" village that filled the valley to the brim. To the soldiers, certainly there was a great herd of horses, but its size increased in the telling, as did the village, in direct proportion to the embarrassment of their defeat.

SOLDIERS FALL BACK, 3:30–3:40

BE 3:30–3:40, **Black Elk** [last 3:10, next 3:40]. As he crawled through the brush in the timbers, Black Elk noticed many Hunkpapas were already in there with him. He heard some admonishing the others to take courage and be brave, for the helpless ones were out of breath from running.

He could not see well back across the flat toward the village because of the billowing dust, but he knew the women were still running and more warriors were approaching. The soldiers continued to fire into the trees, and the leaves fluttered down as they were clipped from the branches above him. Black Elk was mesmerized with the kaleidoscope of floating leaves and shafts of sunlight filtering through the canopy to dapple the ground beneath him.

As he waited under the sheltering trees, his mind recalled the great vision of the Thunder-beings, a vision where Black Elk was presented with powers from the four directions, as well as from the earth and the sky—the houses of the Six Grandfathers. He began to feel stronger. He thought then that the people had become Thunder-beings, able to use some of his power, because he now knew that they would wipe out the soldiers.[122]

OB 3:30–3:40, **One Bull** [last 3:10, next 3:40]. One Bull's suggestion to charge and his exhortation to Wakontonka did not have an immediate effect. In fact, his raised shield only seemed to draw more fire. The bullets flew faster, yet One Bull thought the soldiers were confused, for some fired mounted while others dismounted. In the excitement, two soldiers couldn't hold their horses. The steeds bolted and carried them right into the Indians. "These soldiers didn't last long!" One Bull declared.

Riding with One Bull was Young Black Moon, Swift Bear, White Bull (not One Bull's brother), and Good Bear Boy, the last warrior specifically named by Sitting Bull to accompany One Bull on his fruitless peace mission. They moved across a creek and came to a hill where other Indians were congregating. Since there was to be neither peace nor an immediate charge, One Bull called to the warriors to dismount and shoot back at the soldiers. He noticed the soldier chief also shouting out orders, and three out of every four of his men dismounted, while the fourth remained mounted and held the horses. This new posture did not last long. To counter the Rees who had been threatening the Lakota pony herd, Old Chief Black Moon brought up a large force of Hunkpapa camp police. They not only swept away the Rees, but began to get beyond the soldiers' exposed left flank.

One Bull again raised Sitting Bull's shield. This time he called for the warriors to mount up for a charge. They rushed forward, One Bull leaning down low on his horse's side and clinging to his neck to make himself a smaller target. Old Black Moon had burst around the end of the soldier line about the same time. The soldiers fell back, turning around a few times to shoot as they retreated. One Bull

122. Neihardt, *Black Elk*, 110; DeMallie, *Sixth Grandfather*, 54, 182.

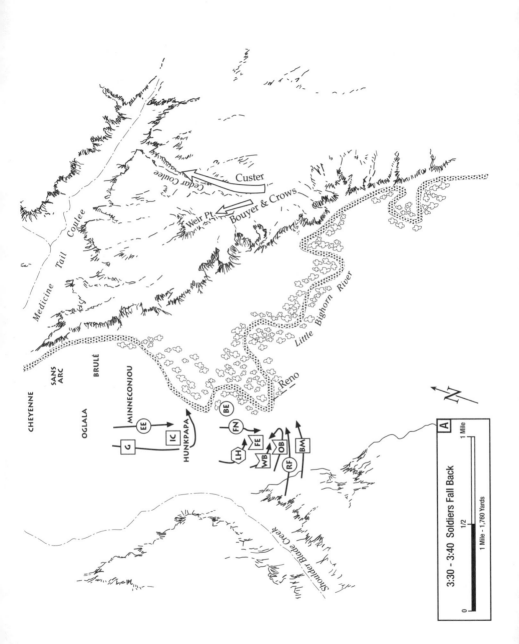

rode right into them and the soldier line was gone, the men scrambling for shelter in the timber along an old dry channel of the river.

As the Indian charge lost impetus and they circled back to regroup, One Bull noticed that Good Bear Boy had fallen, perhaps as close as thirty yards from where the middle company of the soldier line had been. He called to a man named Looking Elk to take Good Bear Boy from the field, but he either did not hear or refused to make the attempt. One Bull raced back to find Good Bear Boy shot through both legs and trying to crawl to safety. Tying him with a rawhide lariat, he hoisted him up on his horse. Making their way to the rear, the pony took a bullet in the hind leg and screamed out in pain. One Bull tried going backwards to hide himself, involuntarily flinching as the bullets screamed past them.[123]

The Minneconjou One Bull a nephew of Sittling Bull, daringly rescued the wounded Good Bear Boy during the fight with Reno. —State Historical Society of North Dakota

123. Miller, "Echoes," 31; Hardorff, *Hokahey!*, 37 38, 42; Utley, *Lance and Shield*, 152; One Bull, Box 104, Folder 6, and Box 105, Notebook 19, Campbell Collection.

FE 3:30–3:40, **Feather Earring** [next 4:50]. The Minneconjou warrior had once been quite an attraction during the social affairs of the village. He had acquired his name because, as a young man at the dances, he had persistently worn earrings made of brightly colored, fluffy plumage that hung down to his knees. Today, on the Greasy Grass, there was much more serious business at hand.

Feather Earring got into the fight early, when an Indian named Lone Dog rode into the camp from the south calling out that the soldiers were right behind him. No sooner had he given the warning than bullets began hitting the tipis. Feather Earring rode against Reno in one of the first attacks. He would have no cause for

Feather Earring was a Minneconjou who received his name from the outrageous plumage he wore. —State Historical Society of North Dakota

merriment at the next dance, however, for in the first charges that took the life of Young Black Moon, and saw the wounding of Good Bear Boy, Feather Earring's own younger brother was shot down. He carried the body of Dog With Horns away from the fighting. Should the bluecoats win the battle, he would have to find a safe place to hide it.[124]

R 3:30–3:40, **Red Feather** [last 3:20, next 3:40]. Anxious for battle, Red Feather had left Crazy Horse waiting for his horses back in camp. He reached the bluffs to the west where many other mounted warriors were pressing for a charge. "Why wait for the women and children to get tired?" Red Feather shouted. "Come on!"

His enthusiasm carried him down the hill about the same moment that Old Black Moon and One Bull were leading their charges. In front of Red Feather were two places where flags were planted. He rode right toward them. Before the charge hit home, however, the soldiers pulled down the flags and began to retreat to the woods behind them. One flag bearer was shot down, but managed to sit up, still clutching the pole. Red Feather thundered past him, striking the man with his quirt. An Indian galloping behind snatched away the flag.

Red Feather pulled to a halt and watched the soldiers fall back into the woods. They had them pressed on two fronts: the mounted Indians confronted the soldiers from the open valley to the west, while the Indians who couldn't catch their horses filtered into the woods on their northern side.[125]

EE 3:30–3:40, **Eagle Elk** [last 3:00, next 3:50]. The sound of bullets being fired from somewhere behind caused Eagle Elk to speed his trek home from the Hunkpapa camp. Arriving at his lodge on a run, Eagle Elk found his brother just driving the ponies in from the river.

As he ran to the tipi, Eagle Elk came across a pony that he recognized as belonging to a relative. He caught the pony and rode him back to his tipi. Eagle Elk secured his gun and traded the relative's pony for one of his own. Now on a fresh horse, he headed for the battle.

The confusion was such that Eagle Elk had only ridden a short way when he saw another Indian riding along, driving more horses that included some of his own. Eagle Elk stopped again to negotiate a quick exchange. Finally he was mounted on one of his best horses. Ahead of him, he could see the young braves rushing on foot toward the soldiers in the woods.[126]

LH 3:30–3:40, **Little Hawk** [next 5:40]. The young Northern Cheyenne had been camping on Reno Creek for three nights before moving down to the Little Bighorn. He was only there one day when the soldiers came. The Indians knew of their presence back on the Rosebud, but the soldiers traveled as fast as the Indian who brought the news.

124. Laubin, *Tipi*, 110; Graham, *The Custer Myth*, 97.
125. Hardorff, *Lakota Recollections*, 82–83.
126. Ibid., 100–101.

Little Hawk got close enough to witness some of the action after the first charge was made. Reno's men came down the Little Bighorn about two miles from their crossing place. The soldiers stopped their charge, halted, and fought for a short while. Then, suddenly they went into the timber near the lodges at the edge of the village. Down they went into a low place near a loop in the river where water used to stand. This did not deter the Cheyennes. They charged in after them.[127]

WB 3:30–3:40, **White Bull** [last 3:20, next 3:50]. Eyeing the flag set up by the soldiers near the timber's edge, White Bull thought of a course of action. "Whoever is a brave man will go get that flag," he yelled. But everyone appeared busy and no one volunteered. White Bull was working himself up to charge after the guidon when soldiers suddenly came and took it down.

The soldiers had been as close to the camp as they ever got. But they removed the flag and immediately fell back into the timber. By this time a great number of Indians had gathered, but no direct charge forced the soldiers back. For a time, individual Indians raced to and fro, drawing fire in acts of bravado, while others hung back and fired from a distance.

By this stage of the battle, White Bull learned that several Indians had already been fatally wounded or killed. In addition to the women and children and the boy Deeds, the Minneconjou Three Bears went down while standing near the Hunkpapa tipis, and the Minneconjou Dog With Horns fell in front of the skirmish line. There was some hot firing on foot in the timber.[128]

FN 3:30–3:40, **Fears Nothing** [last 3:00, next 4:00]. The waiting seemed interminable. More people were fleeing the camps and Fears Nothing was eager to take part in the battle. Yet his horses were far down the valley, below the lodges of the Cheyennes. He was painted up and ready to fight on foot when finally the herders brought his horses in.

Fears Nothing mounted and angled his horse toward the river, threading his way through the Oglala and Minneconjou lodges. He followed the river until he got right up close to the point of woods where Reno's line had been anchored. But the soldier line was no longer there. They had just fallen back into the woods and the Indians were swarming around them on two sides. Fears Nothing had missed the first phase, but now he was ready to fight.[129]

G 3:30–3:40, **Gall** [last 3:20, next 3:50]. As he rode back to the Hunkpapa village, Gall saw evidence of fighting everywhere. He saw Crazy Horse beginning to rush south through the Hunkpapa camp with a great following of braves. He saw Crow King moving in that direction also. Gall fell in with them.

Gall could see a band of Arikara scouts with the soldiers. It made him angry to see other Indians fighting against them, but soon they were chased away. The soldiers were harder to drive out because they were on foot and in the brush and grass. He was about to join a charge, when he heard women on the hill calling

---

127. Greene, *Lakota and Cheyenne*, 62.
128. Ibid., 110–11; Vestal, *Warpath*, 194; Hardorff, *Hokahey!*, 41, 57; White Bull, Box 105, Notebook 24, Campbell Collection.
129. Hardorff, *Lakota Recollections*, 26–27.

"*Daycia! Daycia!* [Here they are!]" Just then, Gall was intercepted by one of his warriors, Iron Cedar, who had been up on the high bluffs east of the river. It was true, Iron Cedar reported, more horsemen were riding north just over the ridge. The soldiers that had been earlier reported kicking up dust far to the east had now shown themselves to be at hand, heading for the Cheyenne camp at the lower end.

It was about two hours after noon as Gall remembered. He glanced at the many Indians who appeared to have gained the upper hand as they pushed back Reno's command, then he glanced to the bluffs. Perhaps he thought to look to the safety of his family, but there was little time. Gall jerked his pony's head toward the river and he and Iron Cedar left quickly to assess the new threat developing against the lower camps. Gall never got into the battle against the soldiers attacking his own village.[130]

◄ DISCUSSION. The mounting pressure from the Indians had forced Reno's hand. Especially on the exposed left, the series of disjointed charges caused him to pull his line back for a better defensive position in the timber. The second skirmish line was formed facing southwest, almost at a right angle to the first. The troops were now protected by the trees and the dry bed of an old loop of the river. East of them, to their rear, was an open glade of a few acres, and the lead horses were kept nearby. The second line extended about 160 yards.[131]

Custer, who left the high ground several minutes before Reno began pulling back, failed to see the maneuver. As Companies C, E, F, I, and I threaded their way down Cedar Coulee, the scout Mitch Bouyer and the Crows Curley, White Man Runs Him, Goes Ahead, and Hairy Moccasin may have kept abreast of the action by continuing along the bluff edge toward a promontory later known as Weir Point.

Down in the valley, the wounding and rescue of Good Bear Boy illustrates the difficulty in placing some events in their correct locale and sequence. Robert Utley wrote that Good Bear Boy was hit while he and One Bull were dismounted and leading their horses through the woods, just prior to the soldiers vacating the timber. Utley noted that there is conflicting testimony; one One Bull interview stated that the wounding occurred during the initial mounted charge, while another indicated that it happened at the end of the timber fight. Utley cited Campbell's Notebook 19 to affirm the incident took place late.[132] Yet, in that notebook, Campbell recorded that One Bull stated:

> Both flanks retreat, middle stands, the[y] retreat last. Bear Good Boy shot & wounded & falls on bank. Sold[iers] back & Ind[ians] go around bend in river. OB goes back for B.G. Boy who was shot in leg & helps him on horse, then OB leads horse back to camp—going backwards to hide himself. Then sold[iers] on horses and line up 5 OB on behind wounded man & goes SW. When horse turned around for OB to get on—horse shot on hip. Then fite at 5—when OB arrives, pulls wounded man off for other to get as his horse limps.

130. Burdick, *Barry's Notes*, 9–11; Marquis, *Custer on the Little Big Horn*, 110; Carroll, *Two Battles*, 102; Graham, *The Custer Myth*, 92.
131. Vaughn, *New Facts*, 156–57.
132. Utley, *Lance and Shield*, 152, 362.

This is not an indication of a late wounding. In fact, the opposite becomes apparent upon studying One Bull's map (see fig. 5). Number 5 represents the fight in front of the Indians' mounted skirmish line. Did Campbell poorly map One Bull's narrative? Perhaps—but the shooting of Good Bear Boy still took place *before* the "fite at 5," and, therefore, prior to the retreat to the timber.

In a subsequent interview, in Box 104, Folder 6, Campbell and One Bull re-phrased the narrative. Good Bear Boy was shot from his horse only thirty yards from the center of the three companies defending at the edge of the woods. One Bull went back to get him, but the rest of the Indians continued the charge. He put a rawhide rope around Good Bear Boy and hauled him up, but the soldiers shot the horse. One Bull helped him to the rear, leading the horse on foot while crossing the level valley under constant fire. When the Indians finally mixed with the soldiers in the woods, One Bull set Good Bear Boy down, got another horse, and returned to the battle. One Bull then killed two soldiers on horseback and a third at the stream bank where Reno crossed over to the east side.

In this narrative, we find the troops still deployed in line in the woods, Good Bear Boy shot *from* his horse (rather than walking dismounted in the woods), and One Bull helping him back to the rear while the Indians continued the attack.

In yet another Campbell interview, in Notebook 41, One Bull indicates that there were five very brave Hunkpapas behind him in the Reno battle: Good Bear Boy, (Young) Black Moon, Swift Bear, and White Bull, and another whose name he had forgotten. Only One Bull and Good Bear Boy lived, and Good Bear Boy, "was shot first & OB saves him."

In Box 110 of Campbell's notes, One Bull says he went straight to the battle without riding his family to safety. He identifies the fifth Indian riding with them as "Young Kansu." He also says that Good Bear Boy was shot first, before One Bull's horse and before White Bull and Swift Bear.

More corroboration of an early wounding comes from White Bull. In Campbell's Box 105, Notebook 24, we find:

> Before the sold[iers] go back to [the] timber young Soo [Sioux] "Dog With Horns" gets shot & the sold[iers] retreating to timber & Good Bear Boy gets shot in hip & Lone Bull saves him—then sold[iers] reach timber & untie horses & run across river.

Again we find Good Bear Boy shot and saved before the soldiers reached the timber. In addition to the narratives and map, we need only turn to the time and terrain constraints to cement an early wounding scenario. Had Good Bear Boy been shot while creeping through the timber just before Reno's "charge" to the river, One Bull would have had to pull his friend out of harm's way, carry or walk him to the rear on a lame horse, set him down, find a remount, and return to the fray in time to kill two retreating soldiers on horseback and a third one while crossing the river. The soldiers would have been long gone.[133]

---

133. Despite these indications of an early wounding, Greene, *Lakota and Cheyenne*, 56, presents an excerpt from a 1930 issue of *Sunshine Magazine*, in which a man named Pretty Bear is wounded. In this version, One Bull kills soldiers on the run to the retreat crossing, goes back to get Pretty Bear, carries him *toward* the river, then drops him off again before crossing over himself.

In 1876, the three-year-old racehorse Vagrant won the second running of the Kentucky Derby. Churchill Downs in 1876 had a one and one-half mile track—about the same distance Reno's horsemen ran from the timber to the river. Assuredly, the loaded, tired cavalry horses would not cover the distance in the two minutes or so that it would take a Derby contender. Yet, lashed by fleeing troopers in fear of losing their scalps, the horses would certainly have galloped the mile and a half in four or five minutes. Had Good Bear Boy been wounded late in the action, One Bull would still have been carrying him away in the opposite direction while the troops were splashing across the Little Bighorn.

One Bull's rescue of the wounded Good Bear Boy occurred relatively early in the valley action. This illustrates the necessity of combining a careful reading of the primary evidence within a framework of time and terrain. Of course, even with all the care exercised, one can never be 100 percent certain.

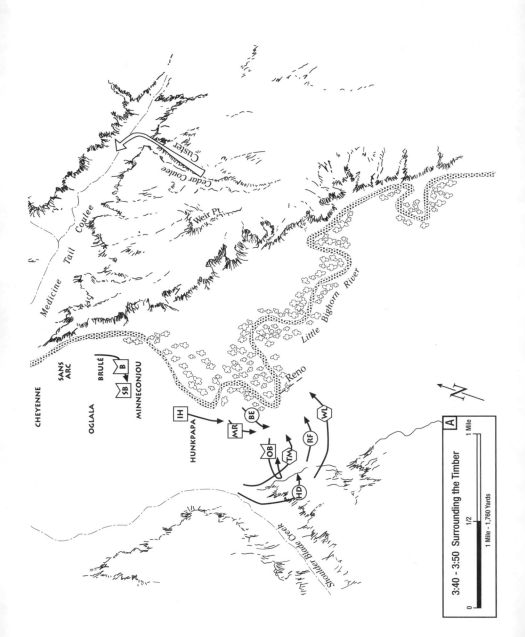

CHEYENNE

SANS
ARC

OGLALA

BRULÉ

MINNECONJOU

HUNKPAPA

Medicine Tail Coulee

"Custer"

Cedar Coulee

Weir Pt.

Little Bighorn River

Reno

Shoulder Blade Creek

B

SB

IH

MR

BE

OB

TM

RF

HD

WL

N

A

3:40 – 3:50 Surrounding the Timber

0   1/2   1 Mile

1 Mile – 1,760 Yards

SURROUNDING THE TIMBER, 3:40–3:50

SB 3:40–3:50, **Standing Bear** [last 3:10, next 4:30]. As he went down off Black Butte and ran barefooted back to the village, Standing Bear looked across the river. At first, it appeared that the Hunkpapas and Oglalas were fleeing. After he waded back across the Greasy Grass and made it to his lodge, the initial panic was over. The Indians began to gather in the camp.

The excitement of people and horses dashing to and fro, the colors and noises blending into a cacophony of swirling sight and sound were almost too much for Standing Bear to comprehend. He heard voices all over, all at one time, as if the entire village was talking at once. "It seemed that all the people's voices were on top of the village," Standing Bear remembered.

After remaining transfixed for a time, Standing Bear noticed Beard ride in with the horses. No words passed between the brothers as Standing Bear caught his gray pony and went off to get ready for battle. Upriver he could see that the Indians were no longer fleeing, but were now charging up close to the soldiers. "Hurry up! We shall go forth!" called Standing Bear's uncle. They would have to hasten to get into the fight.[134]

B 3:40–3:50, **Beard** [last 3:20, next 4:10]. Having located his pony, Little Yellow Horse, Beard helped drive the remainder of the herd back from near the mouth of Medicine Tail Coulee to the Minneconjou camp. When he arrived, members of his family cut out their horses to get ready for the fight. As Standing Bear led his gray off, perhaps Beard wondered why his younger brother had not been tending to the horses at the river. In any event, he had more to think about right now.

Beard had little time to paint up Zi Chischila properly for battle. He took a minute to braid up his tail, then he mixed up some white paint to daub a few spots of hailstones on his own forehead. The hailstones would be his protection. Beard gathered up his bow and arrows, hopped on his buckskin pony, and was ready to help defend the camp.[135]

HD 3:40–3:50, **He Dog** [last 3:10, next 3:50]. When Reno's men approached, the Hunkpapas were the closest to the attack and many were forced to fight on foot. They went up to the point of timber and held the soldiers back. In the Oglala camp, He Dog had a greater opportunity to properly prepare for battle and took advantage of the extra minutes. "I was slow in getting my horse," he admitted.

When ready, He Dog rode to the bluffs and climbed up on a hill to the west of where Reno's skirmish line had been just a short time ago. He had been pushed into the timber, but now the problem was how to get him out. Indians from all tribes were arriving—all that could get to their horses. They waited only for someone to give them the word and lead them in another charge.[136]

---

134. Neihardt, *Black Elk*, 114–15; DeMallie, *Sixth Grandfather*, 185.
135. Miller, "Echoes," 38.
136. Hammer, *Custer in '76*, 206.

WL 3:40–3:50, **Wooden Leg** [last 3:10, next 3:50]. After his father had roped his favorite horse for him, Wooden Leg was free to prepare for battle. He emptied his war bag, jerked on some new breeches, and pulled on a good cloth shirt and a pair of beaded moccasins. Mixing his paints and peering into a little mirror, he drew a blue-black circle around his face.

His father, Many Bullet Wounds, strapped a blanket on his horse and tied the rawhide lariat into a bridle. "Hurry," he urged Wooden Leg. The young Cheyenne was not yet finished, however. Wooden Leg painted in the circle on his face with reds and yellows. Then he combed his hair, thinking that it properly should be oiled and braided. "Hurry," his father said again. Wooden Leg just looped a buckskin thong around his hair and tied it close to the back of his head. He grabbed his bullets, caps, and powder horn. Now he was ready.

Finally he rode as fast as he could in the direction his brother had gone and where all the rest of the young men were going. The air was so full of dust he could not see clearly, but there was no necessity for him to see far. He trailed along with many other Indians on horseback.

Wooden Leg angled out to the south and west, beyond the Hunkpapa camp. The Indians had been dashing to and fro in front of the soldiers, who stood in the level valley and fired back at them with their rifles. Not many bullets struck home, but thousands of arrows fell among the soldiers. Wooden Leg, one of the few Cheyennes on this part of the field, went along with a throng of Lakotas until they got beyond and behind the white men.

By the time Wooden Leg got to the front lines however, the soldiers had already mounted their horses, retreated, and were hiding themselves in the timber. Some of the soldiers' Indian scouts remained fighting, although most had fled up the valley or across the river and into the hills. Wooden Leg thought they were Crows or Shoshones.

More and more Lakotas arrived to extend the encircling line around the timber. They sent arrows into the trees and were answered with bullets, causing them to hang back out of lethal range. Soon, Wooden Leg thought, the soldiers would be surrounded and would not have many hours left to live. Already the Lakotas were creeping forward to set fire to the brush.[137]

RF 3:40–3:50, **Red Feather** [last 3:30, next 3:50]. West of Reno's position in the trees, Red Feather pranced about on his pony, wondering what course of action to take next. The soldiers would be wise to stay in the woods, he thought. They could shoot from there and the Indians would have a tough time dislodging them without taking many casualties.

Somewhat puzzled, Red Feather saw two troopers try to get away. They were overtaken and killed. Dust and smoke surrounded the woods. There was still no effective way to get close to the soldiers from this open side of the valley. Another Indian voiced what Red Feather had been contemplating. "Give way; let the soldiers out," the brave shouted. "We can't get them in there."

---

137. Marquis, *Wooden Leg*, 218–20.

Stalemated for a short while, Red Feather's attention was distracted by another force of approaching warriors arriving in a cloud of dust. It was Crazy Horse. His friend had finally succeeded in getting his horses and men together. Now they would all join together and go against the soldiers.[138]

BE 3:40–3:50, **Black Elk** [last 3:30, next 3:50]. Hearing the hoofs of the soldiers' horses thrashing about in the brush ended Black Elk's ruminations of Thunder-beings. Just then, Indians on the hillside to the west could be heard calling, "Hokahey!" and crying out the tremolo. Everyone began to holler, "Crazy Horse is coming!"

It was true. Black Elk could hear the shrill call of the eagle bone whistles and the thunder of the charging ponies. Crazy Horse was coming, riding his white-faced horse. Now there was sure to be a hot fight.

Black Elk peered through the obstructing timber to the south. The soldiers who had come crashing down the dry riverbank into the brush now seemed to be going back up again. It became "a bad mixture" of soldiers and Indians, said Black Elk. The scene was a jumble of shooting and shouting, obstructed by the brush and trees. Black Elk went deeper into the timber to follow the action.[139]

IH 3:40–3:50, **Iron Hawk** [last 3:20, next 4:00]. Realizing that the action was sweeping past him, Iron Hawk rushed into his tipi to get dressed for war. Bullets whizzed by outside and he was so nervous that he could barely braid an eagle feather into his hair. All the while, he had to restrain his excited pony from pulling free from his rope. Crowds of warriors rode by upstream, yelling, "Hokahey!" Iron Hawk hurriedly rubbed red paint all over his face. He did not have a gun, so he grabbed his bow and arrows and ran outside.

Iron Hawk rode a short distance toward the woods. He saw the Indians gathering so thick that he thought surely the soldiers would be run over where they stood. Watching from near the timber, his speculation was about to become reality.

Crazy Horse had entered the action. Having finally collected his warriors, the Oglala war leader made a dash for the soldiers in the timber and crashed right into them. The warriors that had assembled along the banks saw the movement and heard the shouts of Crazy Horse's men. They too, "advanced furiously with great yelling, coming down on the flank." One side or the other would have to break.[140]

TM 3:40–3:50, **Two Moon** [last 3:10, next 3:50]. Two Moon had been haranguing the Cheyennes near the sacred lodge of *Issiwun* (*Esevone*) for some time, trying both to rally the warriors and to calm the women and children. He cautioned the fleeing women to go slowly, for he, Two Moon, would keep the soldiers out of the camp.

Two Moon moved slowly and deliberately up the valley. By the time he reached the fighting, quite a number of his warriors had already gathered. Reno's soldiers had gone into the brush. Two Moon rode again in front of his men and gave

138. Hardorff, *Lakota Recollections,* 83–84.
139. DeMallie, *Sixth Grandfather,* 182.
140. Neihardt, *Black Elk,* 120–21; Hardorff, *Lakota Recollections,* 64–65.

another brave-up talk, saying that today the Indians would win the fight or he would die in the attempt. Prancing about on his white horse, Two Moon then wheeled, called for the warriors to charge, and galloped off toward the soldiers in the timber.[141]

OB 3:40–3:50, **One Bull** [last 3:30, next 3:50]. One Bull and Good Bear Boy hobbled along on their lame pony in a southwesterly direction, still on the level prairie between the soldiers and Indians. One Bull became covered in the blood of both Good Bear Boy and the pony. As they moved out of the firing line, One Bull could hear the grating sounds of the broken bones in Good Bear Boy's legs rubbing together.

At least they had their lives. Not so lucky was Young Black Moon, who was killed shortly thereafter in front of the soldiers in the timber. One Bull continued across a little creek that ran out of the western hills. He pulled the wounded man off the pony for another Indian to take care of and returned to the fight.[142]

MR 3:40–3:50, **Moving Robe** [last 3:10, next 3:50]. Moving Robe and her father, Crawler, waited near the fringe of woods until the command to charge was given. The soldiers kept up a sharp fire, but the warriors were able to move close to their position by hugging the edge of the woods.

Finally the order to charge was given by Hawk Man. They galloped toward the troopers, who were all on foot and shooting straight. Moving Robe saw Hawk Man drop dead off his horse as he rode with his warriors. However, the Indian charge was stubborn. The soldiers ran to their horses and began to mount.[143]

← DISCUSSION. Reno continued to hold his second skirmish line in the timber along a loop of dry riverbed, but the situation did not look promising. Custer had not followed down the valley in support as Reno assumed he would. Unbeknownst to him, Custer had made his way to the junction of Cedar Coulee and Medicine Tail Coulee and turned left toward the river. Reno's three companies were virtually surrounded. Scout George Herendeen thought most of the Indians had gotten into the timber by passing around them up the valley and coming in on the left from the direction of the hills. Yet, so far, possibly only two men had been killed. Pvt. George M. Smith of Company M might have been one of the men described by One Bull as riding his frantic horse right into the Indian lines. Sgt. Miles F. O'Hara, also of Company M, died on the first skirmish line just before retreat to the timber.[144]

The Indians had taken more casualties than the soldiers. In addition to those killed earlier, the Hunkpapas also lost Young Black Moon and Hawk Man. As was generally the case, most of the Indians fought as individuals, yet One Bull, Two Moon, Hawk Man, Old Black Moon, and others led small contingents. However, it

---

141. Hardorff, *Lakota Recollections*, 135–36.
142. Miller, "Echoes," 31; One Bull, Box 105, Notebook 19, Campbell Collection; Hardorff, *Hokahey!*, 38.
143. Hardorff, *Lakota Recollections*, 94.
144. Nichols, *Reno Court*, 265; Richard G. Hardorff, *The Custer Battle Casualties: Burials, Exhumations and Reinterments* (El Segundo, CA: Upton & Sons, 1989), 141–42, 144.

was Crazy Horse who proved to be the main catalyst in galvanizing the Indians to press the final yards to the timber. It is clear that a number of them assumed the fight would be brought to a successful conclusion as soon as he made his appearance.

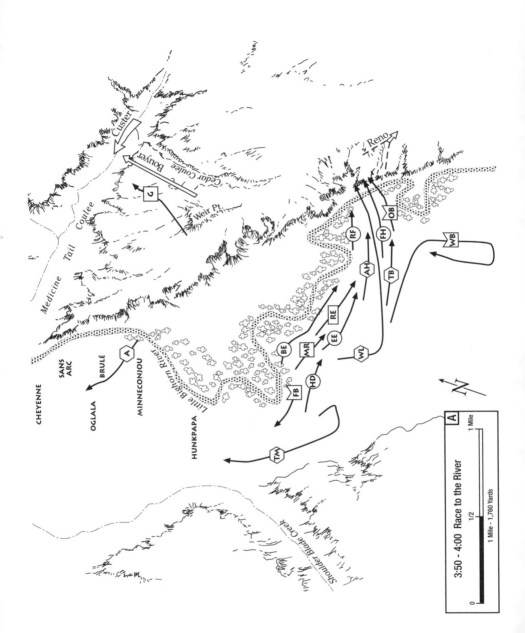

CHEYENNE

SANS
ARC

OGLALA

BRULÉ

MINNECONJOU

HUNKPAPA

Custer

Bouyer

Cedar Coulee

Medicine Tail Coulee

Weir Pt.

Reno

Little Bighorn River

Shoulder Blade Creek

3:50 – 4:00 Race to the River

1 Mile – 1,760 Yards

1/2

0   1 Mile

N

A

RACE TO THE RIVER, 3:50–4:00

HD 3:50–4:00, **He Dog** [last 3:40, next 4:20]. He Dog had surmised that the Indians needed only one person to take charge and direct them in a massive assault on the soldiers in the timber. For He Dog, Crazy Horse appeared to be the catalyst. All along the encircling line in the valley the Indians moved forward.

He Dog joined them, coming down the western hills and heading toward the point of woods. Just as the charge began, however, the soldiers burst out of the trees in two detachments. They rode up the river as fast as they could. He Dog got into the chase, singling out the soldiers' Indian scouts and helping to kill some of them.[145]

TB 3:50–4:00, **Tall Bull** (Hotuga Kastatche, or Hotoa qa ihoois) [next 4:20]. The twenty-two-year-old warrior carried a famous hereditary name among the Cheyenne, although he most certainly did not wish to share the fate of his famous Dog Soldier namesake, killed in the Battle of Summit Springs in 1869.[146] Tall Bull said the leaders of the Cheyennes at the Little Bighorn that day were Two Moon, White Bull (Ice), and Lame White Man, the last being Tall Bull's brother-in-law.

The first attack by Reno was a surprise, Tall Bull declared. The Lakotas may have known about the coming of the soldiers, but the Cheyennes did not. Reno brought his men down to Little Sheep Creek (Little Bighorn), where he crossed over and charged the upper Lakota village. When the people ran away, Tall Bull thought the soldiers set some of the lodges on fire.

The people of the lower villages heard the commotion and rushed south. Many of them ran up on a high hill west of where the fighting was. When the Indians charged down on the soldiers, they retreated into the timber. It looked like they didn't even stop, but ran right through the timber and out the other side. Tall Bull finally got into the forefront of the battle at the point where the soldiers tried to cross the river. Not all were successful, for Tall Bull noted, "the Indians kept killing them right along."[147]

WL 3:50–4:00, **Wooden Leg** [last 3:40, next 4:00]. As Wooden Leg watched some Lakotas enter the timber, he realized the encirclement was almost complete and a decisive action would occur soon. While waiting for the big charge to commence, Wooden Leg pulled his pony to a startled halt.

Suddenly, the hidden soldiers came tearing out of the woods on horseback. They burst out on the side where Wooden Leg had reined up. In fact, they were headed like a flying arrow straight at him. Wooden Leg whirled his horse, lashing it madly to escape the charging troopers. The Indians riding near Wooden Leg also joined in the hasty retreat.

The next time Wooden Leg happened to look over his shoulder, however, the soldiers were no longer galloping at his heels. They were not going directly up the

---

145. Hammer, *Custer in '76*, 206.
146. Dog Soldiers, the most militant and elite of the Cheyenne soldier societies, filled social and military purposes and acted like camp police. Their power was broken at the Battle of Summit Springs, July 11, 1869.
147. Hammer, *Custer in '76*, 212–13; Greene, *Lakota and Cheyenne*, 53.

valley, but had angled southeast toward the river. They were running away. Wooden Leg stopped for a few seconds to comprehend the situation. He and his companions gave a shout, and whipped their ponies into a swift pursuit.

A great throng of Lakotas were pressing after them. Wooden Leg's retreat from what he thought was a charge had actually placed him in the lead for a chase. The soldier horses seemed to be tired and the Indian ponies quickly gained on them.

Wooden Leg fired four shots with his six-shooter, but did not know whether he hit his targets. He saw a Lakota shoot arrows into a soldier's head and back, and watched the soldier tumble off his horse. Men crashed to the ground after taking blows from war clubs or stabs from lances. Riderless horses ran among the wounded and dying men. The Lakotas jeered at their opponents, calling out, "You are only boys. You ought not to be fighting. We whipped you on the Rosebud. You should have brought more Crows or Shoshones with you to do your fighting."

Wooden Leg found himself riding with Little Bird. They maneuvered a fleeing trooper between them and lashed him from each side with their pony whips. It seemed to be a brave thing not to even waste any bullets on him. The soldier, however, pointed his revolver and sent a bullet into Little Bird's thigh. Wooden Leg immediately crashed the elk-horn handle of his whip onto the soldier's head, dazing him. He was then able to seize the man's rifle and wrench it from him, dragging the strap from over his head. The trooper fell to the ground. The jam of onrushing Indians swept Wooden Leg on.

Wooden Leg saw three soldiers separated from the others and riding off up the valley. The Cheyennes Sun Bear, Eagle Tail Feather, and Little Sun joined some Lakotas in pursuit. Wooden Leg turned his attention back to the main action.

At the riverbank, Wooden Leg witnessed the mob of floundering soldiers thrashing about in a rush to cross the water. Exhilarated, he dashed into the crowd, using his captured rifle to club two of them off their horses and into the river. While some of the pursuing warriors stopped at the river, Wooden Leg and some others crossed to continue the fight.[148]

WB 3:50–4:00, **White Bull** [last 3:30, next 4:00]. White Bull was about to join the other Indians in a charge when the soldiers suddenly took their run, fleeing south, upriver, looking for a place to cross. The moment they turned tail, the Lakotas were swarming at their heels, shooting arrows, striking them with war clubs and the butts of their rifles. It was like a buffalo hunt.

White Bull watched most of them plunge into the river and up the steep bluffs, scrambling to the top. However, three soldiers could not get across. They continued up the flats on the west bank and White Bull and some Cheyennes took off after them. One of the soldiers careened toward the river and escaped in the timber. Of the two that continued south, one angled up a gulch and climbed the benchlands to the west. The last rode on to the mouth of the creek where Reno's soldiers had first crossed over, where he dashed in to hide himself in the brush.

---

148. Marquis, *Wooden Leg*, 220–23.

White Bull had his sights on one escapee riding a gray horse. Although he fired at him, he failed to hit him. Tiring of the long chase that took him farther away from the main action, White Bull reined up and trotted slowly back down the valley, giving his horse a rest.[149]

FB 3:50–4:00, **Flying By** (Keya Heyi) [next 4:10]. Flying By was the twenty-six-year-old second son of the Minneconjou leader Lame Deer. He had one older brother, Foolish Heart, and two sisters. That day, Flying By was slow in getting to the battle. Like many others, he was made aware of the soldiers' approach by some Lakotas who had lost horses and were out to the east searching for them. They returned to camp, bringing word of soldiers coming from a direction they did not expect.

Flying By was still preparing for war when the attack was made on the Hunkpapa camp. When he arrived, the soldiers had just burst out of the timber and were retreating to the river. Flying By probably thought this would prove to be a short battle as he kicked his horse forward in a belated pursuit.

Although the soldiers were running, the bullets wildly whizzing about still proved deadly. Flying By had barely begun his race when his horse took a bullet and went down in the dirt. Just like that, he was out of the chase. He watched the last of the soldiers disappear into the river with the Indians swarming behind them, then hiked back to the village to look for another pony.[150]

TM 3:50–4:00, **Two Moon** [last 3:40, next 4:00]. Just as Two Moon, Crazy Horse, and others began the charge toward the timber, the soldiers came out of the woods. The Indians drove them back up the valley. The fighting men were all mixed together—Indians, then soldiers, then more Indians. All of them were shooting and the air was full of smoke and dust.

Two Moon watched as one trooper left the main body and went off in an opposite direction across the valley. He charged after him and succeeded in knocking the trooper off his horse.

Looking toward the east, Two Moon could see the soldiers dropping into the riverbed like buffalo fleeing, having no time to look for a good crossing. Warriors were all around them and beginning to chase them up the hill.

Two Moon's attention was attracted by a riderless soldier horse that came running by him. He caught up to it, calmed it down, and searched it. Luck was with him, for there were many good things tied to the saddle, including plenty of cartridges and a round can half full of whiskey. Satisfied with the battle's progress, and pretty well assured that the soldiers would be defeated, Two Moon headed back to camp.[151]

RE 3:50–4:00, **Runs The Enemy** [last 3:20, next 4:00]. With the wind blowing the smoke into the soldiers' faces, Runs The Enemy thought it would be a

---

149. Ibid., 222; Hardorff, *Lakota Recollections*, 111; Vestal, *Warpath*, 194.
150. Hammer, *Custer in '76*, 209; A. F. Johnson to Walter Camp, Chicago, 19 November 1917. Robert Ellison Collection, Denver Public Library.
151. Hunt, *I Fought with Custer*, 213; Hardorff, *Lakota Recollections*, 136.

good time for a charge. Almost as an answer to his notion, the warriors in the valley began to rush forward.

As if on cue, the soldiers stampeded. The smoke and dust made it difficult to see the troopers as they retreated toward the river, but the Lakota were fresh, and soon caught up with them. Runs The Enemy thundered past a black man in soldier dress, then slowed to watch the scene. The black man turned on his horse and shot an Indian right through the heart. Indians fired back and riddled his horse with bullets. The horse collapsed, rolled over on its back, and pinned the black man long enough for other Indians to close in on him. Runs The Enemy spurred his horse on past.

They drove the soldiers until they rolled and tumbled into the river, which was deep at that point. The land along the river was heavily wooded. Some of the soldiers ran there to hide, others went across the river and up the hill. When the soldiers began their climb up the bluffs, Runs The Enemy believed the battle had ended.[152]

EE   3:50–4:00, **Eagle Elk** [last 3:30, next 4:00]. By the time Eagle Elk had secured his best horse and ridden around the extension of timber, the Indians had succeeded in driving the soldiers out of the woods. He arrived in the middle of the chase, witnessing two Indians riding down a trooper. One of the Indians, riding a white horse, used what looked like a sword to kill the soldier. The other Indian, riding a black horse, went down. The riderless steed ran back toward camp. Eagle Elk saw his cousin Crazy Horse catch the black pony and bring it back.

As Eagle Elk went along the line of the retreat, his brother rode up to him and asked to use his Winchester. Eagle Elk agreed to trade guns. Next, Eagle Elk rode by a dark-skinned man he thought to be a Hunkpapa who had been fighting with the soldiers. The man was sitting on the ground. A woman came up to him and appeared to be pointing at him. A relation of hers had been killed in the battle and she was angry for revenge. The man on the ground asked not to be killed, because he would be dead in a short time anyway. The woman said, "If you did not want to be killed, why did you not stay home where you belong and not come to attack us?" Eagle Elk did not see the weapon until she drew her arm back. The first time she pointed the gun at him, it did not go off, but the second time she shot and killed him. Eagle Elk thought the woman's name was Her Eagle Robe (Tashina Wamnbli).

Eagle Elk rode farther upriver where the Indians had chased the soldiers. The creek at the crossing point was flooded and deep. He watched as the warriors killed the troops in the water as they tried to swim across.[153]

RF   3:50–4:00, **Red Feather** [last 3:40, next 4:00]. Crazy Horse's arrival ignited the warriors' move against the soldiers in the timber. Yet, even as the Indians moved toward the soldiers, the soldiers galloped out of the woods and veered off up the river.

152. Dixon, *Vanishing Race*, 172–73.
153. Hardorff, *Lakota Recollections*, 101–2.

*The Greasy Grass River (Little Bighorn), downstream
of where many of Reno's fleeing troopers splashed across.*

Red Feather rode along as close as he dared, but the soldiers' use of six-shooters kept the Indians back for a while. Red Feather aimed for the soldier horses. He saw one trooper slide from his saddle, catch his foot in the stirrup, and get dragged all the way through the creek.

In the woods near the river, the Oglalas killed one Ree scout (Bloody Knife). Below the point where the soldiers crossed, Red Feather saw two men, dressed in white shirts and blue trousers. He and Kicking Bear went after them.[154]

FH 3:50–4:00, **Flying Hawk** [last 3:10, next 4:00]. Although Flying Hawk thought the Oglalas following Crazy Horse got their horses and guns "as quick as they could," considerable action had already occurred. Reno had already made his brief fight on the skirmish line, retired to the timber, and was about to make his move for the river.

Flying Hawk's brother, Kicking Bear, and Crazy Horse were in the lead. The first fighting they were involved in was when the soldiers came out of the thick timber. The dust was so heavy they could hardly see. Flying Hawk's group got right in among the retreating soldiers and killed many with bows and arrows and tomahawks.

They chased the soldiers to the riverbank, where they tried to cross over. The bank was about twelve feet high and steep at that point. Some got off their horses

---

154. Ibid., 84.

and tried to climb out on their hands and knees. Flying Hawk watched Crazy Horse. He was in the forefront, killing the troopers with his war club, pulling some right off their horses where they slowed at the steep banks. Kicking Bear matched Crazy Horse's deeds by killing many men in the water. The soldiers that managed to escape went up the hill to dig holes for protection.[155]

AH 3:50–4:00, **American Horse** [last 3:00, next 4:00]. American Horse had been among the first of the Cheyennes to reach the fighting above the upper village. The others were delayed because they did not have their horses tied near their lodges. American Horse saw Reno's men charge down the flat, then go into the timber and stop. The Indians circled all around them.

When the soldiers mounted up again and came back out onto the flats, the Cheyennes and Lakotas charged them. The troops ran for the river and the Indians galloped right up to them, knocking some of them off their horses as they ran. "It was like chasing buffalo, a grand chase," American Horse recalled.

At the river, other soldiers were knocked into the water. The survivors clawed their way up the gulches and to the blufftops. American Horse stopped on the west bank and searched among the bodies of the dead troopers. Occasionally the Indians would discover a wounded trooper and quickly finish him off. They found many fine things, including tobacco, cartridge belts, and uniforms. Some dressed up in the blue uniforms. This was, for the most part, done by the warriors, for the women and old men who had fled had not yet returned.[156]

MR 3:50–4:00, **Moving Robe** [last 3:40, next 5:00]. The charge that began with Hawk Man's death was so stubborn that the soldiers ran to their horses, mounted them, and rode swiftly toward the river. Moving Robe watched the Indians ride right in among the troopers and unhorse several of them with blows from their tomahawks. They chased the soldiers to the river, where their horses plunged down the banks and swam across. She saw some warriors ride right into the water with the soldiers, tomahawking them as they tried to make the other shore. Eventually some soldiers did cross the river and climb the bluffs.[157]

OB 3:50–4:00, **One Bull** [last 3:40, next 4:00]. When One Bull removed Good Bear Boy from the field and returned to the fight, the soldiers had already broken for the river. He was so angry, he knew he could never make peace. Charging in the wake of the retreating troops, he managed to kill two on horseback and a third in the river.

Noticing four soldiers on foot that had somehow gotten across, One Bull charged after them, trying to ride them down. Just then, however, he saw his uncle waving and calling to him near the riverbank.

One Bull broke off the chase and rode over to Sitting Bull. "Let them go!" the medicine man said. "Let them live to tell the truth about the fight!" Sitting Bull then looked worriedly at One Bull and said, "Nephew, you are wounded. Go to

155. McCreight, *Firewater*, 112.
156. Powell, *Sacred Mountain*, 1014, 1016; Greene, *Lakota and Cheyenne*, 49.
157. Hardorff, *Lakota Recollections*, 94.

the women and have your wounds treated." One Bull laughed. His uncle had seen the blood of Good Bear Boy and his pony all over his legs and thought he was badly hurt. He explained what had happened.

"You have done well," Sitting Bull praised his nephew. "You put up a good fight. Now go help defend the women and children and old ones. More soldiers may come." But One Bull's anger was not yet gone, and he continued up the bluffs to see if the soldiers were truly defeated.[158]

BE 3:50–4:00, **Black Elk** [last 3:40, next 4:00]. Black Elk worked his way along the river, dodging the tangle of brush and trees, working his way to the left toward the sound of increased fighting. Suddenly he burst out of the timber into the open and was caught in the whirlwind of men and horses weaving in and out and heading upstream.

Black Elk saw a Lakota charge one of the soldiers and try to grab his horse. The soldier took aim with his revolver and shot the warrior off his horse; then, shortly after, he dropped two more Indians with well-placed shots. The Indians were so angry it was nearly impossible to check them, Black Elk insisted. They became "plum crazy."

Black Elk followed the retreating soldiers. Up the creek a little way he came to a river bend and he and two other boys about the same age plunged in. Upon emerging, Black Elk noticed something shiny on the ground. He had found himself a six-shooter. He looked around to assess the situation. Indians were weaving in and out of the trees; most of them were ahead of him and chasing the soldiers. The chaos made Black Elk feel very small—too small to even shoot at anyone.

He rode back out into the open flat where dead and wounded soldiers lay. Black Elk joined the other Indians in stripping the bodies and taking everything they had—clothes, guns, and ammunition. Right near the river where he had jumped in, he saw a soldier lying on the ground, still twitching from his wounds. Black Elk stared at him a moment, when another Indian came up and said, "Boy, get off and scalp him." The young, thirteen-year-old warrior felt a slight lump in his throat. He looked down at the kicking soldier, then up at the warrior, then down again. He swallowed hard as he slid off his pony's back and reached for the hilt of his knife.[159]

A 3:50–4:00, **Antelope** [last 3:10, next 4:00]. Antelope had been watching and listening from her spot in the brush by the river east of the Minneconjou camp for upwards of forty minutes. It was a good vantage point. She did not wish to join the rest of the women fleeing downriver. She heard the sounds of battle changing from place to place as the soldiers and Indians maneuvered across the flats and through the timber.

After a time the sounds of fighting grew fainter, and it seemed that the white men were going away, with the Indians following them. Antelope peered south, across and down the east bank of the river. Just then, she got a glimpse of the soldiers crossing the river, many of them on foot. The Indians were right behind,

---

158. Miller, "Echoes," 31; One Bull, Box 105, Notebook 19, and Box 104, Folder 6, Campbell Collection.
159. Neihardt, *Black Elk*, 111–12; DeMallie, *Sixth Grandfather*, 182–83.

shooting and beating them. Antelope dashed out from her refuge and began to run as fast as she could to the Cheyenne camp, about one mile north of where she had been hiding.[160]

G 3:50–4:00, **Gall** [last 3:30, next 4:00]. Gall had gone with Iron Cedar to personally confirm the report that more soldiers were approaching behind the line of bluffs. Cresting the high ground east of the river, they found several companies of soldiers riding about two miles east of the camp, kicking up dust and heading for the lower village.

The Hunkpapa warrior Gall failed to get into the Reno battle, but went up the bluffs to see Custer's battalion approaching. —Little Bighorn Battlefield National Monument

---

160. Marquis, *Custer on the Little Big Horn*, 84.

Gall thought that the company mounted on white horses was a pretty sight, heading downstream as if on parade. He did not know whose men they could have been, for Crook's troops did not have so many white horses. As they marched along the high land going northwest, Gall was not sure whether they meant to fight, for they were not headed directly toward the Indians.

A few more Indians joined Gall and Iron Cedar as they watched these troopers descend a coulee leading into the valley of the Greasy Grass. The Indians dismounted and sat down on a mound on a vantage point in the hills above the coulee. The man who appeared to be the cavalry leader rode alone with his orderly about three or four hundred yards ahead of his command. Gall was only about six hundred yards away, in full view of the troops, watching them file down the ravine. Just then it looked like the leader spotted the Indians off to his left, along the bluffs bordering the south side of the coulee. He halted and became cautious, waiting for the rest of his command to come up. To Gall, it looked like this was the nearest the soldiers ever got to the river.[161]

← DISCUSSION. By this time, Major Reno had decided the situation had become intolerable enough to risk evacuating the position. He gave an oral order to the company commanders for the troops to leave the timber. Troop A was first to form, then Troop M. Company G was scattered through the woods with the horses and did not receive a definite order to leave. As the troops formed in the clearing, their defensive fire nearly ceased and the Indians were able to move in closer. Volleys from the thickets, possibly including shots fired by the Cheyennes Turkey Leg, Crooked Nose, and Old Man, hit Company M Pvts. Henry Klotzbucher and George Lorentz.[162] The Ree scout Bloody Knife, next to Reno, took a bullet in the head, splattering brains and blood in the major's face. The disconcerted leader ordered a dismount, then, shortly after, a remount. The battalion, at least those who got the word, headed east through the underbrush, then sprang out of the woods in several columns to the slightly higher prairie to the south.

Most of the soldier casualties occurred after the move to the river commenced. Along the retreat route fell Lt. Donald McIntosh of Company G, and his men, Sgts. Martin Considine and Edward Botzer, farrier Benjamin Wells, and Pvts. John Rapp and Henry Seafferman. Additional M Company men who fell were Cpls. Henry M. Scollin and Frederick Streing, and Pvt. David Summers. The Company A losses included Cpl. James Dalious and Pvts. William Moody and John Sullivan. Guide Charley Reynolds and interpreter Isaiah Dorman also went down within a hundred yards of leaving the timber.[163]

The several groups of charging Indians, including the one led by Crazy Horse, did not directly force the troops out of the timber. The soldiers happened to break out about the time the Indians hit—a serendipitous circumstance for the Indians,

---

161. Carroll, *Two Battles*, 104; Burdick, *Barry's Notes*, 9; Graham, *The Custer Myth*, 90, 94.
162. Powell, *Sacred Mountain*, 1014.
163. Stewart, *Custer's Luck*, 362–70; Hardorff, *Battle Casualties*, 124–25; Vaughn, *New Facts*, 157–58; Sandy Barnard, *Shovels & Speculation: Archaeology Hunts Custer* (Terre Haute, IN: AST Press, 1990), 23–29. The last publication sheds light on the 1989 discovery of a skull and other skeletal remains half buried on the riverbank at Reno's crossing, tentatively identified as belonging to either Sergeant Botzer or Private Moody.

as they were immediately close enough to engage the troopers in combat. Several Indians likened the action to a buffalo hunt. Yet, the casualties were not all one-sided. In the mad fighting between the timber and the river crossing, three more Indians fell: the Two Kettle Chased By Owls and the Hunkpapas White Bull and Swift Bear, the last two being brothers of the band leader Crow King.[164] Even so, the kill ratio was almost five to one in favor of the Indians.[165]

Seemingly singled out for special attention was the black interpreter Isaiah Dorman. Dorman had been employed for some years at Fort Rice, had married a Hunkpapa woman, and was known familiarly among a number of Lakotas as "Teat." They did not take kindly to his riding with the attacking soldiers. After Dorman's horse went down, Pvt. Roman Rutten recalled galloping past him and seeing him down on one knee making a stand. "Goodby, Rutten," he called out. George Herendeen said that from the trees he could see the Indians shooting at Dorman and pounding him with clubs. He was later found with pistol balls in his legs, skin stripped from his body, and a kettle of his own blood sitting by his head. Pvt. John Burkman said an iron picket pin was thrust through his testicles, pinning him to the ground, while Pvt. Theodore Goldin said he heard that the interpreter's penis was cut off and stuffed in his mouth.[166]

Dorman's demise was also noted by both Runs The Enemy and Eagle Elk, the latter reconstructing a conversation between the victim and his slayer, a woman whose name he remembered as Her Eagle Robe. It may be that the woman wreaking destruction on Dorman's body was actually Moving Robe. The two names are quite similar, and Eagle Elk perceived the vengeance behind the woman's enthusiasm as she spoke to the wounded black man with a semblance of familiarity.

There is a discernible personal detachment in Moving Robe's narrative between the point where she saw Hawk Man shot as she moved in to join the attack at the fringe of the woods (3:40–3:50), and later, when she and her father go to fight the soldiers attacking the lower end of the village (5:00–5:10). In both of these segments, Moving Robe discusses her own actions. In this middle segment (3:50–4:00), which would include the time of Dorman's mutilation, she does not mention her own movements, but concentrates instead on the action she observes taking place around her. The death of "Teat" is not mentioned. It is possible that Moving Robe deliberately omitted speaking of her participation in the killing of Dorman when she told her story in 1931, perhaps still fearing retribution for the savage attack so many years before. Furthermore, at the end of her tale, Moving Robe left us with more food for thought. "In this narrative," she said, "I have not boasted of my conquests."[167] If it was Moving Robe who concentrated on the wounded black man, she certainly slaked her thirst for revenge for the death of her young brother, Deeds.

---

164. Hardorff, *Hokahey!*, 42–43, 57. Similar Indian names continue to cause complications. The Hunkpapa White Bull, brother of Crow King, should not be confused with the Minneconjou White Bull, brother of One Bull, nor with the Cheyenne White Bull (Ice or Ice Bear), brother of Antelope.

165. Graham, *Story of the Little Big Horn*, 47, places the number of soldiers who died in the retreat at twenty-nine. Robinson, *Good Year to Die*, 184, somehow believes all twenty-nine died while actually crossing the river!

166. Hardorff, *Lakota Recollections*, 102; Hardorff, *Battle Casualties*, 148–50.

167. Hardorff, *Lakota Recollections*, 94, 96.

Though savagely put to death, was Dorman the recipient of one small act of kindness before his demise? Historian Robert Utley offers evidence that Sitting Bull himself might have succored Dorman. Surrounded by Indians, including Two Bull and Shoots Walking, Sitting Bull rode up to the wounded "Teat," ordering, "Don't kill that man, he is a friend of mine," then dismounted to pour him a drink of water from a buffalo horn.[168] If this occurred, it was very uncharacteristic of Sitting Bull, given his previous reactions in similar circumstances.

This is not to say that Sitting Bull would never befriend an enemy. He saved a captured young Assiniboine (Little Assiniboine, or Jumping Bull) from death and adopted him as a brother. He gave asylum to Johnny Bruguier, who was fleeing a white man's arrest warrant. He saved and "adopted" Frank Grouard from white justice and Gall's death threats. Yet, when the latter two "turn coats" returned to scout for the whites, Sitting Bull's hospitality turned to wrath, especially in Grouard's case. Sitting Bull vowed to kill Grouard himself, and no peacemaking could appease his ire.[169]

The chances are slim that Dorman, another "turn coat," would be saved and comforted by Sitting Bull in the midst of a battle where Dorman was trying to kill Sitting Bull's own family. One might also wonder why Sitting Bull took precious moments to obtain a buffalo horn cup prior to the fight, when he had little enough time for a warrior's proper battle preparations. White Bull commented on Sitting Bull's dress. It was "rush doings," he affirmed. He wore nothing special, just the shirt and leggings he already had on, with no time to affix one feather.[170] Sitting Bull certainly did not hurriedly enter the fray, yet spend extra time strapping on drinking paraphernalia to fight in a well-watered valley. Each reader's own predilections may be the deciding factor in whether to accept this incident as truth.[171]

By this time, the first hour of the battle had ended. That the Indians were caught unaware and were still leery about the developing battle is evidenced by Low Dog. Even after Reno had been driven back, he called for caution. "I told my people not to venture too far in pursuit for fear of falling into an ambush," Low Dog said.[172]

In the valley, Sitting Bull and a number of warriors will return to the village. Others will chase Reno up the cutbanks and bluffs on the east side of the Greasy Grass. From the high ground of Weir Point, the mixed-blood scout Mitch Bouyer and the Crow scout Curley watched Reno's retreat from the timber. Signalling to Custer, they hurry to pass this important information on to him. Gall waits nearby on a hill, noting the troops' delay. Some Indian women who ran to the eastern bluffs to escape Reno also discover Custer's battalion. They will return to warn the village. The battle will shift out of the valley and into the hills. The scales slowly tip in the Indians' favor.

---

168. Utley, *Lance and Shield*, 153; Bear's Ghost to Frank Zahn, Box 104, Folder 4, Campbell Collection.
169. Utley, *Lance and Shield*, 23, 94, 124, 168.
170. White Bull, Box 105, Notebook 24, Campbell Collection.
171. William E. Lemons, "History by Unreliable Narrators: Sitting Bull's Circus Horse," *Montana The Magazine of Western History* 45, no. 4 (autumn/winter 1995): 65, 69–70. Lemons has discovered "so many appalling errors" recorded by Frank Zahn that anything he said about Plains history "must be questioned." The Dorman story, incorporated into African-American history, comes mostly from Zahn. Lemons has shown that the veracity of both Zahn and his informant, Bear's Ghost, has been compromised.
172. Graham, *The Custer Myth*, 75.

III

Vantage

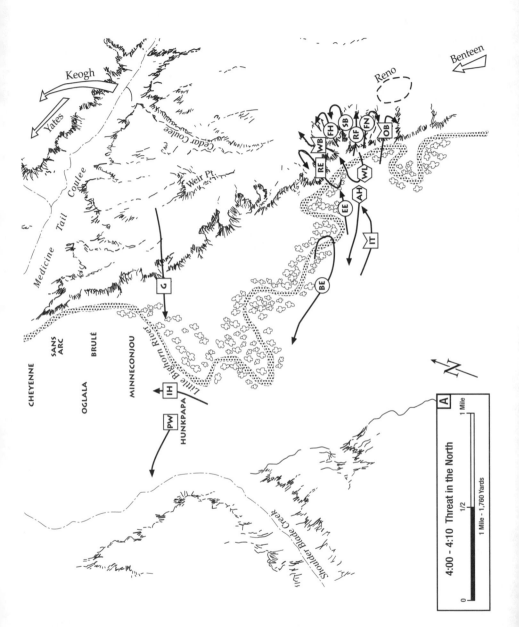

Keogh

Yates

Reno

Benteen

Cedar Coulee

Weir Pt.

Medicine Tail Coulee

Little Bighorn River

RE
WB
FH
SB
RF
FN
OB
WI
AH
EE
TT
BE

G

IH

PW

CHEYENNE

SANS
ARC

OGLALA

BRULÉ

MINNECONJOU

HUNKPAPA

Shoulder Blade Creek

N

A

4:00 - 4:10 Threat in the North

0   1/2   1 Mile

1 Mile - 1,760 Yards

THREAT IN THE NORTH, 4:00–4:10

G 4:00–4:10, **Gall** [last 3:50, next 4:10]. The troopers in the coulee halted when they caught up with their commander. Gall watched the soldier chief put field glasses to his face to scan the bluffs where the Indians sat, barely six hundred yards distant. Gall thought that the halt was made perhaps because they suspected they were in a tough scrape, and were waiting for the rest of the command to come up.

In any event, there were still many undefeated soldiers heading in a northwesterly direction, and the lower camp was in danger. "I saw what was going on, and left the hill, Reno Hill," Gall stated, "and ran for the battle."[173] Gall made his way back over the bluffs dividing Medicine Tail Coulee from the Greasy Grass. He would warn the camp of this new threat. Meanwhile, the soldiers began to move up the next ridge to the north.

Cedar Coulee's junction with Medicine Tail Coulee in the middle distance. One of the knolls to the left may have been where Gall watched Custer descend the coulee.

---

173. Burdick, *Barry's Notes*, 13; Graham, *The Custer Myth*, 90, 92. It is apparent from the context that Gall was not talking about Reno Hill per se, but rather the northern extension of the bluffs beyond Reno Hill.

IT 4:00–4:10, **Iron Thunder** [next 4:10]. The twenty-eight-year-old Minneconjou, brother of Chief Hump, knew nothing about any attack until the bullets of Reno's men came crashing through the camp. Everything was in such confusion and the horses were so frightened that he could not catch his mount for quite awhile.

When he finally caught his pony and readied for battle, Iron Thunder rode up the west side of the river to the upper side of the camp and around a small ash grove at the bend. There he saw that the warriors had already driven the white men off and were running after them. He followed in their wake. Near the river there were a great number of Indians on horseback crossing after the soldiers. Iron Thunder went after them.[174]

WL 4:00–4:10, **Wooden Leg** [last 3:50, next 4:10]. Up on the flats of the east bank, Wooden Leg watched as the Cheyenne Whirlwind engaged one of the Ree scouts. They bravely charged each other, firing almost simultaneously. Both of them dropped.

On a knoll farther east there was another scout firing at them from behind some sagebrush. Wooden Leg and some other warriors got around behind him. As they approached, a bullet hit the Ree. Wooden Leg rushed forward. The scout raised himself up as if to fire once more, but Wooden Leg again used his rifle as a club to crash the barrel down on his head. With that, other Indians swept in to beat and stab him to death. Wooden Leg took the scout's gun, but gave it to a Lakota who had none. He would keep the soldier's short-barrel carbine that he had taken earlier.

Temporarily satiated, Wooden Leg returned to the west side of the river where Indians were searching the dead soldiers. He found some tobacco and two pasteboard boxes with about forty cartridges. Now he would not have to use his captured carbine as a club. Feeling brave, Wooden Leg splashed back across the stream and spurred his mount to the hilltop.[175]

EE 4:00–4:10, **Eagle Elk** [last 3:50, next 4:20]. Eagle Elk had seen the angry woman kill the dark-skinned soldier and witnessed the warriors kill more men in the river. He admitted, "I was not doing very much, but was keeping back and watching."

He saw two Ree scouts on the east bank, singing as they made their way up the hill. A number of Indians charged the Rees, who shot down two of them, a Cheyenne named Whirlwind and a Sans Arc, Elk Stands Above. A stripped Indian charged up to one of the Rees and they fought, tumbling to the ground. More shots were exchanged. Eventually, the Lakota and Cheyenne warriors were able to overcome and kill their Ree opponents. To Eagle Elk, it appeared that all the retreating Rees and soldiers had been killed.[176]

---

174. Graham, *The Custer Myth*, 79.
175. Marquis, *Wooden Leg*, 224–25. The Ree who Wooden Leg helped kill was probably Little Brave.
176. Hardorff, *Lakota Recollections*, 102–3. The two Rees who put up such a good fight were probably Little Brave and Bob Tail Bull.

RF 4:00–4:10, **Red Feather** [last 3:50, next 4:10]. Red Feather and Kicking Bear overtook the two men in white shirts and blue trousers that they had been chasing. They were soldier scouts. "Those two are Indians—Palani!" Kicking Bear shouted.

Red Feather took aim and shot the horse out from under one of them. Kicking Bear followed the other and shot him twice. Red Feather jumped down and finished him off with his knife.

Looking around for more enemies, Red Feather noticed about ten soldiers escaping up the hill and rode after them. On top he saw the arrival of another group of soldiers with pack mules. It was still early, Red Feather guessed about ten in the morning, when the soldiers began their hilltop defense.[177]

WB 4:00–4:10, **White Bull** [last 3:50, next 4:10]. Returning from his abortive upriver chase of the fleeing troopers, White Bull pulled up near the stream, just a little too late to witness any of the hand-to-hand combat that had just occurred on its banks. He did notice a few soldiers and Indians across the river that were still fighting, but he couldn't catch up so he halted.

White Bull took a few long-range shots at distant soldiers on the bluffs. Since many braves had crossed the stream, White Bull decided to follow. It was not much of an obstacle, he thought; fairly wide, but not even deep enough to swim.

The last soldiers got to the hilltop when White Bull pulled up at the side of a hill with some other Indians. He had lost track of Sitting Bull since leaving him back at the village and did not see him cross the river, nor was he with this bunch on the crest. However, White Bull saw something of much greater import.

"Where we were standing on [the] side of [the] hill we saw another troop moving from [the] E[ast] toward [the] N[orth] where [the] camp was moving." A new course of action would have to be quickly decided upon.[178]

OB 4:00–4:10, **One Bull** [last 3:50, next 4:20]. One Bull made his way up the bluffs with another Lakota whom he did not know, but who turned out to be a good shot. As four soldiers went uphill the Lakota aimed his rifle and shot one of them off his horse. While dodging bullets from the others, One Bull may have thought of the consequences of disobeying his uncle. Still, he continued a little farther to see what the soldiers would do next. From a new vantage point, his uncle's caution struck home.

There were more troops coming, leading what appeared to be pack mules, although they were still south of the mouth of a creek flowing out of the east. But even worse, there were troops already to the north. Soldiers were even now beyond the Indians on the bluffs and were heading toward the other end of the camp. Sitting Bull was right. One Bull would have to hurry back to help with the women and children.[179]

---

177. Ibid., 74, 84–85.
178. White Bull, Box 105, Notebook 24, Campbell Collection.
179. One Bull, Box 105, Notebook, 19; Box 104, Folder 6, Campbell Collection.

AH 4:00–4:10, **American Horse**[last 3:50, next 4:20]. American Horse had been looting the bodies of the dead troopers west of the river while Reno's survivors climbed the hill. When he tired of this he turned back to watch the action on the ridges. Just then he spotted a pack train of mules approaching from the south, moving toward the soldiers on the hill.

American Horse never crossed the river, but moved back among the dead soldiers on the west bank. Suddenly, he heard a man's voice calling out that more troops were moving to attack the lower village, American Horse's own people. He spun his horse around and quickly headed north.[180]

FN 4:00–4:10, **Fears Nothing** [last 3:30, next 4:30]. Fears Nothing saw Reno's men fall back across the Greasy Grass. Some stragglers, however, were caught between Reno's main body and the river. They retreated upstream to the point where Reno crossed, but most were killed along the banks before they could escape.

Fears Nothing reached the Greasy Grass at a point a little below where Reno had crossed, at about the same time the fugitives reached the bluffs. From the north bank he could hear an Indian calling that more soldiers were coming down from behind the ridge. Crossing over, Fears Nothing topped the bluffs in time to see the pack mules approaching. He clambered back down and, once in the valley, galloped north toward the mouth of Water Rat (Medicine Tail) Creek.[181]

RE 4:00–4:10, **Runs The Enemy** [last 3:50, next 4:10]. As the valley fight wound down, and thinking the battle over, Runs The Enemy began to ride back to camp when he noticed more activity to the east. Two men in the hills were waving blankets as hard as they could. Crossing over with another Indian, he heard the signalers yell that "the genuine stuff was coming, and they were going to get our women and children."

Runs The Enemy continued to the crest with some other Indians. Peeping over the top he saw more soldiers advancing. It was a sight he would never forget. "As I looked along the line of the ridge they seemed to fill the whole hill," he said. "It looked as if there were thousands of them, and I thought we would surely be beaten." Runs The Enemy put his heels to his pony and raced downhill, across the river, and back down the valley.[182]

FH 4:00–4:10, **Flying Hawk** [last 3:50, next 4:10]. Flying Hawk watched the surviving troopers make their way up the hill where they began to dig holes for protection. He, along with Crazy Horse, Red Feather, Kicking Bear, and others, rode along the crest, feeling close to victory. Yet, the soldiers still had fight left in them, for more of them appeared with pack horses, and they began to fire at the Indians.

Though they could have dealt with the soldiers in their immediate front, there was another problem brewing in the other direction. Additional soldiers were seen

180. Powell, *Sacred Mountain*, 1016–17; Greene, *Lakota and Cheyenne*, 49.
181. Hardorff, *Lakota Recollections*, 27, 33.
182. Dixon, *Vanishing Race*, 174.

*The bluffs east of the Greasy Grass River where Runs The
Enemy could see Indians signaling with blankets.*

on a hilltop to the northeast, heading to attack the lower end of the village. This
new development stirred the Indians to renewed action. They readied their horses,
checked their weapons, and went out to meet the new threat. Flying Hawk and
Crazy Horse left the crowded bluff to head back downriver.[183]

SB 4:00–4:10, **Short Bull** (Short Buffalo—Tatanka Ptecila) [next 4:30]. The
youngest brother of He Dog and a nephew of the great Oglala leader Red
Cloud, Short Bull was in his early twenties at the time of the Little Bighorn battle.
It was about six days (actually eight) after the Rosebud fight, as Short Bull remembered it, that, "Custer ran into us."

Short Bull was fully engrossed in fighting Reno, helping drive him out of
the valley and into the hills. Jubilant on his prancing pony and flushed with
excitement, Short Bull never noticed Custer coming until Crazy Horse rode
up with his men.

"Too late! You've missed the fight!" Short Bull called to him.

"Sorry to miss this fight!" Crazy Horse laughed. "But there's a good fight coming over the hill."

---

183. McCreight, *Firewater*, 112–13.

Short Bull looked where Crazy Horse pointed. For the first time he saw Custer and his bluecoats pouring over a hill. "I thought there were a million of them," he said.

"That's where the big fight is going to be," Crazy Horse predicted. "We'll not miss that one."

Crazy Horse joked about it, Short Bull observed. He did not appear the least bit excited. Then Crazy Horse wheeled his pony back down the hill, followed by his men. Short Bull made a quick decision. Leaving Reno's defeated troops on their hilltop, he turned and rode north after Crazy Horse.[184]

BE 4:00–4:10, **Black Elk** [last 3:50, next 4:20]. Slipping off his pony's back, Black Elk stared at the soldier he was about to scalp and nervously unsheathed his knife. It was not too sharp, and of course this *wasichu* (the Lakota term for a white man) would happen to have short hair, making for a difficult first-time operation. He began to cut.

The man was very much alive! He twitched and ground his teeth from the pain. Black Elk cut through as fast as he could, then pulled out the pistol he had just found and finished the soldier off with a shot to the forehead.

The thirteen-year-old boy had his first scalp. He held up the trophy to show his companions, but did not know whether to exult or feel sadness for the life that had been taken. Black Elk advanced no farther from the river bend, about halfway between the village and the soldiers on the hill. He and his companions turned back downstream. He would go to his mother to show her his prize.[185]

PW 4:00–4:10, **Pretty White Buffalo** [last 3:20, next 4:10]. Remaining in the village, Pretty White Buffalo watched the battle unfold. The young braves had beaten the soldiers back in less time than it takes the shadow of the sun to move the width of a tipi pole. As she learned, there were two score or more of bluecoats dead on the field, and her people took their guns and cartridges.

While this was going on, stragglers, among them the old man who had killed the buffalo east of the river in the morning and women and children who had been digging wild turnips, all cut off from the camp when the soldiers approached, began filtering back to the village. They had seen Long Hair's approach and heard the gunfire and had secreted themselves in the timber along the river until the guns fell silent.

Yet, there was still wild disorder in the village, for word came that more soldiers were coming, from down at the ford by the Cheyenne and Sans Arc camps. Again, women and children shrieked and got in the way of the warriors. They were ordered out of the village, so they would not interfere with the men trying to give battle. This time, as the braves went singing down the river to the north, Pretty White Buffalo finally quit the village to make her way to a hill behind the camp.[186]

184. John M. Carroll, ed., *The Eleanor H. Hinman Interviews on the Life and Death of Crazy Horse* (Nebraska Historical Association: Garryowen Press, 1976), 19, 41.
185. Neihardt, *Black Elk*, 112; DeMallie, *Sixth Grandfather*, 183.
186. McLaughlin, *My Friend the Indian*, 45.

IH 4:00–4:10, **Iron Hawk** [last 3:40, next 4:20]. From a spot near the timber not far from his lodge, Iron Hawk had watched Crazy Horse go against the soldiers. He watched them retreat from the woods and saw the Indians move right in amongst them on horseback, using bows and arrows and war clubs, knocking many of the troopers from their mounts.

As the fight moved so swiftly out of the timber and to the south, Iron Hawk was left behind in the dust. He went back to his lodge, made sure the feather in his hair was braided properly, and was finally ready to do battle. Now, however, a new alarm was heard. More soldiers were coming at the other end of the village, but nobody knew how many were down there.

An Indian named Little Bear rode up to Iron Hawk on a pinto pony with a beautiful saddle blanket. "Take courage, boy," he said. "The earth is all that lasts!" Iron Hawk found he could procrastinate no further. He followed Little Bear and others downstream to meet the new threat.[187]

YN 4:00–4:10, **Yellow Nose** (Sapawicasa) [next 4:10]. Born into the Ute tribe about 1849, Yellow Nose was captured by the Cheyenne Lean Bear when he was about nine years old and remained affiliated with them the rest of his life. Early in the spring of 1876, he left the Indian Territory (Oklahoma) to visit the Northern Cheyenne relatives of his wife.

On the Little Bighorn, they stayed in the Cheyenne camp, farthest north down the river. That Sunday morning about noon, Yellow Nose was bathing in the stream when he heard the firing of guns. Custer's approach from the east was a surprise to Yellow Nose, for he expected no soldiers from that direction.

Yellow Nose was delayed in rallying to the alarm due to the absence of his ponies, which had been driven away to graze. It was quite some time before he mounted up and prepared for battle. In fact, he was much too late to get into the fight beyond the Hunkpapa camp, but it mattered little by then. The Indians had discovered more troops right across the river. Some Cheyennes had already gone to fight Reno, but Yellow Nose and others crossed the river where a small stream entered from the east.

Yellow Nose wended his way up a small promontory formed by that small stream (Medicine Tail) and the main river. There were the troops, advancing toward them along a divide that ran back from the Little Bighorn. Galloping at first, the soldiers slowed to a trot when they saw the Indians were not as few in number as it must have first appeared. Yellow Nose and his companions grew greatly excited as they demonstrated on the ridge, shouting out their war whoops.[188]

A 4:00–4:10, **Antelope** [last 3:50, next 4:30]. Leaving her hiding place along the river when she saw the soldiers being driven up the bluffs, Antelope began to run back to her camp, about one mile to the north. There was still great excitement in the camps she passed. Old men helped the young ones dress and

187. Hardorff, *Lakota Recollections*, 65; Neihardt, *Black Elk*, 121.
188. "Yellow Nose Tells of Custer's Last Stand," *Bighorn Yellowstone Journal* 1, no. 3 (summer 1992): 14–15.

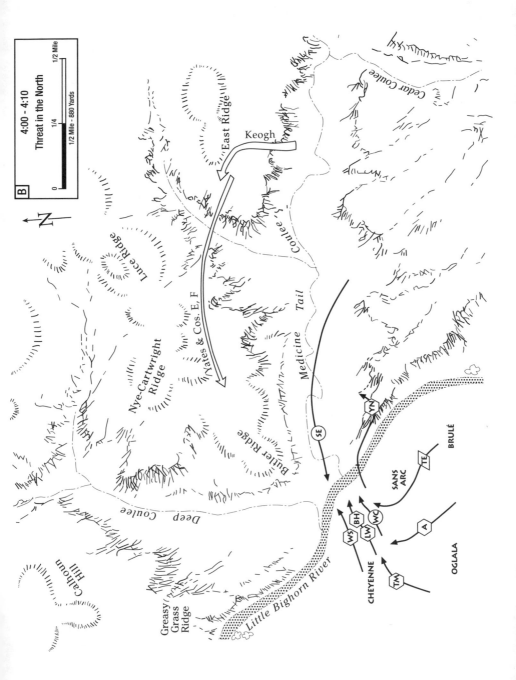

4:00 – 4:10
Threat in the North

0   1/4   1/2 Mile – 880 Yards

1/2 Mile

N

East Ridge

Keogh

Cedar Coulee

Luce Ridge

Yates & Cos. E, F

Cedar Coulee

Nye-Cartwright Ridge

Medicine Tail Coulee

Butler Ridge

Deep Coulee

Calhoun Hill

Greasy Grass Ridge

Little Bighorn River

SE

YN

TE

BRULÉ

SANS ARC

WS

BH

LW

WC

A

OGLALA

CHEYENNE

TM

paint for battle. Some women brought in war horses from the herds, others were busy taking down the tipis, a few were loading pack horses, and still others carried nothing, but ran away with only their children in hand. Antelope saw one Lakota woman jumping up and down screaming, because she could not find her little boy.

There were clouds of dust kicked up by the horse herds, as well as from those of the camp police, men of the Kit Fox Society, picketed close by. At first, mounted Indians were still heading to the fighting south of the Hunkpapa camps, but before Antelope could reach her lodge, there had been a shift in their focus.

As she breathlessly neared her tipi, the men were wildly riding back in the other direction. She thought they were running away, but soon learned what had happened. An old Cheyenne was calling, "Other soldiers are coming! Warriors, go and fight them!"

Antelope paused to peer off in the direction the old man had indicated. Across the river to the east of the Cheyenne circle she could see a few Indians, and beyond them, on a high ridge, came more bluecoat soldiers.[189]

TM 4:00–4:10, **Two Moon** [last 3:50, next 4:10]. Seeing the Lakotas driving the soldiers up the hill, and satisfied with the horse he had caught, Two Moon returned to his camp. Thinking the danger over, he stopped the women from carrying off the lodges and tried to quiet them down. As he rode around on his white horse, calling out news of the victory, he heard a man cry out, "Some more soldiers [are] coming! There are more soldiers now than up above." Quickly, Two Moon had to change his orders, telling the women once again to pack up and be ready to move.

He looked toward the river. "While I was sitting on my horse," Two Moon said, "I saw flags come up over the hill to the east." It appeared that they were riding in columns of fours, formed in three squadrons with a little space in between. Again there was much excitement, for they knew there would be another battle. Two Moon called to the warriors to get ready for the big fight, then headed for the river.[190]

SE 4:00–4:10, **Shave Elk** (Eccoca Taskla) [next 4:10]. A member of Big Road's Oglala band, Shave Elk was not ready to fight when Reno first attacked. While some Indians went to the hills to decide on a course of action, Shave Elk went after his horse.

The first fighting in the valley was almost over when Shave Elk rounded up his pony. He looked across the river, saw other bands of Indians gathering on the east side, and decided to join them. He and another Lakota rode up Medicine Tail Coulee and turned south and east toward the hill where Reno's soldiers had retreated. They had not gone far, however, when they discovered another group of soldiers coming down the ravine. Shave Elk quickly turned around and headed back to the ford, shouting the warning.[191]

189. Marquis, *Custer on the Little Big Horn*, 84–85.
190. Hunt, *I Fought With Custer*, 213; Hardorff, *Lakota Recollections*, 136–37; "Two Moons Recalls the Battle of the Little Bighorn," *Bighorn Yellowstone Journal* 2, no. 1 (winter 1993): 10.
191. Bruce R. Liddic and Paul Harbaugh, eds., *Camp on Custer: Transcribing the Custer Myth* (Spokane: Arthur H. Clark Company, 1995), 121–22, 125.

TE 4:00–4:10, **Two Eagles** [next 4:20]. A Brulé Lakota born in 1858, Two Eagles fought independently at the Little Bighorn, for his camp was small and the Brulés fought wherever they liked, mixed with other tribes, or with relatives or friends. It was, Two Eagles said, "everybody for himself."

There was much confusion during the fight with Reno. The women and children were in tears, but Two Eagles left them with a determination that the Indians would persevere. He had barely returned to his camp after helping defeat Reno when he learned that more soldiers were coming. Across the river, opposite the Sans Arc tipis, he could see them.

Two Eagles studied the scene. It looked like two Indians were out reconnoitering east of the stream. Beyond them, some soldiers were riding down from a high point toward the ford, while others stayed back in the hills. Two Eagles rode toward the ford to confront the mounted troops.[192]

WC 4:00–4:10, **White Cow Bull** [last 3:10, next 4:10]. Thirty or forty minutes had passed since he had watched Two Moon and other Cheyennes head south to the fighting. White Cow Bull opted to stay near the buffalo hat lodge with his friends Roan Bear and Bobtail Horse. They speculated about what was happening beyond the Hunkpapa camp. The sounds had receded and it seemed as if the fight was over when Bobtail Horse shouted, "They are coming this way! Across the ford! We must stop them!"

White Cow Bull looked to the east and saw more soldiers coming down the coulee. Suddenly, it did not seem so important to stand around and guard the lodge of *Issiwun*. They trotted out to meet the soldiers.

Presently they were met by an older Cheyenne, Mad Wolf, riding a bony old horse. He argued for caution, saying that they should not charge the white men just yet, for they were too many. Rather, they should wait for their brothers to help them. He rode with them for a while, continuing to say that they had no chance against a whole army. Finally, Bobtail Horse told him, "Uncle, only the Earth and Heavens last long. If we four can stop the soldiers from capturing our camp, our lives will be well spent."

They stopped behind a low ridge near the ford to make use of the slight cover it afforded. White Cow Bull could see five Lakotas racing down the coulee ahead of the soldiers, dodging their bullets. Then Bobtail Horse pointed to the bluffs beside the ford. On top were three Indians. From their dress and hairstyle they appeared to be Crows. Bobtail Horse said, "They are our enemies, guiding the soldiers here."

The Crows were shooting at the Lakotas. Bobtail Horse fired his muzzleloader at them and White Cow Bull opened up on them with his repeater, hoping to give the Lakotas a chance to reach safety.[193]

192. Hardorff, *Lakota Recollections*, 141–45.
193. Miller, "Echoes," 33.

BH 4:00–4:10, **Bobtail Horse** [next 4:10]. The Cheyenne and Elk Scraper Society warrior Bobtail Horse had been out dancing all night. He was still
sleeping while many people were going to fight Reno's soldiers, and he was only
half awake when he heard a great rumbling noise from the quickening battle. Bobtail Horse tried to get ready, but the boys who were in charge of some of the horses
were late in bringing them in. By the time they were brought to his lodge, almost
all the women had run to the hills.

After he mounted up he prepared to go to the Reno fight, but first he happened
to look to the east. "It was not long before noon when I first saw Custer," Bobtail
Horse said. In the hills was "a body of soldiers coming down a little dry creek; not
in it, but following down by it." He quickly rode out to meet the threat.

*The Cheyenne Bobtail Horse was one of the first to cross the river and
confront Custer's battalion.* —Little Bighorn Battlefield National Monument

Bobtailed Horse
Cheyenne Indian
was a warrior
at Custer's last
battle.

Approaching the river, Bobtail Horse was joined by other Cheyennes, including Calf, Roan Bear, and Dull Knife. They struck across the river to meet the bluecoats. There they could see Custer's soldiers riding after five Lakotas who were running from them. The soldiers fired at them while they were still two miles away from Bobtail Horse and his group. When the troops got within three-quarters of a mile of the river they turned their attention from the five Lakotas and charged toward the river and the camp.[194]

WS 4:00–4:10, **White Shield** [next 4:10]. The Northern Cheyenne White Shield was the son of Spotted Wolf, one of the bravest of the old-time warriors. He fought with distinction against Crook at the Rosebud, using the medicine of his father's kingfisher to overcome his enemies.

The morning of the Little Bighorn fight White Shield and his friend Blackstone had been fishing downstream from the camp. From time to time, he sent his young nephew, Dives Backward, out to the hills away from the river to catch grasshoppers to use as bait. The last time the lad returned, he said to his uncle, "I saw a person go by wearing a war bonnet. They must be looking for someone." White Shield rode up the hill to take a look. He heard distant shooting and saw people running about. The camp appeared to have been attacked, so he hurried toward it.

When White Shield got to the camp, he found most of the men were gone. However, his mother had remained and was leading his war horse to and fro in front of their lodge. He asked her for his war shirt, but she told him a man named Bullet Proof had just come to take it to wear himself. White Shield would have to go to battle without it. Still, he would carefully make his medicine as his father had shown him, tying the sacred kingfisher in his scalp lock. While dressing, he saw troops approaching the river, divided into what appeared to be seven groups. One gray horse company could be seen a long way off. "The horses were pretty white," White Shield commented. Other Cheyennes and Lakotas had seen them too, for some had already made their way across the ford to meet them.

At last, White Shield was ready. While the Gray Horse Company was coming on fast, making for the river, White Shield circled around and came in below them. He overtook a group of Cheyennes, including Roan Bear, Bobtail Horse, and one other. Alongside White Shield rode Lame White Man, also called Mad Wolf, Mad Hearted Wolf, or Rabid Wolf, one of the bravest and wisest men in the tribe. The small band crossed the river in the face of the approaching bluecoats.[195]

194. Bobtail Horse, Notebook 348, September 1908. Grinnell Manuscript Collection, Braun Research Library, Southwest Museum, Los Angeles, California. It is very likely that, after many years, Bobtail Horse confused Dull Knife with Lame White Man. Both were older, respected chiefs, but Dull Knife was not at the Battle of the Little Bighorn. White Shield's narrative confirms this.

195. George Bird Grinnell, *The Fighting Cheyennes* (Norman: University of Oklahoma Press, 1956), 337–38, 350; Powell, *Sacred Mountain*, 1010, 1020; White Shield, Notebook 348, September 1908, Grinnell Manuscript Collection, Braun Research Library, Southwest Museum, Los Angeles, California. Willis T. Rowland, the part-Cheyenne interpreter also known as Long Forehead, suggests that the Cheyenne Rising Sun may have also been one of the first at the crossing. See Richard G. Hardorff, *Cheyenne Memories of the Custer Fight: A Sourcebook* (Spokane: Arthur H. Clark Company, 1995), 142.

◄ DISCUSSION: There are additional questions concerning Sitting Bull's where-abouts during and after the Reno fight. Robert Utley contends that Sitting Bull crossed east of the river below Reno's hill, conferred with One Bull, then went up the bluffs. He told One Bull to let the whites go, but One Bull disobeyed and pursued the soldiers, after which he reunited with Sitting Bull. The two of them rode north, along the bluffs east of the river toward the troops in the north. On the bluffs above Medicine Tail Coulee, Sitting Bull urged other warriors to fight, but told One Bull to stay. However, One Bull again disobeyed his uncle. Sitting Bull crossed back to the west side at Medicine Tail ford and finally went to the west side of the valley with the women and children.[196] Once again, somewhat ambiguous testimony leads us to opt for another sequence.

Sitting Bull apparently did get to the river where Reno crossed, for One Bull met him there; and since he was there, he certainly could not have spent much time searching for drinking water to give to Dorman. At the river Sitting Bull saw blood on One Bull. One Bull told him it was Good Bear Boy's blood. Although Campbell recorded the incident as occurring on the east bank, one might wonder how the wounded Hunkpapa's blood remained on One Bull after the dunking he received while splashing in the river. The actual notes from Box 105, Notebook 19, are:

> Few sold[iers] got to R[iver]. OB k[illed] 2 in R[iver] & 1 across R[iver]. Then SB arrives on E[ast] side R[iver] and tells OB to quit. SB says OB well spent seeing blood then OB tells, wounded man's blood.

It appears that from this point, Sitting Bull may have returned to the camp through the valley, for Campbell recorded that One Bull said:

> SB [goes?] from Reno field to W[est] of Chey[ennes], looking N[orth], on flat W[est] of camp, at 8 [see fig. 5]. No one climbed hill (bench).

In another interview, written by Campbell in Box 105, Notebook 41, One Bull was to have said:

> SB went to battle with arrow for protection only—not to fite. After Reno battle, SB went to C[uster]. OB on one side of river with C[uster] & SB & other guards went to watch women. SB did tell One Bull to go to women after battle above— & guard women for fear of other troops but OB & other knights went to C[uster] by east side of stream from Reno before going to women. OB not in C[uster] Battle—then returned to SB, other knights & women. SB stayed with women all the time and could see C[uster] Battle across river—SB with w[omen] & child[ren] to guard them against another possible attack of 3rd group of white men——enuf men to handle C[uster] Battle—stayed here from noon to almost sundown— about 1 mile from Custer on hill.

In yet another inquiry, in Box 104, Folder 6, Campbell said One Bull told him:

> OB followed 4 men up cliff then crossed river and returned on other side when see battle at other end of camp—SB not with him—was guarding women who were retreating N[orth] W[est] over hill.

---

196. Utley, *Lance and Shield*, 153–55.

Gray Whirlwind said that when the warriors crossed the river, they waited up a coulee for Sitting Bull to catch up. When he arrived, he told them to go on and fight, and Gray Whirlwind did not see Sitting Bull after that.[197]

One Bull may have disobeyed Sitting Bull once, going up the bluffs to see if Reno was truly defeated, and Sitting Bull may have followed up a coulee to Reno Hill. But it appears that Sitting Bull returned to the village shortly afterwards, for One Bull said he was not with Sitting Bull after their meeting at the river. When Sitting Bull left, One Bull probably realized that, being his uncle's bodyguard and adopted son, it was not wise to ignore his instructions. He headed back to guard the women, but by which route is uncertain. One interview said he returned along the east side of the river, and another indicates he went along the west bank.

A third interview, given to John P. Everett in the 1920s, may, in fact, solve what seem to be mutually exclusive alternatives. In this narrative, One Bull said he crossed back to the west bank, rode downstream to the vicinity of the Hunkpapa village, and then recrossed to the east bank.[198] This is the scenario we will follow.

In any case, it does not appear that Sitting Bull went north along the east bank of the river, and One Bull did not twice disobey him. Although these are not incidents that had any great impact on the battle, they are important when we are attempting to correctly reconstruct individual movements. Utley did a prodigious amount of work in his biography of Sitting Bull, and, as we have seen, the sources all too often appear contradictory. He was more concerned with the panorama of Sitting Bull's life than with his exact movements at the Little Bighorn. We are more concerned with each participant's peregrinations during one historical afternoon, and will necessarily pay stricter attention to the narratives as they interlock with the time/space framework.

Several Indians, including One Bull, Fears Nothing, and Red Feather, commented on seeing the arrival of the pack mules upon reaching the blufftops. It appears that they witnessed the arrival of the advance elements of Captain Benteen's Companies D, H, and K. The pack mules, under Lieutenant Mathey, with their Company B escort under Captain McDougall, would not be up for another hour or more, long after these Indians had gone north to meet Custer. It is possible they saw horsemen moving up the ridge, later learned that a pack train did reach Reno's position, and naturally assumed that what they saw were the pack mules. Then again, some of them, well placed on a high bluff, may well have seen the pack train approaching down Reno Creek (off the southwest edge of our A maps).

More important than these Indians' discovery of additional troops in the south was the shock of finding that troops were also north of them, in a position to interpose themselves between the warriors and the village. As they crested the bluffs north of Reno, or climbed the vantage point of high ground later known as Sharpshooter's Ridge, the danger became apparent. Moving along a ridge above Medicine Tail Coulee, less than two miles away, was Custer's battalion. That it was indeed a shock to the Indians is shown in the reactions of Runs The Enemy and

197. Gray Whirlwind, Box 105, Notebook 14, Campbell Collection. The Gray Whirlwind notes were graciously supplied by Robert Utley.
198. Greene, *Lakota and Cheyenne*, 56.

Short Bull, one saying it looked as if thousands of bluecoats filled the hill while the other likened them to a million. Custer had surprised them not once, but twice.

A factor that some battle students may not have fully considered at this point is that this was a *mutual* discovery. While the Indians could see Custer on his ridge, Custer could see the Indians appearing on the bluffs. Not only could he see the Indians, but he very possibly could see Benteen's approach! He had been told of Reno's repulse by Mitch Bouyer while down in the coulee. He moved the command to a vantage point on the ridge above to assess the rapidly changing situation. From there, he decided to send Companies E and F, under Capt. George W. Yates, to make a demonstration toward the ford and village, hoping the threat would be enough to draw off the warriors pursuing Reno. With the remaining Companies, C, I, and L, under Capt. Myles W. Keogh, Custer would continue northwest, staying to the high ground as long as possible to continue an open line of sight in *both* directions, toward Reno-Benteen and the ford. Reno and Benteen would assuredly unite to follow the Indians that Custer drew toward his command. From a good position farther north, undetermined as yet, Custer could turn and confront

The spot where the Indians crested the bluffs in pursuit of Reno. They discovered Custer's battalion on a ridge to the north beyond Cedar Coulee, on the middle horizon.

the Indians while Reno and Benteen would come in to close the back door. He
would still have the Indians caught between the two commands. This mutual discovery, while Custer moved near the crest of what has been called Luce Ridge,[199]
set off the chain of events that would eventually lead to the Lakota victory.

Realization that there was a double discovery clears up some of the confusion
that attends discussion of this segment of the battle. Some contend that Custer
waited a long time in Medicine Tail Coulee, a "fatal" delay that caused him problems later. Apparently Colonel Graham and researcher Walter Camp both believed
there was a hiatus of three-quarters of an hour in the coulee. The argument is
carried further by battle students Bob Doran and William Hedley. The former
contends that there was a thirty-minute time discrepancy in Medicine Tail Coulee,

---

199. Recent scholarship has challenged our conception of the terrain that heretofore has been labeled "Luce
    Ridge"; see Bruce A. Trinque, "Elusive Ridge," *Research Review: The Journal of the Little Big Horn Associ-
    ates* 9, no. 1 (January 1995): 2–8. Whereas maps in John Gray's *Custer's Last Campaign*, Richard Hardorff's
    Markers, Artifacts and Indian Testimony, and James Welch's *Killing Custer* show Luce Ridge as the sharply
    defined feature one mile north of Weir Point, Trinque's study of Edward S. Luce's correspondence
    indicates that Luce was describing the terrain angling off the Nye-Cartwright Ridge complex. The real
    Luce Ridge lies across the North Fork of Medicine Tail Coulee, on the next ridge to the northwest.
    Trinque has labeled the old, "false" Luce Ridge as "East Ridge" (nomenclature I use in this study).
        Continuing his investigation, Trinque believed the confusion may have stemmed from an artifact
    map produced in Jerome Greene, *Evidence and the Custer Enigma*, which shows that army relics were
    found on East Ridge. Trinque contacted Greene for clarification. Apparently the artifacts that appear to
    be on East Ridge were actually found on Luce Ridge, adjacent to Nye-Cartwright. They appear off the
    mark simply because of the distortion inherent in placing large artifact symbols on a small map.
        Although the confusion over which ridge is really "Luce's" has been cleared up, the question re-
    mains: Was Custer ever on East Ridge? While no artifacts have been found there, in this time-terrain
    framework it is still too early for Indians to have initiated any relic-producing encounter. Then again,
    since Benteen's and Reno's men heard volleys, cartridges resulting from signal-firing may yet be there
    awaiting discovery. Has anyone searched East Ridge? Battle student Thomas E. Bookwalter has been up
    there several times. In a letter to me dated 17 September 1995, he said white stakes similar to those used
    along Blummer-Nye-Cartwright Ridge had been scattered along East Ridge, indicating someone has
    marked some discoveries. It is my contention that troops ascended East Ridge for reconnaissance pur-
    poses and it is the prime location for a mutual sighting by each party.
        The idea that from East Ridge Custer may have been able to see Benteen approaching was also
    suggested by Trinque in correspondence to me. To test the possibility, I trekked south along the blacktop
    road from the visitor center to Medicine Tail Coulee on the 117th anniversary of the battle. I then went
    along the bluffs on the south side of the coulee to a knoll where I thought Gall may have observed
    Custer some 600 yards distant. I then crossed the coulee and ascended East Ridge, from which it is quite
    easy to view the crest of the bluffs where the Indians appeared after climbing up from the river. Looking
    south from the *west* end of East Ridge, Cedar Coulee is the gunsight to the bluffs, lying between Weir
    Point to the west and Sharpshooter Ridge to the east. Looking south from the *east* end of East Ridge,
    another coulee east of Sharpshooter Ridge provides the line of sight to the Reno entrenchment area.
    Even with less than 20/20 vision, I could see the glint of automobiles in the parking area by Reno's
    marker two miles away; the hills sloping south from that point were also clearly visible—and would have
    been more so to anyone using field glasses. Benteen *could* be seen approaching Reno's hilltop by Custer's
    troops looking from East Ridge. The likelihood that he *was* seen accounts for many of Custer's subse-
    quent actions.
        On a subsequent field trip in September 1994, I walked the bluffs north of Reno's entrenchments
    where the Indians would have come up from the valley. From south of Weir Point, across the head of
    Cedar Coulee, and to the slopes of Sharpshooter's (Wooden Leg) Hill, there is a natural line of sight to
    the north along Cedar Coulee—the same gunsight visible from East Ridge when looking the opposite
    direction. To the north, sitting plump and bare at the end of that channel, is East Ridge, on that day
    graced with some very distinguishable cattle grazing along its southern slope. Short Bull's and Runs The
    Enemy's descriptions of "thousands" or "millions" of soldiers moving along and over a hill certainly
    seems to point to that terrain. Line of sight to Nye-Cartwright Ridge is almost wholly blocked by Weir
    Point and East Ridge. Therefore, I contend that Custer was on East Ridge for a time, even though he
    did no fighting there. It was on East Ridge that the Indians saw him.

while the latter argues that Custer sat in Medicine Tail for half an hour, and even
waited on East Ridge (which he incorrectly labels "Luce" Ridge) for one hour and
on Nye-Cartwright for another hour![200] The contention is made because it is believed that a warning had to be carried from the north by the Indians who discovered Custer, down to the south to the Indians besieging Reno, who then had to
hurry back north to the Medicine Tail ford area in time to confront Custer, who
was approaching the river. In order to make these treks in time, it is postulated that
Custer must have been delayed considerably.

In actuality, how did the Indians chasing Reno "hear" about the soldiers in the
north? Their narratives tell us that they saw them with their own eyes, or heard
about them from other warriors around Reno. On the bluffs, One Bull saw the
"mules" approaching, and the troops in the north. Fears Nothing heard Indians
calling from the east bank that more soldiers were coming, and after climbing up
the bluffs he saw them for himself. Runs The Enemy was riding back north when
he saw two Indians waving blankets. He went up to see a "thousand" soldiers in the
north. Flying Hawk saw "pack mules" to the south and soldiers to the northeast.
White Bull was on the hill when he saw soldiers moving toward the north. Short
Bull was on the bluffs with Crazy Horse and saw "millions" of soldiers on a hill in
the north. Iron Thunder went up the bluffs and was told that more soldiers were in
the north. Wooden Leg was on Sharpshooter's Hill when another Indian pointed
out more soldiers to the north.

The Indians around Reno saw Custer themselves. It was first-hand knowledge.
They did not have to get word from any messengers from the village. In fact, some
Indians in the valley were even informed of the new threat by Indians on the bluffs,
a complete reversal of the traditional explanation. The alacrity with which such a
mass of warriors vacated Reno's vicinity proves that they saw Custer themselves.
And that is just what almost all of the Indians said.

A few exceptions might have occurred in the valley. Red Hawk said he left
Reno only when he "got word" of other soldiers. But where did he get the word?
It could have been, like Runs The Enemy and Fears Nothing, from Indians on or
returning from the bluffs. Eagle Elk, He Dog, and American Horse were in the
valley, but they did not pursue Reno across the river. Thus, they got back soon
enough to get into the early action at the ford. Few, if any, Indians who chased
Reno's troopers across the river could do the same.

The Indians vacated the bluffs around Reno very quickly, and they did it because they had direct knowledge of the situation. Even so, they could not get to the
ford in time. Likewise, the Indians that were closest to the ford to initially meet
Yates's command, were either not in the Reno action, or they did not join in the
full pursuit of his men across the river. The two soldier battalions were initially
confronted by two separate groups of warriors. Two Moon was briefly in the Reno

200. Graham, *The Custer Myth*, 313, 322; Bob Doran, "Battalion Formation and the Custer Trail," 3rd Annual
Symposium, Custer Battlefield Historical & Museum Association (Hardin, MT: CBH&MA, 1989), 16;
William Hedley, "'ps Bring Pacs': The Order That Trapped the Custer Battalion," 4th Annual Sympo-
sium, Custer Battlefield Historical & Museum Association (Hardin, MT: CBH&MA, 1990), 49, 55, 56.

fight, but he found a well-stocked cavalry horse and returned to the village early, in time to hear shouting about more soldiers approaching. Two Eagles also left the Reno pursuit early and returned to the village in time. Antelope was in the village when she heard the warning, as were Pretty White Buffalo, Iron Hawk, Bobtail Horse, and White Cow Bull. White Shield had just returned from fishing downstream.

There was one group of Indians that drove Reno up on the bluffs, and a separate one that first met Yates. Both received their warning first-hand. No messengers were needed in either direction. Although some, such as Shave Elk, rode upstream to spread the word, it was an unnecessary waste of time and energy. Custer did not sit on his duff for an hour or two, waiting for the Indians to send messengers up and back while several hundred warriors shifted positions miles across field and stream. Custer spent some minutes in Medicine Tail and on East Ridge, but there is no mysterious, unaccounted-for gap in his movements. Neither side wasted time.

One might also note a discrepancy between the White Shield and Bobtail Horse accounts vis-a-vis that of White Cow Bull. Whereas White Cow Bull indicated he was on the *west* bank of the river firing at Crow scouts, White Shield and Bobtail Horse said they had already crossed the ford to the *east* side while the soldiers were still at a distance, and they made no mention of anyone seeing or firing at any Crows. Where were the Crows that White Cow Bull could have fired at? For them to be able to fire at Lakotas moving down the coulee, and be close enough for White Cow Bull to fire at them from the west side of the ford, they would have had to have been on the bluffs very near to the ford itself. But these bluffs were occupied by enemies of the Crow, such as Yellow Nose and his companions. Also, the most common repeating rifles available to the Indians at that time were the Henry and Winchester. Tests showed, however, that the most effective range of those weapons was only about a hundred yards, with hits dropping to about 40 percent at three hundred yards, and to virtually zero beyond that range.[201]

It is hard to imagine how a few Crow scouts, after being dismissed from service, could have, or would have wished to, approach within a few hundred yards of the ford without being attacked by other Indians on those very same bluffs. Two companies of the 7th Cavalry did not get that close. Were they farther south on the bluffs, perhaps at the slightly safer distance of one-half mile (880 yards) or more? Then they couldn't have had any hope of hitting the fleeing Lakotas, nor could White Cow Bull have come close to hitting them—indeed, at that distance he probably couldn't even have recognized them as Crows. Then again, perhaps Miller's White Cow Bull was graced with the same exceptional eyesight that enabled Miller's Beard to recognize One Bull at a one-and-a-half-mile distance. An excellent analysis of the Crow's movements was done by John Gray, who showed that the Crows were on the bluffs, but not north of Weir Point.[202] Henry Weibert metal-detected

201. Wesley Krause, "Guns of '76," 6th Annual Symposium, Custer Battlefield Historical & Museum Association (Hardin, MT: CBH & MA 1992), 5–7.
202. John S. Gray, "Couriers of Disaster," *Research Review* 17 (December 1983): 3–4; Gray, *Custer's Last Campaign,* 339–44.

in the area in 1970 and found six fired cartridges about one-quarter mile west of Weir Point right at the bluff's edge. Although he believed these were fired by the scouts Mitch Bouyer and Curly, it shows that there was some firing in the area.[203] In any case, the location is still a mile from the ford. The place where White Cow Bull (or his chronicler) claimed he fired at the Crow scouts just does not appear to be possible, and the spot where he claimed he confronted Custer's men becomes even more of a problem in the next segment.

---

203. Weibert, *Sixty-Six Years*, 47.

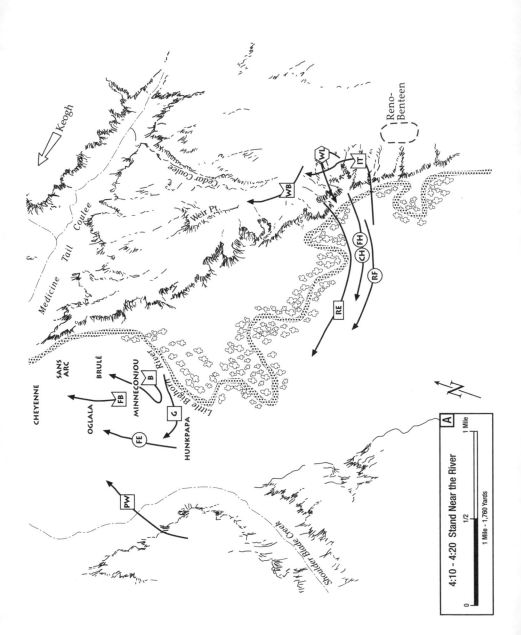

4:10 - 4:20 Stand Near the River

Keogh

Reno-Benteen

Cedar Coulee

Weir Pt.

Medicine Tail Coulee

WL

IT

WB

CH/FH

RF

RE

CHEYENNE

SANS ARC

BRULÉ

MINNECONJOU

OGLALA

HUNKPAPA

FB

B

G

FE

Little Bighorn River

PW

Shoulder Blade Creek

N

A

0   1/2   1 Mile

1 Mile = 1,760 Yards

STAND NEAR THE RIVER, 4:10–4:20

IT 4:10–4:20, **Iron Thunder** [last 4:00, next 4:20]. Following the Indians across the river, Iron Thunder made his way up one of the innumerable gullies toward the top of the bluff. Going around a bend partway up, he stumbled across the body of an Indian whom he quickly recognized, for the two of them had been sworn friends. Iron Thunder knelt down to see if he could do anything, but the man was already dead.

More firing from the soldiers on the hill above shifted Iron Thunder's focus from his friend back to the task at hand. He continued uphill. Just as he reached another group of Indians at the top, a report was heard that another party was coming to attack them, but Iron Thunder could not see any more soldiers from where he was standing. However, he could see other Indians hurriedly moving north. He turned around and went toward them.[204]

HH 4:10–4:20, **Flying Hawk** [last 4:00, next 4:30]. Flying Hawk and Crazy Horse left the crowd and rode back down the river through the valley. For the time being, others would have to contend with the second group of soldiers on the hills to the northeast. Many Indians followed the river down after fighting Reno, without going to the camp, but others had been wounded during the pursuit, and Flying Hawk and Crazy Horse would first help them safely back to camp before returning to the fight.[205]

RF 4:10–4:20, **Red Feather** [last 4:00, next 4:40]. Red Feather had seen the arrival of the pack mules and then heard the alarm that another body of soldiers was coming down from the high ground east of the Cheyenne camp. He left the Reno fight and went as fast as possible to the other end of the valley. Halfway there he discovered a man he knew who was down with a broken leg. Red Feather dismounted to help bind up his leg, then hurried on to the fight.[206]

WL 4:10–4:20, **Wooden Leg** [last 4:00, next 4:30]. After finding ammunition for his captured carbine, Wooden Leg crossed back to the east side of the river and climbed the hill. There he learned from a friend that another Cheyenne named Hump Nose, two years younger than Wooden Leg, had been killed at the river. He was saddened by the news, but resolved to continue fighting.

On the hilltop he joined others who were going around to the left or north side of the place where the soldiers had taken their stand. Finding a position on another hill, Wooden Leg fired back at the soldiers, aiming at no one in particular, for the distance was too great for accuracy.

He had only been there a short time when another Indian said, "Look! Yonder are other soldiers!" Peering downriver, Wooden Leg saw them on the distant hills. The news spread quickly and the Indians began to ride after them. Some went

204. Graham, *The Custer Myth*, 79.
205. McCreight, *Firewater*, 112–13; Hardorff, *Lakota Recollections*, 51.
206. Ibid., 74, 85.

along the hills, while others crossed the river to follow the valley. Wooden Leg guided his horse back down the steep hillside to cross the river and follow north through the valley.[207]

RE 4:10–4:20, **Runs The Enemy** [last 4:00, next 4:20]. Leaving the bluffs where he had seen what appeared to be thousands of soldiers on a hill to the north, Runs The Enemy raced back through the valley to his camp. On the way, he learned the fate of the "black man in a soldier's uniform," whom he had seen go down fighting during the white retreat from the timber. Dorman was "lying there dead."

Reaching the Hunkpapa and Two Kettle tipis, Runs The Enemy found hundreds of Indians milling around, but this time they looked different. He could see fear in their eyes. He called his band together and exhorted them to fight to the death, dramatically taking the ribbons from his hair and removing his shirt and pants. He threw them all away, wearing nothing but his cartridge belt and gun. Runs The Enemy thought of all the Lakota that would fall that day. Resigning himself to a warrior's fate, he said, "I will fall with them."[208]

WB 4:10–4:20, **White Bull** [last 4:00, next 4:20]. From the side of a hill on the bluffs White Bull could see more troops in the northeast. He and other nearby braves quickly decided on a course of action. "We charged," White Bull said. "We went down [the] E[ast] side of [the] river and we rode straight to Custer." He thought it was about three miles from where they left Reno's men to where they would finally reach Custer's troops.[209]

G 4:10–4:20, **Gall** [last 4:00, next 4:30]. It was a rough ride out of Medicine Tail Coulee, over the bluffs, and back across the Greasy Grass. So far, Gall had not been able to get into the fight. If he had hoped all his exertions to bring warning of more troops would earn him laurels, he was probably disappointed, for the alarm had already been spread. Warriors were hurrying through the village to the north, much as they had been heading south, before Gall and Iron Cedar took their detour. All for the better, perhaps, because now the soldiers would not surprise the lower camp.

This gave Gall a moment's respite. It was pointless to check at his lodge for the safety of his family, however, for it appeared that the helpless ones had already fled the village and headed down the valley. Gall would head north to look for them.[210]

FB 4:10–4:20, **Flying By** [last 3:50, next 4:40]. Since his horse was shot almost as soon as he got into the battle against Reno, Flying By missed the early action. Hiking back to his lodge, he noticed that the Hunkpapa and Minneconjou women had been busy taking down the tipis. Securing another pony, Flying By rode to the fight that had begun at the lower end of the camp. From a distance, he could discern more soldiers with four or five flags fluttering as they approached.

207. Marquis, *Wooden Leg*, 225–26.
208. Dixon, *Vanishing Race*, 173–74.
209. White Bull, Box 105, Notebook 24, Campbell Collection.
210. Graham, *The Custer Myth*, 89–90.

Flying By hastened his pace, for it looked as if the soldiers would cross the stream and attack the village.[211]

PW 4:10–4:20, **Pretty White Buffalo** [last 4:00, next 4:30]. She had barely reached a hill west of the camp when Pretty White Buffalo decided it was not the place for her. She wanted to watch the warriors plan to overthrow the soldiers of the Great Father. She could only do that from nearer to the fight that would begin when the soldiers approached the river at the lower end of the village. "I knew," she said, "that no man who rode with Long Hair would go back to tell the tale."

Nearing the river, Pretty White Buffalo could hear the music of the bugles and could see the column of soldiers turn to the left as they marched down the river to attack. In front of her swarmed the warriors of her people, rushing like the wind through the village. The men went to fight, while the women took down the lodges and rounded up the ponies. It was all done quickly and efficiently, as if it had been planned. But there was no plan, no council. The camp was not pitched for a fight and no one had anticipated any. The men would not have set up the camp in such a way as to invite attack from both ends and from the middle. No, thought Pretty White Buffalo, what was happening that day was done while the sun stood still. The Great Spirit had delivered the white men into the hands of the Lakota.[212]

L 4:10–4:20, **Lights** [last 3:20, next 5:10]. Lights had spent almost an hour aiding his friend who had been wounded in the head in front of Reno's skirmish line. He helped him back to the village and did all that could be done. At this time, the warriors who had been fighting Reno headed back through the camp, creating considerable confusion. Lights followed them north.

Nearing the ford, Lights first saw another group of soldiers far to the east at a point that would later be called Nye-Cartwright Ridge. As they neared the river, Lights scanned the landscape. As far as he could tell, there were no Indians east of the river to oppose them. Very quickly, however, Indians swarmed to the crossing in great numbers. The soldiers seemed to change their mind about attacking, and seemed to be looking out for their own safety more than trying to force their way into the village. They dismounted. They got to within one-quarter of a mile of the ford, Lights said. "That was as near as they ever got to the river."[213]

H 4:10–4:20, **Hump** (Etokeah—High Back Bone) [next 4:20]. The Minneconjou, born in 1848, was the older brother of Iron Thunder and one of the most hostile of the non-treaty Lakota. He had been actively fighting the white men since taking a leading part in the 1866 massacre of William J. Fetterman's command near Fort Phil Kearny.

Hump said that the sun was at noon when, without warning, the first white warriors attacked the Hunkpapa camp. He had much trouble getting into the fight, for the horse he had was not his, it was not broken in, and he could not manage it.

211. Hammer, *Custer in '76*, 209.
212. McLaughlin, *My Friend the Indian*, 45.
213. Hardorff, *Lakota Recollections*, 165–66.

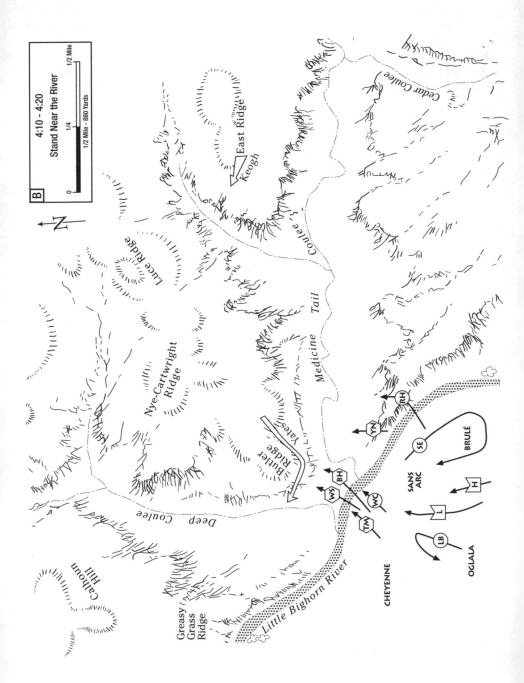

B
Stand Near the River
4:10 – 4:20

0   1/4   1/2 Mile – 880 Yards
1/2 Mile

N

East Ridge

Keogh

Luce Ridge

Coulee 'E'

Medicine Tail

Nye-Cartwright Ridge

Butler Ridge

Yates

Deep Coulee

Greasy Grass Ridge

Calhoun Hill

Little Bighorn River

RH

YN

SE

BRULÉ

SANS ARC

H

L

BH

WS

WC

TW

LB

OGLALA

CHEYENNE

Cedar Coulee

As the women and boys gathered in the herds, Hump finally caught a pony that he could manage better. By the time he was ready for battle, a second group of white warriors had charged. By this time, however, the Indians had gotten together and were ready for them.[214]

TM 4:10–4:20, **Two Moon** [last 4:00, next 4:20]. Two Moon watched Custer's troops marching as if they were going to cross the river, and to him it looked as if they had come right down to the water's edge. At least two Cheyenne guards had been posted on the east bank on each side of the coulee where it emptied into the main river (fig. 6), and Two Moon thought the one to the north of the coulee

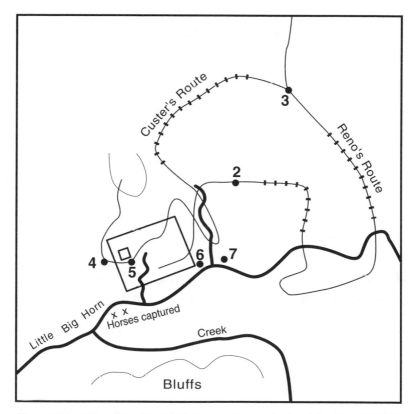

Figure 6. Two Moon Map (A). 2. *This is where Reno made his stand on the hill.* **3.** *This is the place, about three miles from the Little Horn, where Custer halted and separated his forces and sent Reno by the route marked above Reno Creek.* **4. & 5.** *A man in buckskin was shot at 4 and he staggered to 5 and fell.* **6. & 7.** *The two Cheyenne guards posted, and No. 6 fired the first shot at the advancing Custer column.* —Based on a map drawn by Willis T. Rowland (Ricker Collection, Nebraska State Historical Society) in *Big Horn Journal 2*, no. 1 (winter 1993).

fired the first shot at the advancing bluecoats. In addition, a number of Lakotas had already crossed to the east side. Then Two Moon heard a bugle sound and all the soldiers halted.

Indians hurriedly crossed the river, some going upstream and some downstream, trying to get on each side of them. The troopers soon learned that there were more than a few Indian guards facing them, for "almost in an instant the guns commenced to go, increasing to a roar like thunder." The soldiers began to dismount. "Custer had started his last fight," Two Moon declared.[215]

YN 4:10–4:20, **Yellow Nose** [last 4:00, next 4:20]. The war whoops from Yellow Nose and his companions seemed to have an effect on the soldiers, for they slowed from a gallop to a trot and became more cautious. The soldiers fired first, Yellow Nose declared, but the Indians were not intimidated. They returned the fire, especially the Lakotas, many of whom, with ammunition belts around their waists and chests, were better armed than the Cheyennes. Yellow Nose heard the bugles sound, being played by what he called "the regimental band," and the troops all dismounted. Bullets began to fill the air.[216]

WS 4:10–4:20, **White Shield** [last 4:00, next 4:20]. The troops were heading straight for them, and White Shield believed they would force their way across the river. Riding nearby, Mad Wolf (Lame White Man) said, "No one should charge yet. The sold[iers] are too many. Just keep shooting at them." When the Gray Horse Company got close to the river they dismounted, and all the soldiers as far back as White Shield could see stopped and dismounted also.

The Indians began to fire at the Gray Horse Company and the soldiers returned the favor. "It was not long before the Indians began to gather up thick where [I] was," said White Shield.[217]

BH 4:10–4:20, **Bobtail Horse** [last 4:00, next 5:20]. The soldiers had turned their attention from the five fleeing Lakotas, and appeared to concentrate on the ford leading to the camp. As Bobtail Horse and the handful of Cheyennes waited for the inevitable clash, Dull Knife (Lame White Man) began to shoot. Presently, however, he jumped upon his horse and announced, "It's no use. We cannot stop them."

Bobtail Horse would not give up so easily. He said, "Let us get in line behind this ridge and try to stop or turn them. If they get in camp they will kill many women."

In the meantime, the five Lakotas had circled around and come in behind, joining up with them. Bobtail Horse said that his "party had not advanced toward C[uster], but were on [the] bank of [the] L[ittle] H[orn] [on the] same side as C[uster]."

The soldiers charged and Bobtail Horse believed they would cross the river and get into the camp, for they were headed straight for the ford. "The ten I[ndians]

215. Hardorff, *Lakota Recollections*, 137; Hunt, *I Fought With Custer*, 213; "Two Moons Recalls," 10, 13.
216. "Yellow Nose Tells," 15.
217. Grinnell, *Fighting Cheyennes*, 350–51; White Shield, Notebook 348, Grinnell Collection.

were firing as hard as they could and killed a soldier," Bobtail Horse explained. The man's horse ran on ahead and Bobtail Horse caught it. The soldiers finally stopped.

Bobtail Horse used the reprieve to run his captured horse back into camp. There he still found some women among the tipis and he told them that they had better move out of danger. Later, an Indian who had been at the river came back to claim the horse. He declared that he was the one who had killed the soldier, and, as his horse had been wounded, he claimed that the soldier horse should be his. Bobtail Horse gave up the horse, but kept the saddle.[218]

(SE) 4:10–4:20, **Shave Elk** [last 4:00]. Shave Elk splashed across the ford, leaving behind the other Lakotas on the east bank. He entered the village and turned upstream, shouting the warning that more soldiers were coming. All along the steep riverbanks were many dismounted Indians. They moved toward the mouth of the coulee. Shave Elk ceased his tocsins and rode back to the action.

The main body of soldiers, led by a few troopers out in front, moved down toward the river and halted. They had only stopped a short time when the Indians crossed over and attacked them. Both sides began to fire.[219]

(WC) 4:10–4:20, **White Cow Bull** [last 4:00, next 4:20]. Ceasing his fire at the Crows on the bluffs when the five Lakotas splashed safely across the ford, White Cow Bull next turned his attention to the soldiers. Just then a Cheyenne named White Shield joined them. Though he and the Lakotas were armed only with bows and arrows, White Cow Bull was glad to have the extra fighting men. Now there were ten of them to defend the crossing.

Peering at the soldiers who had stopped at the edge of the river, White Cow Bull wondered at the strange, pink, and hairy appearance of them. He had never seen white soldiers before. As they began their charge across the river, Bobtail Horse fired and knocked one from his gray horse into the water. White Cow Bull aimed his repeater at one in a buckskin jacket who appeared to be the leader. Then he shot another soldier who was carrying a flag. They all fell from their saddles and hit the water. With those shots, the soldiers stopped, reined up, got off their horses and began to drag one of the wounded men out of the river. Bullets were still whistling about. Behind him, White Cow Bull heard more war cries. Hundreds of Lakotas and Cheyennes were charging toward them. The soldiers must have seen them also, for those still on horseback got off to fight on foot, and they all began to pull back to the far bank.[220]

(FE) 4:10–4:20, **Foolish Elk** [next 4:50]. The twenty-two-year-old Oglala had not really believed they would be attacked. There was a vague report that soldiers were coming, but Foolish Elk did not know if they were stories about Lone Star (Crook), whom they had just defeated, or some other command. There was little concern, for they thought there were enough Indians camped together to defeat any force that would come against them. Thus, when the fighting started at

218. Grinnell, *Fighting Cheyennes*, 350–51; Bobtail Horse, Notebook 348, Grinnell Collection.
219. Liddic, *Camp on Custer*, 122.
220. Miller, "Echoes," 33–34. Before becoming comfortable with this narrative, be forewarned that I take extreme exception to it in the upcoming discussion.

the Hunkpapa tipis there was little organized resistance. Men of all tribes rushed upriver to join in the fight.

That day, Foolish Elk fought with Crazy Horse. Almost before they got into the battle the Indians had chased the soldiers out of the valley and up into the bluffs. Before they could decide what to do with those soldiers, a second force was seen coming from the east.

Foolish Elk reversed direction and rode back down the valley, but was just a little late to join in the action beyond the ford. He was told that this second group of bluecoats sat on their horses and fired across the river into the village, but did not get into it. He heard that one soldier did ride his horse across into the village and was killed, but Foolish Elk did not see it. Now, many Indians had finally gathered their horses from the hills and were coming up in large numbers.[221]

RH 4:10–4:20, **Red Hawk** [next 4:20]. The Oglala Lakota Red Hawk did not pursue Reno's men across the river. He was in the valley when "one of the Indians gave notice that there were soldiers coming at the other end." Red Hawk reached the area in time to see this second group of soldiers coming down the ridge in three divisions. They did not make it to the river. The first division only got to a point about one-half to three-quarters of a mile from the water.

The Indians that had been pursuing Reno fell back down the river bottom, went through the village, and crossed the Little Bighorn at the only good ford. Many went back up the high hill in the direction that Reno's soldiers had retreated. From the hills they would assail Custer's leading division.[222]

LB 4:10–4:20, **Lone Bear** (Mato Wajila) [next 5:30]. The Oglala Lakota Lone Bear was twenty-nine years old during the summer of 1876, when he fought against Crook and Custer as a follower of Crazy Horse. The first attack that day on the Little Bighorn was a surprise to him, and Lone Bear hardly got near enough to Reno's troops to fight before that phase of the battle had ended.

The next soldiers Lone Bear saw came from the northeast down Nye-Cartwright Ridge. When they first appeared he saw no Indians on the north side of the river. As the soldiers neared the ford, they dismounted and began leading their horses, but they never got to the river. Lone Bear watched as large numbers of warriors, both mounted and on foot, crossed over and started after Custer before he reached the stream. Lone Bear was still on foot, but did not want to fight in that manner. He quickly turned back to his lodge in the Oglala circle to look for his pony.[223]

B 4:10–4:20, **Beard** [last 3:40, next 4:40]. Gathering the horses and painting himself for war had taken up much time. The camp had quieted down quite a bit as Beard made his way to fight the soldiers in the south. On the way, he fell in with four other Lakotas, also heading for the fight. Three of the men appeared to be

---

221. Hammer, *Custer in '76*, 197–98.
222. Hardorff, *Lakota Recollections*, 41–43. The story of Red Hawk was passed on to Eli S. Ricker in 1906 by Nicholas Ruleau, a trader who lived at the Pine Ridge Reservation. The account contains information given by Shot In The Face, Big Road, and Iron Bull, as well as Red Hawk. Yet Red Hawk appears to have contributed most of the story and his name will be used for convenience.
223. Ibid., 153–56.

veterans, for they carried rifles. The other was young, and armed only with bow and arrows, like Beard.

Just then, "one of the veterans went down," said Beard. "I saw my chance to act bravely and filled the gap."

Before they got much farther, however, they heard shooting at the far side of the village, near the Minneconjou camp circle. Beard spun Zi Chischila around and rode fast to meet the new danger.[224]

❧ DISCUSSION. By 4:20, Benteen's Companies D, H, and K—referred to by some of the Indians as the pack mules—reached Reno's men on the bluffs. Custer, with Keogh's Companies C, I, and L, remained on East Ridge, keeping an open line of sight to the river to the west and to the ridges in the south. From this vantage point, Custer could see Captain Yates, with Companies E and F, nearing the ford and Benteen approaching Reno. Indians had begun to appear in greater numbers on the ridgeline separating Custer from the Little Bighorn. Yates was making his demonstration about a half mile from the ford, and additional Indians

Looking down Deep Coulee across the Greasy Grass to the area where the Cheyenne village stood. —Monroe County Library

224. Miller, "Echoes," 38.

were gathering in front of him. If it had been Custer's plan to be a magnet for the Indians, it was working admirably. He now needed to continue north to a junction with Yates, leaving a vacated pocket behind for the pursuing Indians to fill. Reno and Benteen would surely follow from the rear.

Down at Medicine Tail Ford, Yates had no intention of crossing into the camp. Had he wished to have gone right through the dozen or so Indians in his path, he could have done so, but it would have served no purpose and was not part of the plan.[225]

In the village, only a fraction of the people still remained. Many noncombatants had fled northwest, to the flatlands and up on the western bluffs. A number of warriors had gone to Medicine Tail Ford. The greater portion were either in the process of escorting Reno off the field or returning from that action. Yet, somehow, we find that Beard had just left his tipi, joined with four other warriors, and headed south, when "one of the veterans went down" in some sort of mounted charge. Then they heard shooting near the Minneconjou camp and abruptly turned north. A glance at the 4:10–4:20 map shows the problem in tying this action to the time and terrain. The Reno mop-up was two miles away and across the river from Beard when the action at Medicine Tail Ford began. Who were Beard and his four companions charging against? It appears the only way "one of the veterans went down" is if his horse inadvertently jammed its leg in a prairie dog hole. This portion of the account does not fit our framework and must be rejected. But Miller is not yet through with us.

Back at the ford we face more of the conflicting testimony that has caused many a researcher in the past to throw up his hands in frustration. In this case, it is Miller's story of White Cow Bull, which fueled the hypothesis that Lt. Col. George Armstrong Custer was shot and killed while attempting to cross the river. The story has caused more mischief than almost any of the tales that have been circulated about the Battle of the Little Bighorn.

Who were the first Indians to the ford? According to White Cow Bull, it was he, Bobtail Horse, Roan Bear, Mad Wolf, five Lakotas, then White Shield. According to White Shield, it was Bobtail Horse, Roan Bear, one other (Calf, perhaps), and Mad Wolf (Lame White Man). According to Bobtail Horse, it was Calf, Roan Bear, and Dull Knife (Lame White Man). There are always discrepancies inherent in recollections, but one point is noticeable: the conspicuous absence of White Cow Bull.

Who was cautioned by Mad Wolf? White Shield said Mad Wolf rode by his side, and he heard the old Cheyenne's advice but did not mention any response. White Cow Bull said Mad Wolf's caution was answered by Bobtail Horse, before White Shield joined them. Bobtail Horse acknowledged making the response, without mentioning anyone else being involved.

Who shot at Crows on the bluffs? White Cow Bull said that Bobtail Horse first saw them and shot at them. Bobtail Horse made no such claim. Who saw the five Lakotas? White Shield didn't mention them. Bobtail Horse said they were riding

---

225. Robinson, *A Good Year to Die*, 190, believes that there were only two possible reasons that Custer did not cross at Medicine Tail Ford: either the women and children had fled and the village was empty, or he hit the middle of the village and had to continue north to find the far end.

east of the river, and joined them east of the river. White Cow Bull said they splashed across the river to join them on the west bank.

Who mentioned shooting soldiers from their horses into the river? White Cow Bull said that *both* he and Bobtail Horse did. White Shield never mentioned it. Calf never mentioned it. Bobtail Horse made no mention of any such feat, which, if it truly occurred, would have been the highlight of many talks around the nighttime campfires. Other Indians, in addition to White Cow Bull, would have commented about dropping two or three charging soldiers out of their saddles and into the river. From White Cow Bull's narrative, it appears that he, almost single-handed, stopped a full-scale cavalry charge in midstream, but no other Lakota or Cheyenne saw it happen.[226]

In fact, the other Indians involved in the affair near the ford indicated the con-frontation with the soldiers occurred *east* of the river. The fleeing Lakotas were east of the river. George Grinnell's informants said the Cheyennes had already ridden east of the river before the Lakotas met them. Two Moon indicated that at least two Cheyenne guards were firing from east of the river (see fig. 6), while a considerable number of others had already crossed over. Yellow Nose was on a promontory east of the river watching the troopers descend the coulee. Red Hawk witnessed the same. Gall had been there. Antelope saw Indians east of the river with the soldiers behind them. Two Eagles saw Indians reconnoitering east of the stream. The Blackfoot Lakota Kill Eagle said, "The Indians crossed the creek and then the firing com-menced." Wooden Leg said that the first three Cheyennes to cross the river were Bobtail Horse, Roan Bear, and Buffalo Calf, and they fired on Custer while he was "far out on the ridge." Shave Elk said the Indians crossed over the river to attack the soldiers. Lone Bear said the warriors had gone after Custer before he reached the river. He Dog said fifteen or twenty Indians fought the troopers from the east side of the stream; they fought him near the dry creek, but not near the river. Standing Bear also said that the Indians crossed the river as soon as Custer came in sight. They took position behind a low ridge and were reinforced rapidly as more warriors crossed over. "There was no fighting on the creek," Standing Bear said. Bobtail Horse, who was right there, unquestionably indicated they were all on the east bank, on the same side as Custer. Two years after the fight, Hump, Brave Wolf, and White Bull (Ice) told 5th Infantry Lt. Oscar F. Long that the Indians crossed the

---

226. The story of troops being stopped in the river was told in 1890 by war correspondent John Finerty. Using stories attributed to the Crow Curly and the Lakota Horned Horse, Finerty wrote that Custer made a dash to cross the river but was repulsed by Indians using repeaters, losing several men to bullets, water, and quicksand in the process. The story of Custer being shot there may have come from Pretty Shield, the wife of the Crow scout Goes Ahead. She indicated that Goes Ahead was with the troops at the ford, and both Custer and Mitch Bouyer were killed in the water, although Goes Ahead never mentioned this in any of his own narratives. John F. Finerty, *War-Path and Bivouac* (Norman: University of Oklahoma Press, 1961), 130, 137; Frank B. Linderman, *Red Mother* (New York: The John Day Com-pany, 1932), 236–37.

227. Graham, *The Custer Myth*, 53; Marquis, *Wooden Leg*, 381; Hardorff, *Lakota Recollections*, 59; Hammer, *Custer in '76*, 214; Bobtail Horse, Notebook 348, Grinnell Collection; James Brust, "Lt. Oscar Long's Early Map Details Terrain, Battle Positions," *Greasy Grass* 11 (May 1995): 6, 9. It remains a puzzle how some Indian accounts continue to be misread—and even altered—when they don't fit an author's preconceptions. See Schoenberger, *End of Custer*, 141–45. He states that the Indians all fought from the west bank and that White Cow Bull *and* Bobtail Horse claimed Custer was shot into the water, and even changes He Dog's testimony from the "east" side of the river to the "west" side.

river before Custer could possibly have forded. They had already gained a small hill on the north side of the river and placed themselves between Custer and the river.[227]

What action could White Cow Bull have been describing? Was he, perhaps, shooting at soldiers who may have reached a northern ford later in the battle? It does not appear to be, for his testimony and the time sequences place him in the Medicine Tail affair. Did a lone trooper break loose on an uncontrollable horse, as Foolish Elk had heard, and as the Crow scout Curly had seen, and did White Cow Bull shoot this unfortunate runaway?[228] Perhaps this was the trooper that Bobtail Horse said was killed, and whose horse ran close enough for him to capture and take back to the village. Whatever the actual circumstances, it is an almost inescapable conclusion that White Cow Bull could not have been west of the river, looking into the unshaven faces of two or more companies of cavalrymen on the opposite bank, then shooting two of them as they charged across the river, when no one else who was there mentioned it, and when all the other Indians who described the scene placed the action on the east bank, one-quarter to three-quarters of a mile or more from the river's edge. If White Cow Bull was firing from the west bank, he was firing into the backs of all the Indians who were fighting in front of him.

As much as we might have wished to accept all the Indian testimony, the scenario described by White Cow Bull just will not fit. Whether this was his own exaggeration or a misinterpretation by his chronicler, or a little bit of both, is unknown. Perhaps Miller let his desire for good literary copy take precedence over actual events. I would like to think the story has some basis in fact, that White Cow Bull did hit a trooper in the river on a runaway horse, and that the tale has grown out of proportion perhaps because of a slight misinterpretation. In any case, the time is long past due that we lay this story, and the hypothesis it has engendered, to a well-deserved rest: Custer was not shot and mortally wounded in a midstream charge across the Little Bighorn. Once we remove that fiction, we may be better able to understand the remaining phases of the battle.[229]

228. Hammer, *Custer in '76*, 157, 198; John M. Carroll, ed., *A Seventh Cavalry Scrapbook*, vol. 11 (Bryan, TX: Privately published, 1978–79): 4.

229. Regardless of the evidence against it, this interpretation continues to appear. As late as 1995, one writer affirmed, "It was the shooting of Custer at the ford . . . that brought on the debacle." Jack Pennington, "The Reno Court: The Second Cover-up," *Research Review: The Journal of the Little Big Horn Associates* 9, no. 1 (January 1995): 17.

COUNTERATTACK, 4:20–4:30

IT 4:20–4:30, **Iron Thunder** [last 4:10]. Iron Thunder moved north along the ridge. It looked as if most of the Indians were traveling in the direction of a circle, moving along the outer perimeter, but Iron Thunder decided to cut the circle by heading straight north. Farther along the ridge he climbed a knoll. There he could see the soldiers coming down toward the village.

Just yesterday, Iron Thunder had returned from a war party against the Crows. He had only one horse, and since Indians do not shoe their horses, its feet were worn out. The cumulative effects of that raid and today's battle had taken their toll. "I got half-way back to where [the] Long-Haired Chief and his men were," he said, "[and] my horse was so lame I could go no further." Iron Thunder got within about two miles of Custer when the Indians charged. He led his lame pony down the bluffs to the village. He was out of the fight.[230]

WB 4:20–4:30, **White Bull** [last 4:10, next 4:30]. Joining with White Bull on his ride north were the Lakotas Iron Lightning (Iron Thunder?), Owns The Horn, and Shooting Bear As He Runs, and two Cheyennes. As they twisted their way along the bluffs, the troops they had been watching vacated the ridge they were on, and the Indians lost sight of them. "[I] Couldn't see Custer," White Bull said, "as he was in [a] canyon."

When White Bull crested the high ground later known as Weir Point, the soldiers once again came into view. Now they were about one mile away and he began closing the range. There were "many little bunches of Indians" pursuing the soldiers, but White Bull didn't know how many for sure. He was certain Sitting Bull had gone back, and thought Pizi (Gall) must have been in camp at this time. Still ahead of White Bull, the soldiers kept moving north.[231]

OB 4:20–4:30, **One Bull** [last 4:00, next 4:30]. Although he wished to continue the fight with the soldiers he had seen in the north, One Bull realized that Sitting Bull's concerns for the women and children were valid. He crossed over to the west bank and went north down the valley. He rode with the Lakota who had been on the bluffs with him, shooting at the four escaping soldiers.

By the time they got back to the vicinity of the Hunkpapa camp, One Bull could see a group of Lakota horsemen up on the bluffs to the east, and his curiosity

---

230. Graham, *The Custer Myth*, 79.
231. White Bull, Box 105, Notebook 24, Campbell Collection. White Bull's statement that he lost track of Custer when he went in a canyon was rendered by Hardorff in *Lakota Recollections*, 112, as White Bull "could not see Custer as he was in company," a transcription that does not quite make sense in context. However, White Bull was not representing "Custer" as a single individual. Rather, "Custer" was a generic name for the troops that appeared in the north, as opposed to "Reno" in the south. When reading Campbell's original handwriting, it seems plain that he was writing "canyon." White Bull, in a time-terrain framework that would place him in the Weir Point area moving north, didn't lose track of Custer (the man) in a company, but he did lose track of Custer (the battalion) as it left East Ridge and went down in the "canyon" beyond the ridge. The move off the ridge will also be noted by Two Eagles and Wolf Tooth.

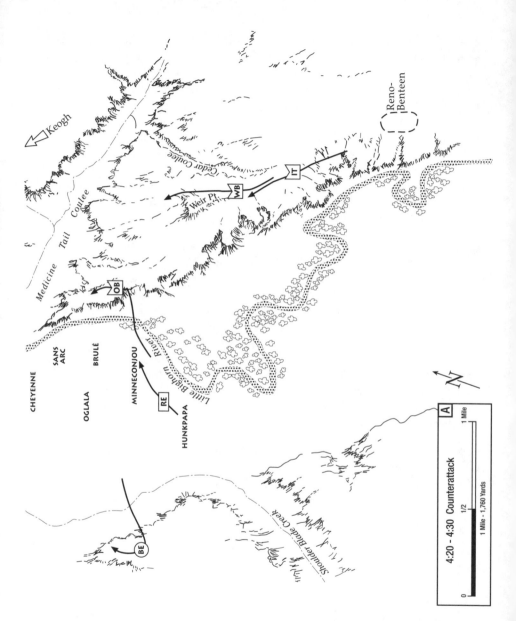

CHEYENNE

SANS
ARC

BRULÉ

OGLALA

MINNECONJOU

HUNKPAPA

Keogh

Medicine Tail Coulee

(Cedar Coulee)

Weir Pt.

Reno-
Benteen

Little Bighorn River

Shoulder Blade Creek

N

A

4:20 - 4:30 Counterattack

0   1/2   1 Mile

1 Mile - 1,760 Yards

got the best of him. The two decided they would again cross to the east side and take in the situation.

Urging their panting ponies up the hill, they approached the Lakotas. One Bull could not help but boast a bit, telling how he had just finished killing a lot of soldiers, and showing them the tomahawk he had used in the process. He said that he wished to continue on up to help kill the other (Custer's) soldiers, but that Sitting Bull told him not to go. He rode a bit farther to where he could clearly see the Lakotas and Cheyennes fighting. The shooting became heavy. Finally, reluctantly, One Bull turned his pony's head away from the action and headed for the ford.[232]

RE 4:20–4:30, **Runs The Enemy** [last 4:10, next 4:40]. In the Hunkpapa and Two Kettle circle, Runs The Enemy had stripped down for the second phase of the battle when Sitting Bull made an appearance. He could remember every one of his words: "A bird, when it is on its nest, spreads its wings for defense, but it can cackle and try to drive away the enemy. We are here to protect our wives and children, and we must not let the soldiers get them." Sitting Bull danced on his pony from one end of the line to the other. "Make a brave fight!" he called out. Again, Runs The Enemy rode out to the battle.[233]

YN 4:20–4:30, **Yellow Nose** [last 4:10, next 5:40]. As the bullets filled the air, Yellow Nose could no longer restrain himself. On his fleet, wiry pony, he had edged closer and closer to the white horsemen. Now, almost spontaneously, the Indians burst forth and headed for the soldier line.

Yellow Nose found himself in the lead, ahead of other noted Cheyenne warriors such as Contrary Belly and Comes In Sight, the latter having had the dubious distinction of being rescued by his sister, Buffalo Calf Road, only eight days earlier in the fight with Crook on the Rosebud.

A color bearer rode toward Yellow Nose, with his guidon poised outward like a spear. Yellow Nose accepted the challenge, and they closed like a pair of jousting medieval knights. On the top end of the flagstaff was a brass ferrule that in the heat of battle, Yellow Nose mistook for a rifle. With a nimble dodge and a quick lunge, Yellow Nose wrested the "rifle" from the trooper's hands.

He gave a shrill whoop and held the captured guidon high in the air for all to see. Here was a deed that would be remembered by the old-timers until their dying days. Yellow Nose pranced about on his pony. The soldiers, heretofore making a stand, now began to pull back.[234]

WS 4:20–4:30, **White Shield** [last 4:10, next 5:50]. Perhaps because he did not have his war shirt, White Shield dropped out of the front lines of the battle. After the soldiers and Indians had been shooting for some time, he saw Contrary Belly make a charge down in front of the Gray Horse Troop. The horses of one company became frightened and circled around the men who were holding them.

232. Greene, *Lakota and Cheyenne*, 56, 58.
233. Dixon, *Vanishing Race*, 174–75.
234. "Yellow Nose Tells," 15–16; Grinnell, *Fighting Cheyennes*, 336, 351.

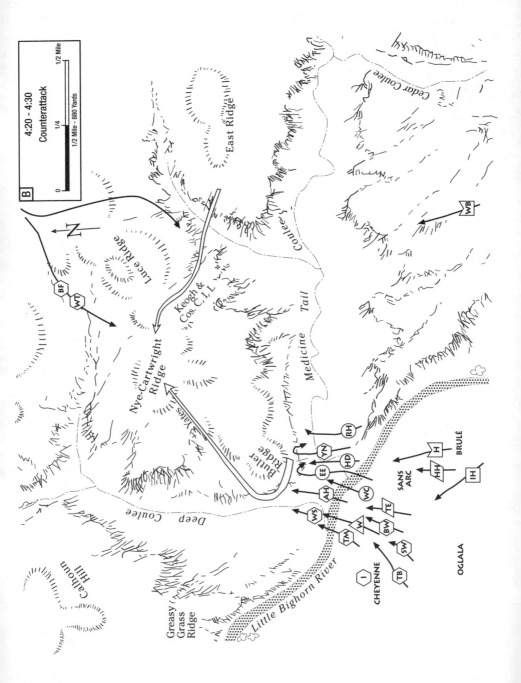

B

4:20 - 4:30
Counterattack

0   1/4   1/2 Mile

1/2 Mile - 880 Yards

1/2 Mile

N

East Ridge

Luce Ridge

BF
WT

Keogh &
Cos. C,I,L

Nye-Cartwright Ridge

Cedar Coulee

Medicine Tail Coulee

WB

Butler Ridge

E. Yates

RH
YN
HD
EE
WC
AH
WK
TM
W
BW
TE
SW
TB
I

H
HH
IH

BRULÉ

SANS
ARC

CHEYENNE

OGLALA

Deep Coulee

Greasy Grass Ridge

Calhoun Hill

Little Bighorn River

When Contrary Belly got back, the Cheyennes began shooting fast. White Shield looked across and saw two men, Yellow Nose and White Shield's half-brother, make a charge on another company off to the southeast. "It was here that Y[ellow] N[ose] got the flag," White Shield said, "snatching it from the ground where it stood and counting coup with it on a sold[ier]."

When Yellow Nose turned and went back toward the Indians, the frightened soldiers' horses broke from their holders and stampeded. The soldiers hung on tightly and did not let go, but some horses managed to escape. White Shield heard someone shout out that the soldiers were moving.[235]

WC 4:20–4:30, **White Cow Bull** [last 4:10, next 5:10]. "Hokahey!" the Lakotas coming from behind White Cow Bull were shouting. "They are going!" It was true. The soldiers were backing up over the higher ground to the north. Bobtail Horse ran to his pony, shouting, "Come on! They are running! Hurry!"

White Cow Bull and Bobtail Horse led the massed warriors out against the faltering troopers. Surely, the other Indians knew they had stood bravely to protect the village and willingly followed them.

Still riding with the Cheyennes, White Cow Bull noticed Yellow Nose making several runs, out in front, braving the troopers' fire. The soldiers' horses were so frightened by the noise that they began to bolt in all directions, and the soldiers had to slacken their fire to grab their horses. At that moment, the Indians, including Comes In Sight and Contrary Belly, charged again. Yellow Nose rushed in and grabbed a guidon. He carried it away and used it to count coup on a soldier, an act that showed more courage than if he had killed him.

White Cow Bull knew he had also been brave in his defense of the ford. He hoped word of his courage would be passed to Meotzi.[236]

EE 4:20–4:30, **Eagle Elk** [last 4:00, next 4:50]. Eagle Elk had stayed at Reno's retreat crossing for a time. Apparently there were soldiers still hiding in the brush and tall grass along the banks, because some Indians were setting fires to drive them out.

Just then he heard the warning that more soldiers were coming. Eagle Elk moved back north through the camps. Riding with eight other Indians, they reached a point just past the intervening bluffs where they could see that the warning was true. There were soldiers on the ridge.

The nine of them crossed the river and were among the first to make a charge. They went right up close to the soldiers. A Cheyenne that Eagle Elk did not know rode out ahead and took a flag away from one of them. Soon thereafter, Eagle Elk thought that the Cheyenne was shot through the heels, and his horse stumbled and broke its legs.

---

235. White Shield, Notebook 348, Grinnell Collection. Clearly, White Shield was near the river at Medicine Tail Ford, before the troops retreated, when he saw Yellow Nose get the flag. *"It was here,"* he said (italics added). It is incomprehensible how one could read White Shield's account and claim that, "This seems to identify Calhoun Hill." See Hardorff, *Memories,* 54.

236. Miller, "Echoes," 34.

Pulling back from the encounter, Eagle Elk noticed many more Indians joining them from across the creek. To the south, he could see another group of Indians charging the soldiers.[237]

HD 4:20–4:30, **He Dog** [last 3:50, next 5:30]. He Dog had joined in the chase of Reno, but broke off the pursuit in the valley when he saw the approach of more cavalry from the south, Benteen's men. He made his way back to the Hunkpapa camp. From there, he headed toward his lodge in the Oglala circle. If he thought

The Oglala He Dog crossed to the east side of the river and opened fire on the advancing soldiers. —Little Bighorn Battlefield National Monument

---

237. Hardorff, *Lakota Recollections*, 103–4. As in the White Shield account, Eagle Elk clearly places the flag capture incident near the river, but Hardorff, *Memories*, 54, uses this to argue for a Calhoun Hill location.

leaving Benteen's men behind would give him respite from the battle, he was mistaken. "We looked and saw other soldiers coming on the big hill right over east," He Dog said. "They kept right on down the river and crossed Medicine Tail Coulee and onto [a] little rise."

He Dog could see that Custer's line "was scattered all along parallel with [the] river." He thought Custer meant to reach the lower end of the camp, but the Indians west of the stream had already left the camp to confront him. Except for a few shots, He Dog stated, there was no general fighting while Custer was down near the river. However, He Dog, along with fifteen or twenty Lakotas, had already gone to the east side of the Greasy Grass, where they exchanged a few shots with the soldiers. He then joined them in an attack near the dry creek. "Custer," He Dog said, "never got near the river."[238]

IH 4:20–4:30, **Iron Hawk** [last 4:00, next 5:30]. Riding downstream with Little Bear and some other Hunkpapas, Iron Hawk neared the ford, where there was fighting going on. The Indians were crossing the river everywhere. It looked like a hundred of them had already confronted Custer, and it didn't appear that the soldiers got anywhere near the river, maybe no closer than three-quarters of a mile. Iron Hawk and a contingent of Hunkpapas continued north along the valley.[239]

HH 4:20–4:30, **Hollow Horn Bear** (Mato Heli Dogeca) [next 5:00]. The Brulé Lakota, son of Iron Shell, was twenty-six years of age at the Battle of the Little Bighorn. He had spent the winter at the Spotted Tail Agency, and was not one of the active year-round roamers. In May 1876, however, he and about twenty Two Kettle Lakotas were out searching for lost ponies when they discovered the Terry Expedition moving west along the Heart River after leaving Fort Abraham Lincoln. After following them for a few days, they eventually located and joined up with Sitting Bull's band, and were in the village about five days before the battle began.

Hollow Horn Bear thought it was about one hour after the fight with Reno began that the second group of soldiers first appeared opposite the lower end of the village. He participated briefly in the Reno action, but was back among the Brulé tipis when he first saw Custer's troops coming over the top of a high ridge in the area of Nye-Cartwright. These soldiers came toward the river, but they only got as far as the ridge south of the south end of Calhoun Hill (Butler Ridge). It was near that ridge where the fight started, Hollow Horn Bear declared. "There was no fighting near the river."

The soldiers fired into the village for a time, but no one was hit. Hollow Horn Bear did not think the soldiers wanted to cross the river when they saw how many Indians were gathering, but even if they had wanted to, the Indians took away their initiative when they carried the attack to them. The fighting was heavy from the start and the soldiers had no choice but to give up ground.[240]

---

238. Hammer, *Custer in '76*, 206–7; Hardorff, *Lakota Recollections*, 75.
239. Neihardt, *Black Elk*, 121; Hardorff, *Lakota Recollections*, 68.
240. Ibid., 177–81.

I 4:20–4:30, **Ice** (White Bull). The elder brother of Antelope and father of Noisy Walking, Ice was a prominent man in the Northern Cheyenne tribe. He had proven to be a brave warrior in the past. Today, Ice was one of three well-respected holy men in the camp, along with Coal Bear, keeper of *Esevone*, and Box Elder, who had dreamed about soldiers attacking.

Ice did not participate directly in the fighting. However, he could see the initial action to the south, including the fires from where some lodges in Sitting Bull's camp had been burned. Now, from the Cheyenne lodges in the lower village, Ice could see more soldiers coming down toward the riverbank and forming in a line of battle. Their charge was met by the Indians. The soldiers stopped, Ice said, "and fell back up the hill."[241]

H 4:20–4:30, **Hump** [last 4:10, next 4:50]. As he studied the white soldier movements, Hump believed it was Custer's intention to cut off the Indians' line of retreat. However, because he did not know where Reno was, or that he had already been defeated, his plan was doomed to fail. When the Indians charged, Hump said, the long-haired chief and his men became confused and retreated slowly back up the hill.[242]

AH 4:20–4:30, **American Horse** [last 4:00]. Not having crossed the river after Reno's fleeing men, American Horse was one of the first to return to the lower village. Reaching the Cheyenne circle he saw Custer's men "coming down the hill and almost at the river."

"I was one of the first to meet the troops," American Horse declared. The Indians and soldiers reached the flat near the river at about the same time. Custer saw the Indians, formed his troops in a line of battle, and fought there for a little while.

Shortly thereafter, the Indian pressure forced the soldiers to give way, and they "were driven up the hill." This was no panic retreat, however, for American Horse said that the troopers remained on horseback, fighting doggedly, all the way up the hill.[243]

BW 4:20–4:30, **Brave Wolf** [next 6:10(a)]. A fighting chief of the Northern Cheyennes and a Contrary at the time, Brave Wolf had been battling Reno's troops until they had fled out of the timber, across the river, and up the hill. He never understood why they left the wooded bottoms, for it seemed like a good place to defend. Had they stayed, Brave Wolf thought, "they would have been all right."

By the time Brave Wolf reached the Cheyenne camp, it appeared that the fighting with Custer had been going on for some time. He could see the soldiers were close to the stream, although none of them had gotten to the west bank. Just as he got to the ford, Brave Wolf saw the soldiers retreat back up the gulch. They were all drawn up in line of battle, shooting well and fighting hard, but there were too many Indians, and the soldiers could not help being killed.[244]

---

241. White Bull (Ice), Notebook 325, August 1895. Grinnell Manuscript Collection, Braun Research Library, Southwest Museum, Los Angeles, California; Powell, *Sacred Mountain*, 1004, 1008.

242. Graham, *The Custer Myth*, 78.

243. Greene, *Lakota and Cheyenne*, 49–50.

244. Ibid., 46; Grinnell, *Fighting Cheyennes*, 349–50, 352–53. As a Contrary, Brave Wolf lived according to special rules and was thought to have special powers. His actions or speech might directly contradict what he was asked or what he wished.

The Cheyenne Brave Wolf had battled Reno's troops and only reached Medicine Tail Ford when the soldiers began to fall back. —Little Bighorn Battlefield National Monument

TB 4:20–4:30, **Tall Bull** [last 3:50, next 5:00]. Tall Bull never pursued Reno's fugitives across the river, but went north to meet the new threat. All the Indians, he said, "rushed back on the west side of the camp," down to a small dry run (Medicine Tail Coulee) that came in from the east. He heard that the first word of Custer's coming was brought in by the women who had gone to the high ground east of the river to overlook the fight with Reno.

Custer's troops got onto the flat near the ford and within gunshot range of the village. The first men who fought Custer were those who did not have time to get their horses and participate in the Reno action, but they did have enough time to cross over and fight near the village. Tall Bull did not see the beginning of the battle. By the time he got there, the soldiers were backing off, fighting for quite a distance, "working up the hill." The Indians had pushed the soldiers to the first rise, "and they were going up the ridge to [the] right of Custer (Medicine Tail) coulee and the Indians [were] driving them." Some were mounted and some were on foot, but not in very good order.[245]

SW 4:20–4:30, **Soldier Wolf.** A seventeen-year-old Northern Cheyenne, Soldier Wolf did not fight in the front lines of the battle, but considered himself "old enough to notice a great many things and to see the reasons for them." As he

245. Hammer, *Custer in '76*, 212–13; Greene, *Lakota and Cheyenne*, 53. Tall Bull's statement that the Indians rushed back to the ford "on the west side of the camp" is another indication of the village's configuration as shown in figure 1. The shortest distance to the ford was from the Garryowen loop of the river, then north on the west side of the camp, avoiding the longer ride and the obstacles they would have encountered had they gone through the village, which generally conformed to the river's course. This is just what Gall did (3:20) when he rode in the opposite direction in the most direct line to get to the Reno action.

understood matters, the first word of Custer's approach was brought by the women who had gathered in the lower village during Reno's attack. They became more frightened as they listened to the firing and decided to cross east of the river to get farther away. Some of these women who went up in the hills discovered Custer coming. They ran back, and their alarm caused some riders to head south to warn the warriors still pursuing Reno.

Now that Custer neared the mouth of the dry creek, the fighting began in earnest. Soldier Wolf said they fought in the bottoms for quite a time, with neither side giving way. The Cheyennes, Lakotas, and white men lost a good number of horses, for their bodies covered the ground. By then, the Indians began to overpower the soldiers. "They fell back up the hill," Soldier Wolf said. Although they retreated slowly, with their faces to the front, two dead soldiers were left behind.[246]

TE 4:20–4:30, **Two Eagles** [last 4:00, next 5:00]. Two Eagles saw that some of the troops had stayed in the hills while others came down toward the camp. There was a large force of Indians defending, and those who approached the ford "did not get down to the river." There was only a fight of short duration before the soldiers were driven off. They were not in a compact body when they retreated, and a few soldiers were killed before the ridge top was reached.

Two Eagles saw the Indians passing to the east bank all up and down the ford area, anywhere shallow water made for a safe crossing. In the distance, he could see that while these troops had come down near the river, another group headed from an eastern hilltop to a ridge farther north.[247]

TM 4:20–4:30, **Two Moon** [last 4:10, next 4:40]. With the gunfire sounding like thunder, Two Moon saw Custer's troops dismount and move slowly back up the ridge, with the soldiers trying to protect their horses by keeping them inside their lines. The Indians circled around them. Their attack had thrown Custer's course (see fig. 7) "about half a mile away from the river."[248]

W 4:20–4:30, **Waterman** [next 5:00]. The twenty-two-year-old Arapaho was one of only five of his tribe to participate in the battle. Slipping out from the agency at Fort Robinson, in present-day Nebraska, Waterman, Yellow Eagle, Yellow Fly, Well-Knowing One, and Left Hand thought they would spend the summer scouting and hunting. They met a Lakota near the Little Bighorn River and were told about the sun dance that was going to be held. The Arapahos thought they would go to the Lakota village "and have a good time."

Their plan did not turn out as they had intended, however, for the Lakotas only made them prisoners, thinking they were scouts for the white soldiers. They were freed only when Two Moon pleaded for them. They were given back their weapons, but Waterman still felt as if he was being closely watched, and was he unable to make his escape. When the soldiers did attack, the Arapahos had no choice but to fight with the Lakotas.

---

246. Greene, *Lakota and Cheyenne*, 51–52.
247. Hardorff, *Lakota Recollections*, 143, 145. The group moving from an eastern hilltop to a ridge farther north was probably Custer coming down off East Ridge on his way to Nye-Cartwright Ridge.
248. Hardorff, *Lakota Recollections*, 137; "Two Moons Recalls," 10.

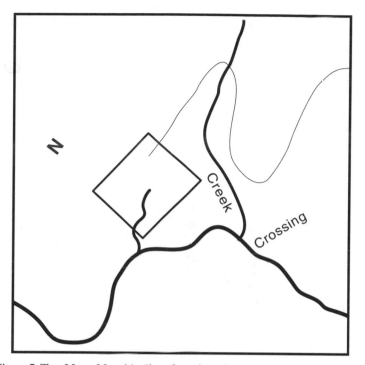

Figure 7. Two Moon Map (B). *Shots from the Indians turned Custer "so that his course was thrown about half a mile away from the river."* —Based on a map drawn by Willis T. Rowland (Ricker Collection, Nebraska State Historical Society) in *Big Horn Journal 2*, no. 1 (winter 1993).

Waterman thought the initial attack by Reno began about nine in the morning. There were not many soldiers, and he was sure they would be beaten back. After they had been driven to the ridge where they dug pits for protection, Waterman heard shooting at the lower end of the village.

He went there as fast as he could. It looked like these troops were trying to cross the river and attack the camp, but the Indians drove them back also. Waterman believed they could have forded the river and attacked the village if they wanted to, for the crossing there was easy, and the Indians had no trouble in going over to drive them back up the hill.[249]

RH 4:20–4:30, **Red Hawk** [last 4:10, next 4:30]. From the hills along the river, Red Hawk had seen the soldiers approach in three divisions. When enough Indians had gathered, they charged down from their high position and met the first division. They drove the first division back to the second division, and then drove both of those back to a third division (see fig. 8).

---

249. Graham, *The Custer Myth*, 109–10.

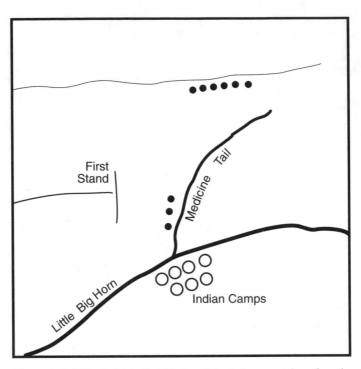

Figure 8. Red Hawk Map. *Red Hawk said the Indians went down from the point, or hill, and met the first division of soldiers. They drove the first division back to the second, and then both of them back to the third.* —Based on a 1906 map by Austin Red Hawk (Ricker Collection, Nebraska State Historical Society).

Although they retreated, Red Hawk had never seen soldiers fight as bravely as they did. He thought several Indians were killed, but did not believe any soldiers had died yet. It looked like the officers were doing their best to keep their men together, but some of their horses became unmanageable, and they would rear up and throw some of their riders.[250]

WT 4:20–4:30, **Wolf Tooth** [next 4:30]. The Northern Cheyenne Wolf Tooth and his cousin Big Foot had made a long, circuitous ride to get in this position. They had been out since early this morning, hoping to sneak past the Kit Fox camp police. White soldiers were known to have been east of the Wolf Mountains, perhaps twenty miles away in the valley of the Rosebud, and it would have been an honor to locate them and strike them first. The military societies had been guarding along the bluffs east of the Little Bighorn. Wolf Tooth and Big Foot had to take their horses far north of the village and hobble them on the west side of the

river, pretending to leave them there so they could be ready the next day. After
dark, however, they crept back, got the horses, and went down to the river, hiding
in the brush all night.

At dawn, early this morning, they could still see the patrols in the hills, so they
remained hidden for some time. Stealthily creeping east, the two Cheyennes met
up with a few more warriors with the same intentions, then a few more, and yet
more again. Soon there was a band of about fifty men heading east, following up a
creek (Custer) that entered the Little Bighorn a few miles north of the village.

They had finally gotten far enough away from the patrols to relax their vigi-
lance and pick up their pace. Then they heard someone holler. Wolf Tooth looked
back and saw a rider, waving and calling to them. They wheeled their horses and
rode to him. He spoke in a Lakota dialect, but Big Foot could translate: "The
soldiers are already at the village!"

The party raced up the creek until they came to a ridgeline that they could
follow back toward the camp. Reaching a high point east of the valley, they found
that the warning was true. There were the soldiers, between them and the village.
As they watched, giving their ponies a chance to rest, the soldiers began to move
down the ridge, heading into a coulee that led to the ford. They disappeared.

Quickly a course of action was decided upon. The band split up, half of them
riding after the soldiers along the south side of the divide, and the rest circling
around to the north to try and cut them off. Finally they caught up with the
soldiers while they were still in the coulee, but they were discovered, and the troops
began firing at them. Though the fight did not last long, Wolf Tooth said, "It was the
first skirmish of the battle."[251]

BE 4:20–4:30, **Black Elk** [last 4:00, next 6:10(a)]. Clutching the scalp he had
taken, Black Elk and his two friends turned back downstream, listening to
the battle receding behind them. When he got back to the Oglala camp he could
see more soldiers on a hill east of the river, maybe three miles away. Beyond the
Santee camp there was a great dust cloud, with many warriors whirling in and out
of it just like swallows.

Learning that his mother had gone to the hills in the west, Black Elk headed
there to find her. He passed by a wounded man who was sitting with his gun and
lance, singing a song of regret that he was unable to participate in the fight. As he
reached the hill, Black Elk also saw a very pretty single woman singing a song of
courage for the warriors, wishing them to fight hard so that she would not be taken
captive.

Finding his mother on the hill, Black Elk held his trophy high so that she could
see. His mother began a shrill tremolo for him, her voice blending in with the
many other women who were singing encouragement for their men. Black Elk felt
proud. He would rest awhile, looking to the east to watch the fight.[252]

251. Powell, *Sacred Mountain*, 1007, 1018; John Stands In Timber and Margot Liberty, *Cheyenne Memories*
(Lincoln: University of Nebraska Press, 1967), 193, 197–98.
252. Neihardt, *Black Elk*, 112; DeMallie, *Sixth Grandfather*, 183–84.

←**DISCUSSION.** In this segment, Custer accomplished about all he had hoped to with Yates's demonstration at the ford. Keogh's battalion fired the volley that was, first, a signal to Yates to begin his withdrawal and, second, a signal to Reno and Benteen to get moving and come to the sound of the guns. The volleys were heard by men of both commands on Reno's hilltop, and by soldiers who had been stranded after the retreat and were still hiding along the banks of the river. Immediately after the firing, Custer left East Ridge to head for the next high ground to the north, the Nye-Cartwright complex, where he would join Yates. White Bull saw Custer disappear off the ridge at this time, as did Two Eagles, Wolf Tooth, and Big Foot.

During this period, the Yellow Nose–guidon incident occurred down at the ford. Historically, it has been one of the most often recalled events of the battle. Geographically and temporally, it has been variously placed. John Stands In Timber, a grandson of Lame White Man and a repository of Cheyenne oral tradition, placed the event late in the fight at the north end of the field near Last Stand Hill. Father Peter Powell, using Cheyenne testimony, placed the event late in the fight in the basin below Last Stand Hill. Hardorff thinks it occurred on the slopes of the hill named for Lt. James Calhoun. Miller understood from his interviews that the event occurred near the ford early in the fight. Eagle Elk saw a Cheyenne that may have been Yellow Nose grab a guidon in an early charge near the ford, but thought that the Cheyenne was subsequently wounded. At the same time, the group of Indians Eagle Elk saw charging against soldiers in the south may have been the southern half of Wolf Tooth's group currently engaged in assailing the rear of Keogh's battalion.[253]

Perhaps the best authority to pinpoint the action is Yellow Nose himself. It is fairly clear from his narrative that he crossed the river onto a promontory above Medicine Tail Coulee and watched troops come down near the river. He and a relatively small band of warriors were among the first to charge. It was on the east bank, in some of the earliest skirmishing with Custer's battalion, that Yellow Nose said he captured the flag.[254]

Confirmation is found in George Grinnell's notes. In his book *The Fighting Cheyennes*, he summarized the action, with rather vague time and place references, as occurring "a long way off to the southeast." Yet a close reading of his own handwritten notebook shows that this statement came from White Shield while describing the first confrontation east of the ford. The notes show that Yellow Nose's charge was not made against the Gray Horse Company, which was closest to the river, but on another one southeast of it (probably Company F), a bit farther back up Medicine Tail Coulee. That White Shield, without his war shirt, probably dropped out of the front lines, maybe even back to the west bank, is indicated by his statement that he had to look "across" to see the two men making a charge.[255] The event did not take place on Calhoun Hill or Custer Hill.

---

253. Stands In Timber, *Cheyenne Memories*, 202; Peter J. Powell, *Sweet Medicine: The Continuing Role of the Sacred Arrows, the Sun Dance, and the Buffalo Hat in Northern Cheyenne History,* vol. 1 (Norman: University of Oklahoma Press, 1969), 117; Miller, *Custer's Fall*, x, 131; Hardorff, *Lakota Recollections*, 104; Hardorff, *Memories*, 54.
254. "Yellow Nose Tells," 15–16.
255. Grinnell, *Fighting Cheyennes*, 351; White Shield, Bobtail Horse, Calf, Notebook 348, Grinnell Collection. I had always been perplexed by Grinnell's rendition of the battle, from Yates's river approach to Last

One may notice that this study depicts Yates's subsequent withdrawal from the river differently from conventional interpretations. Instead of relying on secondary sources for the consensus explanation, one need only look closely at the Indians' own words to find that Yates did not leave the ford and go directly to Greasy Grass Ridge; rather, he retreated back up the divide to Nye-Cartwright Ridge.

To illustrate this, we first need to establish the route Yates took on his way to the lower end of the village. From the many secondary accounts of the battle, the usual assumption is that Yates followed Medicine Tail Coulee, snaking his way along the bottom. In fact, most of the Indians told a different story. Gall saw Custer in Medicine Tail Coulee, but that was near the junction with Cedar Coulee, before he rode up East Ridge. White Cow Bull said they came down the coulee, but that was when they were almost at the river (and we have seen his accounts are not always trustworthy). Others saw the move differently. Bobtail Horse said they came down by a dry creek, but specifically "not in it." Yellow Nose said the troops advanced toward them along the crest of a divide that ran back from the Little Bighorn. Antelope saw them coming from the east on a high ridge. Two Moon saw their flags coming over a hill in the east, and we will see Young Two Moon (4:40) indicate that they came down a steep hill east of the battlefield. Two Eagles said the soldiers came down from Nye-Cartwright Ridge. He explained that while some came riding down from a high point, others stayed back in the hills. Lights saw the soldiers at a point near Nye-Cartwright Ridge. Red Hawk saw three divisions of soldiers coming down the ridge. He Dog saw soldiers coming on a big hill from the east. Eagle Elk saw Custer's soldiers on a ridge. Fears Nothing said Custer came down on top of the ridge northeast of Water Rat Creek (Medicine Tail). Lone Bear said the soldiers came from the northeast and were seen coming down from Nye-Cartwright Ridge. American Horse saw them coming down the hill. Hollow Horn Bear said the soldiers came over the top of a high ridge and advanced as far as the ridge south of the south end of Calhoun Hill.[256]

Anyone walking along the meandering bottoms of Medicine Tail Coulee today would quickly realize the impossibility of seeing across the river and into the valley.

Stand Hill, particularly in regard to the Gray Horse Troop. On pages 350–53, we find them by the river, at the monument, by the river again, near the monument again, over and over. It turns out that Grinnell's notes are clearer than his book. The four pages in question primarily come from White Shield and Bobtail Horse, with lesser contributions from Calf, Brave Wolf, and Ice. In his book, Grinnell would let one narrative run chronologically, then shift into another account from the beginning, without identifying the change in narrator. As a result, there is an overlapping of tales with seeming shifts in time and terrain as described above. It is easier to visualize the sequencing in Grinnell's notes where he at least added parenthetical clarifications such as "Calf goes on with story" or "Now B[ob] T[ail] H[orse] takes up story."

256. Hardorff, *Lakota Recollections*, 31, 180. Of course the label "Nye-Cartwright" was not in general use for this terrain during the times these interviews were given. The Indians would have spoken in terms of "the high ridge" or "the big hill." Even today, the slope that runs toward the river from Nye-Cartwright Ridge and forms the divide between Medicine Tail Coulee on the south and Deep Coulee on the north has never been named. Because the terrain contains the memorial marker for Sgt. James Butler, we will call this feature "Butler Ridge" for ease of identification. Butler Ridge was the "ridge south" that Hollow Horn Bear referred to. Researcher Richard G. Hardorff indicates that the Indian was referring to the western terminus of Calhoun Hill, otherwise known as Greasy Grass Ridge. Read in context and with a respect for the topography involved, one will find that by leaving Nye-Cartwright and going toward the ford, one will not end up on Greasy Grass Ridge. One will, however, traverse Butler Ridge.

One cannot see across the ford until almost the last bench above the creek is reached. In particular, one could not see the tipis that would have been hidden behind the intervening bluffs (Yellow Nose's promontory). Likewise, one standing on the valley floor west of the ford could not see along the twisting course of Medicine Tail. The very fact that troops were easily seen shows they did not make their approach along the streambed—and this is exactly what the Indians said.

Moving down from the Nye-Cartwright area, perhaps just below and south of the backbone of Butler Ridge, solves both difficulties immediately. The panorama of the valley is opened up and the troops are visible. Yates can see the ford and village and the Indians can see him—just what Custer wanted. Contrary to popular conception, and such hypotheses as advanced by authors Henry and Don Weibert, Custer was not trying to hide from the Indians at this place and time.[257]

It seems clear from the Indian descriptions that Yates advanced along Butler Ridge for at least part of the trip toward the ford. We also find Keogh's battalion leaving East Ridge at this time. While Yates was near the river, Two Eagles saw them leaving an eastern hilltop to a ridge farther north. White Bull saw them disappear into a canyon as they left the ridge, and Wolf Tooth saw them move down the ridge into a coulee. It appears the moves were planned to coincide, for about the time Keogh moved north to what we know as Nye-Cartwright Ridge, Yates was pulling back from his sortie and heading east for the same point.

Having established Yates's advance route, we move to the question of his retreat route. In the first place, the Indians described Yates's moves after the initial conflict as a *retreat*. He was driven back. This implies the stopping of his forward impetus and the start of a retrograde movement. The great majority of Indians did not say the soldiers advanced or continued north along the river.[258] They fell back. But to where?

Once again, we need to turn to the eyewitnesses. There is one Indian, Brave Wolf, who said they retreated up the gulch. Yellow Nose said that what had begun as a stand turned into a retreat. Hump just said the soldiers retreated slowly. Others were more descriptive. Tall Bull said they were "working up the hill." They were driven to the first rise, "and they were going up the ridge to [the] right of Custer (Medicine Tail) Coulee." The ridge on the right bank of the coulee is Butler Ridge— the ridge on the left bank does not come down from the high eastern ground and would have been occupied by the Indians, Yellow Nose and others. Waterman said they drove the soldiers back up the hill. Two Moon said the soldiers' course was thrown a half mile away from the river and they were forced back up the ridge. His map (fig. 7) shows the retreat path remained south of Deep Coulee and hooked

257. Weibert, *Sixty-Six Years*, 44–47, 51.
258. Besides some Walter Camp questionnaires, which will be discussed in the next segment, the only instance I can find where an Indian might have alluded to a movement north along the river comes from Calf in Notebook 348, Grinnell Collection. In this instance, Calf indicated that the two companies who charged the river went back to a little knoll, then crossed a deep gulch and climbed a hill on the other side. After this, a parenthetical addition states that these companies were the ones to cross the gulch and go to the present battlefield. It is unclear whether this is Calf's narrative or Grinnell's surmising. Calf was positive about one point: he said, "The dust was so thick they could not see [the] soldiers nor each other nor [the] G[ray] H[orse] Co[mpany]. He knows nothing about what happened for he could see nothing." The one allusion to a move north along the river is still obscured in "dust."

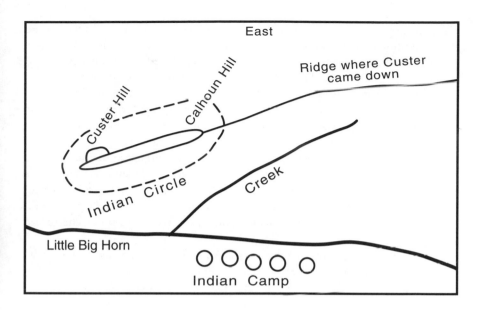

Figure 9. Maps by Standing Bear (top) and Flying Hawk (bottom).
—Based on maps in the Ricker Collection, Nebraska State Historical Society

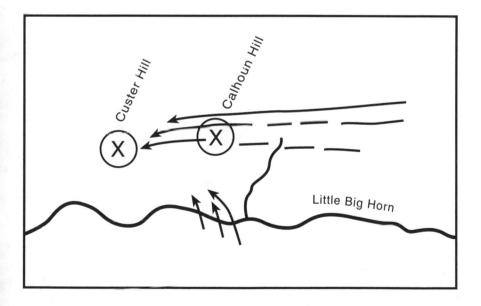

back up Butler Ridge to Nye-Cartwright Ridge. American Horse said they "were driven up the hill." Ice said the soldiers "fell back up the hill." Soldier Wolf used exactly the same words as Ice. Shave Elk said they "chased the soldiers up a long, gradual slope or hill in a direction away from the river."[259] Red Hawk said the divisions (companies) were forced back into one another, and produced a map to illustrate the sequence (fig. 8). The dots, representing the "divisions," show the cavalry went directly back up Butler Ridge, heading toward Keogh. Although they missed the action closer to the ford, Standing Bear and Flying Hawk drew maps (fig. 9) that illustrate the soldiers moved along the high ground in the east, directly to Calhoun Hill. None of these Indian maps or narratives show or tell of the soldiers going from the river directly to Greasy Grass Ridge or Calhoun Hill. In fact, the traditional depiction of Custer coming down one coulee (Medicine Tail) and going back up another one (Deep) is unfathomable after reading the Indian descriptions.

From a number of accounts it appears that Yates retreated up the same terrain he advanced down. There was no reason to move directly to the Greasy Grass–Calhoun Hill complex. Such a move would probably not have appeared to be a retreat to the Indians, and Yates would have been moving away from Custer instead of linking up with him for further instructions. Yet, there are other reasons that may have led to the consensus that Yates and his troops retreated from Medicine Tail Ford to Calhoun Hill. We will note them in the next segment.

---

259. Liddic, *Camp on Custer*, 122–23.

ADVANCE, 4:30–4:40

WT 4:30–4:40, **Wolf Tooth** [last 4:20, next 4:40]. The split band of fifty warriors had done their best to harass the bluecoats as they moved along the ridges. While one group attacked south of the divide, the other, after circling around to try to cut them off, attacked from the north. However, the troopers began firing at them, Wolf Tooth said, and the Indians did not try to get in very close. The Indians dropped back behind the troops and moved higher into the hills. Wolf Tooth and Big Foot hung back, following the soldiers at a safe distance, waiting for another opportunity to strike. They watched as the soldiers moved down the high ridge and crossed the coulee, climbing over to the south end of the ridge where the final battle would take place.[260]

WB 4:30–4:40, **White Bull** [last 4:20, next 4:40]. White Bull rode down from the high ground and crossed the coulee, still following the soldiers. From there until Custer reached Calhoun Hill, White Bull saw that the soldiers were keeping close together. Sometimes they walked and sometimes they trotted, but they always kept on the move. The Indians were getting closer to the soldiers, and some began to fire at them, but the soldiers kept riding, White Bull said.[261]

WL 4:30–4:40, **Wooden Leg** [last 4:10, next 4:40]. After the long ride through the valley, Wooden Leg arrived back in the Cheyenne camp. He could see many Indians moving into the hills east of the river to fight the soldiers. The bluecoats had come along a high ridge about two miles east of the Cheyenne camp, but rode past the camp and were moving to another lower ridge farther downstream.

Not many people were left in the lodges, for most had gone to the west side of the valley or up on the western bluffs. A few were still hurrying back and forth, carrying off their packs. Wooden Leg's father was the only one at his lodge. He told him about the earlier fight, showed him the gun he had captured, and gave him some of the tobacco he had taken.

"You have been brave," Many Bullet Wounds told him. "You have done enough for the day. Now you should rest."

Wooden Leg did not want to stop now. "I can fight better with this gun," he replied.

Realizing that any further protests would be futile, Many Bullet Wounds took Wooden Leg's tired horse and roped a fresh one from the small herd he had held within the circle. While he prepared the pony, Wooden Leg added his sheath knife to his stock of weapons and braced himself for the next fight.

He watched the battle in the hills for a few moments. More Indians flocked from the camps, and still others were coming down along the bluffs from where they had stopped the first group of soldiers.

260 Stands In Timber, *Cheyenne Memories*, 198–99; Powell, *Sweet Medicine*, 115.
261. White Bull, Box 105, Notebook 24, Campbell Collection.

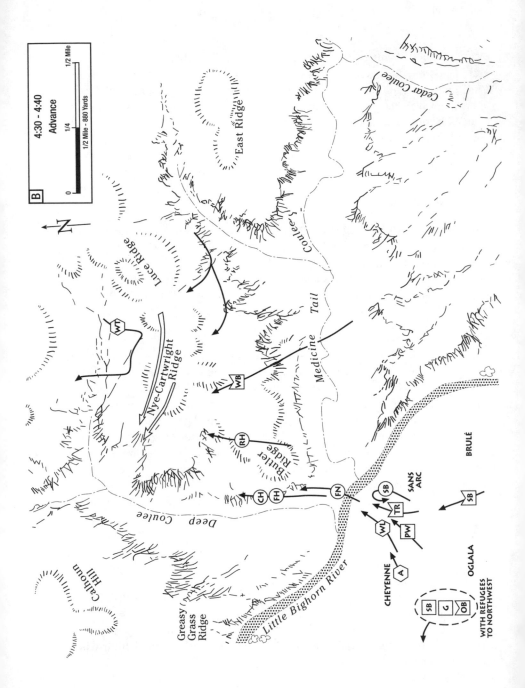

B

4:30 - 4:40
Advance

0   1/4   1/2 Mile

1/2 Mile - 880 Yards   1/2 Mile

N

East Ridge

Cedar Coulee

Luce Ridge

Medicine Tail

Nye-Cartwright Ridge

Coulee

WT

WB

RH

Butler Ridge

CH
FH

FN

Deep Coulee

SB

SANS
ARC

TR

PW

W

SB

Calhoun Hill

Greasy Grass Ridge

Little Bighorn River

CHEYENNE

A

SB   G   OB

WITH REFUGEES
TO NORTHWEST

OGLALA

BRULÉ

Many Bullet Wounds reminded Wooden Leg that his older brother, Yellow Hair, was already out fighting, and that he did not wish to send both of his sons into the fray. As a last caution, he added that Wooden Leg did not have his shield or his eagle wing bone flute. "Stay back as far as you can and shoot from a long distance," Many Bullet Wounds called Wooden Leg rode toward the ford.[262]

A 4:30–4:40, **Antelope** [last 4:00, next 5:00]. Back at her lodge, Antelope watched as many Indians lashed their ponies through the river and made their way up the coulee to the high ridge. Antelope had seen other battles and had always liked to watch the men fighting, though she had been teased about it, for not many women followed the warriors to battle.

This time, however, she had a good excuse, for her nephew, Noisy Walking, had gone into the fight. The young, eighteen-year-old son of Ice and Wool Woman had only this morning participated in the suicide warriors' parade, and had taken a vow to fight to the death in the next battle. Now, the battle was on and Noisy Walking had gone. Antelope was twenty-nine winters old and did not have a son of her own to serve as a warrior. Some women had told her that before Noisy Walking left, he had tied a red scarf around his neck so he could be recognized from a distance. Antelope knew she must go out to be near her nephew, to sing strong-heart songs for him.

"Let me have a horse," she begged her elder brother White Bull (Ice), the Cheyenne holy man. Though he was reluctant, he finally gave his permission. In a moment, Antelope mounted, turned, and raced her pony toward the river at a dead run.[263]

TR 4:30–4:40, **Turtle Rib** [last 3:10, next 5:40]. One of the late sleepers, Turtle Rib did finally manage to get into the Reno fight before it ended, assisting in killing one of the Arikara scouts. It seemed to happen so quickly, he thought the first battle lasted only a few minutes.

Even so, Turtle Rib was still late getting to the ford at the lower end of camp. He passed back through the Minneconjou village. Amidst crying children and stampeding women, he learned of the fight that had occurred near the ford. Soldiers, the Indians said, had come over the hill from the east, but had been driven back. Turtle Rib scanned the hills. The bluecoats were no longer near the river. He decided he would go to fight against the soldiers he could see on the high ground across the river.[264]

FH 4:30–4:40, **Flying Hawk** [last 4:10, next 4:50]. Having dropped off some wounded men in the Oglala village, Flying Hawk and Crazy Horse rode to the ford. Being with the leaders, Flying Hawk could see all the action. The soldiers had come along the second ridge back from the river and had stopped on a high hill above them. Flying Hawk did not see Custer try to go down to the river.

Flying Hawk, Crazy Horse, and many other Indians had crossed the river above Calhoun Hill before the soldiers had come down off the ridge. As they streamed up

262. Marquis, *Wooden Leg*, 226–29.
263. Marquis, *Custer on the Little Big Horn*, 85–86; Powell, *Sacred Mountain*, 1019.
264. Hammer, *Custer in '76*, 201.

The Oglala Flying Hawk followed Crazy Horse across the river and up Deep Coulee after Custer's men. —Nebraska State Historical Society

the gulch from the ford, the soldiers saw them approaching and began to head out. Custer was coming down off the second ridge and heading up onto Calhoun Hill.[265]

SB 4:30–4:40, **Short Bull** [last 4:00]. Short Bull left Reno's men on the bluffs when Crazy Horse had pointed out the bluecoats moving along a hill to the north. He followed Crazy Horse's band back through the valley to the Oglala village, and then down to the Medicine Tail crossing of the Greasy Grass. At the ford, Short Bull reined up. He watched Crazy Horse on his pinto pony, leading his band across the river. As Crazy Horse and his warriors trailed up the draw and disappeared in the dust, Short Bull lost sight of them. Knowing they had the business well in hand, Short Bull dropped back. He had fought enough for the day.[266]

265. Hardorff, *Lakota Recollections*, 50–52; McCreight, *Firewater*, 113.
266. Carroll, *Hinman Interviews*, 40.

FN 4:30–4:40, **Fears Nothing** [last 4:00, next 5:00]. After he left the Reno fight, Fears Nothing had gone directly through the camps and to Water Rat (Medicine Tail) Creek. Custer, he said, had come down from the top of the ridge northeast of Water Rat Creek, but did not make a direct attempt to cross the river. He moved from the high ridge directly to Calhoun Hill.

Fears Nothing crossed at the mouth of Water Rat and went up the coulee with the great majority of Indians. Again, he clarified the action: "The soldiers came up to Calhoun Hill diagonally from the east, and the Indians came up diagonally from the river crossing to Calhoun Hill."[267]

SB 4:30–4:40, **Standing Bear** [last 3:40, next 5:00]. Notwithstanding his uncle's admonitions to hurry, Standing Bear had found a number of reasons to delay his entrance into battle. He found his six-shooter and hung his bow and arrows over his shoulder. A few days earlier he had killed a red bird, which he now fastened in his hair. He had vowed to make an offering if this would keep him from getting hurt in the next fight. Besides, Standing Bear rationalized, he was still only sixteen years old and he did have to wait for the horses for quite awhile.

Finally proceeding to the mouth of Muskrat Creek, Standing Bear learned that the soldiers had come down the second ridge back from the river, but made no attempt to cross, nor did they fire into the village. He could clearly see the soldier companies on the ridge. They "all were together all the time," and they were moving toward Calhoun Hill.[268]

RH 4:30–4:40, **Red Hawk** [last 4:20, next 5:00]. The Indians drove the lead soldier division back to the other two. As they fell back, the troopers tried to keep together, but some horses got away from them. Red Hawk watched the Indians as they forced the soldiers back to Calhoun Hill.[269]

PW 4:30–4:40, **Pretty White Buffalo** [last 4:10, next 4:50]. Pretty White Buffalo had reached the riverbank. She saw the chiefs and the young men riding down to that end of the village. She saw the Cheyennes crossing, and Crazy Horse crossing, and Crow King and his Hunkpapas making their way across the ford and up the ravine.

The ravine they ascended started across from the Sans Arc camp and ran all the way around the butte that Long Hair was moving toward. To get to that butte, Long Hair would have to cross the ravine, but Pretty White Buffalo did not believe he could see all the way down the ravine to the banks of the river where hundreds of warriors were converging.

Pretty White Buffalo moved a little ways back from the river for a better view of the attack that was surely coming. Although she was a woman of the Lakotas, and her husband, Spotted Horn Bull, her uncles, brothers, and cousins were all taking part in the battle, Pretty White Buffalo's heart was sad for the soldiers of Long Hair.[270]

267. Hardorff, *Lakota Recollections*, 31, 33.
268. Ibid., 59; Neihardt, *Black Elk*, 115; Hammer, *Custer in '76*, 215.
269. Hardorff, *Lakota Recollections*, 43.
270. McLaughlin, *My Friend the Indian*, 45–46.

OB 4:30–4:40, **One Bull** [last 4:20]. Finally ending his procrastination on the bluffs, One Bull sped off, crossing at Medicine Tail back to the west side of the river. He rode toward the northwest end of the villages where the helpless ones had been gathering. There, One Bull met up again with Sitting Bull. If his uncle made a comment about his tardiness, neither made mention of it.

One Bull had only been there a short while when the sounds of the distant battle inexorably drew his attention to the east. He looked back at the fighting and could see the troops moving down along a ridge across the river about two miles away. Impatiently, One Bull commented that he should go over to help. Sitting Bull said there were enough Indians over there already. One Bull should stay with the women and children. Besides, in Sitting Bull's sun dance vision, he had seen that the Indians would kill all the soldiers, but they were not to touch the bodies. The soldiers were a gift of God. They should be killed, but their spoils should not be taken; if they were, the Indians would eventually starve, begging at the white man's door. No, it was best to keep away from the soldiers, for after the fight, the temptation to take their possessions would be too great.

From his spot north and west of the village, One Bull could only watch the battle's denouement. He thought he spent most of the day, from noon to almost sundown, circling his charge, never getting closer than one mile to Custer, who was fighting on the hill.[271]

G 4:30–4:40, **Gall** [last 4:10, next 4:40]. Gall reached the area where the women and children had congregated, but after a cursory search he still could not locate his family. He reined up near Sitting Bull and One Bull.

Standing nearby was the twenty-year-old Lakota White Hair On Face. The young man had no pony because he had given it to his mother-in-law and two little girls so they could get away at the outset of the Reno fight. Now on foot, he helped guard the women and children with only his bow and arrows. In front of him he heard Sitting Bull admonishing the warriors not to take things that belonged to the white men. Everyone was talking, so White Hair on Face had difficulty understanding much of the conversation. However, he did note that One Bull and Gall were both there on horseback.

Shortly thereafter, Gall, unsuccessful in locating his family among the refugees, decided he would have to look elsewhere. He pointed his pony south and returned to the Hunkpapa camp.[272]

❦ DISCUSSION. During this segment we find additional Indian narratives that describe Yates's move back to Nye-Cartwright Ridge, and a united battalion moving from there to Calhoun Hill. Antelope watched the warriors riding up the coulee to the soldiers on the high ridge. Pretty White Buffalo saw them stream up the ravine, which the soldiers were soon to cross, toward soldiers on the high ground. Turtle Rib saw soldiers on the high ground. Wooden Leg saw them mov-

---

271. One Bull, Box 105, Notebooks 19, 41, and Box 104, Folder 6, Campbell Collection.
272. One Bull, Box 105, Notebook 41, Campbell Collection.

ing from the high ridge two miles east of camp down to a lower ridge. Standing Bear watched them go directly from Nye-Cartwright Ridge to Calhoun Hill, and stated they were always together. Fears Nothing said soldiers moved directly from the high ridge to Calhoun Hill, while the Indians moved diagonally from the ford to Calhoun Hill. Flying Hawk saw the soldiers on a high ridge. He said the Indians crossed the ford *before* Custer came down from his ridge. The Indian move up Deep Coulee was the catalyst that sent Custer from Nye-Cartwright to Calhoun Hill. He Dog said the soldiers kept together all of the time. After their attack on Luce/ Nye-Cartwright Ridge, Wolf Tooth said the soldiers vacated the hill and moved to the south end of Calhoun Hill. One witness we have not previously heard from, the Hunkpapa Good Voiced Elk, said, "Custer's men at all times were together in one body." They were not formed in a line, nor at intervals, nor were they detached for the purpose of holding any particular point of ground.[273] None of these Indians ever said the soldiers went directly from the ford to Calhoun Hill. None of them said there were soldiers already on Calhoun Hill. They saw the troops, united, moving along the high ridge and going to Calhoun Hill. Custer's five companies were riding together as they reached the final battleground.[274]

Looking north up Deep Coulee, a main attack route for the Indians following Custer's battalion.

273. Good Voiced Elk, Walter Camp interview, 21 May 1909. Ellison Collection.
274. Somehow, Welch, *Killing Custer*, 166, states that Custer was sitting on Calhoun Hill, waiting for Yates, who was still near the river.

There is no mystery in Custer's movements. Some writers have thrown in the towel when trying to decipher the Indian accounts, complaining that they were too inconsistent to rely on. For instance, how could one Indian say that the soldiers came near the river, a second avow that the soldiers moved straight overland without making the slightest attempt at the ford, a third say there was no fight, and a fourth insist there was a fight? These are not inconsistencies. Rather, they illustrate that most Indians made no attempt to expand their narratives beyond what they saw with their own eyes—hence, they were good witnesses. Gall saw Custer far east in Medicine Tail Coulee, before he returned to the village. When he next saw the soldiers, they were on Calhoun Hill. He missed Yates's entire trek, so, naturally, he assumed Custer went nowhere near the river. White Cow Bull was one of the few early defenders near the ford. Yates's men looked frightfully close to the river to him. Other Indians described the shots exchanged with Yates as occurring one-fourth to three-fourths of a mile or more east of the river, back along Butler Ridge. To Hollow Horn Bear, more removed from the action than was White Cow Bull, the fight was nowhere near the river. Fears Nothing, who arrived after Yates had linked back up with Custer, said the troops made no attempt at the river at all. They were all correct from their own point of view. It was up to the chroniclers and synthesizers not to denigrate their accounts as being contradictory, but rather to study them and piece them together into a comprehensive whole.

Why have we remained saddled with this consistent depiction of cavalry moving from Medicine Tail Ford north along the river to Greasy Grass Ridge and Calhoun Hill? Part of the answer must lie in the discovery of the bodies of Custer's men by the Reno-Benteen survivors and the men of the Montana Column on June 27 and 28. Clearly there were tracks leading down to the ford area. At least one body, identified as Cpl. John Foley, was found about the place of Yellow Nose's attack, on the low western terminus of Butler Ridge. About two hundred yards farther up Deep Coulee, the body of James Butler was found, although his memorial marker was later placed higher up near the spine of the ridge we have labeled as Butler's. The soldiers discovered no other bodies in the area.[275] This corroborates Bobtail Horse's statement that one soldier was killed, and Soldier Wolf's contention that the soldiers left two dead men behind when they pulled back.

There were, however, numerous bodies found on Calhoun Hill and its southwestern extension (also known as Finley Ridge). Certainly there were also hundreds of pony tracks leading up to those bodies—tracks made by the Indian horses as well as by the shod hooves of the captured cavalry mounts. The natural inclination would be to follow the path between the bodies and conclude that it was the path Custer's men must have taken. It was ten years later, at the 1886 battle anniversary, that Company K commander Lt. Edward Godfrey recalled seeing tracks all along what would later be called Nye-Cartwright Ridge. Prior to that time he never understood the reason for those tracks being there. The consensus explanation was that all the troops went from the ford up Deep Coulee and to Calhoun

---

275. Hardorff, *Battle Casualties*, 94–95, 110, 113.

Hill—for that was where the bodies were. It was not until Gall told him that white soldiers had ridden back along the high ridges that Godfrey first realized the meaning of the tracks he had seen ten years earlier.[276] The story that Custer went to the ford and then straight to Calhoun Hill began as an incorrect, on-field assumption by the white survivors and rescuers.

One of the men most responsible for perpetuating that interpretation was researcher Walter Mason Camp. We are indebted to Camp for the many years he spent interviewing the Indian battle participants, and our knowledge of the fight would certainly be lessened had he not put forth his efforts. But some of Camp's interviewing techniques have served only to lead us astray. When he met with the Indians personally and allowed them to tell the story in their own words, they *did not* tell of soldiers going from the ford to Greasy Grass–Calhoun Hill. When Camp could not attend his scheduled meetings, he drew up questionnaires for assistants to administer. The questions, of course, were framed by Camp's own preconceptions shaped from his contacts with the white participants. The answers were not unlike what was supplied when the Indians were asked to explain the size of their village in terms of miles—exaggerated or misleading estimates. When left to explain the size of the camp or the path of the troops in their own unprompted words, and in terms of the terrain that they understood, a truer picture was painted.

After years of listening and talking with Indian participants in the battle, Thomas Marquis stressed the importance of letting the Indians "tell their stories spontaneously, without prompting them." The interviewer must never utter a positive contradiction, he explained, for "interjecting of our adverse views may cause them politely to adopt our basis for talk, or more likely, they will excuse themselves from further talking, since old Indians in general abhor verbal arguments."[277]

In Camp's questionnaire interviews, some of the Indians were allowed only two choices: Did the soldiers go from Nye-Cartwright ("E" in fig. 10) to the ford ("B") and then to Greasy Grass Hill ("C"), or did they go from Nye-Cartwright ("E") directly to Calhoun Hill ("D")? A path from the ford ("B") back to Nye-Cartwright ("E") was never offered as an option.[278] We can only wonder what might have gone through the Indians' heads when the correct answer was "None of the above."

However, most of the Indians attempted to conform to the white man's guidelines. Two Eagles and Lights chose the ford ("B") to Greasy Grass ("C"). Hollow Horn Bear was asked if soldiers fell back from the river by way of Deep Ravine ("H") to Custer Hill ("G"), or by way of Greasy Grass Hill ("C") to Calhoun Hill ("D"). This was a tough question, for the very response Hollow Horn Bear gave in his previous answer was that the soldiers were never even near the river! How could they fall back from it to one of Camp's options? Yet, Hollow Horn Bear played by the rules and chose "C" to "D," probably the best guess of the choices given—also a polite adoption of the white man's viewpoint—just as Marquis predicted. Lone Bear was also asked if the soldiers went from the ford to Greasy Grass Hill. At least he was able to break free of the question's constraints and admitted

---

276. Graham, *The Custer Myth*, 94.
277. Marquis, *Cheyennes of Montana*, 244–45.
278. Hardorff, *Lakota Recollections*, 143.

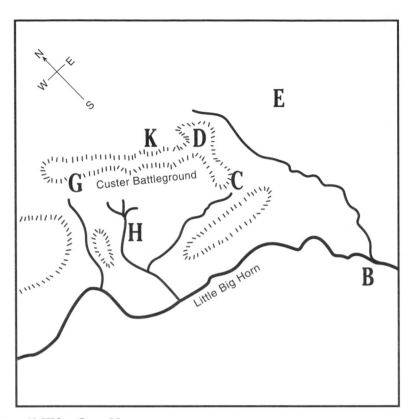

Figure 10. Walter Camp Map. —Based on a map by Walter Camp (Harold B. Lee Library, Brigham Young University).

that he did not see any such move, for at that time he returned to his lodge to look for his pony.[279] Flying By, though he was not given a questionnaire, was still puzzled by Camp's drawing. He told Camp he didn't understand the map, and proceeded to sketch his own rendition of the action, telling Camp that "Custer's soldiers kept together all the time and were killed moving along toward camp." Standing Bear also stood by his recollections. He said Custer's men did not fight by companies, but were together all the time. Camp tried to get Standing Bear to change his story but finally conceded, "[I] could not make him say different."[280] Had more Indians taken Flying By's or Standing Bear's initiative, we may have broken free from an incorrect interpretation decades ago.

Camp's question and answer technique will not necessarily result in a true answer. "It is wrong to coax people in order to elicit preformulated opinions and fictitious choices," said historian John Lukacs. "The very existence of a question may not only influence, it may artificially produce a previously unformed answer

---

279. Ibid., 143, 156, 165–66, 180–81.
280. Hammer, *Custer in '76*, 210, 215. One might wonder just why Camp felt he had to get Standing Bear to "say different," if not for the fact that the Indian did not tell a story that matched Camp's conception of events.

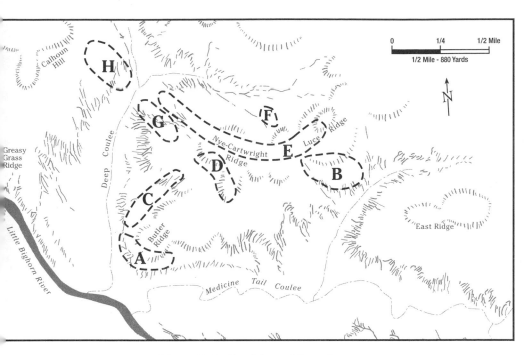

Figure 11. Artifact Map and Legend.

"A" includes ten .45/.55-caliber bullets, four .45/.55 cases, two unfired .45/.55 cartridges, two Colt .45 bullets, one .50/70 cartridge, three .44 Henry cases, three .50 Spencer cases, four brass cavalry insignia, one arrowhead, two half horseshoes, a metal ring, brass grommets, iron snaps, and a Winchester rifle.

"B" includes four .45/.55 cases, three .50/.70 cases, fourteen .45/.55 cases (plus an additional undetermined number), at least three horse skeletons plus additional horse bones, at least three human skeletons plus additional human bones, a saddle and bridle, saddle leather and pommel rings, and horseshoes.

"C" includes two .45/.55 cartridges, a horseshoe, a harness buckle and straps, a leather boot, a leather scabbard, an arrowhead, two human skeletons, and numerous horse bones.

"D" includes four .45/.55 cases, four .45/.55 cartridges, six .56 Spencer cases, twenty-four .50/.70 cases, fifteen .44 Henry cases, nine .44 Henry cartridges, and an Indian bridle.

"E" includes upwards of 480 .45/.55 caliber cases and cartridges, several .50/.70 cases, plus an undetermined number of additional shells, saddle and tack parts, uniform buttons, and buckles.

"F" includes three .44 Henry cases.

"G" includes three human and three horse skeletons plus various bridle and saddle parts.

"H" includes human bones, two horse skeletons, eight .45/.55 cases, two .50/.70 cases, two .50- and one .56-caliber Spencer cases, a .32 rimfire case, two .44 Henry cases, and a Winchester rifle.

or an unformulated opinion—whereby the observation does not only influence the character, it falsifies the essence of the object." In simpler terms, historian Marc Bloch argued that the judge dictates the answers.[281]

Battle student Bruce Trinque, formerly with the armed forces in military intelligence, has commented that the questionnaire interview technique that Camp employed is certain to give the interviewer exactly the answer he is looking for, but not necessarily the truth.[282] By forcing the Indians to choose from a limited set of answers that conformed to Camp's own conceptions of the troop movements, he perpetuated an incorrect interpretation. When the Indians were allowed to tell the story in their own words, they told us the soldiers were forced back to the high ground on present-day Nye-Cartwright Ridge, and then all of them went to Calhoun Hill.

Over the past several decades, artifacts have been discovered that bear out the true Indian testimony. An artifact map (fig. 11) shows some of the terrain the troops traversed, and where some of the action most likely occurred. The relics at "B," in the north fork of Medicine Tail below the Nye-Cartwright and Luce Ridges, may have been from the battle with the southern half of Wolf Tooth's split band of fifty warriors. Likewise, the relics at "F" could have come from the skirmish with the northern group. Artifacts found at "C" and "D" may have been from a combination of Yates's men moving back up Butler Ridge and from the Indians who followed Yates and Keogh. The great number of cartridges found at "E," along Nye-Cartwright and Luce Ridges, show conclusively that the cavalry moved northwest along these crests, returning the Indians' fire. However, there were few or no relics found along the traditional northward line directly from the ford to Greasy Grass Hill and Calhoun Hill.

Although Yates moved back from the ford to Nye-Cartwright Ridge, not as much by coercion as by plan, the Indians thought they had driven him away. United again, Custer had experienced Indian pressure from the south. Indians following Yates increased pressure from the west. Now, he could see more Indians streaming up Deep Coulee, where, given time, they would encircle him on the north. Custer would have to move beyond Deep Coulee to keep them between himself and Reno-Benteen. Had Custer been on the high ground on *true* Luce Ridge just to the east, he might have had his last look back at the rest of the regiment, for from that point one could still catch a glimpse of Reno and Benteen on the bluffs about two and a half miles to the south. Certainly they would be on their way shortly. Perhaps on the next ridge to the north, high and seemingly level, a halt could be made to await the other seven companies. The Indians watched Custer move across Deep Coulee to climb Calhoun Hill.

281. John Lukacs, *Historical Consciousness or the Remembered Past* (New York: Schocken Books, 1985), 83; Marc Bloch, *The Historian's Craft* (New York: Random House, 1953), 118.
282. Bruce A. Trinque, Niantic, CT, to Greg Michno, 2 November 1991.

Pursuit, 4:40–4:50

G 4:40–4:50, **Gall** [last 4:30, next 5:00]. With apprehension, Gall made his way to the nearly abandoned Hunkpapa camp. His lodge was vacant. He extended his search around the point of timber a short distance to the south. There he finally found his family. Dead. His two wives and his three children, killed. The *wasichus* or their Ree allies did get in close enough to the camp to wage their war on the defenseless ones. Gall was crushed. For all his strength and fortitude, he had not been there to protect them.

For a short time Gall mourned, not knowing what to do. Eventually, far-off gunfire brought him out of his trance. He looked north to the hills where the pale-faced warriors were still fighting his people. "It made my heart bad," he said. "After that I killed all my enemies with the hatchet." Gall finally mounted back up and rode for the river crossing.[283]

TM 4:40–4:50, **Two Moon** [last 4:20, next 4:50]. After seeing Custer's course thrown back half a mile from the river, Two Moon crossed the river with a number of Cheyenne warriors. He said that the Indians all came up the coulee from the foot of Reno Hill (Medicine Tail). "I led the Cheyennes as we came up," Two Moon declared. His warriors, men from about fifty lodges, followed Custer down the river and around to the west and northwest.

Custer approached along the ridge from the right (or southeast) of where the battle monument now stands. He marched behind the ridge on the reverse slope of where Two Moons was riding, deploying his men along the entire line of ridge. The Lakotas rode up the ridges on all sides, Two Moon said. "The Cheyennes went up the left way."[284]

RE 4:40–4:50, **Runs The Enemy** [last 4:20, next 4:50]. Runs The Enemy left the Hunkpapa and Two Kettle tipis after hearing Sitting Bull's brave-up talk. As he rode to the battle he saw warriors hidden in the ridges and hills along the river. Fording the creek and making his way up the high ground, Runs The Enemy had a panoramic view of the action. To him, it looked as if the Cheyennes were circling around Custer on the west, and even on the north and east sides. He could see a Cheyenne woman riding with her people, helping them fight the soldiers. He thought there were so many Cheyennes that the only place left for the Lakotas was on the south side. So be it. "We then filled the gap," Runs The Enemy said.[285]

WT 4:40–4:50, **Wolf Tooth** [last 4:30, next 4:50]. When they had drawn back after delivering their harassing fire against the troops on Nye-Cartwright Ridge, Wolf Tooth and Big Foot watched the soldiers move to the ridge where the battle monument now stands. The split warrior bands joined up again and forty or fifty of them continued to follow the troopers, keeping to the north and east of

---

283. Graham, *The Custer Myth*, 89–90; D. J. Benham, "The Sioux Warrior's Revenge," *The Canadian Magazine* 43 (September 1914): 462.
284. Dixon, *Vanishing Race*, 181; Hunt, *I Fought With Custer*, 213; Hardorff, *Memories*, 110.
285. Dixon, *Vanishing Race*, 175.

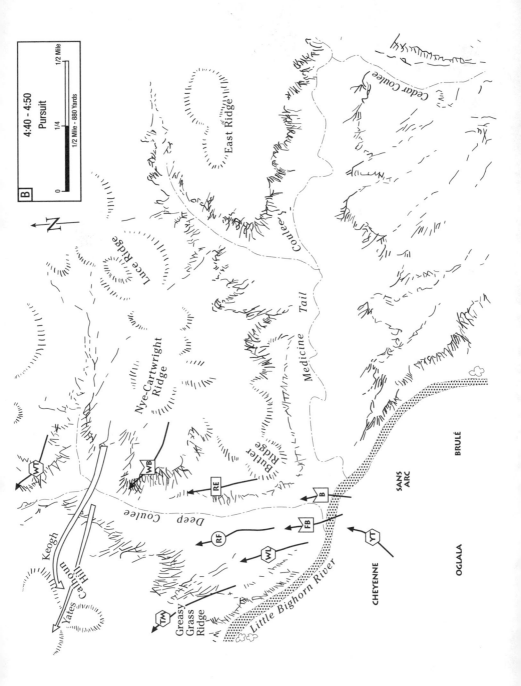

B

4:40 - 4:50
Pursuit

0   1/4   1/2 Mile
1/2 Mile - 880 Yards

N

East Ridge

Cedar Coulee

Luce Ridge

Nye-Cartwright Ridge

Coulee's

Medicine Tail

Butler Ridge

Deep Coulee

Keogh

Calhoun Hill

Yates

WB

RE

RF

WL

FB

B

TM

Greasy Grass Ridge

Little Bighorn River

CHEYENNE

YT

OGLALA

SANS ARC

BRULÉ

them. They followed them across the dry headwaters of Deep Coulee, staying back as a mobile guard. They would cut the soldiers off in case they tried to retreat to the north.[286]

YT 4:40–4:50, **Young Two Moon** [next 4:50]. The twenty-one-year-old Cheyenne was the nephew of Two Moon, and came to be known as Young Two Moon or John Two Moon. He was in the camp on Reno Creek and witnessed his uncle saving the skins of the Arapahos. This day, Young Two Moon did not get into the thick of the fighting, but chose to stay back and watch it from a distance.

He saw nothing of Reno's battle, for it was out of his line of sight. The first Young Two Moon saw of Custer's soldiers was when they were coming down the steep hill east of the battlefield. They were moving at a lope and the Indians were following behind them, but they seemed to pay no attention to their pursuers. The soldiers climbed and turned up on the next little ridge. Young Two Moon followed.[287]

WB 4:40–4:50, **White Bull** [last 4:30, next 4:50]. Although the soldiers kept moving, the Indians inexorably closed the gap. White Bull joined in with a great number of Indians who had come up from the river. They trailed up the draw after Custer. Most of the five cavalry companies had passed the head of the ravine (Deep Coulee) by the time White Bull got close enough to do any shooting himself.[288]

RF 4:40–4:50, **Red Feather** [last 4:10, next 4:50]. Red Feather tried to get to the second body of soldiers as fast as he could, but was delayed in the valley while helping his friend who had broken his leg. By the time Red Feather had splashed across the river, the Cheyennes were already fighting the soldiers, and it seemed as if the Oglalas were acting as reinforcements.[289]

FB 4:40–4:50, **Flying By** [last 4:10, next 5:10]. Lagging behind because his horse had been shot early on, Flying By finally walked and ran his way to the battle. He could see warriors crossing at all points along the river. "When I got to Custer," he said, "Indians had been fighting quite awhile."[290]

B 4:40–4:50, **Beard** [last 4:10, next 6:10(b)]. By the time Beard got to the ford, he could see swirls of dust and hear more shooting on the hills and bluffs across the river. Hundreds of warriors converged. They all joined together and splashed across the ford not far from the Minneconjou camp. Beard raced up the hills, seeking to charge into the thickest of the fighting.[291]

 4:40–4:50, **Wooden Leg** [last 4:30, next 4:50]. Wooden Leg rode across the broad shallows immediately in front of the wide coulee to the east. He fell

286. Powell, *Sweet Medicine*, 115; Stands In Timber, *Cheyenne Memories*, 198–99.
287. Greene, *Lakota and Cheyenne*, 68.
288. White Bull, Box 105, Notebook 24, Campbell Collection; Vestal, *Warpath*, 195.
289. Hardorff, *Lakota Recollections*, 85.
290. Hammer, *Custer in '76*, 209–10.
291. Miller, "Echoes," 38.

in with other Lakotas and Cheyennes, urging their horses up the small valley. As they neared the fight, each Indian chose his own course. While most of them rode to the battle, many left their ponies and crept along the gullies afoot. Yet, hundreds of braves remained mounted, changing position or racing back and forth in front of the soldiers to exhibit their bravery.

The soldiers had moved off the high ridge to travel down the lower ridge downstream of the camp. Though it was natural for tribal members to try to keep together, there was inevitably a mingling of fighters from all the tribes. Wooden Leg swerved up a gulch to his left, toward the north, where he saw other Cheyennes going ahead of him.[292]

✦ **DISCUSSION.** This was a time of movement for both sides. Custer's five companies had crested the high ground of what would be known as Calhoun Hill. There Keogh's battalion of Companies C, I, and L would go into a holding action, Company L deploying first, with C and I moving a bit farther on and down into a swale on the reverse side of a ridge that trailed north. Yates's Companies E and F,

On the slopes of Calhoun Hill, looking toward Nye-Cartwright Ridge in the middle distance.

---

292. Marquis, *Wooden Leg*, 228–30.

this time with Custer accompanying them, continued along the ridge, perhaps taking in the lay of the land with an eye for future maneuvers. Custer was still on the offensive.

The Indians followed in their wake, the majority trailing up Deep Coulee. Others, probably Cheyennes for the greater part, worked their way north nearer the river's course, keeping between the soldiers and the village. Wolf Tooth's and Big Foot's band kept above the head of Deep Coulee. The Cheyenne Red Bird (Young Little Wolf) succinctly summarized this phase of the action. Custer was first seen opposite the ford. He moved parallel with the river, seemingly trying to circle the camp. "After he passed Med[icine] Tail Coulee [the] Indians followed him."[293] Thus, the Indians had not yet surrounded their enemy, but they followed behind and were encroaching on both flanks. Besides the brief encounter on the slopes of Butler Ridge near the ford, and with Wolf Tooth's band near Luce Ridge, there was no heavy contact. Firing had generally been from a distance and not very telling.

---

293. Walter M. Camp, "Camp Manuscripts," Box 7, Folder 5, Lilly Library, Indiana University, Bloomington, IN. Hereafter cited as Camp Mss., IU; Young Little Wolf, Notebook 346, Grinnell Collection. Red Bird later took the name of his famous "uncle," Little Wolf. Red Bird's father, Long Horn (Left Hand), and Little Wolf were cousins.

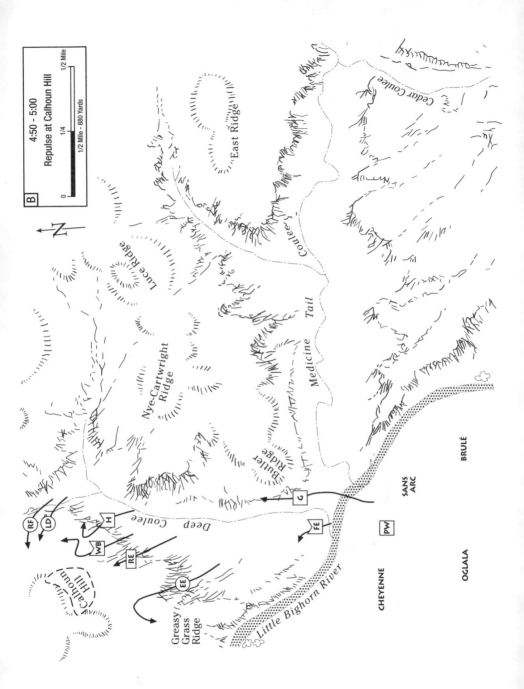

B

4:50 - 5:00
Repulse at Calhoun Hill

0   1/4   1/2 Mile - 880 Yards

1/2 Mile

N

Luce Ridge

East Ridge

Nye-Cartwright Ridge

Coulee's

Medicine Tail

Cedar Coulee

Butler Ridge

Deep Coulee

G

FE

PW

SANS ARC

CHEYENNE

OGLALA

BRULÉ

Little Bighorn River

Greasy Grass Ridge

EE

RE

WB

H

LD

RF

Calhoun Hill

REPULSE AT CALHOUN HILL, 4:50–5:00

PW 4:50–5:00, **Pretty White Buffalo** [last 4:30]. Still near the banks of the Greasy Grass where she had seen Crazy Horse and Crow King cross with their warriors, Pretty White Buffalo finally saw Gall approaching. Not knowing about the death of his family, she thought he must have been engaged in killing and driving off Reno's soldiers from the upper end of the village, and perhaps he had stayed longer to shoot at the ones who had dug in on the hill.

Now, however, Pizi had arrived. Pretty White Buffalo heard him exhorting the Indians to try to frighten the horses of the soldiers, which appeared to be held in small bunches and could perhaps be stampeded. The warriors coming up now appeared to be riding horses taken from the soldiers that had fled to the hills. Others had replenished their guns with captured soldier bullets.

Some women were still driving in the Indian ponies from the northwest, while others chose to follow Pizi when he crossed the river. Pretty White Buffalo saw him cross over and ride along the bench by the river where Long Hair had stopped with his men. She elected to remain behind where she could watch the action.[294]

RE 4:50–5:00, **Runs the Enemy** [last 4:40, next 5:00]. Runs The Enemy joined with the Lakotas who filled the gap in the line south of the soldiers. While they attempted to surround the bluecoats there was very little, if any, firing done by either side. The period of maneuvering ended abruptly, however.

"The Sioux then made a charge from the rear side," Runs The Enemy said, "shooting into the men, and the shooting frightened the horses so that they rushed upon the ridge and many horses were shot." However, the soldiers put up a stiff return fire. The Lakota charge was blunted and they retreated over the hill. Runs The Enemy pulled back with his Two Kettle followers. The soldier fire was strong and he would have to figure out another way to get at them without directly exposing his men to the volleys.[295]

H 4:50–5:00, **Hump** [last 4:20]. Hump had seen the long-haired chief retreat slowly from the river. It seemed like no time at all before the Indians had them nearly surrounded. The chiefs yelled out, "Hi-yi-yi," and the warriors joined in, whipping each other's horses into a frenzied charge.

In the forefront of the first dash, Hump lashed his pony toward the nearest group of soldiers on the hill. Suddenly, bullets ripped the air. His horse was hit and, in the next second, Hump also took a bullet. Horse and rider hit the ground heavily and Hump tumbled to the dirt, nearly knocked senseless. He tried to examine his wound. A ball had entered just above his knee and had torn a path up his leg, exiting near his hip. Hump could not do much more than lay there motionless. He could see the sky. It was a clear day, strangely calm, with no storms or lightning;

294. McLaughlin, *My Friend the Indian*, 45–46.
295. Dixon, *Vanishing Race*, 175.

*The Minneconjou Hump, shown with two of his wives. Hump
was in the forefront of the attack against Calhoun Hill, where he
was badly wounded.* —Little Bighorn Battlefield National Monument

the heavens incongruously serene in contrast to the nearby hell on Hump's hillside.
The rest of the Indians thundered by on horseback.[296]

LD 4:50–5:00, **Low Dog** [last 3:00]. Low Dog had taken some time to recover
from the surprise of being attacked, and had even thought Reno's retreat
was a ploy to draw the Indians into an ambush. By the time all the warriors were
mounted and ready to fight, they had been attacked by another party of troopers
on the other side of the camp.

---

296. Graham, *The Custer Myth*, 78.

"They came on us like a thunderbolt," Low Dog said. The Indians retreated at first, but managed to rally and make a charge of their own. Low Dog called to his men, "This is a good day to die: follow me." They massed their warriors. So that no man should fall back, every man whipped another man's horse as they rushed the soldiers.

The bluecoats dismounted to fire, but did not shoot well. While firing, they had been holding their horse's reins with one arm. The frightened horses pulled them all around and many of their shots went high in the air and did the Indians no harm. Nevertheless, the white warriors stood their ground bravely, and none made an attempt to get away.[297]

WB 4:50–5:00, **White Bull** [last 4:40, next 5:00]. In spite of all the chasing and long-distance firing, White Bull thought the Indians had shot only two soldiers before the whites came to a halt. They stopped straight across from the camp on a rise later to be called Calhoun Hill. White Bull counted what appeared to be four companies.

The soldiers had dismounted, giving the Indians time to gather sufficient force for a charge. White Bull joined in. Riding up a ravine, he passed two Lakotas and two Cheyennes sitting on their horses.

"Only Heaven and Earth last long!" White Bull shouted as he galloped by. They took courage and followed him. The soldiers saw them coming up the draw and began to fire. Though only one of the four companies was shooting, their fire was heavy enough to drive the Indians back. White Bull retreated, realizing that this was not a good point from which to attack the soldiers. He left the group he had been riding with and looked for a new place where he might attack with better results.[298]

RF 4:50–5:00, **Red Feather** [last 4:40, next 5:00]. Although the Oglalas might have been reinforcements, they soon made their presence felt. Red Feather got in with the first charge against some of Custer's soldiers who were firing on foot. They were sweeping in and it looked like there was a good chance of success. Red Feather thought some of the soldiers were retreating back to their horses. Just then, his own pony was hit and its knees buckled under. Red Feather was dumped to the ground. When he regained his bearings, he saw the Indian charge had not dislodged the soldier line. He would have to continue the fight on foot.[299]

EE 4:50–5:00, **Eagle Elk** [last 4:20, next 5:10]. Having participated in the first charge on Butler Ridge near the ford, Eagle Elk pulled back for a time to watch the action. More Indians crossed the creek. Again they closed in, but the soldiers were shooting fast and straight, and the Indians were thrown back.

Eagle Elk saw a riderless, yellow spotted pony gallop past, its owner probably a victim of the soldier gunfire. Just then, he saw an Indian running back toward the

297. Graham, *The Custer Myth*, 75.
298. White Bull, Box 105, Notebooks 23, 24, Campbell Collection; Miller, "Echoes," 35.
299. Hardorff, *Lakota Recollections*, 85, 87.

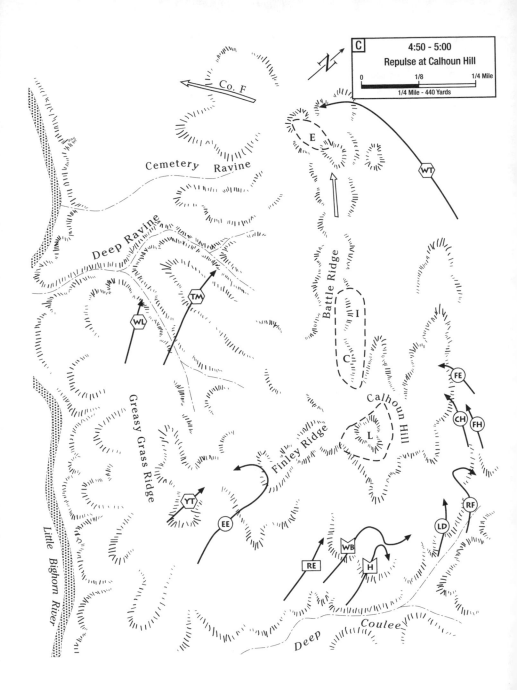

C | 4:50 – 5:00
Repulse at Calhoun Hill

0   1/8   1/4 Mile
1/4 Mile – 440 Yards

Co. F

Cemetery Ravine

Deep Ravine

Battle Ridge

E

WT

I

C

Calhoun Hill

FE

CH FH

L

WL

TM

Finley Ridge

Greasy Grass Ridge

YT

EE

RF

LD

RE

WB

H

Little Bighorn River

Deep Coulee

river. He had been shot through the jaw and was covered with blood. Eagle Elk's brother also noticed the wounded Indian, and they both went over to help him. After doing what they could, the brothers turned and went back after the soldiers.[300]

FE 4:50–5:00, **Foolish Elk** [last 4:10, next 5:50]. Foolish Elk had crossed the river at the broad ford with Crazy Horse, but saw other Indians crossing farther downstream. There were so many that he wondered how such a small force of soldiers would stand a chance against them. Many warriors went between Custer and the river, while others kept coming up the coulee and getting around to the east of him.

While Custer followed the line of ridges, the Indians were staying abreast of him by following the hollows and ravines. Foolish Elk rode up Deep Coulee with the warriors that were circling to the east, or on Custer's right, as he headed downstream. On the high ground known as Calhoun Hill, Foolish Elk saw the soldiers make what he considered a charge. Now the battle became furious.[301]

FH 4:50–5:00, **Flying Hawk** [last 4:30, next 5:00]. As Custer went up Calhoun Hill, Flying Hawk, Crazy Horse, and others continued up the gulch (Deep Coulee) to a place in the rear of the soldiers. On Calhoun Hill a detachment of soldiers turned to make a stand, while others continued along the ridge to the far end that would later be called Custer Hill. Troops were on Custer Hill while the soldiers on Calhoun Hill were giving battle.[302]

FE 4:50–5:00, **Feather Earring** [last 3:30, next 6:10(a)]. During the midst of a battle was not the time and place to locate a site and properly prepare a body for burial. Feather Earring carried off his brother Dog With Horns's body and secreted it away in some bushes. Perhaps he would have time to return later. Experiencing the anguish, sadness, and desire for revenge that many Lakotas were assuredly feeling that day, Feather Earring finally readied himself to renew the fight.

He reached the ford area after the second group of soldiers fired on the village. This group did not get across the river. Instead, the Indians who had crossed the Greasy Grass upriver from where the soldiers were riding now went up the ravines in great numbers and cut off Custer's soldiers from the first group of soldiers back on the high bluffs. Feather Earring saw many Indians circle around behind the troops to the east. All the while, the soldiers were making a stand on the ridge, and they were fighting very hard.[303]

WL 4:50–5:00, **Wooden Leg** [last 4:40, next 5:10]. Most of the Indians left their ponies safely behind in the gulches while they crept along other ravines, steadily closing in on the soldiers. Wooden Leg stayed back, minding what his father had told him. He could see that the Indians used their bows and arrows more than their guns. From their hiding places they could loft the arrows in high

---

300. Ibid., 104.
301. Hammer, *Custer in '76*, 198–99.
302. McCreight, *Firewater*, 113; Hardorff, *Lakota Recollections*, 51–52.
303. Graham, *The Custer Myth*, 97.

curves, to fall upon the soldiers from above. The falling arrows hit the horses in their backs and caused them to plunge and kick, knocking down the soldiers. The warriors who used rifles had to stand up and expose themselves long enough to shoot, a much more dangerous proposition.

From his vantage point, Wooden Leg thought most of the firing was slow, at long distance, and was kept up for an hour or more. All the while the Indians could see the white men because they kept to the high ground, the soldiers and their horses silhouetted on the skylines of the ridges. The warriors remained hard to see, using the gullies and clumps of sagebrush for cover, jumping up quickly to shoot, then crawling a little farther. The bluecoats were being surrounded little by little, and very few Indians had been hit by the soldier bullets during this time.[304]

WT 4:50–5:00, **Wolf Tooth** [last 4:40, next 5:10]. Although Wolf Tooth and his band had remained north of the soldiers in case they tried to ride in that direction, the soldiers did not do as they expected. Instead, they veered off west, toward the river, riding down the ridge to a level place near the present cemetery. Wolf Tooth's forty or fifty warriors pursued them for a short distance, managing to shoot at them for awhile, but the soldiers kept moving down toward the river.[305]

YT 4:50–5:00, **Young Two Moon** [last 4:40, next 5:40]. Young Two Moon watched the soldiers climb the hill, where they turned and moved down the ridgeline. The troopers stopped at intervals as they moved along. The Gray Horse Company halted at the place where the present monument is, while others moved on. There were four lines, the last about opposite of the camp.

When the soldiers reached these positions, Young Two Moon, who was near the river on a hillside, ran with some others to catch their horses. He moved closer to the fight.[306]

TM 4:50–5:00, **Two Moon** [last 4:40, next 5:00]. Two Moon and a number of Cheyenne warriors had turned north from the ford, keeping abreast of the soldiers who moved along the ridgeline. As the soldiers rode, they detached groups along the ridge. Those soldiers dismounted and led their horses over the reverse slope away from Two Moon. The remainder continued along the ridge until they rode behind the hill where the monument now stands. There they turned down into the valley where he could no longer see them.

The group that had stopped on top where the gravestones are today were riding gray horses. Two Moon watched them deploy out in the open. Unlike the other troops, the men with the gray horses dismounted, but each one held his own horse. Not a shot was fired all the while. Both sides were making their preparations.[307]

---

304. Marquis, *Wooden Leg*, 230–31.
305. Powell, *Sweet Medicine*, 115; Stands In Timber, *Cheyenne Memories*, 199.
306. Greene, *Lakota and Cheyenne*, 68.
307. "Two Moon Recalls," 11; Dixon, *Vanishing Race*, 181.

⤎ **DISCUSSION.** By this time, readers familiar with the battle may have noted a variance in my tracking of Gall's movements. Traditionally, Gall is shown leading hordes of warriors up Deep Coulee in an overwhelming attack that crushes the defenders of Calhoun Hill. Yet, now we find the first large-scale assault on Lieutenant Calhoun's position has come and gone, and Gall is nowhere to be found.

Gall was surprised in camp, as were all the Indians, almost without exception. He left his family to ride north, beyond the Cheyenne circle, to round up his horses. He circled back to the Hunkpapa tipis, where Iron Cedar found him and convinced him to go to the bluffs to scout the approach of a second body of troopers. He sat on a knoll south of Medicine Tail Coulee watching Custer. He returned to the village, found it abandoned, and went to look for his family among the refugees. He was seen there with Sitting Bull and One Bull. He returned to the Hunkpapa camp, where he finally discovered the fate of his family.

Although this is not all spelled out clearly in Gall's several and sometimes contradictory narratives, a few salient issues help in reconstructing his moves. At the reunion ten years after the fight, Gall gave a poignant description of the death of his family, which still brought tears to his eyes. Although Gall's story has been discounted by Richard Hardorff, it goes a long way in explaining his prior and subsequent actions.[308] It was only after the discovery, he said, that he "fought with the hatchet." He also said he did not fight against Reno. These two points guide the reconstruction of his actions. When he returned from getting his horses, he had not yet found his family dead; if he had, his rage assuredly would have led him into the Reno fight still in progress only a half mile away. Had he found his family dead early, he would not have left the battle to sit calmly on a hill watching the white soldier leader scan the hills with his binoculars. From that point, Gall did not follow Custer north, nor did he go to Medicine Tail Ford to gather warriors for a charge. Had he taken either course, he would have seen Yates move toward the river; but Gall insisted that the soldiers made no such move. For Gall to miss this he must have gone from the upper coulee back to the camp, which was nearly deserted. He is next seen by White Hair On Face, on horseback near Sitting Bull and the refugees. Finally riding back to the campsite, he finds his family. He mourns. He thirsts for revenge. He takes up his hatchet. Only after this does Gall finally make it to the ford, where he is seen by Pretty White Buffalo, crossing after the likes of Crazy Horse, Crow King, and the others.

Contrary to some secondary studies of the battle, Gall was not one of the first at the ford. He did not confront Custer there, nor did he chase at his heels, leading hundreds of warriors up Deep Coulee.[309] Gall did not participate in the Reno fight, and he was late to the Custer fight. He acknowledged he was not in com-

---

308. Hardorff, *Hokahey!*, 32. The contention is that Gall's story was stimulated by a large sum of money.
309. Weibert, *Sixty-Six Years*, 54; Don Weibert, *Custer, Cases & Cartridges: The Weibert Collection Analyzed* (Billings, MT: By the Author, 1989), 172; Graham, *Story of the Little Big Horn*, 88; Graham, *The Custer Myth*, ix, 95; Welch, *Killing Custer*, 159–61, 166–68; Ambrose, *Crazy Horse and Custer*, 440. Welch claims Gall "fought the longest and the hardest of any warrior that day." He avers that Gall led the fight against the soldiers in the timber (although Gall told us emphatically that he did not get into the Reno fight at all. See Graham, *The Custer Myth*, 92). Welch also states that Gall led hundreds of warriors across the river chasing at Yates's heels. To top this, Ambrose claims Gall blocked Custer at the river with 1,500 Hunkpapas!

mand of anyone. As for followers, one would be very hard-pressed to find any warrior who claimed to have ridden with Gall that day. One Bull thought the Hunkpapa Bad Soup might have been with Gall,[310] and Iron Cedar is another possibility, yet not one warrior could ever remember seeing Gall participating in, let alone leading, any assault up Deep Coulee or around Calhoun Hill.[311] Contrast Gall with Crazy Horse, who truly led an assault force: virtually everyone saw him.

Maps showing Gall's move up Deep Coulee in a sweeping arrow of attack against Calhoun Hill are deceiving.[312] They may depict his battle movements, but they certainly convey an erroneous impression of him as a leader of a large force of warriors. The arrow labeled "Gall," could just as well be labeled "Flying Hawk," "Red Feather," "Runs The Enemy," or "Hump," or any other one of possibly five hundred warriors who took that path. Gall's reputation as the bellwether of a great throng of warriors instrumental in crushing Custer was mostly the result of later machinations by the Standing Rock Reservation Agent James McLaughlin.[313] With this in mind, it is time to stop portraying Gall as the nemesis of the defenders of Calhoun Hill.

Years later, the Lakota Bobtail Bull recalled seeing Sitting Bull yelling words of encouragement at the start of the Reno action. He did not see Sitting Bull in the Custer fight, but he did not know if Gall was even there at all. Young Two Moon, on the fringe of the action from Calhoun Hill to Custer Hill, commented, "I don't know where Gall was." White Bull fought in the Calhoun-Keogh sectors, but said he did not see Gall anywhere. White Bull characterized Gall as "a good advertiser," and he "laughed at Gall's fame" at the Little Bighorn. Willis Rowland, interpreter and associate of many of the Indian battle participants, thought it was very improbable that Gall ever aimed to command anyone. "I have yet to find an Indian," Rowland stated, "who saw Gall in the battle or did not smile at the claim that he directed it."[314]

Most likely, more women than warriors followed Gall across the river. By the time he got to Calhoun Hill, two hours of fighting had passed, an assault had been made and broken, and much of the drama had been played. If he got to "hatchet" anyone, it was the flotsam left behind after the battle had swept on by. Gall was not the force behind Calhoun's destruction. He contributed almost nothing to the ultimate Indian victory.

Back on the hilltop four miles to the south, Reno's and Benteen's men were busy with their own problems. Major Reno had been down the bluffs, looking for the body of his adjutant, Lt. Benjamin H. Hodgson, who was said to have been

---

310. One Bull, Box 105, Notebook 41, Campbell Collection.

311. Robert M. Utley, "Sitting Bull," *Greasy Grass* 10, no. 4 (May 1994): 4–5.

312. Godfrey, *Custer's Last Battle*, 23; Evan S. Connell, *Son of the Morning Star* (New York: Harper & Row, 1984), inside cover; Kammen, Marshall, and Lefthand, *Soldiers Falling*, 225; Utley, *Cavalier in Buckskin*, 184; Graham, *Custer Myth*, ix; Weibert, *Sixty-Six Years*, end map; Sarf, *Little Bighorn Campaign*, 205, 225.

313. Neil C. Mangum, "Gall: Sioux Gladiator or White Man's Pawn?" 5th Annual Symposium, Custer Battlefield Historical & Museum Association (Hardin, MT: CBH&MA, 1991), 35; Marquis, *Custer on the Little Big Horn*, 110–11.

314. Old Bull, Bobtail Bull, Box 105, Notebook 11, Campbell Collection; White Bull, Box 105, Notebooks 4, 24, Campbell Collection; Willis Rowland, Box 106, Notebook 52, Campbell Collection; Hardorff, *Memories*, 156.

killed during the river crossing. Lt. Luther R. Hare was sent back down the trail to speed up the pack train. Many of the soldiers could hear heavy gunfire, some of it sounding like volley firing. The cacophony prompted Capt. Thomas B. Weir to ask Reno for permission to move his Company D downstream toward the sound of the firing. Reno denied him permission.[315]

On Custer's field, Captain Keogh's battalion deployed along the ridgeline: Calhoun's L Company farthest south, Capt. Thomas Custer's C Company in the middle, and Keogh's I Company farthest north. Lieutenant Colonel Custer rode with Yates's battalion. Company E, under Lt. Algernon E. Smith, deployed just beyond the ridge's northern end, and Custer probably continued toward the river with Captain Yates's F Company.

The Indians had been following the troops since they had pulled back from Butler Ridge near the ford. The firing, which had been long-range and desultory for the most part, now became heavier. Calhoun's halt enabled the Indians to mass for the first large-scale charge, in which White Bull, Red Feather, Runs The Enemy, Hump, and others participated. The heavy soldier fire drove them back and was heard on Reno's hill. Horses screamed and men were thrown to the ground, although surprisingly few warriors were killed or wounded. Realizing that a charge up the open ground would not dislodge the bluecoats, the braves broke off the action and circled around, seeking another approach.

To the north, Wolf Tooth, on the land side of the soldier ridge, and Two Moon, on the river side, both saw some of the companies change direction and leave the ridge. The five companies were strung out, and the Indians formed a U-shaped line around them. Soon the time would be ripe to press the issue to its conclusion. About one hour remained in the lives of Custer's soldiers, and one hour until the Indians had won their greatest triumph.

---

315. Gray, *Custer's Last Campaign*, 316–18.

IV

Vortex

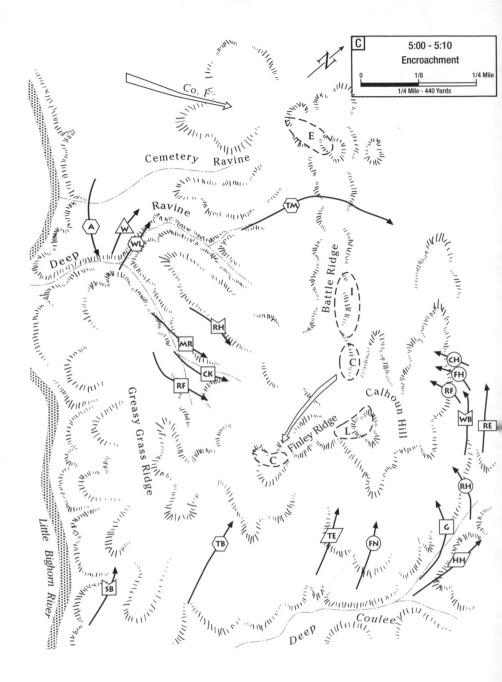

Co. F.

Cemetery Ravine

Ravine

Deep

E

C

5:00 - 5:10
Encroachment

0   1/8   1/4 Mile
1/4 Mile - 440 Yards

A   W   WL   TM

Battle Ridge

I

RH

MR   C

CK

RF

Finley Ridge   L

Calhoun Hill

CH
FH
RF
WB   RE

C

RH

G

Greasy Grass Ridge

TB

TE   FN

HH

Little Bighorn River

SB

Deep   Coulee

Encroachment, 5:00–5:10

A 5:00–5:10, **Antelope** [last 4:30, next 5:10]. Obtaining a pony from her brother White Bull (Ice), Antelope had dashed to the ford, crossing over just behind the lead warriors. As she rode directly up the broad (Deep) coulee, she could see that the soldiers had lined themselves out on a long ridge a little nearer to the river than the high one where they were first seen.

As she worked her way east and then north of the soldiers, she rode past many Indian ponies, left back in the gulches while their owners were crawling up the gullies toward the soldiers on the ridge. They too had dismounted, and there was a long-range exchange of fire. Since there were no trees on the high slopes, the soldiers were at a disadvantage, for even when they tried to take cover, the smoke from their guns showed exactly where they were hidden. Meanwhile, the Indians sent hundreds of arrows arcing high into the air, to fall onto them from above.

Antelope kept searching for Noisy Walking, but on the east and north sides she found only Lakotas. Though there was some intermingling of tribes, the warrior societies liked to band together because they knew each other's ways. Since she saw none of her people on that side of the field, she rode on.

From the north side of the ridge, Antelope circled around to the west side. Still, she could not find her nephew. After about half an hour of riding, Antelope trotted between the ridge and the river, making her way to the south side. Approaching a large ravine, she began to find some Oglalas, but many more Cheyennes. Here she would intensify her search.[316]

W 5:00–5:10, **Waterman** [last 4:20, next 5:20]. After the soldiers had gotten to the top of the hill, Waterman followed after them, riding with some Cheyennes. Though he had gotten separated from Left Hand and the other Arapahos, he found it safer to stick with a band who had not been as hostile toward them as the Lakotas had. Early in the action, Waterman stayed with some warriors in a small gulch below the hill that the soldiers held. As the fight progressed, he moved up the hill, closing in on the bluecoats.[317]

TM 5:00–5:10, **Two Moon** [last 4:50, next 5:10]. Two Moon watched the Gray Horse troopers on the hill dismount and prepare for battle. Impatiently, he wanted to charge right in, but he too had to wait for more warriors. All the while, Two Moon said, the Lakotas and Cheyennes "came up the valley swarming like ants toward the bunch of gray horses" on the hill.

As soon as he could get his men ready, Two Moon ordered the charge, calling to his Cheyenne brothers: "Come on, children; do not be scared!" They sprang forward, yelling and firing. The charge went right up the sloping ground to the hill where the first line of gravestones are today. However, their shock tactics did not have the desired effect. "The soldier fire was so heavy that the Cheyennes had to

316. Marquis, *Custer on the Little Big Horn*, 86–87; Powell, *Sacred Mountain*, 1019–20.
317. Graham, *The Custer Myth*, 110.

Two Moon led a group of Cheyenne warriors against the Gray Horse Troop on Custer Hill. —Little Bighorn Battlefield National Monument

fall back," Two Moon admitted. They veered off, breaking to the right and cresting the ridgeline. Two Moon led his band out of the line of fire of the grays on the west slope, and down into the valley on the reverse slope. There, gaining temporary respite, Two Moon and his Cheyennes met up with another band of Lakotas.[318]

SB 5:00–5:10, **Standing Bear** [last 4:30, next 5:10]. Crossing at the mouth of Muskrat Creek, just north of the Santee camp, Standing Bear could see nothing but Indians swarming up against Custer. Guns were being fired repeatedly. Standing Bear made his way up the hill toward the action, but he stayed back a short distance, not joining "the fronters," where the bravest warriors congregated.

---

318. Dixon, *Vanishing Race*, 181; "Two Moon Recalls," 11.

Just west of the Custer soldiers, Standing Bear rode past a Lakota named Long Elk. The man's horse was wounded and he himself had been hit in the face. His mouth was full of blood, which dripped all over him. This was the first thing Standing Bear saw as he neared the battle, and he knew it was a wise decision to remain with those in the rear who were not so brave.[319]

RE 5:00–5:10, **Runs The Enemy** [last 4:50, next 5:10]. Because the heavy fire from the soldiers had driven the Lakota charge back, Runs The Enemy decided to try a different tack. He left his men in a protected gully south of Calhoun Hill and told them to hold their position. Runs The Enemy rushed around the hills, heading north. He would ride for the far end of the soldier line to see what opportunity might open up.[320]

TE 5:00–5:10, **Two Eagles** [last 4:20, next 5:40]. Two Eagles followed the progress of the soldiers up to Calhoun Hill. They stayed mounted the whole time, until the Indians got close enough to shoot some of the horses. When the horses became unmanageable, the soldiers were forced to dismount. Some horses had been getting loose since the beginning of the fight, and the Indians broke away to chase after them.

Two Eagles worked his way up the slope to a point just east of, and midway between, Calhoun Hill and its southern extension (Finley Ridge). From there he could see a number of troopers coming from the north side of the ridge. They were not running away, Two Eagles noted. From their manner he thought that perhaps they were only going for water. A detachment of at least eight of them took up position at the southern end of the ridge.[321]

FN 5:00–5:10, **Fears Nothing** [last 4:30, next 5:10]. Fears Nothing rode up Deep Coulee from the river. The soldiers had spread themselves out in a line along the ridge, but one group moved down closer to the Little Bighorn. The present-day grave markers running in a line down toward the river from Calhoun Hill mark where the soldiers once stood. This, said Fears Nothing, is where the battle began in earnest. The bluecoats there made a valiant effort to check the Indian advance, and there a good many of them died.[322]

RH 5:00–5:10, **Red Hawk** [last 4:30, next 5:40]. The troopers made their first stand on Calhoun Hill and on the ridge (Finley) running from there toward the river. "At this place," said Red Hawk, "the soldiers stood in line and made a very good fight." They delivered volley after volley into the Indian ranks. However, because of the great number of Indians, the firing did not seem to have a perceptible effect.[323]

---

319. DeMallie, *Sixth Grandfather*, 185.
320. Dixon, *Vanishing Race*, 175.
321. Hardorff, *Lakota Recollections*, 148–49. The extension of ridge that runs south and west from Calhoun Hill and about halfway to Greasy Grass Ridge has been called "Finley" or "Finckle" Ridge, after C Company Sgts. Jeremiah Finley and August Finckle, whose bodies were identified there after the battle.
322. Ibid., 31–32.
323. Ibid., 43.

TB 5:00–5:10, **Tall Bull** [last 4:20, next 6:10(a)]. Tall Bull got to the battle in time to see Yates being driven back up Butler Ridge. For some time after that there was little firing while the soldiers and Indians maneuvered for a better position. Tall Bull didn't hear any heavy shooting until the soldiers reached the Calhoun Hill area. It was there, and down that hill toward Greasy Grass Ridge, that he heard the first sustained volleys. There, said Tall Bull, was where the real fighting began.[324]

Hollow Horn Bear, a twenty-six-year-old Brulé, thought the first stand made by the soldiers was on Calhoun Hill and Finley Ridge. —State Historical Society of North Dakota

---

324. Hammer, *Custer in '76*, 213.

HH 5:00–5:10, **Hollow Horn Bear** [last 4:20, next 5:40]. In moving to the ridge where the final fighting occurred, Hollow Horn Bear thought the soldiers kept together fairly well. They shifted positions, but no stand was made at one place to enable another troop to move elsewhere. In fact, Hollow Horn Bear believed the troops were in good order at the start of the fight, and kept their organization even while moving from point to point.

The first time the soldiers "bunched," said Hollow Horn Bear, was when they reached Calhoun Hill and the ridge (Finley) that ran down from it. Here, "when the soldiers made the stand nearest to the village," some soldiers dismounted to fire at the Indians. Those who remained mounted held the horses of the ones fighting. This was the only place Hollow Horn Bear saw the soldiers fight in this manner. From there he rode around the ridge and out of sight of the river.[325]

G 5:00–5:10, **Gall** [last 4:40, next 5:30]. In the wake of many other Indians, Gall made his way across the river. After the Reno fight, he said, leaders such as Crow King and Crazy Horse were afraid the soldiers marching to the north end of camp would get the women and children. They had raced back through the camp. Crow King turned right and went up a deep gully where Custer could not see him. In the upper part of the gully he could creep up very close to the soldiers on their south side. Crazy Horse went up another deep ravine and came up very close to the troopers on their north side.

Up Deep Coulee, Gall struck the trail the soldiers made while riding north, although his tracking skills were not needed at this point, for the battle was already raging in front of him. While Crow King and his warriors were shooting from the south side, Crazy Horse was behind the hill, shooting from the north. Gall came up on the east end. He could see soldiers falling. "They were on foot," Gall said, "and most of their horses were in the upper part of the ravine where Crazy Horse was."

Finally he was able to take part in the battle. Noticing that some troopers held the horses while others shot the guns, Gall said, "We tried to kill the holders, and then by waving blankets and shouting we scared the horses down the coulee, where the Cheyenne women caught them." The soldiers fought hard, Gall said. They fought standing in lines along the ridge and they never surrendered. However, once the horses had stampeded it was impossible for any of the soldiers to escape.[326]

CK 5:00–5:10, **Crow King** (Patriarch Crow—Kangi Yatapi). The Hunkpapa chief had lost two brothers, Swift Bear and White Bull, in the fight against Reno's soldiers. By the time the second band of white warriors came, Crow King was ready for revenge. By then, all the warriors and horses were together and ready, and about eighty Hunkpapas followed him into the fray.

At first, the parties commenced firing at long range. When the greater portion of warriors came together in front of the soldiers, they rushed their horses at them.

325. Hardorff, *Lakota Recollections*, 181–83.
326. Burdick, *Barry's Notes*, 11, 13; Graham, *The Custer Myth*, 92; Benham, "Warrior's Revenge," 462.

The Hunkpapa chief Crow King led about eighty warriors against Finley Ridge and Calhoun Hill. —Montana Historical Society

Crow King led his men up one ravine, while more Indians rode around the other side, circling, until the soldiers were nearly surrounded.

When Custer's forces saw how they were beset, they dismounted. "They tried to hold on to their horses," Crow King said, "but as we pressed closer they let go [of] their horses." Riderless mounts scattered across the hills and ran to the river, but the soldiers still kept in order and fought like brave warriors. Although Crow King was firing from south of the ridge, heavy pressure from Indians on the opposite side seemed to crowd the soldiers toward the main camp.[327]

327. Graham, *The Custer Myth*, 77; Hardorff, *Hokahey!*, 43.

`MR` 5:00–5:10, **Moving Robe** [last 3:50]. Moving Robe had been in the bottomlands and timber as Reno's men retreated to the bluffs. When word was given that another body of soldiers was attacking the lower end of the village, she and her father, Crawler, rode back in that direction. The young warriors also turned north, riding in columns of fives and singing a victory song.

With a number of Hunkpapas, they rode farther down the Greasy Grass, beyond the main ford, to a crossing just below a beaver dam where the water was not very deep. Making their way up a ravine, they were able to approach the soldier position from the flank. Moving Robe saw the horse holders trying to control the reins of eight to ten horses each. They were not having an easy time. The Indians began waving blankets, frightening the horses. As some of them broke away from the troopers, the scene became chaotic.

"On the ridge just north of us," Moving Robe said, "I saw blue-clad men running up a ravine, firing as they ran. The valley was dense with powder smoke. I never heard such whooping and shouting." Nearby, she could hear the Minneconjou Lakota Red Horse shouting, "There is never a better time to die!"

Moving Robe saw Indians everywhere. Crow King was attacking the soldiers from the south, and others—Cheyennes, she believed—were attacking from the north. Long Hair's troopers appeared to be trapped in a little enclosed valley. It was a hotly contested battle.[328]

`RF` 5:00–5:10, **Rain In The Face** [last 3:10, next 5:30]. Rain In The Face had taken quite some time to get back to his tipi and prepare for the fight. He had been carrying his stone war club, but also gathered up his gun and bow and a quiver full of arrows. Just as he was about to set out after Reno, another body of soldiers appeared at the edge of a long line of cliffs across the river.

All of the mounted Indians rode downstream to the ford. Men of all tribes were mixed together—Oglalas, Minneconjous, Cheyennes, and some Hunkpapas. Rain In The Face noticed that most of the warriors riding with him were very young men. The foremost braves crossed the stream and followed the white men until they had them almost surrounded. Finally the soldiers dismounted and began to fire into the camp.

Riding among the Hunkpapas, Rain In The Face was surprised to see the familiar face of Tashenamani (Moving Robe). Her brother had been killed and now she held his war staff over her head, exhorting the warriors.

"Behold, there is among us a young woman!" Rain In The Face shouted. "Let no young man hide behind her garment!" He knew those words would make the men brave. Rain In The Face thought that Tashenamani, leaning forward on her charger, was as pretty as a bird. Always when a young woman was in the forefront, it caused the warriors to vie with one another in displays of valor. The battle increased in intensity and both sides fought bravely.[329]

328. Hardorff, *Lakota Recollections*, 94–95.
329. Eastman, "Rain-In-The-Face," 18.

RF 5:00–5:10, **Red Feather** [last 4:50, next 5:30]. With his horse killed, Red Feather worked his way up a gully on his hands and knees. Above him, the dismounted soldiers continued to fire. After the repulsed charge, many Indians left their ponies behind and crawled up the gulches, although they could not get in very close. If Indian or soldier exposed his head, a flurry of gunfire would kill him or drive him down. About this time, some soldiers' horses got loose and the Indians picked them up.

Red Feather crawled up behind a little roll of ground. He could see the soldiers were on one side of the hill while the Indians were on the other, with a slight rise between them. All about him were young warriors. Only one old man accompanied them so close to the fighting. He wore a shirt and had his hair tied behind his head. Shouting words of encouragement, he was an inspiration to the young braves.

The long-range sniping continued, with the Indians using many more arrows than bullets. Whenever Red Feather chanced to raise his head high enough for a better glimpse of the action, he could see the soldiers fighting hard from the ridges. In their exertions, they all seemed to have lost their caps.[330]

FH 5:00–5:10, **Flying Hawk** [last 4:50, next 5:40]. While the soldiers were making a stand on the hill, Flying Hawk was in a gully on the north side holding his horse. Crazy Horse came up and gave him his pony to hold also. Flying Hawk watched Crazy Horse crawl up a ravine to a position where he could see the soldiers. From there he began to fire at them as fast as he could load.[331]

WB 5:00–5:10, **White Bull** [last 4:50, next 5:10]. Breaking off the attack on Calhoun Hill after the first charge failed, White Bull looked for a new approach. "When they ran me out of the ravine," he said, "I rode south and worked my way over to the east of the mounted bunch of soldiers." There he met Crazy Horse and his band of warriors. The Oglala war chief wore plain white buckskins and let his hair hang loose with no feathers in it, White Bull observed. He had white spots of hail painted on his face for protection, and he was said to have been bulletproof. White Bull would see how the famous Oglala war chief fought.[332]

← DISCUSSION. The first assault on Calhoun Hill had been repulsed. Many of the attacking Indians pulled back and moved east and north, looking for another approach. As Keogh's battalion was occupied with Indians to the south and east, a number of warriors began infiltrating up the Calhoun Coulee branch of the Deep Ravine, threatening the western flank.

Among these Indians were a significant number of Hunkpapas. Since they were the first to fight Reno, and perhaps remained engaged with him for a longer time than some of the other tribes, they were among the later arrivals to face Custer. By the time the Hunkpapas reached the lower camp, other tribes had already gone up

330. Hardorff, *Lakota Recollections*, 87.
331. McCreight, *Firewater*, 113.
332. Hardorff, *Lakota Recollections*, 115; White Bull, Box 105, Notebook 24, Campbell Collection; Miller, "Echoes," 35; Vestal, "Man Who Killed Custer," 6–7.

*The mouth of Deep Ravine, where many Indians crossed the
Greasy Grass to attack Custer's battalion.* —Monroe County Library

Deep Coulee in front of them, and they moved farther downstream before crossing. There are several corroborating narratives. According to Iron Hawk, the
Hunkpapa gathering point was at the foot of the gulch (Deep Ravine) that led up
to Custer Hill. Flying Hawk indicated that a number of Indians "went across at the
lower crossing west of Custer Hill," where they caught some soldiers' horses and
went up to the fight. Two Moon said that some Lakotas "crossed at the lower place
and waited in the breaks concealed west of the monument."[333] Moving Robe,
Crawler, and a number of their Hunkpapa tribe crossed at the Deep Ravine Ford
(Cheyenne Ford) near a beaver dam, and Moving Robe said the Hunkpapas fought
from the south side of the ridge. Gall also said Crazy Horse fought from north of
the ridge while the Hunkpapa Crow King fought from the south side. Rain In The
Face saw Moving Robe riding with the other Hunkpapas, which also places him
in the same vicinity. Moving Robe heard the Minneconjou Red Horse shouting
to the braves, so he, too, must have been on the river side of the main ridge. When
we realize that a number of Indians viewed the ridge as running east-west, we can
more easily understand their statements of warriors fighting from either its north
or south side.

　　　To counter this infiltration, at least a portion of one company was moved from
the north side (or east side, depending on one's perception) of the main (Battle)

333. DeMallie, *Sixth Grandfather*, 190; Hardorff, *Lakota Recollections*, 52; "Two Moon Recalls," 13.

ridge, down to Finley Ridge. Two Eagles, Fears Nothing, Red Hawk, and Tall Bull commented on the soldiers moving down to, or firing from, that new position.

The troopers were still putting out a heavy volume of fire, because in this time segment, we again find officers and men back on Reno Hill and trapped down in the valley, commenting on hearing distant volleys.[334]

The failure of the first Indian charge and the heavy return fire led to more Indian movement, infiltration up the gullies, long-range firing, and several blanket-waving incidents, some of which were successful in stampeding horses.

Using terrain and proximity restrictions, we might speculate that the battalion's led horses were kept in two main areas. Companies I and C may have held their mounts in Keogh Coulee, which would have been in the low ground just east of Battle Ridge and north of Calhoun Hill. Company L probably held their horses in the low sag just behind, or northwest of, their position on Calhoun Hill, or perhaps a little farther downslope at the head of Calhoun Coulee. The men who moved from east of Battle Ridge over to Finley Ridge were probably detached from Company C, since a number of their dead were later identified on that ground. It was

Looking from Greasy Grass Ridge to upper Calhoun Coulee behind Finley Ridge, where some of Company C's or Company L's horses may have been held.

---

334. Gray, *Custer's Last Campaign,* 317–18.

not a full company-sized movement, for Two Eagles described it as at least eight men. Other Company C men, including Sgt. Edwin Bobo, were later found dead in Keogh Coulee, illustrating the likelihood of Company C having deployed in two platoons. Most likely, the C Troop platoon holding Finley Ridge held its horses directly behind in upper Calhoun Coulee. The blanket-waving Indians south and west of the ridge would have run off the sorrels of Tom Custer's Company C and the bays of Calhoun's Company L, while those frightening the horses to the north and east would have stampeded more sorrels of Company C and the bays of Keogh's Company I.

To the far north, the grays of Smith's E Troop remained near what was to become Last Stand Hill and the cemetery grounds. The bays of Yates's F Troop, most likely in the company of Custer, were seen by Two Moon and Wolf Tooth continuing down toward the river, disappearing from sight for a time. We do not know just what Custer was planning with this maneuver. He may have simply been verifying another avenue of operations, either for advance or retreat, keeping his options open. He may have thought of making an attack on the women and children who could be seen fleeing northwest down the valley. Perhaps it was another feint to draw the Indians away from his own rear battalion, while awaiting the advance of Reno and Benteen.

The Cheyenne historian John Stands In Timber indicated that warriors hidden in the brush along the river at a far northern crossing had fired at soldiers who neared the ford, driving them back. In a story similar to that attributed to White Cow Bull, the Cheyenne Hanging Wolf said the Indians' gunfire knocked a trooper off his horse, and the soldiers fished him out of the river and took him along when they retreated. The troops then went to the present-day cemetery grounds, where they waited for about twenty minutes.[335] A move to this far northern ford does seem to have occurred, although more corroborating narratives would be helpful.

While F Company was on its trek to the river, Two Moon charged against E Company but was deflected back over to the east side of the ridge. Warriors all around were closing in on the troopers, but Custer was not yet surrounded. His five companies, at least upon F Company's return, were essentially in a line along Battle Ridge: C, L, I, E, and F, from south to north. No defensive perimeter had been established, for Custer did not see the situation as being serious enough to "fort up" for a hard fight. He was still thinking offensively. So were the Lakotas and Cheyennes.

---

335. Stands In Timber, *Cheyenne Memories*, 199.

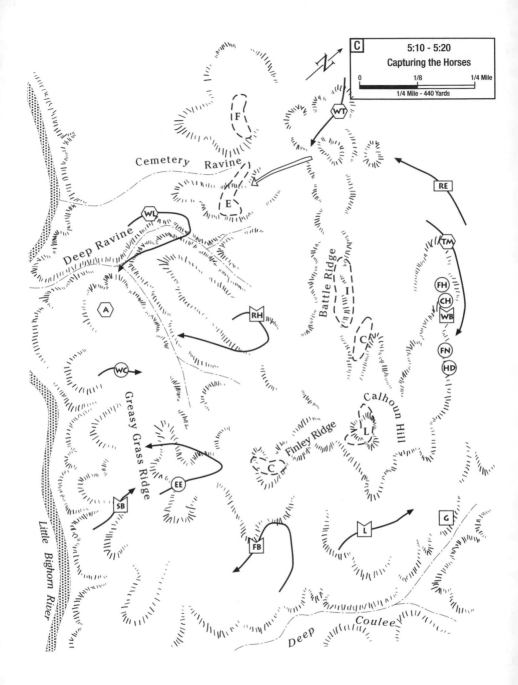

WT

F

RE

Cemetery Ravine

E

WL

Deep Ravine

TM

Battle Ridge

I

FH

CH

WB

A

RH

C

FN

HD

WC

Calhoun Hill

L

Greasy Grass Ridge

Finley Ridge

C

EE

C

SB

L

G

FB

Deep Coulee

Little Bighorn River

Capturing the Horses, 5:10–5:20

WB 5:10–5:20, **White Bull** [last 5:00, next 5:20]. White Bull impatiently rode his pony back and forth in a ravine behind the lines. The fight here had also degenerated into a long range sniping, with Crazy Horse joining in the shooting.

More Indians gathered and it seemed to White Bull that it was high time to press the issue. He rode up to Crazy Horse and suggested that they make a charge together, to go after some of the nearest of the soldiers' held horses. Although Crazy Horse might have had his face painted with hailstones for protection and was considered bulletproof, White Bull said he "backed out" of the charge. Very well. If anyone was going to set an example, it would have to be White Bull.[336]

TM 5:10–5:20, **Two Moon** [last 5:00, next 5:30]. Two Moon's band rode over Battle Ridge to the east side partly as a result of the Gray Horse Troop's gunfire, but also to avoid the bullets of the Lakotas. A number of them had crossed at the lower ford and moved up in the breaks west of where the monument now stands. Their hot fire following on the heels of Two Moon's charge helped persuade the Cheyennes to vacate the dangerous open slopes southwest of the hill where the Gray Horse troopers fought.

Below Battle Ridge on the east side, Two Moon's band met up with Lakotas coming from the south. Along the soldier line, he remembered seeing troops on white, bay, and black horses. He dismounted his panting white charger and told his men to wait, and to take a few minutes rest while they reloaded.[337]

FN 5:10–5:20, **Fears Nothing** [last 5:00, next 5:40]. Fears Nothing moved with the Indians east of Calhoun Hill and then worked his way north along Battle Ridge. He could see that Custer had formed a line all along the ridge. About halfway up the line, the Lakotas met up with another band of Indians (Two Moon's) who had enveloped the ridge after crossing over its nose to the northwest. He thought those Indians must have crossed the river at one of the lower fords. Seeing this band approaching from an almost opposite direction, Fears Nothing thought that surely the soldiers must have been completely surrounded.[338]

L 5:10–5:20, **Lights** [last 4:10, next 5:40]. Lights thought the soldiers kept in company formation and in good order, from Custer's approach to the river, then back to the Calhoun Hill area. The shooting had not been vigorous, but it was continuous for the entire distance.

Lights followed the Indians up Deep Coulee and took a position just northeast of the ridge (Finley) running down from Calhoun Hill. From there he had a good view of the action. He did not think any Indians had gotten to the long (Battle) ridge ahead of Custer, but along Finley Ridge they did get on both sides of him.

---

336 Miller, "Echoes," 35; Vestal, "Man Who Killed Custer," 7; Hardorff, *Lakota Recollections*, 115.
337. Dixon, *Vanishing Race*, 182–83; "Two Moon Recalls," 11, 13. There were some dark bay horses in Custer's five companies, but no blacks.
338. Hardorff, *Lakota Recollections*, 31–32.

Lights did not see the soldiers make any charges. From his position on the Deep Coulee slope of the ridge he could not see any of the held horses. It looked as if all the soldiers remained mounted. They did not leave their horses until the mounts were shot from underneath them, were taken away by the warriors, or stampeded. Whatever the cause, a good number of soldier horses were captured alive and, although some were wounded, many still had ammunition in the saddlebags.[339]

EE 5:10–5:20, **Eagle Elk** [last 4:50]. After they helped the Indian who had been shot in the jaw, Eagle Elk and his brother turned their attention back to the soldiers. Together, they decided to make a charge. As they dashed their ponies toward the hill, the heavy gunfire brunted their enthusiasm and they swung back.

Riding for safety, Eagle Elk looked back for his brother, but could only see a riderless pony running off. About the same time, he saw four soldiers' horses stampeding free. Eagle Elk thought his brother might have been shot, but the lure of four big cavalry steeds was too tempting. He dashed after the horses.

After a successful chase, Eagle Elk caught a bay and a sorrel whose bridle reins were still tied together. He gave one to another Indian. At that moment another horse was shot. Although it looked like the bullet entered its head near the ear, the horse did not drop, but ran around in circles. The entire scene was painted with dust, screams, whizzing bullets, and confusion.

Another Indian came up to Eagle Elk and told him, "Your cousin [brother?] is shot off his horse. He is lying over there." Eagle Elk did not go back to look for him, for about that time he discovered his brother, unhorsed but unharmed. He heard another warrior call out and point to where a man had been shot through the head. Eagle Elk and his brother went to the spot. They found the warrior on the ground. He wore a decorative bird on his head and a bullet had gone right through the bird and the man's head. At this point the brothers were behind a ridge, out of the line of the soldiers' fire, and there was little danger. The shootings Eagle Elk had witnessed within the last minutes had been enough to convince him of the good sense in staying away from the front lines. Eagle Elk dropped out of the fight.[340]

FB 5:10–5:20, **Flying By** [last 4:40, next 5:50]. Because his horse had been shot, the fight was going on for a while before Flying By got there. He heard that Custer had driven the Indians toward the river at first, but when enough warriors went over, it was Custer who was soon surrounded.

Flying By did not see another soldier charge after he approached the battlefield. The soldiers got off their horses to fire, and some were unable to hold on to their mounts, for the Indians captured many. As loose cavalry horses stampeded toward the river, Flying By was lucky enough to run one down after it had slowed sufficiently to enable him to approach it. Climbing on his new mount and back in his element, he was able to round up a few other strays. Flying By left the fight to drive his prizes back to the relative safety of the camp.[341]

---

339. Ibid., 166–69.
340. Hardorff, *Lakota Recollections*, 104–5.
341. Hammer, *Custer in '76*, 209–10.

The twenty-six-year-old Minneconjou Flying By had his horse killed in the Reno fight, but captured another near Calhoun Hill. —State Historical Society of North Dakota

SB 5:10–5:20, **Standing Bear** [last 5:00, next 5:40]. Leaving Long Elk to make his way to the rear nursing his bloody jaw, Standing Bear crested a ridge to get a better view of the fight. The Indians who had crossed at the mouth of Medicine Tail had spread out both ways around Custer. Between Calhoun Hill and where the monument presently stands, the Indians moved along on both sides of the soldier ridge. It looked as if they had completely surrounded Custer's troops on both hills.

From his position in the rear, Standing Bear saw a soldier horse that had broken away and gotten through the front ranks of the warriors. He caught it and tied it up. A short while later he came across another Indian with blood in his mouth. The man stood and fell, rising, walking dizzily, and falling again. Standing Bear held back, trying to keep out of range of the deadly soldier bullets.[342]

342. Ibid., 215; Hardorff, *Lakota Recollections*, 59; DeMallie, *Sixth Grandfather*, 185.

WL 5:10–5:20, **Wooden Leg** [last 4:50, next 5:20]. Most of the time Wooden Leg kept away from the front, leaving his older brother, Yellow Hair, to do the close fighting. He could see the Indians inexorably creeping closer to the whites on the ridges. However, the long wait eventually got the best of him. Wooden Leg dismounted, tied up his pony in a ravine near the river, and crept up a gulch with the other warriors.

The encroaching Indians finally forced the soldiers to take action. About forty troopers came galloping from the east part of the ridge down toward the river, directly toward the spot where many of the Cheyennes and Oglalas were hidden. In front of Wooden Leg the Indians began flowing back, off the low ridges, out of the upper gullies, and back into a deep gulch. Wooden Leg pulled back with them. From a vantage point, he looked back to see that the soldiers had stopped and gotten off their horses, taking up a position on a low ridge that the Indians had just vacated.[343]

A 5:10–5:20, **Antelope** [last 5:00, next 5:20]. Although she had completely circled the soldiers on the hills, Antelope was unable to find Noisy Walking. Reaching a deep gulch where she saw many Cheyennes, she continued her search. All around, the Indians were using the gullies, or dodging from knoll to knoll, gradually creeping closer to the soldiers.

"On the southern side, where I stopped to watch the fight," Antelope said, "almost all of the Cheyennes and Oglala Sioux had crawled across a deep gulch at the bottom of a broad coulee south of the ridge where were the soldiers, and about half way between them and the river." This slow fighting had been kept up for a long time, without great harm done to either side.

Finally a band of soldiers on the high ridge mounted up and came riding down the broad coulee toward the river. The Cheyennes and Oglalas hidden there quickly got back into the deepest parts of the gulch or climbed out of it until they got to the ridge just south of it, the ridge where Antelope was watching. The soldiers who had galloped down halted and got off their horses along another ridge, a low one just north of the deep gulch.[344]

RH 5:10–5:20, **Red Horse** [next 5:20]. Like most of the Indians, the Minneconjou chief Red Horse had been surprised by Reno's attack, but, unlike most of the men, he had been caught one mile from camp, digging turnips with four women. By the time he returned to the council lodge there was no time to give orders. The women ran and the warriors went to fight the soldiers who had attacked the Hunkpapas.

When the Lakotas drove the soldiers across the river, another group threatened the lower camp and, like a whirlwind, the Indians rushed north. While Red Horse made his way up to fight this second group of soldiers, he couldn't help but worry that the first soldiers on Reno's hill would charge the Indians from the rear. When they did not, he thought they must have run out of ammunition.

343. Marquis, *Wooden Leg*, 231, 234.
344. Marquis, *Custer on the Little Big Horn*, 87.

The Minneconjou chief Red Horse saw the soldiers making a charge against the Indians, temporarily driving them back. —Little Bighorn Battlefield National Monument

Red Horse thought this second group of soldiers made five brave stands as the Indians drove them back. However, as the Lakotas closed in on one group making a stand, another band of soldiers in their rear charged down at them. The Lakotas fell back. They retreated a short way and then halted, as did the troopers. It was as if the bluecoats had gone as far as they dared, and the Indians fell back only as much as they had to. They stopped and turned, said Red Horse, "and the Sioux and the soldiers stood facing each other."[345]

---

345. Graham, *The Custer Myth,* 61–62.

RE 5:10–5:20, **Runs The Enemy** [last 5:00, next 5:20]. Having left his men below Calhoun Hill, Runs The Enemy headed north to see where else they might be able to press a successful attack. He rushed around the hills on the back side of the soldier ridge and came up on the far end of the field where the monument now stands. In the coulees all around him were hundreds of Indians. They had dismounted, tied their horses in a bunch, and gotten down in the coulees, shooting at the soldiers from all sides. Runs The Enemy worked his way closer to the top.[346]

WT 5:10–5:20, **Wolf Tooth** [last 4:50, next 5:20]. Wolf Tooth, Big Foot, and their band of warriors broke off their firing when the soldiers continued down toward the northern ford. After a short time, however, the bluecoats pulled back to the level ground near the present cemetery. There they halted.

Wolf Tooth and the other braves moved in, taking positions behind the ridge where the monument stands. From that vantage point, Wolf Tooth could see that some of Custer's men had gone down into the center of the basin below. The soldiers of the Gray Horse Company dismounted and moved up afoot to the lower bank of the basin, down near the Deep Ravine, where they were confronted by many Indians. Some troopers lay down on the ground to fire. Others advanced, running, while covered by the rifles of the men lying prone. Wolf Tooth believed that if the soldiers had pulled out then, before the fighting got heavy, they might have gotten away to join up with Reno. But the wait at the cemetery and in the basin had sealed their fate. More warriors lined up behind the ridge, and soon Wolf Tooth thought that a retreat in that direction would be impossible. In addition, the Indians from the river side were putting out some heavy fire.[347]

WC 5:10–5:20, **White Cow Bull** [last 4:20, next 5:40]. After being repulsed at the river, the soldiers swarmed out over the higher ground to the north, shooting as they went. Still riding with the Shahiyelas (Cheyennes), White Cow Bull kept between the soldiers on the ridge in front of him and the river at his back. Out on the ridge, the soldiers had split into two bands. Most of them were now on foot and shooting fast, so as far as White Cow Bull could see, the Indians made no more mounted charges.

At a midway point along a ridge (Greasy Grass), White Cow Bull found suffi- cient cover and began to return the soldiers' fire. He considered himself a good shot, and since he had one of the few repeating rifles carried by any of the warriors, he felt it was his duty to use it the best way he could. From his position between the two bands of soldiers he kept up a hot fire, first at one, then at the other. "It was hard to see through the smoke and dust," he said, "but I saw five soldiers go down when I shot at them."[348]

---

346. Dixon, *Vanishing Race*, 175.
347. Stands In Timber, *Cheyenne Memories*, 199–200; Powell, *Sweet Medicine*, 116; Hardorff, *Memories*, 170. In the last account, John Stands In Timber indicates that Wolf Tooth took him across the battlefield in 1916 and showed him the places where the action occurred. He was definite that the Gray Horse Troop moved from the present cemetery area south toward the Deep Ravine.
348. Miller, "Echoes," 34.

❧ DISCUSSION. By this time the Indians' long-range firing and blanket-waving had the desired effect of stampeding some of the cavalry horses. Standing Bear, Eagle Elk, and Flying By were some of the beneficiaries of the activity.

The Indians had been encroaching in all quarters except in the far north. First, Keogh's battalion responded to the southern threat by deploying a platoon of Company C to counter the Indians in Calhoun Coulee. On the opposite end of the ridge, Company F had returned from its scout to the lower ford and halted on the cemetery grounds. Indians filtered up all of the numerous upper fingers of the Deep Ravine. Their fire was an increasing nuisance to Yates's battalion, which, from its vantage point on the high ground north end of the ridge, could see the Indians posing a serious threat to Keogh. Company I, deployed on the reverse side of Battle Ridge and preoccupied with Crazy Horse's group to the east, probably had no idea of the threat creeping up from the west.

Company E was probably sent down from the monument area to check the Indians getting too close to Keogh's rear and to clear out the central Deep Ravine watershed of infiltrators threatening its own position. The fact that E Troop once held the monument area was amply demonstrated by Two Moon. Participating in a great council held on the battlefield in 1909, Two Moon was interviewed among the memorial stones of Last Stand Hill. "Those who were on the hill where the monument now stands, and where I am now standing," he declared, "had gray horses and they were all in the open."[349] That Company E subsequently vacated the spot was attested to by Wolf Tooth, through his step-grandson, John Stands In Timber. The soldiers who returned from the ford occupied the cemetery for about twenty minutes. When Wolf Tooth and his party went to the monument ridge, the Gray Horse troop had gone down into the basin below, a fortuitous move for Wolf Tooth's band, for now they were able to fire toward the cemetery and the ravine (Cemetery Ravine) below it from the protection of the ridge.[350]

Another corroboration of the deployment comes from Flying Hawk. Although fighting with Crazy Horse on the northern (or eastern) opposite slope of the ridge at the time, Flying Hawk learned of the action afterwards. "When Custer got nearly to the lower end of the camp, he started to go down a gulch," he explained, "but the Indians were surrounding him, and he tried to fight. They got off their horses and made a stand but it was no use. Their horses ran down the ravine right into the village."[351]

Eyewitnesses such as Wooden Leg, Antelope, and Red Horse, respectively, told how the soldiers "came galloping," "came riding," or "charged" down against the Indians, who retreated momentarily in surprise. Although the retreat would be of short duration, the maneuver did have favorable short-term results: Indians were forced back, and the makings of a rough, rectangular, defensive perimeter were established by the soldiers. On the other hand, it was a forced move, made as a reaction to Indian initiative. Almost imperceptibly, on both northern and southern flanks, Custer had relinquished control of events as he passed from offense to de-

349. Dixon, *Vanishing Race*, 181.
350. Stands In Timber, *Cheyenne Memories*, 199–201.
351. McCreight, *Firewater*, 114.

fense. The cavalry, most effective as a mobile, offensive threat, had taken up a defensive, reactionary posture. They were reduced to countering the Indian leads in uneven terrain, with a poor field of fire, and faced by a more numerous, mobile, and elusive foe. The situation was a potential disaster for the U.S. Army and a golden opportunity for the Lakotas and Cheyennes.

As in other instances where we cannot place every individual with absolute accuracy, White Cow Bull again presents us with a problem. After leaving the ford, his narrative becomes vague. Since he hoped Meotzi would hear of his courage, he remained riding with the Cheyennes. Since many Cheyennes and a number of fellow Oglalas stayed between the river and the ridge near the Deep Ravine, we can reasonably place him in that sector. White Cow Bull also stated that after the initial assaults, the Indians made no more mounted charges, which means he was probably not east of the ridge to see the coming Crazy Horse-White Bull sorties. He said he took position on a ridge and saw the soldiers split into two bands, and that he was close enough to fire at both with his repeater. There is a likely site on the north end of Greasy Grass Ridge where a cluster of six or eight .44 Henry cartridges, fired from either a Henry or Winchester Model 1866 repeater, were found during archaeological excavations in the 1980s.[352] Being able to kill five soldiers from either E Troop north of the Deep Ravine, or from C Troop on Finley Ridge, would have been a remarkable feat from that spot, more so than dropping two soldiers into the river at Medicine Tail Ford. Scoring five hits from that distance is very unlikely; however, the act of shooting from that point is very possible. There we have placed White Cow Bull.

The placement of Red Horse is also tentative. We deduced Moving Robe's position in Calhoun Coulee, and we know that she heard Red Horse shouting orders to his men. Red Horse said that Custer's men made five stands, and while moving against one of the groups of soldiers, another band of soldiers in their rear charged them, causing the Lakotas to fall back. Where could this have occurred? Since Red Horse was known to have been in the Calhoun Coulee area, it seems reasonable to assume that he was concerned with, and *facing,* the troops in his front, which would have been the "rear" of both the Company C platoon on Finley Ridge and Company L on Calhoun Hill. It is also possible he was one of those moving up the middle forks of Deep Ravine, threatening the "rear" of Company I just over Battle Ridge. In either case, a soldier charge from Red Horse's rear would, by definition, have come from *behind* him out of an unexpected quarter. This would preclude the likelihood of a charge by Companies C, L, or I, which were in his front. No other Indian narratives indicate any of these units left their position to charge anywhere.[353] The deployment of the Company C platoon, seen by Two Eagles and Fears Nothing [5:00-5:10], might be interpreted as that "charge." Upon first glance it could be considered a possibility, but it occurred a short time earlier and Red Horse would not have been presenting his backside to them.

---

352. Scott et al., *Archaeological Perspectives* (Norman: University of Oklahoma Press, 1989), 161.
353. Some researchers have depicted Company C as the unit that left the ridge to force back the Indians, but we shall show that from Indian testimony, time, terrain, casualties, and common sense, this is not the case. Fox, *Archaeology, History,* 152–54; Hardorff, *Lakota Recollections,* 139–40.

The ride of Company E fits the bill. Flying Hawk learned of its move "down a gulch." Wolf Tooth fired on it in the basin. It came against Red Horse's "rear," drove Wooden Leg out of Deep Ravine, and was seen by Antelope to have evicted a number of Indians from their forward positions.

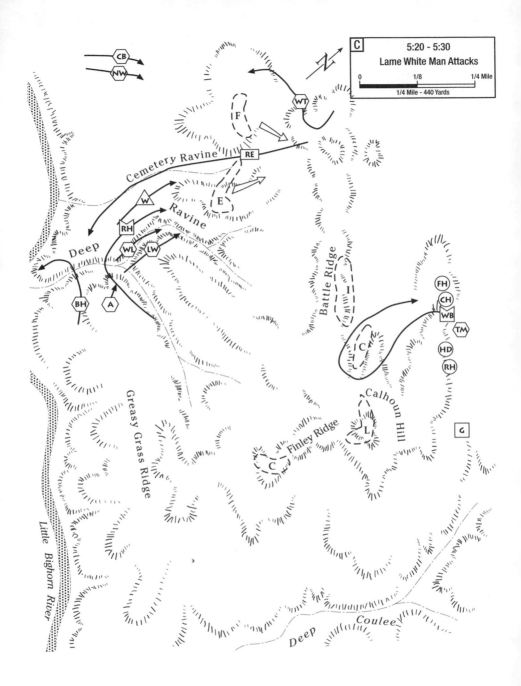

C

5:20 - 5:30
Lame White Man Attacks

0   1/8   1/4 Mile

1/4 Mile - 440 Yards

CB

NW

WT

F

Cemetery Ravine

RE

W

E

Ravine

RH

Deep

WL   LW

BH   A

Battle Ridge

I

C

FH

CH

WB

TM

HD

RH

Calhoun Hill

Greasy Grass Ridge

Finley Ridge

L

C

G

Little Bighorn River

Deep Coulee

LAME WHITE MAN ATTACKS, 5:20–5:30

WB 5:20–5:30, **White Bull** [last 5:10, next 5:30]. The stalemate in the fighting did not please White Bull. If Crazy Horse would not join him in a charge, he would go on his own. White Bull whipped up his pony and took off toward what appeared to be a gap in the soldier line. He was riding bareback, leaning low, and hugging the pony's neck.

Carbines popped down the line as White Bull took his center run. He dashed right between two troops, then cut behind one of them. At the end of their line was another gap. He cut through again and headed back, riding clear around one of the troops. He led a charmed life that day. "The soldiers shot at me but missed me," White Bull said. "I circled back to my friends." These reckless charges, bold to the point of foolhardiness, were ostentatious enough even for the proudest warrior. "I thought I would do it again," White Bull declared. Pulling up near Crazy Horse, he shouted, "Hokahey, brother! This life will not last forever!" Then he called out, "This time I will not turn back."[354]

RE 5:20–5:30, **Runs The Enemy** [last 5:10, next 5:30]. Runs The Enemy worked his way out of a coulee and up the north slope of the knoll at the far end of the ridge. A number of Indians were nearby on the crest. Below in the basin, Runs The Enemy could see the held horses of Company E. It was too tempting for many of the warriors.

"From the point that juts out just below where the monument stands," Runs The Enemy said, "about thirty of us got through the line, firing as we went, and captured a lot of Custer's horses and drove them down to the river."

The Indians, some of them very likely from Wolf Tooth's band of forty or fifty, galloped through the basin and down Cemetery Ravine, stampeding a number of Lieutenant Smith's grays and possibly some of Yates's bays. There was no need to corral them when they reached the creek. The horses were so thirsty, Runs The Enemy said, that the moment they reached the water they just stood there and drank. It was easy to get off their own ponies and catch hold of the bridles. The saddlebags were loaded with shells and blankets and all the items that the soldiers carried. It had been quite a coup.[355]

W 5:20–5:30, **Waterman** [last 5:00, next 5:30]. As Waterman closed in on the soldiers on the hill, it appeared that they must not have been keeping tight rein on their horses. Above him, amidst the noise and powder smoke, some Indians had broken through and either captured or stampeded a number of them. They came galloping down to the river, where they were caught by other Indians. Waterman noticed that they were mostly grays and a few sorrels.

Now the soldiers were on high ground, but the loss of their horses must have left them on foot and almost surrounded. Waterman, still with the Cheyennes, saw

354. Miller, "Echoes," 35; Vestal, "Man Who Killed Custer," 7, Hardorff, *Lakota Recollections*, 115.
355. Dixon, *Vanishing Race*, 175–76.

one of their chiefs, named White Man Cripple (Lame White Man), about to lead the warriors in a charge. He would join in.[356]

BH 5:20–5:30, **Bobtail Horse** [last 4:10]. The Elkhorn Scraper warrior had temporarily solved his horse problems and returned to the fight. He moved downstream in the footsteps of many of his fellow Cheyennes, keeping between the soldiers and the river. Near the far end of the field, he saw the soldiers charge the Indians.

"Their charge was from above, from the hills," Bobtail Horse said, "so that the soldiers who charged were the last two co[mpanie]s of the command." Undaunted, after the soldiers charged, the Indians charged right back toward the Gray Horse Company. At that point, the soldiers were standing in sort of an "L" formation. The Indians were on foot and behind ridges, only about forty feet from the soldiers, who were out in the open.

Some of the soldier horses got away and stampeded through the warriors, knocking them down and running some of them over, such as the son of Red War Bonnet. Only Bobtail Horse and one other Indian went after the horses. The others stayed to fight. Although the gray horses got loose and ran, they did not leave the battlefield. In hot pursuit, Bobtail Horse caught two and continued across the river at a dead run.

Back again at his lodge, he told his women to hold the horses and not to let them go. As he jumped off his pony, they saw that he was slightly wounded and seized him. His women said to him, "Since you have got away alive, we will not let you go back." Bobtail Horse had to stay and watch the rest of the fight from afar.[357]

WL 5:20–5:30, **Wooden Leg** [last 5:10, next 5:30]. When the white soldiers moved down from the ridge, the Indians fell back. Wooden Leg, without his horse, scrambled back through the gullies with them. When he looked back, however, he saw the soldiers were no longer pursuing. They had stopped along a low divide and dismounted.

Somewhat sheepishly, the warriors may have wondered about their precipitous flight. Already some had begun crawling back up the gullies. Just then, Lame White Man rode onto the scene. The old Southern Cheyenne chief had been nearby watching the Indians' retreat. There was no cause for it. Sitting tall on his horse, he

---

356. Graham, *The Custer Myth*, 110.
357. Grinnell, *Fighting Cheyennes*, 352; Powell, *Sacred Mountain*, 1020, 1023; Bobtail Horse, Notebook 348, Grinnell Collection. Confirmation that Bobtail Horse was speaking of Company E, as one of the "last two" companies of the command that made the charge down from the hill at the north end of the field, comes from several deductions. (1) All through Grinnell's notes, the Gray Horse Company and its companion (probably Company F), are referred to as "the two companies." (2) The sequence of notes immediately preceeding Bobtail Horse's narrative is told by Calf, whose narrative has brought the Gray Horse Troop up to the monument area. He begins to describe their charge, when Bobtail Horse cuts in to finish up the story. (3) Bobtail Horse said it was the Gray Horse Company that the Indians charged. (4) Bobtail Horse referred to the Gray Horse Company as being on the right when they "strung down toward R[iver]." He also said the companies "went to right" while moving along the ridge. In this context, right is north. By deduction and by direct statement, it is clearly Company E, with gray horses, that made the sortie down from the ridge on the northern part of the field, and that the Indians counterattacked.

shouted to all the warriors within earshot to come back and fight. With a bit of admonition and a large helping of brave-up talk, the warriors responded enthusiastically. Then Lame White Man raised his arm and called out that now was the time. "Come," he cried. "We can kill all of them."[358]

A 5:20–5:30, **Antelope** [last 5:10, next 5:30]. From her spot on the north end of Greasy Grass Ridge, Antelope saw the soldiers chase the Indians back into the deepest parts of the gulch or onto the ridge with her. The Cheyenne chief, Lame White Man, had been hiding close to where the soldiers had gotten off their horses on the low ridge. Now he called out to the young men, and they began creeping back to him. Antelope also heard the Oglala chiefs calling to their braves, and they too returned to the fight. Within a few minutes, hundreds of warriors were wriggling along the gullies, once more circling around the soldiers. After a little while, Antelope heard Lame White Man call out, "Young men, come now with me and show yourselves to be brave!"[359]

RH 5:20–5:30, **Red Horse** [last 5:10, next 5:30]. The soldier charge had chased the Indians back, when it suddenly lost impetus. The Lakotas stopped running and both adversaries stood facing each other, as if unsure of what action to take. The Lakotas acted first.

"Then all the Sioux became brave and charged the soldiers," Red Horse explained. The Indians advanced back up the gulches. After only a short distance, some of the bands began to separate and surround the soldiers. The long-distance firing had abruptly ended and the battle took on a new intensity.[360]

WT 5:20–5:30, **Wolf Tooth** [last 5:10, next 5:30]. On the ridge, those remaining in Wolf Tooth's and Big Foot's band continued to fight, but they had to be very careful all the time. The horse-stealing charge by thirty or more warriors had depleted their ranks, and some soldiers were returning. The bluecoats must have realized their mistake in leaving the high ground, for shortly after their move they were fired upon from the rear and they lost a number of their held horses. Despite the fire of Wolf Tooth's band, a number of soldiers returned to the hill, and the Indians had to use caution and take better cover.

Before long, Lakota criers came along behind the line, calling out to get ready and watch for the suicide boys, a group of young men who had taken a vow to fight to the death in the next battle. The criers said they were getting ready down by the river, and would soon come up and charge the soldiers. All Indians were told to wait for the suicide warriors. When they rushed in, all should then jump up together for hand-to-hand fighting. The soldiers would be attacked from two sides and would not have a chance to shoot.

Although Big Foot knew the Lakota language, many Cheyennes could not understand the criers, but individual Lakota warriors explained what had been said. Wolf Tooth pulled back from the ridge to await the suicide boys. As he peered

---

358. Marquis, *Wooden Leg*, 231.
359. Marquis, *Custer on the Little Big Horn*, 87–88.
360. Graham, *The Custer Myth*, 62.

intently through the dust, he could see them beginning to ride up from the river in the west.[361]

◄ DISCUSSION. Besides the acts of bravado by White Bull, the southern half of the battlefield was relatively static during this period. Such was not the case in the north and west. After retreating before the rush of Company E's downhill deployment, the Indians realized the "charge" was not being pressed, and they too halted in their tracks. From out of nowhere, the Indians heard the exhortation of the "old" Cheyenne chief Lame White Man. They rallied to his call.

Since he subsequently perished in the fight, Lame White Man's story is found in the narratives of his grandson, John Stands In Timber. A Southern Cheyenne, Lame White Man had been with the northern branch for so long that he, his wife, Twin Woman, and his children, Crane Woman and Red Hat, were considered part of the Northern Cheyennes. In Little Wolf's absence, Lame White Man was chosen to be the spokesman for the Elkhorn Scraper Society.

The night before, during the "dying dance," about twenty warriors, including Lakotas and several Cheyennes, had taken a suicide vow to fight to the death in the next battle. Among those Cheyenne were Cut Belly (Open Belly), son of Roman Nose; Closed Hand (Fist, or Black Bear), son of Long Roach; Limber Hand (Limber Bones), son of Horse Roads; Roman Nose (Hump Nose), son of Red Robe; Noisy Walking, son of Ice; and Little Whirlwind. The ceremony lasted long into the night.[362]

Early on the morning of the battle, the same warriors were assembled for a parade through the villages. Starting on a hill to the west of the camp, the procession wended its way across the valley. Lame White Man was up early. "I must go up there and ride down in the parade with my boys," he told Twin Woman. "I must follow my boys."

The suicide boys set out, older men riding alongside of them, shouting out their names for all to hear. Lame White Man led in the singing of one of the chief's songs, while the others joined in. Antelope also was there, proudly watching Noisy Walking. In the Cheyenne camp they paraded past the tipis, but walked in silence past the sacred buffalo hat lodge, for none were permitted to make noise close to the home of *Esevone*. The procession circled the village, and, as it cleared the camp,

---

361. Stands In Timber, *Cheyenne Memories*, 200–201; Powell, *Sweet Medicine*, 116; Powell, *Sacred Mountain*, 1027.

362. The idea of "suicide boys" in the battle is another point of contention. Sincerely believed in and documented by Stands In Timber in *Cheyenne Memories*, 60–61, 67, 87, 186, 189, 202, 225, the idea that families would let their young sons take a suicide vow is questioned by contemporary authors. See Hardorff, *Hokahey!*, 41, and Welch, *Killing Custer*, 172. Yet, self-sacrifice was not at all unknown. There were instances when a warrior would stake himself out on a battlefield to die so that others might live. In Hassrick, *The Sioux*, 32, 74, 100, 294, we are told that it was a Lakota maxim that it was better to die in battle than to live to be old, that war demanded sacrifice, that sacrifice of life could be worth the price, and that even self-destruction was a proven method of securing recognition from one's fellow men as well as from the gods. Perhaps "suicide boys" was just a poor translation of a Native American concept whites could not easily understand. Whatever one wishes to call these young boys, they certainly did their "job," as we shall see.

the singing began again until the people marched back to their starting point. With the ceremonies concluded, all departed for their tipis, while Antelope went with another woman to the Minneconjou camp and Lame White Man joined his friend Tall Sioux for a bath in his sweat lodge near the river.

Thus were they engaged when the soldiers struck. Lame White Man returned to his lodge to clear his family away from danger. There he found Twin Woman, his son Red Hat, and his daughter Crane Woman, almost ready to travel. Still stripped from the sweat bath, Lame White Man had no time to put on his proper war clothing. He wrapped a blanket around his waist, grabbed a belt, moccasins, and a gun, and jumped on his horse. The family dashed off, heading for the hills.

The Cheyenne Lame White Man is shown sitting next to Wild Hog in an 1873 photo. He led a charge against Company E north of Deep Ravine. —Nebraska State Historical Society

About halfway there, Lame White Man had a change of heart. He called to his wife, "I must go across the river. I must follow my boys."[363] Leaving his family, he turned and rode to the battle. By that time, Custer was approaching the ford. Lame White Man joined up with Bobtail Horse, White Shield, Roan Bear, and a few others.[364] He cautioned them against rashness. But the young warriors did not heed him. Perhaps stung by their remarks about being overly cautious, Lame White Man may have resolved then and there to prove to himself and to all who could see that, at thirty-seven years of age, he was still a warrior to be reckoned with. After the soldiers pulled back from the river, Lame White Man made his way north. He was in the Deep Ravine area when Company E made its sally, forcing the Indians back.

Now was the time to show he was not an old man, but still a brave who could fight with the best of them. The warriors milling around rallied to Lame White Man's challenge. Up the gullies and around the ridges he led them. In minutes, hundreds of Indians began to encircle E Troop in its vulnerable position. Bobtail Horse said that the Indians got as close as forty feet to the exposed soldiers. Companies L and C had repulsed the first concerted rush of warriors south of Calhoun Hill about a half hour earlier, but this second major assault was not to be denied.

The move of Company E from the hilltop left a vacuum in the basin behind the lines. Wolf Tooth and Big Foot took advantage of the situation by moving to the ridgeline to fire down on the troopers. Better yet, an opportunity opened up for Runs The Enemy and about thirty others to charge down from an unexpected quarter and cut out a number of held horses. Waterman saw the grays going to the river, and Bobtail Horse was able to catch two after Lame White Man's charge.

---

363. Stands In Timber, *Cheyenne Memories*, 194–96; Powell, *Sacred Mountain*, 1005–7, 1009, 1019–20.

364. The confusion of Indian names at times is no more evident than with Lame White Man. During this incident he was identified as Mad Wolf, Mad Hearted Wolf, and Rabid Wolf. He has also been called White Man Cripple, Walking White Man, Bearded Man, and Moustache. Bobtail Horse even confused him with Dull Knife. In Hardorff, *Memories*, 52, Mad Wolf was identified as a 51-year-old Cheyenne who survived the fight, to later die in 1905. Some of this confusion may stem from Hardorff's misreading of Grinnell's handwritten notes. For instance, one statement by White Shield (p. 58) is scribed as: "White Bull's son, Mad Wolf or Limber Bones, charged among the soldiers and was killed." In a following footnote, Hardorff faults White Shield for mistaking Mad Wolf or Limber Bones for White Bull's (Ice's) son, then tells us Noisy Walking was White Bull's son. Certainly White Shield already knew this, and this was *not* what he was saying. The actual handwritten notes appear as: "W[hite] B[ull's] son, Mad Wolf & Limber Lance charged among [the] sold[iers] & were killed." Clearly White Shield was talking about three individuals whom we know were killed: White Bull's son (Noisy Walking), Mad Wolf (Lame White Man), and Limber Lance (Limber Bones or Limber Hand). The fact that Lame White Man was also called Mad Wolf by the Indians is also borne out in Little Hawk's narrative (Little Hawk, Notebook 348, Grinnell Collection). He said Mad Hearted Wolf, or Rabid Wolf, was always in the front of the fighting. He was killed in the Custer fight and was found dead in the very midst of the soldiers. The Sioux took him for a scout and scalped him, but when they found he was a Cheyenne they brought the scalp back. As we shall see, this corresponds almost perfectly with information supplied by those such as Wooden Leg, Tall Bull, and Standing Bear when speaking about Lame White Man. Willis Rowland (Long Forehead) also reported that Thunder Walking (Noisy Walking) and Walking White Man (Lame White Man) rode into the midst of the troops and were killed (Hardorff, *Memories*, 143). In addtion, the fact that Lame White Man was also known as Mad Wolf was amply demonstrated by Peter Powell in *Sacred Mountain*, 1020.

Quickly, Yates or Custer must have seen that this was an unacceptable situation and sent a platoon, possibly elements of both companies, back to the high ground recently vacated by Company E. Wolf Tooth made note of the move, for he told of men fighting their way back to the hilltop, moving in fits and starts, covering each other as they returned. Now there were soldiers in the basin and on the hilltop, and his band had to exercise more care when shooting and exposing themselves to the soldier fire.

Custer had formed a perimeter, albeit a poor one, thinly manned or completely unmanned in some sectors. He was on the defensive. From this point on, the situation deteriorated rapidly for the men in blue, while the Indians fully seized the initiative they would not relinquish.

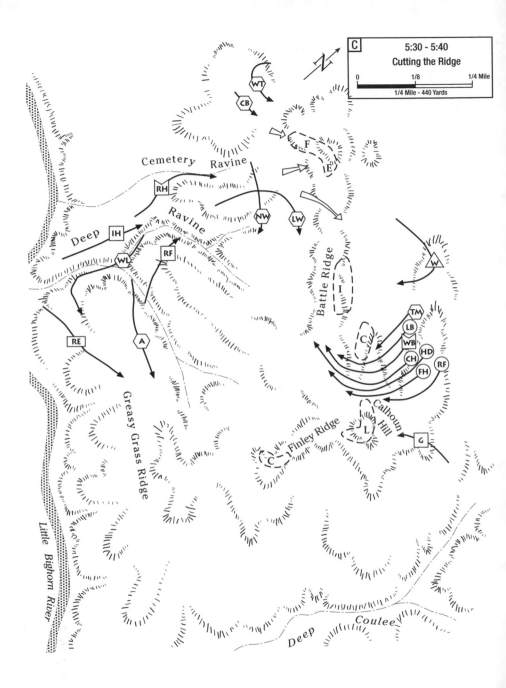

WT

CB

Cemetery   Ravine

RH

F

E

Deep

IH   Ravine

NW   LW

WL

RF

W

Battle Ridge

I

C

TM

LB

WB

HD

CH

FH

RF

RE

A

Calhoun Hill

L

G

Greasy Grass Ridge

Finley Ridge

C

Little Bighorn River

Deep   Coulee

CUTTING THE RIDGE, 5:30–5:40

A 5:30–5:40, **Antelope** [last 5:20, next 5:40]. When Lame White Man called the braves to him, Indians on all sides of the soldiers jumped up. There were hundreds of them, more than Antelope thought could hide in the gullies. There must have been twenty Indians for every soldier. Their charge frightened the trooper's horses and they broke for the river.

Antelope saw one soldier panic and shoot himself in the head with his revolver. Then another did the same, and another. By the time the Indians got close enough to count coup on a living enemy, not many soldiers were left to fight.

The day was hot and the soldier horses ran to the river to drink, where they were captured by warriors as well as by the women and old men. The warriors remaining on the hillside were able to get many guns and cartridges from the dead soldiers. With these they went crawling to different parts of the ridge where the main body of soldiers still fought.

Antelope had been singing strongheart songs for her nephew, hoping he would hear her, but she still had not seen him. Suddenly her heart thumped in fear when she saw a warrior leading a horse with a wounded rider. She thought he looked like Noisy Walking and she galloped closer to the two men. However, both of them were Lakotas. Frustrated and anxious, she decided to head to the fight on the east end of the ridge.[365]

WL 5:30–5:40, **Wooden Leg** [last 5:20, next 5:40]. Lame White Man's words helped the warriors rally. All around, the Indians began jumping up, running, dodging, going down, and running again toward the soldiers. To Wooden Leg, it looked like many of the whites went crazy, turning their guns on themselves instead of shooting at the Indians. Yet, the fighting was deadly for a number of Indians. Cut Belly was mortally wounded while riding across the level cemetery area, and Noisy Walking and Lame White Man also took bullets during the attack. Wooden Leg said about fifteen Indians were killed by Custer's men, and "more of them fell during the first close fighting, when Lame White Man led us and himself was killed, down toward the river, than fell at any other one section of the field."

But the battle was over almost before it began. The Indians took the guns of the soldiers and used them to shoot at the others on the high ridge. Wooden Leg didn't follow through with the charge, but went back down the gulch to look for his horse.[366]

RH 5:30–5:40, **Red Horse** [last 5:20]. When the Lakotas got their courage up, they went after the soldiers in a solid body. After going but a short distance they separated, spread out, and encircled the soldiers. Red Horse saw the white officers riding in front of their men, and could hear them shouting out orders.

365. Marquis, *Custer on the Little Big Horn*, 88–89.
366. Marquis, *Wooden Leg*, 231–32, 268, 379.

Even though virtually surrounded, the soldiers put up a stiff resistance, for it was in this charge that the Lakotas lost most of their men. Red Horse thought that 136 Indians were killed and 160 were wounded in that phase of the battle. Regardless, the soldiers were overwhelmed. "We finished up this party right there in the ravine," Red Horse declared.

The Lakotas were able to take the guns and cartridges off the dead soldiers. Red Horse got a gun and two ammunition belts, with only about seven cartridges missing. Now they were better armed and were able to turn their attention to the remaining soldiers on the hill.[367]

WT 5:30–5:40, **Wolf Tooth** [last 5:20]. Wolf Tooth had pulled back to watch for the suicide warriors. They rode up from below, near the river, and burst onto the scene over the level ground of what is now the Custer National Cemetery. At this time, the soldiers were grouped in the basin and near where the monument now stands. Some of the suicide warriors coming from the north turned and stampeded the soldiers' gray horses. Others rushed right in to attack the soldiers. At the same time, Indians coming from the south out of the Deep Ravine frightened more of the gray horses.

With a number of bluecoats engaged in hand-to-hand fighting, the Indians with Wolf Tooth were able to approach the ridge again and fire into the melee from another quarter. Some soldiers who still had horses attempted to mount them and ride up to the hilltop, but most were cut off. Right behind the suicide boys followed more warriors, including Lame White Man, mounted conspicuously on his pony. They rushed in with hatchets, spears, clubs, and rifles. The fighting was furious and there was little time for anyone to take careful aim. Soldiers ran uphill, downhill, and under the edge of the ridge, scattering to one side or the other.

In the confusion, Closed Hand was quickly killed, Noisy Walking received a mortal wound, and Lame White Man went through the soldiers in the basin only to fall near the ridge crest. Wolf Tooth thought it was quite a mess. "All I could see were tomahawks, hatchets, and guns raised above the heads of the warriors through the dust," he said. The dying soldiers moaned, "How! How!" but the warriors never understood what they meant. They just killed them.[368]

RF 5:30–5:40, **Rain In The Face** [last 5:00, next 6:10(a)]. Having broken free from the spell cast by Tashenamani on some of the warriors, Rain In The Face moved north with the flow of battle. By this time it appeared that the troops were surrounded, with Indians on two sides and the river on the third. Rain In The Face heard the order to charge. "There were many very young men, some of whom had only a war staff or a stone war club in hand," he observed. These young braves "plunged into the column, knocking the men over and stampeding their horses."

The soldiers had mounted up and started back, but when the charge began they were forced to dismount and fight. The white companies were "separated into

367. Graham, *The Custer Myth*, 60, 62.
368. Stands In Timber, *Cheyenne Memories*, 201; Hardorff, *Memories*, 170–71; Powell, *Sacred Mountain*, 1027–28; Powell, *Sweet Medicine*, 117. According to Powell, Closed Hand (Fist or Black Bear) the suicide warrior, is not to be confused with Black Bear, the Cheyenne council chief.

general divisions, facing different ways." Rain In The Face saw them firing their guns as fast as they could load them, while the Indians chiefly used arrows and war clubs. Through the confusion and swirl of battle, Rain In The Face noted that there seemed to be two distinct methods of movement among the Indians. "One body moved continually in a circle, while the other rode directly into and through the troops."[369]

IH 5:30–5:40, **Iron Hawk** [last 4:20, next 5:40]. It had been quite a while since Iron Hawk watched the Indians cross over at the ford and go up after the soldiers. He rode north down the valley with a contingent of Hunkpapas. Across the river, he could see Custer riding along and the Indians starting to surround him. He stopped at the foot of a deep gulch that led down from Custer Hill and ran into the Little Bighorn. Many Hunkpapas congregated there.

Although the ravine was an avenue for the Hunkpapas to make their way up to the battlefield, Iron Hawk continued to hang back. After all, he was still young, only fourteen years of age, and it was not expected that he be in the forefront of the battle. Eventually, however, Iron Hawk crossed over and cautiously worked his way up until he got on the field between the ridge and the river. Others of his tribe, such as Rain In The Face, were also in the fight nearby.[370]

RE 5:30–5:40, **Runs The Enemy** [last 5:20, next 5:40]. At the river, Runs The Enemy let the cavalry mounts drink while rummaging through their saddlebags. He was able to take some cartridges but would have to leave the horses behind if he was to return to his men and get back in the fight.

He rode upriver and then east, completely circling Custer's position by the time he returned to his warriors. The soldiers were still on the hill fighting, a number of them with their horses held nearby.[371]

WB 5:30–5:40, **White Bull** [last 5:20, next 5:40]. Immediately after announcing his intention of cutting through the soldier line a second time, White Bull kicked his pony and sprang forward. His reckless courage was infectious, and Crazy Horse and the other warriors were not to be outdone. The Lakotas swept forward.

White Bull ran at the last company near Calhoun Hill before cutting to the ridge crest toward a gap in the line. The many Lakotas who joined in the charge seemed to break the soldiers' courage. Amid the dust and confusion, the Indians were able to ride in among the soldiers and pull them right off their horses.

It was a wonderful opportunity to count many coups. For the Lakota brave, the striking of a blow upon an enemy was the most glorious deed he could perform, and his rating would depend on the number of coups he could gather. The first strike was the greatest honor, and the man who had done that could wear an eagle feather upright in his hair. Shooting or scalping an enemy were creditable, but not as honorable as a coup.

369. Eastman, "Rain-In-The-Face," 18.
370. Hardorff, *Lakota Recollections*, 66–67; DeMallie, *Sixth Grandfather*, 190.
371. Dixon, *Vanishing Race*, 176.

The area east of Battle Ridge where Crazy Horse and White Bull led the charge that cut the soldier line. Gravemarkers of Company I men appear in the background.

White Bull found many an opportunity on this run. He first saw a soldier get hit by a bullet and waver in his saddle. White Bull quirted his pony, but the soldier fell to the ground just as he got there. He jumped off his pony, struck the soldier with his quirt, and yelled "Onhey! I have overcome this one!" He gathered up the man's pistol and cartridges.

Indians galloped past. White Bull hurriedly mounted and came upon a soldier on a played-out horse. The man tried to spin around with his carbine and take aim, but White Bull was too quick. He grabbed the trooper by the shoulder of his blue coat and jerked him off his horse. The carbine fired into the air, the man screamed and fell to the ground. White Bull had another coup. Behind him he noticed Crazy Horse charging up to strike the man for the second time.

White Bull burst over the hogback of the ridge between the second and third companies and rode to the west side. He could see that the attack had forced some of the first company to run toward the second, while the third company (Keogh's) started south in the direction of the first two.

The sorrels and bays crossing madly to and fro drew White Bull into a horse chase. He was about to capture one when another Indian cut him off and took the prize. Instead, White Bull spied a soldier on foot, threatening Indians on all sides with his carbine. He charged straight at him. The soldier fired and missed. White Bull rode him down and counted a third coup. The Lakota Bear Lice followed up with a second strike.

By this time the third company stopped its southern move. Some crossed the ridge to head downhill, possibly to join another bunch fighting nearer the river (the fourth company of grays), while others moved north toward the far end of the ridge. The braves around White Bull were in a battle frenzy, dashing madly about, striking targets of opportunity and yelling "Try!" to keep encouraging each other.

Just then, White Bull's pony went down from bullets in the shoulder and ribs. Suddenly he found himself on foot in the midst of this chaotic battle swirling about him.[372]

RF 5:30–5:40, **Red Feather** [last 5:00, next 5:40]. The adversaries had been lying there for some time shooting at each other. The stalemate abruptly ended, however, when Crazy Horse came up on horseback. He blew on his eagle bone horn, and just that quickly the Indians were off.

Red Feather, still on foot, watched Crazy Horse ride between the two parties. The soldiers fired, but could not hit him. The Indians got the idea that the soldiers had emptied their guns, and they immediately followed in Crazy Horse's wake. "They charged right over the hill," Red Feather declared.[373]

LB 5:30–5:40, **Lone Bear** [last 4:10, next 5:40]. Lone Bear had seen the soldiers coming down from the high ground to the east. Indians had crossed the river to meet them, but Lone Bear returned to his lodge to look for his pony. By the time he returned to the fight, the soldiers had gathered in a body around Calhoun Hill. They reached the long ridge first and the Indians followed behind.

Lone Bear went up Deep Coulee and then along the north side of the long ridge, where he joined in with Crazy Horse's band. When the Oglala leader made his run, Lone Bear joined in the charge. He cut across the ridge about halfway between where Keogh's company fought and Last Stand Hill.[374]

TM 5:30–5:40, **Two Moon** [last 5:10, next 5:40]. Two Moon and his followers had pulled up for a rest after crossing to the east side of the ridge. There they fell in with the Lakotas, and the Cheyennes and Lakotas each took turns making runs at the soldiers.

Two Moon reloaded his gun and they were ready. They fired into the first troop (Keogh's), which was very nearby. Then they went forward. Two Moon said that in the first big charge, when all the Indians swept in together, it appeared that nearly one whole band of soldiers was killed.[375]

---

372. Hardorff, *Lakota Recollections*, 114–16, 124; White Bull, Box 105, Notebook 24, Campbell Collection; Vestal, "Man Who Killed Custer," 7–8; Miller, "Echoes," 36.
373. Hardorff, *Lakota Recollections*, 87–88.
374. Ibid., 156, 158.
375. Ibid., 137; Dixon, *Vanishing Race*, 181–82.

W 5:30–5:40, **Waterman** [last 5:20, next 6:10(a)]. Waterman continued over the ridge in the wake of Lame White Man's assault. "The soldiers were on the high ground," he said, "and in one of the first charges we made a Cheyenne Chief named White Man Cripple was killed."

Now on the east slope, Waterman noted that Two Moon then took command and led the Cheyennes through the rest of the fight. On this side of the field, watching through the air heavy with powder smoke, Waterman saw the Indians dashing by on horseback, hugging close to the sides of their ponies so the soldiers' bullets would not find them. He saw Crazy Horse riding up close to the soldiers, yelling to his warriors. All the bluecoats were shooting at him, but he was never hit. Waterman thought Crazy Horse was the bravest man he ever saw.[376]

HD 5:30–5:40, **He Dog** [last 4:20, next 5:40]. After He Dog helped to drive the soldiers away from the ford, the action moved rapidly away from him. The soldiers stayed mounted and kept moving. They were "all together all [of the] time," and did not fight by companies as they moved to Custer Ridge.

The soldiers stopped along that ridge, one group (Keogh's) taking position in the hollow on the slope away from the river. By this time the Indians had finally gotten all around, and He Dog reentered the battle.

The fighting began in the Finley area and kept up all along. About midway along the ridge from Calhoun Hill to where the monument now stands was a small gap at the crest. At this point, He Dog joined Crazy Horse in a charge that broke right through the soldier lines, cutting them in two. Fighting was going on everywhere.[377]

G 5:30–5:40, **Gall** [last 5:00, next 5:40]. Gall reached the Calhoun Hill area after the first Indian charge had been repulsed. He helped in the effort to stampede the soldiers' horses, but the bluecoats tenaciously kept their hilltop positions, with Calhoun's men fighting as skirmishers. There was a temporary stalemate with neither side giving way.

Gall and the other warriors steadily closed in on Calhoun's knoll. A large number of them dismounted and advanced up the slope far enough to be able to see the soldiers while standing, but protected when lying down. They jumped up, fired quickly to expose themselves only for an instant, then ducked back down. Thus they drew the soldiers' fire and made them waste their ammunition.

Gall gathered his followers under the protection of the slope. When all was ready, he signaled to them. The dismounted warriors rose to fire, the mounted Indians whipped their ponies forward, and every voice could be heard calling out the war whoop. The whole mass of warriors rushed upon the troopers defending Calhoun Hill.[378]

376. Graham, *The Custer Myth*, 110.
377. Hammer, *Custer in '76*, 207; Hardorff, *Lakota Recollections*, 75.
378. Benham, "Warrior's Revenge," 462; Graham, *The Custer Myth*, 91, 95.

← DISCUSSION. In the north, the combination Lame White Man–suicide attack had overwhelmed Company E on the low divide between Cemetery Ravine and Deep Ravine. A few fugitives may have run for cover in Deep Ravine, but the majority of survivors fought their way back uphill. The suicide boys, striking hardest against what may have been a platoon of Company F on the present-day cemetery grounds, also forced their fugitives to retreat back to what would become Last Stand (Custer) Hill. The fury of their attack was attested to by Wolf Tooth and Rain In The Face.

Although the execution was over quickly, it was not all one-sided. Wooden Leg said Open (Cut) Belly went down in the vicinity of the "stone lodge" on the present cemetery grounds. He said Noisy Walking was also hit during the charge, making his way into the upper reaches of Deep Ravine before collapsing, later to be found by friends and relatives, still clinging to life. Lame White Man himself rode nearly to the ridge top before being hit. The spot of Noisy Walking's mortal wounding was marked by the Cheyennes, which, according to John Stands In Timber, was about 150 feet south of the present-day marker set for his grandfather, Lame White Man.[379] These sites were three to four hundred yards south of the present monument, on the river side of the crest of Battle Ridge.

Many more Indians became casualties. Wooden Leg thought about fifteen Indians were killed on Custer's field, and most of them were hit in the Lame White Man assault. Red Horse said a total of 296 warriors were killed or wounded in this episode. Although his numbers are grossly exaggerated, his perception of a great killing indicates the action was deadly and a significant number of Indians became victims of the soldiers' fire. Some writers have placed this scene late in the fight, but the large number of Indian casualties associated with it precludes its occurrence in the mop-up stages of the battle.

The placement of Lame White Man's attack has been the subject of controversy. For many years it was assumed that he assaulted troops on the divide between Cemetery Ravine and Deep Ravine, down the slope from Custer Hill, where we have placed it. Of late, however, that view has been challenged, the revisionists placing the attack in Calhoun Coulee against elements of Company C.[380] As much as I would like to be in tune with this revisionism, and as much as I have challenged established conventions in this examination, I do not find that the historical record justifies shifting the attack site. The old explanation still follows most closely with the Indian narratives.

Wooden Leg's account has been studied in regard to the Lame White Man attack more thoroughly in another work,[381] but a summary of those arguments is

---

379. Stands In Timber, *Cheyenne Memories*, 204; Powell, *Sweet Medicine*, 119.
380. The traditional placement of Lame White Man's attack has been advanced by many historians, including Thomas B. Marquis, Charles Kuhlman, William A. Graham, Robert M. Utley, Peter J. Powell, Neil C. Mangum, Douglas D. Scott, and the Cheyenne tribal historian John Stands In Timber. The revisionist interpretation has been forwarded by Richard A. Fox Jr. and Richard G. Hardorff, and a map showing Lame White Man attacking in Calhoun Coulee appears in the national park's own 1988 edition of the Custer Battlefield Handbook.
381. Gregory Michno, *The Mystery of E Troop: Custer's Gray Horse Company at the Little Bighorn* (Missoula, MT: Mountain Press, 1994), 268–73.

appropriate here. First, Wooden Leg said the Lame White Man assault took place inside the present fence around the field and at its lower side. When Wooden Leg gave this information to Dr. Marquis, there was a fence entirely around the field and across Deep Ravine. Lower, in battlefield context, is at the end opposite the Calhoun Coulee–Finley Ridge side—north, not south. Second, Wooden Leg said the soldiers who moved downhill stopped on a low ridge. The Finley Ridge area where some of Company C's men were found is on some of the highest terrain on the field, rising 40 to 60 feet above Greasy Grass Ridge and 120 feet above Deep Coulee. Third, Wooden Leg went to the east end of the field after the Lame White Man attack. He was not already at the east end. Fourth, Wooden Leg said the troopers killed by Lame White Man's attack were killed in the ravine where he later found Noisy Walking, which was in the Deep Ravine watershed, not Calhoun Coulee. Fifth, Wooden Leg found Lame White Man's body after walking up the coulee where he had discovered Noisy Walking, another corroboration of the Deep Ravine watershed site. Sixth, Thomas Marquis was the interpreter for Wooden Leg and a dozen other Cheyennes. They told him where the Lame White Man attack took place: against soldiers on a low ridge "about 500 yards down the gulch slope from the present monument."[382] All these considerations verify the conventional interpretation as correct. Our discussion (5:40) of artifacts on Calhoun Hill will further support tradition.

Likewise, the Antelope (Kate Bighead) narrative has been used to support the new interpretation. The revision received a boost when anthropologist Richard A. Fox Jr. suddenly realized that many Indians visualized Battle Ridge as lying on an east-west axis, whereas most whites viewed it in north-south terms (it actually runs northwest to southeast).[383] Fox reasoned that because Kate saw the ridge as lying east-west, the ridge that the troopers (Company E or C) rode to could not have been the divide north of the Deep Ravine, because Kate's "north" was actually "east," and east was to the Calhoun Hill side.[384]

It does appear that Antelope viewed the ridge as running east-west, but this does not alter her description of the terrain. In the course of her search for Noisy Walking, she circumnavigated Battle Ridge, stopping south of the ridge to watch the fight. There she saw a troop gallop down to a low ridge just north of the deep gulch. No matter which angle one tilts Battle Ridge, if it lies east-west and Antelope said she stopped south of it, then her position must be about ninety degrees removed from both the east and west ends, somewhere to the river side of the ridge and about midway between the two points. Likewise, north would be directly across the ridge, about midway between the east and west ends. From the south side she saw the troop go to a low ridge north of the deep gulch. From her probable vantage point, Company E would be in the direction of Custer Hill, on a low ridge north of the deep gulch (actually northwest of Antelope's position). Also from that spot, Company C would be in the direction of Calhoun Hill, on a high

---

382. Marquis, *Last Bullet*, 159.
383. Andrew Ward, "The Little Bighorn," *American Heritage* 43, no. 2 (April 1992): 84. Fox said, "As soon as I figured that out, it was like the gears in a clock slipping into place."
384. Fox, *Archaeology, History*, 149–51.

ridge and not across any deep gulch (actually northeast of Antelope's position). Fox's insistence that when Kate said "south" she really meant "west," and when she said "north" she really meant "east," becomes rather strained.

What is important here is to view Antelope's testimony either in all-white or all-Indian terms. We cannot shift between the two at our convenience. No matter how *we* visualize the ridge—east-west or north-south—it is clear that Antelope was between Battle Ridge and the river, with the deep gulch in front of her. She saw Lame White Man attack a troop on a low ridge on the far side of the deep gulch. The only site that fits the description is the spot where Marquis's Cheyenne informants told him the event occurred: five hundred yards below the present monument on Custer Hill. Wolf Tooth showed John Stands In Timber where the attack occurred: in the basin near the Deep Ravine after the Gray Horse troop moved down from the hill. George Grinnell's informants, Bobtail Horse and Calf, also told him the Gray Horse Company was near the monument when they attacked and were counterattacked by the Indians.

Some evidence for a Lame White Man assault in the Finley-Calhoun area comes from the Cheyenne Red Bird. In 1918 he told Walter Camp that the Indians followed Custer after he passed the upper reaches of Medicine Tail Coulee. Camp's notes (see fig. 10) read: "Only line on Custer ridge was from C to D. I was there Lame White Man charged them here & chased them to Keogh where he (L.W.M.) was killed."[385] Unfortunately, we are again faced with the problems of Camp's alphabetical map references and wonder how true to reality Red Bird's statements were in relation to the letters on the map. Red Bird (Young Little Wolf) also told Grinnell that he couldn't see much of the battle because he had lost his horses. Another account that possibly places Lame White Man near Yellow Nose in the Calhoun area is a 1929 interview between Walter Campbell and Young Two Moon, where the text reads that the Walking White party made the first charge, "side of hill."[386] However, the Cheyennes interviewed by Grinnell do not mention Lame White Man in the fighting around Calhoun Hill, but they do refer several times to Yellow Nose, Contrary Belly, or Comes In Sight as being the leading protagonists in that phase of the battle.

Red Horse also made note of the very large number of Indian casualties in the Deep Ravine–Cemetery Ravine area and around Custer Hill. In addition to Cut Belly, Noisy Walking, and Lame White Man, other Indians killed in the area include Closed Hand (Black Bear), Limber Bones, Red Horn Buffalo, and Black White Man.[387] Contrast this to the lack of Indian casualties associated with the Calhoun Coulee–Finley Ridge–Calhoun Hill area. The sector that appears well defended in the historical record actually had very few associated Indian casualties. Hump and Long Elk were wounded in the vicinity, but no named deaths were recorded there. In fact, most of the wounds and deaths occurred in the north. Richard Hardorff's study of Indian casualties inadvertently confirms this. Of the

---

385. "Camp Mss.," IU, Folder 5, Box 7.
386. Young Little Wolf, Notebook 346, Grinnell Collection, Hardorff, *Memories*, 155.
387. Marquis, *Wooden Leg*, 268; Stands In Timber, *Cheyenne Memories*, 204; DeMallie, *Sixth Grandfather*, 191, 194.

locations of the sixteen kills in the Custer fight, nine are listed as "unknown," and of the remaining seven, none are placed in the Calhoun-Finley area.[388] Therefore the revisionist interpretation of the Lame White Man attack site would make his assault virtually bloodless. Wooden Leg told us a different story. He said almost all of the Indians killed were hit in the first close fighting during the Lame White Man attack, more "than fell at any other one section of the field."[389] With the possible exception of the unnamed Indian who Eagle Elk saw hit in the head, no Indian death sites were recorded on the southern half of the field where the revisionists place the attack. Time, terrain, casualties, and interlocking historical narratives point to the fact that Lame White Man attacked a troop in the Cemetery Ravine–Deep Ravine area, not in the Calhoun Coulee–Finley Ridge area.[390]

We might approach the question of the Lame White Man attack site on a different tack. What would the consequences have been if he did attack in the south? First, there should have been some Indian deaths there. Had the attack bowled over the Company C platoon on Finley Ridge, the Indians would quickly have been in the rear of Company L on Calhoun Hill, which, being surrounded, would have collapsed within minutes. There would have been no profusion of Indian .44 Henry cartridges near the Calhoun Hill crest (fig. 12-A). White Bull and Crazy Horse would not have made a run at the "last" company before cutting the soldier line because there would have been no line left there to cut. White Bull would not have subsequently crested the ridge to see the grays finishing their retreat from below Custer Hill, because Lame White Man would not have attacked them below Custer Hill. Without the assault, Wolf Tooth would not have seen the grays fight their way back uphill. Lame White Man's body probably would have been found in Calhoun Coulee instead of three hundred yards from Custer Hill. All the casualties Red Horse associated with the Deep Ravine watershed would not have been there. All the dead bodies of men and horses found on the slopes of Custer Hill, positioned in response to an attack from the west and south, would not have been there but would probably have been discovered on the south and east slopes instead.

The horse barricades and the positions of the dead on the slopes of Custer Hill are very strong arguments for the Lame White Man attack occurring in that sector. Companies E and F were not overwhelmed solely by about twenty hyperactive teenagers with a death wish. The southwest slope of Custer Hill graphically

---

388. Hardorff, *Hokahey!*, 82. Hardorff may believe a furious fight occurred around Calhoun Hill, but his own casualty study belies that conclusion. This is developed further in the 6:10B discussion segment.

389. Marquis, *Wooden Leg*, 379.

390. The Park Service, according to former chief historian Douglas C. McChristian, changed its official depiction of the Lame White Man attack to the Calhoun Coulee location because of archaeological data and a re-examination of Indian accounts. I do not find that the evidence, old or new, warrants the change. But perhaps there were other considerations. McChristian wrote, "The Service has an obligation to the public to give them a return, if you will, on their investment in the archaeology projects. If the public does not benefit by solid new evidence, then one must question the justification for such projects." Certainly, public funding is important for continued research, but we must wonder about the accuracy of historical interpretation when it stems from a bureaucracy that has on its agenda a desire to give the public a "return" in order to keep money flowing in to finance the next project. Douglas C. McChristian, Crow Agency, MT, to Greg Michno, Westland, MI, 3 August 1992.

illustrates that there was a hell of a fight—a fight continuing for quite some time before the flotsam of Companies C, I, and L arrived. The defenders of Custer Hill were not concerned with events to the north, east, and southeast while fighting for their lives against a threat from the west and southwest.[391] The very positions of the dead below Last Stand Hill is a reductio ad absurdum to the Lame White Man–Calhoun Coulee attack argument.

About the time Lame White Man and the suicide boys were finishing driving the troopers back to the ridge, the White Bull–Crazy Horse ride began. Significant numbers of Indians participated in or witnessed the charge. While the first attack on Calhoun Hill failed, this one succeeded, perhaps because it was more concentrated or better led, or perhaps because it wasn't an attack at all in the strict sense of the word, but rather an episode of derring-do, its purpose only to show off the bravery of each individual warrior. Whatever the actual motive, many mounted warriors split the soldier line, likely between Companies L and C, and then continued to the crest and over the ridge. The warriors were probably surprised by the ease of their feat. A bravery run turned into a major penetration. There was no need to rush back, dodging bullets in a deadly game of cat-and-mouse. Here was an opportunity to wreak havoc on the shocked troopers. While Lame White Man had disrupted Companies E and F in the north, the survivors were able to stabilize the situation by taking position on what was to become Last Stand Hill. The White Bull–Crazy Horse penetration was not to be remedied. It marked the beginning of the rapid deterioration of Custer's ephemeral perimeter. If the Indians could exploit their advantage, there would be many coups yet to be counted.

---

391. For a thorough discussion of this topic, see Bruce A. Trinque, "The Defense of Custer Hill," *Research Review: The Journal of the Little Big Horn Associates* 8, no. 2 (June 1994): 21–31.

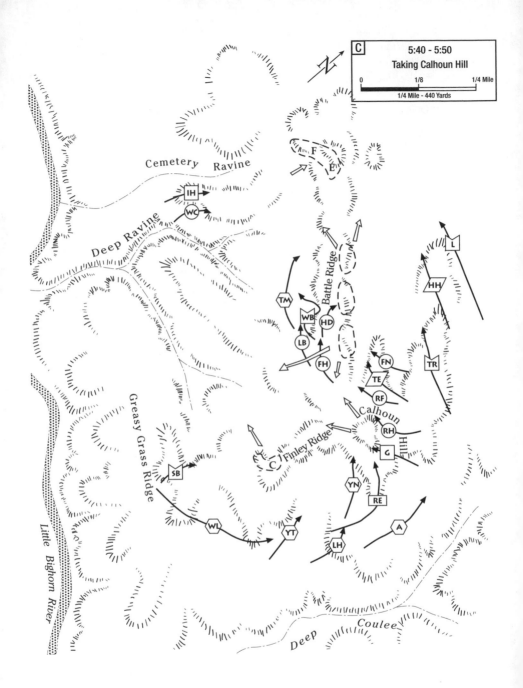

Cemetery   Ravine

Deep Ravine

IH

WC

F

E

Battle Ridge

TM

WB

HD

LB

FH

L

HH

FN

TE

TR

RF

Calhoun

RH

G

Finley Ridge

C

SB

YN

RE

WL

YT

LH

A

Greasy Grass Ridge

Little Bighorn River

Deep   Coulee

TAKING CALHOUN HILL, 5:40–5:50

YN 5:40–5:50, **Yellow Nose** [last 4:20, next 6:00]. Ever since he had helped force back the soldiers near the ford, Yellow Nose had been conspicuous in his bravery. The Indians had been trying to get in the rear of the troops and gain the cover of the east slope of the ridge that the soldiers held. However, the bluecoats held the ground to their advantage, and the Indians, in trying to dislodge them, exposed themselves to a galling fire.

At first, the soldiers knelt to take deliberate aim, with every fourth man holding the horses. As the confusion increased, many soldiers took their own horses to be ready in case the battle went against them. Unfortunately for the soldiers, the horses grew wild with fright and their rearing and plunging made it impossible for the soldiers to shoot accurately. Some hobbled their horses. When the Indians charged through the line there was no time to cut the hobbles and man after man was killed beside his horse.

The troopers shifted around on the high ground. Some moved toward the river and some away from it. Others drew together. The men, now on foot, moved north along the ridge trying to reach the Gray Horse troopers at the far end. Finally, the soldiers who had held the east slope of the ridge for much of the battle were driven to the west slope.

Yellow Nose, although he later gave away his captured guidon to a woman, had been making good use of it during the fight. As the Indians dashed through the soldiers' lines, Yellow Nose charged after the fleeing troopers, striking them left and right with the guidon, counting many coups. Contrary Belly and Brave Bear rode nearby, inspired by his courage.

The soldiers raced headlong down the straight ridge, turning their backs to the charging Indians. The warriors rode in among the troopers. Now, many warriors in addition to Yellow Nose were striking the running men with their quirts and lances.[392]

YT 5:40–5:50, **Young Two Moon** [last 4:50, next 5:50]. After catching his horse, Young Two Moon moved closer to the fight. He saw the Indians struggling up the gulch northeast of the soldiers like ants rushing out of a hill. There were several charges made but no real fighting had been done.

Young Two Moon got close enough to identify Yellow Nose. The Ute-Cheyenne made two dashes toward the soldiers, but swung back to his people, encouraging them, calling out, "Let us charge." There were three companies on the ridge. The third one closest to the river had moved back a little toward the second. It looked like the Indians were trying to drive them all along the ridge toward the Gray Horse Company in the north.

For the third time Yellow Nose charged, but still the others did not follow him. All the while, Indians were getting farther around to the north, trying to surround

392. "Yellow Nose Tells," 16, Powell, *Sacred Mountain*, 1024.

the soldiers. Finally, the fourth time Yellow Nose called for a charge, the Indians mounted up and followed him. This time they crowded the companies and they began to run down the ridge.[393]

LH 5:40–5:50, **Little Hawk** [last 3:30, next 5:50]. Having dallied on the fringes of the fight for the past two hours, Little Hawk finally crossed the river and went up the ravine the Indians used (Deep Coulee) in approaching Custer. The first thing he saw was the Cheyenne chief Comes In Sight riding up and down in front of the soldiers, drawing their fire.

Moving in, Little Hawk noticed Contrary Belly and Yellow Nose making a charge. They rode partway toward the soldiers, then turned their horses and rode back. The troops were all dismounted at this time, fighting on foot. About the time the two Cheyennes returned from their bravery run, an officer was killed. As he fell from his horse, the other soldiers mounted up. Now was the time to make another charge. Yellow Nose and Contrary Belly dashed forward again, and this time they were followed by the rest of the Indians. The soldiers ran north along the straight ridge.[394]

G 5:40–5:50, **Gall** [last 5:30, next 5:50]. Many minutes had gone by while the warriors below the slopes of Calhoun Hill prepared for the assault. When Gall signaled, both the mounted and dismounted braves rushed forward, with every voice yelling the war cry. The soldiers defending the hill were overwhelmed by the mass of warriors sweeping up from below. Their own momentum carried them across the crest. Just like that it was over. Almost as an anti-climax, Gall remarked on the brevity of the action. "We either killed or ran over these and went on down to where the last soldiers were."[395]

SB 5:40–5:50, **Standing Bear** [last 5:10, next 5:50]. For the past half hour Standing Bear had been in the vicinity of Greasy Grass Ridge, taking care of the horse he had caught and keeping out of the range of the soldier bullets. The bluecoats had dispersed their forces along the top of the long ridge between Calhoun Hill and Custer Hill, where they had been fighting all the while. Finally, as Standing Bear watched, the soldiers on Calhoun Hill gave way. They fell back along the ridge, trying to unite with those still alive at the farther end. The Indians followed close behind.[396]

RH 5:40–5:50, **Red Hawk** [last 5:00, next 6:00]. Red Hawk had been at the Calhoun Hill end of the ridge throughout most of the long-range firing. Although the soldiers had delivered many volleys, not much damage had been done. To Red Hawk, the Indians appeared to come like an increasing flood that could not be checked.

"The soldiers were swept off their feet," he said. "The Indians were overwhelming. Here the troopers divided and retreated on each side of the ridge."

393. Greene, *Lakota and Cheyenne*, 68.
394. Ibid., 62.
395. Graham, *The Custer Myth*, 95; Burdick, *Barry's Notes*, 13.
396. Hardorff, *Lakota Recollections*, 59.

As the Indians pushed to the hilltop, the survivors of L Troop abandoned their position. The warriors were able to take the guns and cartridges off the dead soldiers and become even more active in the struggle. They put the captured weapons to use against the fleeing troopers.[397]

RE 5:40–5:50, **Runs The Enemy** [last 5:30, next 5:50]. Back with his men, Runs The Enemy could see the soldiers were still fighting on the hill. But that did not last long. "Just as I got back," he said, "some of the soldiers made a rush down the ravine toward the river, and a great roll of smoke seemed to go down the ravine."

As the soldiers retreated down the ravine, more Indians who had been in the gulches by the river advanced up to meet them. Another clash sent the surviving troopers right back up the hill again. Those still alive had no choice but to fight, and "they made a stand all in a bunch," Runs The Enemy observed. The fire from the Indians now came from nearly every side.[398]

WB 5:40–5:50, **White Bull** [last 5:30, next 5:50]. On foot after his pony was shot, White Bull looked left and right, trying to assess the rapidly changing situation. From the ridge crest he could see the confusion the Indians had caused. Soldier horses from the first and second companies (Calhoun and Tom Custer) had mixed in with horses of the third company (Keogh), and the scene was painted on a canvas of swirling colors. From the river side, the fourth company, the ones with the white horses, also seemed to have lost their mounts. The men started to run to the top of the hill, but many did not make it. They had to lay down and start shooting.

Some soldiers from the third company rode to the south, but only one got away. He managed to get some distance from the battlefield before his horse was shot from under him and he was killed. On the ridge, Bear Lice rode up to White Bull, leading a captured bay. He gave the horse to White Bull. Through the smoke and dust White Bull saw a soldier on foot, wounded in his left thigh. He had a revolver in one hand and a carbine in the other. He stood firm and shot well and the Indians could not get near him. White Bull circled around and rode him down from his back side, counting the first coup. Brave Crow followed close behind to strike second.

White Bull noticed that the soldiers were not running straight. Some went toward the river, some toward the far end of the ridge. White Bull now found himself on the river side of the ridge. Below him was another white trooper on foot, threatening the Indians with his rifle much as the previous soldier had done. White Bull went after him.[399]

RF 5:40–5:50, **Red Feather** [last 5:30, next 5:50]. When Crazy Horse led the Indians in a charge over the ridge, the other Indians swept after him. The soldiers got to their horses and tried to get away. Red Feather, still on foot, rushed forward, yelling as loud as he could.

397. Hardorff, *Lakota Recollections*, 43–44.
398. Dixon, *Vanishing Race*, 176.
399. Hardorff, *Lakota Recollections*, 113–16; Vestal, "Man Who Killed Custer," 7–8.

There was a deep place in the timber that the soldiers could have run to for defense, but instead they took to the open country. This made it easier for the Indians to catch them, and Red Feather joined in in shooting the retreating soldiers from behind.

Most of the Indians charging right in among the soldiers were younger men, inexperienced and reckless. The older warriors held back for safety. The daring young braves were the ones to capture most of the soldier guns and ammunition, but they also suffered the most casualties.

Some of the soldiers who were able to mount their horses and retreat were met by Indians coming across the ridge from the river side. The collision caused the soldiers to ride off on a slant. One trooper riding a sorrel with white legs tried to get around the Indians. They took off after him and shot at him, but could not catch him. It appeared that the soldier was about to get away when they saw smoke, heard the report of a gun, and saw him fall off his horse. Red Feather learned that the soldier had shot himself.

As he moved toward the ridge where the breakthrough had occurred, Red Feather came upon an officer who was shot through the stomach. The man was sitting on the ground, holding a gun in his hand. Red Feather tried to take the gun away, but the officer dropped the gun and grabbed him. The attack by a nearly dead white man almost scared Red Feather to death himself. His grip was only broken when another Indian came up and shot the officer again. Red Feather took the officer's gun and examined it. It could not have been fired anyway because it was too smoked from shooting and cartridges were stuck in it.[400]

LB 5:40–5:50, **Lone Bear** [last 5:30, next 6:00]. Lone Bear joined in the close-in fighting that occurred as a result of Crazy Horse's charge across the ridge. He thought the stands made by the soldiers on Finley Ridge and Calhoun Hill were of relatively short duration. It seemed to Lone Bear that the longest stand and the hardest fighting took place in the action he was involved in. It was in the fight with Keogh's company that many horses were killed and the battle became fiercest.[401]

FN 5:40–5:50, **Fears Nothing** [last 5:10, next 6:10(a)]. Fears Nothing spent most of the battle with the Indians on the north side of the ridge held by the soldiers. When they were forced out of their position by the Indian attacks, one soldier broke away from Calhoun Hill. He galloped off on horseback and managed to get a long way off before he was killed by pursuing warriors.[402]

TR 5:40–5:50, **Turtle Rib** [last 4:30, next 6:10(b)]. For the past hour Turtle Rib had been hanging back, content to watch the battle from long range. He had gone up Deep Coulee to the north and east side of the ridge on which the soldiers had taken position.

When he got close enough to see the action, there was a running fight going on between the Indians and some soldiers on foot. Other troopers who managed to

400. Hardorff, *Lakota Recollections*, 85–86, 88.
401. Ibid., 157–58.
402. Ibid., 32–33.

keep their horses appeared to be stampeded. Some troopers were going toward the end of the ridge where the monument now stands, while others were trying to ride back the way they came. Those remaining on foot seemed to be the coolest and fought the hardest.

There was much dust and smoke and the Indians were running all around shooting into the soldiers. Turtle Rib saw one soldier mount up and ride across a hollow trying to get away. Two Indians took up the chase. Turtle Rib sped off after them.[403]

HD 5:40–5:50, **He Dog** [last 5:30, next 6:10(a)]. After He Dog joined the attack that cut the ridge, the soldier position became untenable. Indians were still on the far side with the bluecoats, while a number of Lakotas were now on the river side of the same ridge, perhaps only forty yards away. The troopers were in the valley between, being fired at from two sides.

One trooper on a stocking-legged horse got away riding toward the north. His horse was very fast. The man turned around occasionally to fire back, and the warriors who pursued him were about to give up, when he suddenly shot himself with his own revolver. He Dog also heard it said that the soldier had been beating his horse to speed it up when the revolver accidentally went off, killing him. In any case, he did not succeed in escaping.

Custer's men made no charges while fighting along the ridge, but were concerned with saving themselves. Horses stampeded loose and ran toward the river, where the Indians caught them. He Dog watched some of the cut-off soldiers fight their way to those at the end of the ridge, while other soldiers tried to get away toward the river. It mattered little, for they were all killed.[404]

FH 5:40–5:50, **Flying Hawk** [last 5:00, next 5:50]. Flying Hawk saw the results of the Indian fire as wounded soldiers dropped off their horses one by one. "When they found they were being killed so fast," Flying Hawk said, "the ones that were left broke and ran as fast as their horses could go to some other soldiers that were further along the ridge toward Custer."

From Calhoun Hill they retreated, fighting as they went. On the northeast side of the ridge, a body of men (Keogh's) made a stand, firing a few more shots before the Indian pressure forced them back. Most of them were killed, but of the remainder, Flying Hawk said, "we rushed them on along the ridge to where Custer was."

One man (possibly Lt. Henry M. Harrington of Company C) was driven back along the ridge with the rest of the command, from Calhoun Hill all the way to Custer Hill. Upon arriving there, however, he did not stop. The soldier kept right on going, escaping from the field before the remaining soldiers were surrounded. Flying Hawk said the man fired two shots back at his pursuers. He got about half a mile away before he fell.[405]

 5:40–5:50, **Two Eagles** [last 5:00, next 6:00]. Two Eagles slowly made his way from below Finley Ridge, around Calhoun Hill, and up the north side

403. Hammer, *Custer in '76*, 201–2.
404. Ibid., 207; Hardorff, *Lakota Recollections*, 75–76.
405. Hardorff, *Lakota Recollections*, 51–52; McCreight, *Firewater*, 113.

of the long ridge. By this stage of the fight the battle was fluid, with much movement between Calhoun Hill and Custer Hill. The Indians tried to keep hidden in
the draws below the crown of the ridge, but the situation necessitated fighting at
close quarters. Finally, the Indians had surrounded the soldiers except for the area
northwest of Custer Hill.

Most of the bluecoats moving toward Custer Hill had lost their horses. They
made a weak stand in the Keogh area, but about ten or twelve soldiers, upon
reaching that point, made a dash to the river. They ran down on a line about
halfway between Finley Ridge and the Deep Ravine (Calhoun Coulee), but then
scattered a little while going down.[406]

L 5:40–5:50, **Lights** [last 5:10, next 5:50]. From the Deep Coulee side of Finley
Ridge, Lights worked his way around the soldiers to the north side of the
ridge and headed northwest. The Indians generally stayed in the gullies and kept
the soldiers near the tops of the ridges. Most of the soldiers were mounted as they
moved along Battle Ridge. Those on foot were in that predicament because their
horses had been shot or stampeded. Lights believed the soldiers were killed while
fighting. They did not appear to be running away, but only giving ground because
of the superior number of Indians.[407]

HH 5:40–5:50, **Hollow Horn Bear** [last 5:00, next 6:10(b)]. Moving north
and east around Calhoun Hill, Hollow Horn Bear did not see the soldiers
make any charges. In fact, they were moving all the time and seemed drunk. By the
time the soldiers got to the place where Keogh's company had taken position,
warriors had already captured the guns and ammunition of the dead soldiers at
Calhoun Hill.

"Many of the soldiers at this point tried to get off the top of the ridge and make
their escape," Hollow Horn Bear declared, but they "got in a pocket, or trap, where
they were easily killed." It did not seem to matter where the soldiers went by this
time, for the Indians were on the ridge and in the gullies. In fact, Hollow Horn
Bear thought that there were so many warriors in the fight that they only got in
each other's way. He did not stop to join the battle, but continued to ride north.[408]

TM 5:40–5:50, **Two Moon** [last 5:30, next 5:50]. The dust rose like smoke and
the braves swirled past the troopers like water around a stone. Two Moon
and his Cheyenne warriors broke through the soldiers and crested the ridge to the
river side. Jubilant, yet somewhat disorganized after the charge, Two Moon rode
back through his men, telling them to get ready once more.

Looking north, he could see the company with gray horses on the far end of the
ridge, apparently still in the position where they repulsed Two Moon's band earlier.
He told his men that once more they would have to fight hard and shoot good. "I
rode my horse back along the ridge again," he said, "and called upon my children

406. Hardorff, *Lakota Recollections*, 146–48.
407. Ibid., 167–69.
408. Ibid., 182–84.

to come on after me." Many Cheyennes had already been killed, but this would not be the end of it. "I whipped up my horse and told them to come on, that this day was the last day they would ever see their chief." After that brave-up talk, Two Moon sped off toward the Gray Horse troopers on the hilltop. The Indians followed him, yelling and firing.[409]

IH 5:40–5:50, **Iron Hawk** [last 5:30, next 6:00]. As Iron Hawk made his way uphill from the river, the soldiers were retreating along the ridge to Custer Hill. The Indians following close behind were able to pick up arms and ammunition and could now use those instead of bows and arrows.

Iron Hawk was riding up to the hill that Custer was defending when he pulled his horse to a halt. Another Indian called out, "He is going." Iron Hawk looked over to see a handsome Cheyenne wearing a spotted war bonnet and a shawl made from an animal skin. The Cheyenne rode past Iron Hawk and continued uphill to circle right in front of the soldiers. He returned near the group of Hunkpapas with Iron Hawk, then started around for another run. The soldiers shot at him but could not hit him. Returning again to the Hunkpapa band at the head of the gulch, he gesticulated and said "Ah, ah."

Standing next to Iron Hawk, Little Bear asked, "Cheyenne friend, what is the matter?" The Cheyenne began to undo a belt made of hair that was tied around his waist to secure the animal hide. When he took the belt off, many bullets began to drop out of it. Iron Hawk was impressed. The Cheyennes were very sacred, he thought, and this man was bulletproof.[410]

WC 5:40–5:50, **White Cow Bull** [last 5:10]. After shooting his repeater at two bands of troopers from his position on Greasy Grass Ridge, White Cow Bull moved north. Across the Deep Ravine, he stopped for a time to watch a lone warrior show his courage.

A Shahiyela wearing a spotted war bonnet and a robe of mountain lion skins rode out all alone. "He's charging!" an Indian shouted. White Cow Bull watched him race up to the long ridge where one band of soldiers was defending. They stood there holding their horses and putting out a steady fire, but they could not hit the Shahiyela. He charged in almost close enough to touch them, then rode around in circles with the bullets kicking up dust all around him.

When he returned, the Indians with White Cow Bull cheered. "Ah! Ah!" he said, which meant "yes" in Shahiyela. Then the brave unfastened his belt and opened his robe. Many spent bullets fell to the ground. It was quite a feat. White Cow Bull grinned while thinking about such courage.[411]

A 5:40–5:50, **Antelope** [last 5:30, next 5:50]. Unable to find Noisy Walking after Lame White Man's charge, Antelope rode to the east end of the main ridge. As she circled the position she noticed many Indians running toward the end

---

409. Hunt, *I Fought With Custer*, 213; Hardorff, *Lakota Recollections*, 137; Dixon, *Vanishing Race*, 182.
410. Hardorff, *Lakota Recollections*, 67; DeMallie, *Sixth Grandfather*, 190–91; Neihardt, *Black Elk*, 121–22.
411. Miller, "Echoes," 34.

of the ridge, and the soldier horses there were breaking away. By the time she approached close enough to see what was taking place, she found that all of the white men were dead.

As they had done after the Lame White Man attack, the victorious Indians immediately went among the dead and took their guns. Antelope did not see how the soldiers were killed, but thought perhaps that many of them took their own lives.[412]

WL 5:40–5:50, **Wooden Leg** [last 5:30, next 5:50]. The warriors that Lame White Man led had made short work of the troopers above the ravine. After they were dead, Wooden Leg went back down the gully to find his horse. Mounting up, he rode out of the gully and made his way back upriver before cutting over to the east end of the main ridge. On the way up, the sounds of gunfire had lessened considerably. By the time Wooden Leg rode up to Calhoun Hill, all the soldiers there were dead.

Meeting another Cheyenne, Wooden Leg was told that four soldiers had broken away and tried to escape back along the trail from where they had come. Three were killed quickly, but the fourth made it across a gulch and over a ridge before the pursuing Lakotas caught up with him. His horse was tired and as the Lakotas gained on him he put his revolver to his head and shot himself.

As the battle moved north, Wooden Leg raced his horse around the hillside and up the ridge where Indians were still fighting a band of soldiers on the north slope. The fight was over on this portion of the field.[413]

⬿ DISCUSSION. One of the first braves to go over the crest of Battle Ridge to the west side, White Bull was in time to see the remnants of the Gray Horse troop making their way back to Custer's Hill. Immediately following, Two Moon crossed over to see the grays on the same hill. To him, they had not moved. In actuality, they left the hilltop soon after they had repulsed Two Moon's charge, then they had been beaten back by Lame White Man's attack just prior to the Cheyenne chief's return to the western slope. Two Moon thought they had "stayed right out in the open" the whole time.[414]

Confusion reigned at the site where the Indians penetrated the line. The troops' response was tentative, bordering on an outright inability to take any remedial action. Those north of the break began to move toward Custer Hill, while those south of the break headed toward Calhoun Hill. Some even went to the west side of the ridge in the direction of the river. Surely, some Indian commentary concerning troopers running down a ravine that is typically depicted as Deep Ravine, must have alluded to the fugitives from Companies I and C in Calhoun Coulee.

With the cutting of the lines we find the first of innumerable Indian accounts mentioning troopers fleeing from the battlefield. Fears Nothing and Wooden Leg told of one or more men escaping from Calhoun Hill to the south before either being killed or committing suicide. Red Feather and He Dog told of an escapee on

412. Marquis, *Custer on the Little Big Horn*, 89.
413. Marquis, *Wooden Leg*, 232, 234.
414. Hardorff, *Lakota Recollections*, 138.

a sorrel or stocking-legged horse breaking away from the Keogh area and eventually shooting himself. Flying Hawk said a man rode from the Keogh area past Custer Hill before he was killed, and White Bull said a soldier went from the Keogh area to the south before being killed. Turtle Rib saw a soldier dash across a hollow and he joined in the chase himself. The stories vary in detail, but amply illustrate one point: there was a serious shock to the integrity of the Custer battalion's lines—so serious that a number of men thought flight was the only way to save their lives.

In this segment we again find a problem with some of White Cow Bull's testimony. D. H. Miller recorded the Oglala as saying that one soldier on a sorrel horse broke away from the others and rode off down the ridge. Two Cheyennes and a Lakota chased him, but the soldier's horse was fast and they couldn't catch him. "I saw him yank out his revolver and thought he was going to shoot back at these warriors," White Cow Bull said. "Instead he put the revolver to his head, pulled the trigger, and fell dead."[415]

At first glance there is nothing extraordinary in his statements. A significant portion of some Indian testimony was based on oral tradition. Witness, for example, Wooden Leg and Antelope, whose narratives match closely in many respects. White Cow Bull's story of this incident also may have been based on nothing more than tradition, and it could have been accepted as such, were it not for the disturbing fact that he used the word "I" to describe the action.

With the exception of Wooden Leg, who was told of the incident after reaching Calhoun Hill, every one of the previous Indian descriptions of the event came from a warrior stationed on the north and east sides of the ridge, away from the river. In addition, Foolish Elk was east of the ridge, but did not see the incident. He admitted he heard it from other eyewitnesses. The mounted, escaping troopers went north, or east, or southeast back in the direction from which they had come. At this time, White Cow Bull was near Iron Hawk watching the "bulletproof" Cheyenne make runs at the soldiers from halfway down the western slope toward the river. The fleeing trooper on his sorrel horse was probably a mile or more away from White Cow Bull on the *opposite* side of an intervening ridgeline. The "I saw him . . ." story of either White Cow Bull or his recorder is not believable.

Did we perhaps place White Cow Bull in the wrong spot on the field? Was he really north of Battle Ridge and close enough to "see" what a trooper really did with his revolver beyond hill and dale from a distance of a half mile or more? If so, then he could not have been witnessing the Shahiyela make his bravery run against Custer Hill. In either case there is an inconsistency. Miller's informants seem to be graced with extraordinary powers. Beard sees One Bull in a crowd from one and a half miles away. White Cow Bull sees and shoots at Crows from almost that distance. He stops a soldier charge in midstream when the soldiers never got close enough to charge into the stream. He sees a trooper shoot himself in the head from a position where it would be impossible to view such an action. Had White Cow

---

415. Miller, "Echoes," 34.

Bull simply stated that he heard of the incident, we could have accepted it. Then again, perhaps he did. Perhaps the extraordinary deeds derive less from Miller's informants than they do from Miller's imagination in the retelling.

A related concern lies with the informants' corroborations. Usually an edifying connection can make an account ring true, but such a large number of corroborations may be too much of a good thing. In 1931, Standing Bear told John Neihardt of his uncle's premonition of an upcoming battle. In Miller's 1957 publication he credited Beard with the same story. In the early 1930s, One Bull told Walter Campbell about riding out to meet Reno's men. According to Miller, Beard says he saw One Bull actually make that ride. In a book first published by George Grinnell in 1915, Cheyennes said that Mad Wolf (Lame White Man) cautioned the Indians about attacking the soldiers near the ford. Miller's White Cow Bull was there to hear the warning. In 1932, Frank Linderman wrote that the Crow Pretty Shield said her husband, Goes Ahead, indicated that Custer was shot into the water while attempting to charge across the river. Miller's White Cow Bull claims to be the one who shot him. Many Indians told of Yellow Nose capturing a guidon. White Cow Bull was there to see it. In 1931 Iron Hawk told Neihardt of watching the "bulletproof" Cheyenne make runs at the troops. Miller's White Cow Bull stood nearby and described the incident almost verbatim. Indians on the east side of Battle Ridge said they saw an escaping trooper put a bullet in his head. White Cow Bull said he, too, witnessed it. After the fight, Antelope heard about an Indian woman who punched a sewing awl into Custer's ears. Who was there to witness the action? White Cow Bull, of course.

Historian Marc Bloch made some observations pertinent to this situation. If we confine ourselves to simple, blunt statements, there will not be many ways to describe a fight, he said. "But should two witnesses describe the battle in exactly the same language or, despite a certain variation of phrasing, with exactly the same details, we should unhesitatingly conclude that one of them had copied the other or that both had copied a common model. In effect, our reason refuses to admit that two observers, necessarily posted at different parts of the field and endowed with unequal powers of attention, could have noted the same episodes, detail for detail." If the two accounts claim to have been taken from reality, Bloch said, "then at least one of them must be lying."[416]

We might add another possibility to Bloch's assessment. In our situation, the Indian informants might simply have been repeating oral tradition, but if that is so, then the first person "I saw" and "I did" needs to be removed. The unity of the entire affair is joined by rather weak links because there is a limit to coincidence. The number of possible witness combinations is so immense that their spontaneous repetition is nearly inconceivable. There is a similarity of evidence that vindicates and a similarity that discredits, said Bloch. Somehow, its criticism must rest upon one's instinctive judgment.[417] The very fact that so much of the Indian testimony is *similar,* yet *not exact,* is a telling point for the truthfulness of their stories.

---

416. Bloch, *Historian's Craft*, 114–15.
417. Ibid., 115–16.

Vindicating evidence from perhaps 90 percent of our informants allows us to interlock pieces of the puzzle to construct the story of the Little Bighorn with a certain degree of confidence, the distractions of Miller's manipulations notwithstanding.

The dilemma of Companies I and C in Keogh Coulee must have been alarming in the extreme. In addition to the Indians from the Crazy Horse–White Bull penetration, warriors from the suicide boys–Lame White Man attack were cresting the ridge from the west side. There were now Indians on both sides of the soldiers while they maneuvered in the narrow alley in between. The route to the north must have appeared more open, but the troops on Custer's knoll were a bit farther away than those to the south. The route south to Calhoun's command was closer, but had just been cut off by the Indians. Individually, the men took the course of expediency. Some went north, some south, some west, and a few tried to flee the scene altogether.

The Indian assault on Calhoun Hill serendipitously coincided with the White Bull–Crazy Horse breakthrough. Gall's almost nonchalant description of the ease of rolling over the Calhoun Hill position, which previously proved a hard nut to crack, indicates some other factor had entered the equation. Company L was unfortunately faced with an approaching enemy in front, while witnessing all too clearly the dissolution of its comrades to the left and rear. Control must have evaporated on Calhoun Hill. The surviving soldiers abandoned their position and headed north, trying to link up with Company I and the northern platoon of Company C.

The Indians attacking Calhoun Hill, including Gall and a host of nameless, unremembered faces, triumphantly rushed to the vacated hilltop. Down on Finley Ridge, that most unlucky platoon of C Company, heretofore admirably holding its own, could see nothing of the disaster occurring over the crest in Keogh's sector. In addition, the men probably knew little about Calhoun's abandonment of the hill until it was too late, when they must have noticed men in blue streaming north beyond their own left and rear. Most assuredly they realized their predicament when the Indians on Calhoun Hill began firing into their left flank. The situation went from tentatively stable to hopeless in moments.

This scenario is enhanced by examining the archaeological record. In a rough oval about one hundred to two hundred yards east and south of Calhoun Hill a large number of battle-related artifacts were found, including cartridges and bullets from both army and Indian weapons. The 1984–85 discoveries were so unexpected and plentiful, particularly the number of .44 Henry cartridges, that members of the dig named the artifact concentration "Henryville" (see fig. 12). They concluded that the Indians there must have "poured intense fire" into Calhoun's men.[418]

In 1991, I walked the site with a number of visiting Custer Battlefield Historical and Museum Association members. Comments were made about how remarkably close the Indians were to the men on Calhoun Hill, about the hubris they exhibited by fighting it out virtually toe-to-toe, in plain contempt of the fighting prow-

---

418. Scott et al., *Archaeological Perspectives*, 126.

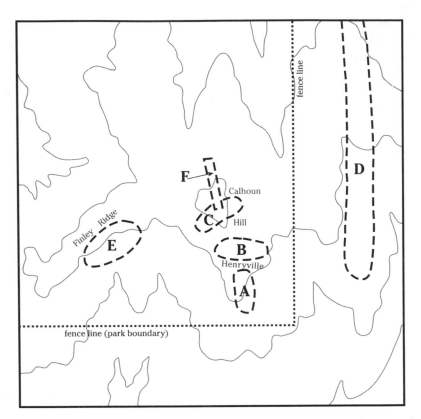

Figure 12. Artifact Map: "Henryville." A. *About 32 Indian cartridge cases.* **B.** *About 13 Indian cartridge cases.* **C.** *About 9 Indian cartridge cases.* **D.** *About 108 Indian cartridge cases, including .50/.70s, .44s, and .56s.* **E.** *About 9 Indian bullets.* **F.** *About 5 Army cartridge cases.*

ess of their white adversaries. This assessment somehow did not "feel" right at the time, but the consensus opinion was approved, and we walked on. However, upon another examination of the field in 1994, and after piecing the Indian narratives together into a comprehensive whole, there is reason to believe a more valid alternative exists.

The Indians simply *did not* shoot it out toe-to-toe with the soldiers on Calhoun Hill. The narratives clearly show that, with the exception of a bravery run or two, or a few quick, slashing attacks, the Indians chose not to expose themselves in the open to the soldiers' fire. They fought from long range, protected by intervening terrain. Grinnell's Cheyenne informants told him the same story. "The Indians state positively that they did not kill the troops by charging into them," he reported, "but kept shooting them from behind the hills." Red Horse indicated the fight was "carried on at a distance," or continued "at long range." The Lakota Yellow Horse indicated that Custer kept his ground clear to the last. The Indians did not mingle among the soldiers and fight them hand-to-hand. Rather, they kept their distance, the soldiers holding them at bay until all but a handful had been shot down. Only then did they close in.[419]

At numerous sites from the Reno Hill sector, through Nye-Cartwright Ridge, and on to the north of Custer Hill, the artifact patterns support this contention. After many years of relic hunting in the area, local ranchers Henry and Don Weibert confirmed this pattern. Very few Indian positions were within three hundred yards of the soldiers, while many were seven to nine hundred yards away. Artifacts showed that "safety in distance" was the Indian way of fighting.[420]

The fact that Indians fought from a safe distance was no revelation to the nineteenth-century army. Colonel Gibbon, whose 7th Infantry was to play a part in the rescue of the 7th Cavalry survivors, was certain of that very point. Indians fought as individuals, he said. They took advantage of every inequality of ground, of every stump, stone, or buffalo wallow. They never fought in masses except in the most desperate circumstance. Though individuals would partake in an exceptional act of bravery, Gibbon affirmed, "these are usually isolated cases of bravado, and generally performed at a safe distance."[421] Circling a wagon train or a fort, massed charges, and hand-to-hand combat with an unrouted foe are perceptions we have gotten from Hollywood movies, not from reality. The Weiberts' artifact discoveries only confirmed what our nineteenth-century ancestors already knew, but what we, today, have forgotten because of a half century of watching "B Westerns" at the movies.[422]

What appears to have been a toe-to-toe fight at Henryville was just that—an appearance. Calhoun Hill had been abandoned before the warriors took their positions on the south and east slopes. There, a rough east-west line ("B" in fig. 12) of about thirteen .44 Henry cartridges just below the crest shows they did some firing at Calhoun's retreating men or at Tom Custer's or Keogh's men to the north.

An even more pronounced north-south line of about thirty-two cartridges ("A" in fig. 12) also exists just below the crest. There are several reasons to contradict speculations that these Indians blasted away from this line against soldiers on Calhoun Hill. First, Fox estimated that the thirty-two cartridges came from about twenty repeaters. These theoretically could have been deposited in as little as three or four seconds of firing, which would hardly constitute sustained action. Second, as I have argued, the Indians were still cognizant of the safety factor. They did not duel it out with anyone at Napoleonic smoothbore range. Third, from one hundred to two hundred yards south of the Calhoun crest, they did not have a line of fire to the retreating Company L men on the opposite slope. Fourth, a group would not form

419. Grinnell, *Fighting Cheyennes*, 353; Graham, *The Custer Myth*, 60; John M. Carroll, ed., *Who Was This Man Ricker and What Are His Tablets That Everyone Is Talking About?* (Bryan, TX: by the author, 1979), 18–19.
420. Weibert, *Custer, Cases*, 123–25, 161–62.
421. John Gibbon, "Arms to Fight Indians," *Bighorn Yellowstone Journal* 3, no. 2 (spring 1994): 11–12.
422. For further reading about western movies and American culture, see Paul Hutton's "From Little Big Horn to Little Big Man" or Richard Slotkin's *Gunfighter Nation: The Myth of the Frontier in Twentieth-Century America* (New York: HarperCollins, 1993).

a north–south line and then shoot to the north (or to the south), unless they lacked concern for potentially knocking the head off the next man in front. A north–south line is formed to shoot either east or west, and there were no soldiers to the east. The line could only have been set up to fire to the west. The only place where soldiers could still have been holding their ground within line of sight from that north–south line below Calhoun Hill was to the west, out on Finley Ridge. Finally, there were about nine Indian bullets found impacted on the eastern slopes of Finley Ridge; they must have been fired from the east—from Henryville. There were also about six Indian bullets found some three hundred yards in a straight line beyond the Finley position; these could have been overshots from Henryville. Simply put, Calhoun Hill was abandoned before Finley Ridge. The Indians at Henryville were primarily firing into the left flank of the men on Finley Ridge.[423]

Studies have been done on firearms identification and cartridge case distributions to identify on which parts of the battlefield individual Indian weapons were used. Some of the same Indian rifles were shown to have been used at both Greasy

Looking southwest from the Henryville Indian position to Finley Ridge.

423. An alternative scenario was suggested by Bruce Trinque in a letter dated 29 November 1994. He didn't think Calhoun Hill had to be completely abandoned before the Indians took Henryville. He wondered if perhaps Keogh or Calhoun simply made a tactical error in placing their firing line, giving up control of the southern slope of Calhoun Hill. As a result of choosing short-term safety from enemy fire by hiding behind the military crest (as opposed to the more genuine long-term security provided by control of the approaches to the position), Calhoun gave the Indians a close-in foothold to disrupt the integrity of the entire position.

Grass Ridge and Henryville. Concomitant theories have suggested that the cartridge case distribution indicated one of two things: either the Indians moved in two broad lines, from Greasy Grass Ridge north and from Calhoun Hill north, or they moved from Greasy Grass Ridge east to Calhoun Hill and then north.[424]

Ballistics evidence from fired cartridges can show that one weapon was fired on two parts of the field, but it cannot tell us which firing occurred first. The theory of two Indian movements to the north does not take into consideration the east-west movement of the Indians and shift of the weapons. The second theory takes this into consideration and is more sustainable. Yet, the Henryville anomaly still sticks in the craw. We must accept an east-west axis of Indian movement in this sector, but we need not assume that the west (Finley) side fell before the Indians moved to the eastern (Calhoun) side. During the forty or more minutes of fighting that occurred, there was ample time for Indians to move between the two positions. Warriors could have fired from Greasy Grass, moved down into Deep Coulee, circled below the Finley position, and come up to fire again toward Finley from the recently abandoned Calhoun-Henryville position. As indicated, the north-south line of Indian cartridges below Calhoun's crest makes this scenario the most plausible. The Indians would not have been blasting away toe-to-toe with Calhoun's men and they would not have been firing back to Finley Ridge had they already overrun the position.

Archaeologists tell us that from physical relics they can deduce human behavior, which seems reasonable enough. But whose behavior? Archaeologists are themselves subject to the same forces as historians: they both perceive the past, conceive ideas, and manipulate data and theory relationships within their own socio-cultural matrix. Their responses are dependent on data, but also on their historical imaginations, which in turn are affected by their understanding of the present.[425] In other words, if one is predisposed to see a tenacious defense eventually overcome by a fanatical offense, then one might easily postulate a "whites of their eyes" fight at shooting-gallery range.

In this case, uncharacteristic Indian behavior has been postulated: the warriors "poured intense fire" into Calhoun's men from a hundred yards away. This tells us less about nineteenth-century Indian behavior than about twentieth-century ethnomorphic conceptions of that behavior.

Richard Fox Jr. was aware of the north-south cartridge line on Henryville ("A" in fig. 12), which he said represented about twenty repeating rifles. He thought some of the fire from Henryville went west. Yet, although he saw the pattern, he did not follow it through to its logical conclusion—that Indians fired at soldiers on Finley Ridge before it was abandoned. Fox postulated a different scenario. He also saw a north-south line of five army cases ("F" in fig. 12) that he said denoted a soldier line on Calhoun Hill, just north of the north-south Indian line at Henryville.

424. Scott et al., *Archaeological Perspectives*, 129; Bruce A. Trinque, "The Cartridge-Case Evidence on Custer Field: An Analysis and Re-Interpretation," 5th Annual Symposium, Custer Battlefield Historical & Museum Association (Hardin, MT: CBH&MA, 1991): 74.

425. Ian Hodder, *Reading the Past: Current Approaches to Interpretation in Archaeology* (Cambridge: Cambridge University Press, 1986), 17–18, 31, 99.

That line, he said, must have fired to the west, because terrain may have blocked the line of sight to the east, and relic finds in that direction, beyond the park boundary line, were few in number. Certainly Fox was aware that the valley east and north of Calhoun Hill was a major avenue for the circling Indians, but apparently he did not have access to, or chose not to make use of, Weibert's study that showed fifty Indian weapon relics had been found along that very portion of the field ("D" in fig. 12). Yet he did cite Greene's compilation, which showed fifty-eight Indian artifacts in the same terrain where he said they were "few in number."[426] Either unaware of or ignoring the relic concentrations to the east, Fox concluded that the five-case skirmish line must have been firing to the west, against Indians moving up from the Greasy Grass Ridge and Calhoun Coulee areas (which in turn may have stemmed from his belief that Lame White Man overwhelmed troops in that sector). Having gotten into this predicament, Fox concluded that the north-south Indian line on Henryville, immediately below the north-south soldier line on Calhoun Hill, must have formed up to fire *north,* at close range, into the left flank of the western facing soldiers![427] This is an inaccurate assessment of the relics based on a mistaken premise. We must realize that artifacts tell us only as much as we are predisposed to read into them. The bottom line of archaeological evidence is that its utility is still governed by human foibles and it must be used with caution.

The Indians did not radically alter their fighting style when they reached Calhoun Hill. For the most part, they still fought from a distance, against targets retreating from Calhoun Hill, against those in Keogh Coulee, and against targets on Finley Ridge approximately three hundred yards away. And here we find another argument against the Lame White Man–Calhoun Coulee attack scenario: had Lame White Man overwhelmed the Finley position, as claimed by the revisionists, there would be no north-south line of Henry cartridges on Henryville. There would probably have been no Henryville, period.

To the defenders of Finley Ridge—fighting Indians to their right on Greasy Grass Ridge, to their front in Deep Coulee, and now, surprisingly, to their left on Calhoun Hill where Company L once secured their flank and from where Indian bullets now began finding them—the result must have been devastating. Like the men on Calhoun Hill, they probably were not bowled over by a mass of warriors but abandoned their position because an intolerable, unexpected development broke their morale. They fell back in surprise and fear. Visceral self-preservation superseded the need to maintain unit cohesion.

White Bull said the soldiers did not run straight. Red Feather said Indians met soldiers along the ridge and the soldiers went off on a slant. Turtle Rib said some soldiers ran north, while others went back the way they came. Hollow Horn Bear said some troopers ran into a pocket. He Dog saw some run north, while others ran for the river. Two Eagles saw ten or twelve soldiers run for the river. Runs The Enemy saw soldiers run down a ravine, meet more Indians, and then run back

---

426. Fox, *Archaeology, History,* 100, 103–6; Weibert, *Custer, Cases,* 43, 160–61, 308; Jerome A. Greene, *Evidence and the Custer Enigma: A Reconstruction of Indian-Military History* (Golden, CO: Outbooks, Inc., 1986), 57, end map.
427. Fox, *Archaeology, History,* 110–11.

uphill. Julia Face, daughter of the Oglala Face, said some soldiers ran from the Finley area to Calhoun Hill, then over to the Keogh area, and finally to the Deep Ravine.[428] Clearly the officers had lost control of their units. Once the soldiers turned their backs to run, the Indians had no scruples about a close-range chase, which to them was much like running down stampeding buffalo. When Antelope and Wooden Leg reached the vicinity of Calhoun Hill, the soldiers had already fled or were dead on the field. The battle was decided. From now on it was only a matter of time.

---

428. Hardorff, *Lakota Recollections*, 191.

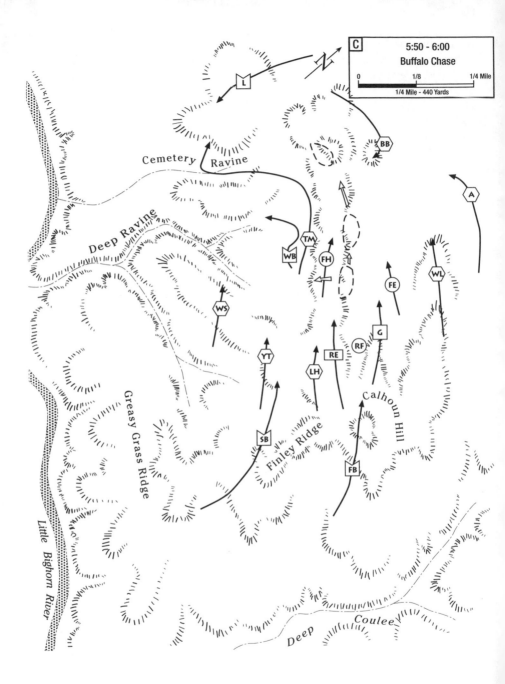

Cemetery Ravine

Deep Ravine

Greasy Grass Ridge

Little Bighorn River

Finley Ridge

Calhoun Hill

Deep Coulee

L

BB

A

TM

WB

FH

WL

FE

WS

G

RF

RE

YT

LH

SB

FB

BUFFALO CHASE, 5:50–6:00

RE 5:50–6:00, **Runs The Enemy** [last 5:40, next 6:10(b)]. The soldiers, who had first run downhill and then uphill, finally managed to make a short stand. However, another charge was made and they retreated along the ridgeline. Said Runs The Enemy, "It looked like a stampede of buffalo."

As the soldiers fell back along the ridge, Runs The Enemy's Two Kettle tribesmen finally became closely engaged, hitting the retreating bluecoats from one side as other Lakotas attacked them from another direction. The soldiers broke and divided: some of them went down the eastern slope of the hill, and some of them went down toward the river.[429]

LH 5:50–6:00, **Little Hawk** [last 5:40, next 6:00]. When the soldiers abandoned the hill and ran north along the straight ridge, the Indians were off after them. The warriors, said Little Hawk, "chased them like buffalo and as long as they had their backs toward [the] Indians the Indians rode right in among them."

Even so, during the run up the ridge while the opponents were all mixed together, Little Hawk did not think many soldiers were slain. He did believe that it was during this part of the fight that Noisy Walking was killed. Still, the soldiers ran and did not turn until they reached the knoll where the monument now stands.[430]

SB 5:50–6:00, **Standing Bear** [last 5:40, next 6:00]. After the soldiers had fallen back from Calhoun Hill, Standing Bear began to follow in their wake. He moved up to a hill (Finley). There he saw one soldier lying dead, then another. Also lying among them were a few Indians, but Standing Bear said, "I don't know how they got killed together, because I wasn't down there." The battle shifted north and he continued along the ridge.[431]

FE 5:50–6:00, **Foolish Elk** [last 4:50]. For the past hour Foolish Elk had been on the east side of the ridge watching the battle. Neither side had seemed able to gain the advantage, until finally "the battle became furious."

Although he did not see any soldier get away, Foolish Elk heard four other eyewitnesses tell of one who did manage to ride off on a very swift horse. He heard that the man got a mile or two away before pulling out a pistol and killing himself.

Foolish Elk worked his way into a gully closer to the action. There he saw Keogh's soldiers killed on the side of the hill as they "marched" toward the high ground at the end of the ridge. It did not look like any of them made a stand, for they were constantly moving along toward the far end. The men still on horseback did not stop to fight, but rode ahead as fast as they could go. However, the dismounted troopers put up some resistance, for they were shooting as they passed along.[432]

---

429. Dixon, *Vanishing Race*, 176.
430. Greene, *Lakota and Cheyenne*, 64. We shall see that Noisy Walking was found in the upper Deep Ravine after the battle, still clinging to life.
431. Hardorff, *Lakota Recollections*, 59; DeMallie, *Sixth Grandfather*, 185.
432. Hammer, *Custer in '76*, 199.

WB 5:50–6:00, **White Bull** [last 5:40, next 6:10(a)]. Now mounted on the captured bay Bear Lice had given him, White Bull rode down the west side of the ridge. There he saw another white soldier protecting himself by aiming his rifle at the circling Indians. White Bull slid off his horse and started for him on foot.

The soldier, tall, well-built, with yellow hair and a mustache, saw White Bull coming and tried to bluff him with his rifle. White Bull rushed in anyway and the soldier threw his weapon at him. Dodging the missile, White Bull charged into the soldier. They grabbed each other and fell to the ground. Wrestling there in the dirt, dust, and smoke, was like fighting in a fog. The soldier tried to grab White Bull's rifle away, but White Bull lashed him in the face with his quirt, thereby counting another first coup. The soldier let go, then grabbed the rifle with both hands. White Bull struck him again.

Although White Bull may have had more experience in hand-to-hand combat, the soldier was very strong. He punched White Bull in the jaw and shoulders, then he grabbed his long braids in both hands, pulled their heads together until only inches apart, and tried to bite off White Bull's nose.

"Hey, Hey," White Bull cried. "Come over and help me!" He thought the soldier would kill him. Bear Lice and Crow Boy came running. They tried to hit the soldier, but the combatants were locked together, swirling through the dirt in such a tumble that most of their blows fell on White Bull, knocking him dizzy. Yelling at the soldier to scare him and wrestling with all his might, he finally broke free. The soldier drew his pistol, but White Bull managed to grab it from him. He pummeled his foe with it three or four times, knocked him down, and finally shot him in the head and in the heart. He took the pistol and a cartridge belt.

"*Ho hechetu!*" White Bull said. "That was a fight, a hard fight. But it was a glorious battle, I enjoyed it. I was picking up head-feathers right and left that day."[433]

WL 5:50–6:00, **Wooden Leg** [last 5:40, next 6:00]. Leaving Calhoun Hill, Wooden Leg raced his horse to a hillside on the north side of the soldier ridge. Indians were all around a band of soldiers on the north slope. He dismounted, but fired only two shots at long distance with his captured rifle. There were so many Indians behind the clumps of sagebrush, crawling near the soldiers and jumping up and down to shoot, that Wooden Leg thought he might hit one of his own men.

Hundreds of men and boys were circling beyond gunshot range, watching the fight from a distance. The ridge to the north of the soldier ridge was crowded with them. Suddenly, Wooden Leg saw one trooper break away from the north slope of the ridge and run across a gulch and toward the next hill to the north. Wooden Leg guessed the soldier must have thought there were no Indians in that direction, but several jumped up and ran after him. The soldier crossed the gulch and stopped. Wooden Leg thought the soldier killed himself with his own revolver.

433. Hardorff, *Lakota Recollections*, 116; Vestal, "Man Who Killed Custer," 9. This was the encounter that led Stanley Vestal to conclude that White Bull had killed Custer. However, the fight took place too far downslope from the hilltop where Custer's body was found. Utley, *Lance and Shield*, 364, states that nowhere in Campbell's notes from White Bull does the Indian claim responsibility for killing Custer.

A young Cheyenne named Big Beaver dashed down to the dead man and got his gun and cartridges. Another Cheyenne scalped the soldier and hung the hair on a clump of sagebrush.

Watching the incident from nearby, Wooden Leg next noticed a wounded Lakota walking slowly toward the gulch, trying to leave the battle. He wobbled dizzily, fell down, and got up again. As he passed close by Wooden Leg, he noticed the man had his whole lower jaw shot away. The sight made Wooden Leg sick. He turned away and began to vomit.[434]

BB 5:50–6:00, **Big Beaver** [next 6:00]. Like so many of his tribesmen, the seventeen-year-old Cheyenne had been quite surprised when word was brought that the soldiers were coming to fight them. Big Beaver rushed out to find his pony, only to be cautioned by his father. "Son, you are too young to fight," he said, "and as there are lots of fighting men here, they will not need you." Big Beaver did not listen. Although he did not own a gun, he gathered up his bow and arrows and rode off.

Since the Cheyennes were located on the north end of the camp and nearest to the battleground, Big Beaver trailed north along the river. Crossing over, he turned right, or east, and came up toward Custer Hill from the north side. He tied up his pony and left him behind at a safe distance, then crawled the rest of the way up a coulee, finally reaching a point just north and a little east of where the present monument now stands.

In front of Big Beaver was a Lakota wearing a warbonnet. The warrior would jump up and shoot toward the soldiers on the hill, then would fall down, reload, and crawl ahead again. Big Beaver watched the Lakota perform this action several times, crawling close behind him. Finally, when the Lakota jumped up to shoot once more, a bullet struck him square in the forehead.

Suddenly Big Beaver realized the serious nature of this fighting business. "I thought it was no place for me so I turned and crawled back," he declared.[435]

A 5:50–6:00, **Antelope** [last 5:40, next 6:10(a)]. Antelope watched the Indians crowd the soldiers along the ridge from both sides, inexorably pushing them westward. She followed behind, keeping back out of bullet range. North of the ridge she stopped on a little hill to watch. By then, the Indians were all around the soldiers on the north slope, and the soldiers horses had all been chased away or killed.

Antelope saw the remaining white fighters collect in a group at the west end of the ridge. There must have been hundreds of warriors for every white soldier still alive. They shifted from shelter to shelter, each trying to get close enough to count coup on a living enemy.

434. Marquis, *Wooden Leg*, 232–34.
435. "Big Beaver's Story of the Custer Battle," J. A. Blummer Manuscript, Little Bighorn Battlefield National Monument, 53.

The seventeen-year-old Cheyenne Big Beaver crawled close to Last Stand Hill and saw a warbonneted Lakota get shot in the head. —Little Bighorn Battlefield National Monument

Hundreds of Indian heads popped up and down. They would take a quick look, then move up a little farther. The soldiers must have seen their heads, but had to have been puzzled at which to shoot, for no sooner could they take aim than the Indians would disappear and move elsewhere. The soldiers kept behind their dead horses, and, likewise, the Indians could only catch quick glimpses of them, but it was easy enough to know where they were.

Antelope had been watching a crowd of Indian boys and older men on the surrounding hills. The men called out advice to the warriors who were hidden close to the soldiers. As the battle continued, however, they all began to move in. In their desire to strike coups some of the youths got in too close. Antelope saw one Lakota boy pitch forward, killed. The older men still called out for them to be cautious. "Be careful. Wait," they cried.[436]

FH 5:50–6:00, **Flying Hawk** [last 5:40, next 6:10(a)]. Flying Hawk took part in the fighting along the gulch on the north slope of the ridge, driving the retreating soldiers. At one point the bluecoats tried to make a stand, the third attempt, and succeeded in rallying for a few minutes.

However, the stand was short-lived. The Indians killed most of the soldiers, and the survivors fell back to Custer Hill, fighting and falling all the way. "Other Indians came to us after we got most of the men at the ravine," Flying Hawk said. "We all kept after them until they got to where Custer was. There was only a few of them left then."[437]

G 5:50–6:00, **Gall** [last 5:40, next 6:00]. As Gall and other warriors took the ground recently vacated by Calhoun's men, he could see the troopers falling back to the north. In his eyes, they retired step by step until forced back to the ridge where they all finally perished. "They were shot down in line where they stood," Gall commented. As fast as the soldiers were killed, their horses were herded up and driven toward the women and old men, who eagerly gathered them up.

To Gall, Calhoun's company appeared to fight as skirmishers, while farther along the line, "Keogh rallied his company, which was all killed in a bunch." The other companies broke, and the men "were shot down individually as they fled in confusion from the field."[438]

FB 5:50–6:00, **Flying By** [last 5:10, next 6:00]. Flying By rode his captured cavalry horse and a few other strays back to camp. He searched the saddlebags and found some extra ammunition. Having secured his prizes he saw the battle was still in progress and decided to return.

Crossing again at the ford, he rode up a coulee and over to the gully on the east side of the long ridge where the fighting had just been. Flying By wended his way along the gully, gingerly stepping around the flotsam of the battle. Scattered about on the ground were the bodies of the many soldiers who had already been killed.[439]

RF 5:50–6:00, **Red Feather** [last 5:40]. The battle was sweeping on past Red Feather, who was still on foot since his horse had been shot. After the scare he had when trying to take the pistol from the wounded officer, he decided he would stay back and let the younger braves take the battle to the bluecoats.

He did not follow the retreating soldiers any farther. Instead, he found enough items of interest scattered about in the immediate vicinity. Red Feather began

---

436. Marquis, *Custer on the Little Big Horn*, 89–90.
437. Hardorff, *Lakota Recollections*, 51; McCreight, *Firewater*, 113.
438. Graham, *The Custer Myth*, 89, 91.
439. Hammer, *Custer in '76*, 210.

gathering up saddlebags, getting four good ones. In them he found coffee and more ammunition. He found a little can with some liquid in it. He smelled it and tasted it. "It was whiskey," Red Feather recalled. He would savor his good fortune for a while before deciding whether to return to the battle.[440]

TM 5:50–6:00, **Two Moon** [last 5:40, next 6:00]. Now on the western slope of Battle Ridge, Two Moon again spotted the Gray Horse Company. Rallying his men once more, he led them on a charge directly at these troopers defending the northern end of the ridge. The Cheyennes galloped straight toward the knoll, but this encounter ended much as had the first.

"I could not break the line at the bunch of gray horses," said Two Moon, "and I wheeled and went to the left down the valley with the line of soldiers facing me as I went, firing at me, and all my men firing at the soldiers."

Riding partway down the valley, Two Moon reached safer ground, then cut back up on another ridge to view the action. The soldiers on the hilltop were still pouring out a heavy fire. "The White Horse Troops fought with signal desperation," Two Moon said. "If the others had not given up, but had fought with equal stubbornness of the White Horse Troop, Custer would have driven the Indians from the field."[441]

YT 5:50–6:00, **Young Two Moon** [last 5:40, next 6:00]. Following north in the wake of Yellow Nose's charge, Young Two Moon pulled up short of the far end of the ridge. There, as the soldiers got down partway toward the Gray Horse Company, the fire from that unit drove the Indians off and a number of the fugitives were able to reach them safely.

Although some soldiers were killed when they all banded together on the hill, the fire from the Gray Horse troop was coming so fast that the Indians retreated over the hill to the northwest (Cemetery Ridge). Under the protection of the ridge they dismounted and began firing at the remaining soldiers who were retreating to the top of the hill.[442]

WS 5:50–6:00, **White Shield** [last 4:20, next 6:10(b)]. White Shield had gone north, keeping between the soldiers and the river. He could see the Gray Horse Company standing its ground where the monument is now, but the other companies were running. Some went away from the river and some went toward the river. "The I[ndian]s charged from all sides," said White Shield, "and [the] co[mpanie]s came together a little."

It looked like four of the soldier groups were able to hold their horses, while three lost theirs. One company that lost its horses "was near where the road goes now," said White Shield, and "they were all on foot going toward the G[ray] H[orse] Co[mpany]."

White Shield got around on that side for a closer look. It appeared that one-half of the company moving toward the grays had lost their rifles and were fighting

440. Hardorff, *Lakota Recollections*, 88.
441. Dixon, *Vanishing Race*, 182; "Two Moons Recalls," 10.
442. Greene, *Lakota and Cheyenne*, 69–70. Young Two Moon described the terrain the Indians went out of sight behind as the hill toward the location of the later Crow Agency.

with six-shooters. "It was close fighting, almost hand to hand up that hill," White Shield said.

The Gray Horse troopers were dismounted. Their fire kept the Indians off one side of the hill, but the Indians on the other side cut across in front of them during their pursuit of Keogh's men. Men of the three companies (Keogh, Calhoun, Tom Custer) still surviving were about a half mile from the grays. Soon, all of them tried to move north to unite with the Gray Horse Company, but most of them were killed. Finally, the remaining soldiers also lost their horses. The remnants managed to make it to the Gray Horse Company on foot.[443]

L 5:50–6:00, **Lights** [last 5:40, next 6:00]. Lights had moved north and west below the main ridge until he took a position just west of Custer Hill. He did not know of any stands being made in the Keogh area. If one was made, it must have been short. On this side of the field, however, the soldiers were definitely making a stand. In fact, the fighting became a little too warm for Lights. He moved away from the hilltop and made his way back down toward the deep gully.[444]

❦ DISCUSSION. In general, Indians were reluctant to come close and trade bullet for bullet with a cohesive, unbeaten foe. Their preference for safety in distance, however, did not apply once their enemies turned to run. The Indians would be on a fleeing foe in an instant. Colonel Gibbon commented on the folly of mounted flight: "In running away from an Indian on horseback," he said, "the average horseman of the service is almost as much at the mercy of his pursuer as is the buffalo." Col. Richard I. Dodge wrote that the surest form of death on the plains was to turn one's back on an Indian. Capt. Thomas French echoed the statement when he wrote that to turn one's back on Indians is throwing life away. Custer himself knew the Indians would have "a buffalo hunt" whenever soldiers turned their backs and ran.[445]

Indeed, this is nearly what the battle along Keogh Coulee degenerated into during this segment—a buffalo hunt. Runs The Enemy and Little Hawk made this comparison, as did Julia Face, wife of the Brulé Lakota Thunder Hawk. The Indians were not on the high ridges in front of the soldiers, she said. Nor did Custer's men ever charge the Indians. "The Indians acted just like they were driving buffalo to a good place where they could be easily slaughtered," she said.[446] For the swift-riding Indians, the affair was becoming less of a battle and more of a game.

The confused fighting and virtual stampede of the troopers in and around Keogh's Coulee was the ineluctable result of the Indian breakthrough. In the south, troopers of Company L made a good show, at least in the early stages. In the north, Yates's battalion, particularly Company E, continued to put up stiff resistance. They made

443. White Shield, Notebook 348, Grinnell Collection.
444. Hardorff, *Lakota Recollections*, 167–68.
445. Gibbon, "Arms to Fight Indians," 15; W. Kent King, *Massacre: The Custer Cover-Up* (El Segundo, CA: Upton & Sons, 1989), 241; T. R. Fehrenbach, *Comanches: The Destruction of a People* (New York: Da Capo Press, 1994), 128, 299. Fehrenbach also added that "the sight of fleeing enemies spurred every feral killing instinct."
446. Hardorff, *Lakota Recollections*, 187, 189.

the best fight of all. In the middle, where Crazy Horse and others cut the line, the conduct of Company I left something to be desired. Although Keogh has been portrayed as a hard-drinking, hard-fighting, battle-toughened veteran, his Indian-fighting experience in the 7th Cavalry was almost nil.[447] His company was the weak link whose exploitation tipped the scales for the now-inevitable Lakota triumph.

About this time, 5:30 to 6:00, is when several secondary accounts tell us the battle ended. One, by John Gray, sets 5:50 as the time when some of Reno's and Benteen's companies left Weir Point to return to Reno Hill—a pullback caused by the appearance of an increasing number of Indians in their front.[448] Traditionally, the story is that the Indians only chased Reno *after* they had finished with Custer. But "Custer" is not dead yet. The apparent discrepancy in timing has an explanation. What was seen from the perch on Weir Point was probably the destruction of the troops on Calhoun-Finley Ridge. When the soldiers made their appearance on the high ground, they saw the Indians riding around and shooting—and the Indians saw them. Earlier, one group of braves chased Reno up his hill while a second confronted Custer at Medicine Tail Ford. Likewise, the first Indians to initially confront the troops near Weir Point were not those still fighting the remnants of Custer's battalion.

The Indians were cognizant of Reno's force possibly coming to Custer's aid. Red Horse voiced their fears when he acknowledged, "While this last fight was going on, we expected all the time to be attacked in the rear by the troops we had just left." Indians were posted between the commands to prevent any junction. Red Horse heard orders given. "Sioux men, go watch the soldiers on the hill and prevent their joining the different [Custer's] soldiers." Some of the Indians stripped the clothing off the dead troopers, dressed themselves in it, and went back and attacked Reno's command.[449] Warriors headed for the soldiers on the Weir Point skyline *before* the Custer fight was over.

Where did these braves get soldiers' clothing in sufficient quantities to attire themselves for a new attack on Reno? Some could have been picked up in the valley, but the first large, concentrated quantity became available immediately following the destruction of Companies L and C in the Calhoun Hill area. The probability that troops made their appearance on Weir Point about this time is shown by the reaction of the Indians. They were watching for them, they saw them, some had just finished dressing in the clothing of Calhoun's dead, and a significant number went south to chase them off Weir Point and back to their entrenchments.

447. Melbourne C. Chandler, *Of Garryowen In Glory: The History of the 7th U.S. Cavalry* (Annandale, VA: Turnpike Press, 1960), 18, 40, 41; Adjutant General's Office, *Chronological List of Actions, &c., with Indians from January 15, 1837 to January, 1891* (Ft. Collins, CO: Old Army Press, 1979), 24–63. Keogh missed participating in Custer's 1867 campaign, missed the Washita Battle, missed the 1873 Yellowstone Expedition, and missed the 1874 Black Hills Expedition. A list of thirty-one 7th Cavalry actions between its formation in 1866 and June 25, 1876, shows Keogh was the commanding officer in only one action. On May 27, 1867, at Pond Creek Station, Kansas, Keogh led Company I in a short "fight" with the Indians that resulted in no casualties to either Indian or trooper.
448. Gray, *Custer's Last Campaign*, 320, 372.
449. Graham, *The Custer Myth*, 60, 62.

The Oglala warrior Low Dog shot one of Custer's last escaping troopers.
—Little Bighorn Battlefield National Monument

Two Indians who went after Reno's men when they noticed the soldiers on Weir Point were Low Dog and Little Sun. Low Dog had participated in the initial attack against Calhoun Hill (see the 4:50 segment). After that check, he pulled back for a time. Low Dog and Littlesun then headed upriver when soldiers first appeared in the south (per Gray, about 5:25). In the words of John Stands In Timber, "Low Dog and Little Sun were two warriors that went back and forth between the fights."

After Reno retreated from the high ground, the two Indians were going back toward the Custer fight when a soldier on a fast horse broke from Custer's lines and galloped toward Reno Hill. The lone rider got past several Indians, and Low Dog and Little Sun gave chase. The soldier crossed Medicine Tail Coulee and looked like he might get away. Low Dog, however, was a good shot. He jumped off his horse, took aim, and knocked the man off his horse, just before he went over a knoll. Two or three other Lakotas chased after the soldier's horse, but Little Sun did not see whether they caught it. The site was about halfway up Medicine Tail Coulee, between its mouth and Cedar Coulee.[450]

There were plenty of Indians to go around. Although many stated that they didn't go after Reno until the last of Custer's men were killed, apparently there were still many others who did take that very course of action. Young Two Moon indicated as much. Middle-aged and young warriors were in the Custer fight, he said, but many Indians were not. There were enough left, "so remainder charge[d] Reno while Custer battle is on."[451] The Indians who were in the village, posted between the commands or leaving the fight after Calhoun's destruction, were in sufficient number to force Reno's and Benteen's men into a hasty retreat. Many battle episodes ran concurrently. The dusty men looking through field glasses from atop Weir Point did not witness the final fight on Custer Hill.

This also may be an opportune time to reassess the role played by Crazy Horse, much as we did with Gall. Readers familiar with secondary accounts of the battle

A view up Cedar Coulee with Weir Point in the background. Custer's battalion came down this avenue, while some Indians used the same route to chase Reno and Benteen off of Weir Point while the Custer battle was still being fought.

450. Margot Liberty, "Oral and Written Indian Perspectives on the Indian Wars," in *Legacy: New Perspectives on the Battle of the Little Bighorn,* ed. Charles E. Rankin (Helena: Montana Historical Society Press, 1996), 134–35.
451. Hardorff, *Memories,* 158.

may wonder when this work will address the Oglala's legendary sweep out of the north. The battle is rapidly approaching its denouement, but Crazy Horse has not yet begun his legendary ride. When will Crazy Horse rush through the valley, gathering one thousand warriors, crossing the river far to the northwest, swinging east to thwart Custer's moves, then finally sweeping down from his northern position to crush the unsuspecting troopers?

They won't read of it here. It did not happen. It is an incorrect story perpetuated during the past century by novelists, journalists, and historians.

The first storytellers of the late nineteenth century wrote almost exclusively from the white point of view and took little notice of what path Crazy Horse or any other Indian may have traced across the battlefield. By the turn of the century, however, a new pattern was being established. Crazy Horse was elevated in the chroniclers' eyes. His feats of leadership and daring, his supposed ability for quick, concise thinking and planning, combined with an astonishing strategic and tactical sense, led to his depiction as the archetypal warrior supreme.

Early-twentieth-century writers, from archdeacon novelist Cyrus T. Brady to the full-blooded Santee medical doctor Charles A. Eastman, told of Crazy Horse's lightning fighting between Reno's and Custer's battalions. He could be south of the village at one moment, only to circle around and hit Custer from the north "in the twinkling of an eye." Crazy Horse, "as quick as a flash," could size up the situation and outwit Custer "in a very few minutes."[452]

While operating at such a torrid pace, Crazy Horse was still able to stop in the village, ascertain how the battle was developing, then circle around to attack Custer from the northern ravines. Crazy Horse could do this even while leaving his ponies behind at the river crossing, creeping with his warriors up behind Last Stand Hill, and hiding "for a long time" waiting for Custer to blunder into them.[453]

The "Strange Man of the Oglalas" could fight the whites in attack after attack until his horse failed him. He could get a fresh mount, council with Sitting Bull, gather Cheyenne warriors, sweep around the far northern edge of Custer's ridge, and block the escape route just as Custer himself reached the top. The greatest deeds of the day were said to have been planned by Crazy Horse.[454]

An even more romanticized account has Crazy Horse leading one thousand warriors through the village to the north and back down to the ridge where the Oglala may actually have met the lieutenant colonel himself, lance to carbine, eye to eye, "spears high in the air, their glistening points aimed right at Custer." Then Crazy Horse crushed everything in his path, winning the battle not with his courage but with his brain.[455]

---

452. Brady, *Indian Fights and Fighters*, vi, vii, xvi, 238, 254; Charles A. Eastman, *Indian Heroes and Great Chieftains* (Boston: Little, Brown, 1918), 99–100.

453. George E. Hyde, *Red Cloud's Folk: A History of the Oglala Sioux Indians* (Norman: University of Oklahoma Press, 1937), 270; Kuhlman, *Legend Into History*, 12, 193; Greene, *Evidence and the Custer Enigma*, 35.

454. Edgar I. Stewart, *Custer's Luck* (Norman: University of Oklahoma Press, 1955) 436–37; Miller, *Custer's Fall*, 138; Sandoz, *Crazy Horse*, 328–31; Mari Sandoz, *The Battle of the Little Bighorn* (Philadelphia. J. B. Lippincott, 1966), 127.

455. Ambrose, *Crazy Horse and Custer*, 438–45.

In another version, Custer was supposedly sitting atop Calhoun Hill, assessing Crazy Horse's move north down the valley. He then led his battalion toward the river near the mouth of Deep Ravine. By the time Custer approached the river, Crazy Horse had led his minions in a semicircle around the northern hills to appear behind Custer on the ridge he had just vacated.[456] This trip was six times the distance Custer traveled. Had Custer been galloping at the norm of nine miles per hour, Crazy Horse must have been cruising at fifty-four miles per hour—freeway speed. This was quite an accomplishment, even for one with hailstones and lightning painted on his face.

As late as 1994, in a book that professed to tell the Indian side of the story, James Welch repeated the same tale of Crazy Horse coming out of the north, although he did acknowledge that there was "pretty convincing evidence" to the contrary. Nevertheless, he continued in the established mode: Gall attacked Calhoun Hill before Crazy Horse even appeared on the field—a situation exactly reversed from reality.[457]

The number of such tales is voluminous. All share the traditional narrative of Crazy Horse sweeping out of the north.[458] The accounts of Crazy Horse's deeds that day run from near possibilities to virtual impossibilities. Yet their sheer number must give pause to those who would question their accuracy. How can we contend that it did not happen that way? The answer is found in eyewitness accounts combined with the logical restrictions of time and terrain. Crazy Horse's actions must be analyzed in exactly the same manner as we have been examining all the Indian movements.

We are assured of Crazy Horse's participation in the Reno fight, for numerous warriors—including Two Moon, Black Elk, Iron Hawk, Eagle Elk, Red Feather, Short Bull, and Flying Hawk—either saw him there or fought with him. Could Crazy Horse have subsequently vacated the southern arena near Reno's retreat crossing at approximately 4:15, done all the things the white narratives credit him with, and yet be approaching Calhoun Hill about 4:45?

Crazy Horse would have had to ride about three miles back to his own village. From there he would have had to go another two miles down the valley to the far northern crossing, then another mile and a half east to reach Last Stand Hill from the north, then another mile south to get southeast of Calhoun Hill where many Indian eyewitnesses placed him. The entire circle is more than seven miles long.

John S. Gray's time-motion analysis of troop movements at the Little Bighorn indicates that Custer rode seven miles from the divide in the Wolf Mountains to the lone tipi site on Reno Creek in one hour and forty-eight minutes. Traveling at a quicker pace than the regulars, Lieutenant Varnum and his Crow scouts headed directly down Reno Creek from the divide and were at the mouth of No Name

456. Weibert, *Sixty-Six Years*, 57–59.
457. Welch, *Killing Custer*, 168, 305.
458. For additional examples of this interpretation, see Evan S. Connell, *Son of the Morning Star* (New York: Harper & Row, 1984), xiv; Graham, *The Custer Myth*, ix; Scott et al., *Archaeological Perspectives*, 127; Utley, *Cavalier in Buckskin*, 190–91. Apparently Utley has reevaluated the situation, for he dropped the "Crazy Horse from the north" scenario in his 1993 *Lance and the Shield*.

Creek, a seven-mile ride that took one hour and ten minutes. Col. Nelson A. Miles of the United States 5th Infantry visited the battlefield in June 1878 and measured the distance from Reno's hilltop to the knoll of Custer's Last Stand. Miles's cavalrymen walked the four miles in fifty-eight minutes.[459]

In a flat-out seven-mile race, Crazy Horse assuredly would have surpassed the cavalry's rate of movement. But he did not beeline between two points. According to the white interpretations, he was delayed at the Reno fight and delayed back in his camp when he gathered his warriors. He changed ponies. He councils with Sitting Bull. He watched the battle develop in the hills to the east of the river while he planned his next moves. He did not know where Custer was going, but he went north—away from the fight—to intercept him. He left his ponies at the northern river crossing and crept up to the battlefield. He waited in the northern ravines before attacking. Using the time and terrain constraints implicit in these interpretations, Crazy Horse could have taken one hour to complete his circle, given the absolute minimum of activities charged to him, or over two hours, had he taken all the actions ascribed to him. By then the battle would have been over. Crazy Horse may have arrived in time only to witness the women stripping the soldiers' dead bodies. We have seen that Big Beaver was one of the Indians who actually did take a northern route along the river, going east up a coulee, leaving his horse behind and crawling up to the battle area from the north. We have also seen that Big Beaver arrived only in time to witness the final action around Last Stand Hill.

However, we need not rely solely on time and terrain restrictions to illustrate the extreme unlikelihood of such a wide northern sweep. The Indians told us where Crazy Horse went. We have followed his progress back to the village, where Flying Hawk said they dropped off some wounded braves. They immediately went to Medicine Tail Ford, where Short Bull and Pretty White Buffalo commented on Crazy Horse crossing the river. He was next placed in the area of Calhoun Hill by numerous Indians who fought with him that day, including Foolish Elk, Lone Bear, He Dog, Red Feather, and Flying Hawk. White Bull rode from the bluffs where Reno had retreated directly north on the east side of the river. He approached Calhoun Hill up the Deep Coulee avenue, but was driven out by heavy gunfire. He worked his way east where he joined who else but Crazy Horse and his men, already there fighting. Had Crazy Horse gone on his mythical northern sweep, or done half the deeds ascribed to him, he would not have been fighting near Calhoun Hill in this phase of the battle.

Crazy Horse was very reticent about speaking to white recorders about his battle deeds. He told his medicine man, Chips (Encouraging Bear), about the battle, but he had little to say regarding the Custer portion of the fight. What seemed to occupy his thoughts, according to Chips, were episodes in the Reno conflict, the charge of the Ree scouts, and how many Lakota were killed. After he surrendered in 1877, Crazy Horse gave an account of the battle through his spokesman, Horned Horse. According to that account, the initial assault was a surprise. The Indians had

459. Gray, *Custer's Last Campaign,* 251–52; Nelson A. Miles, *Personal Recollections and Observations of General Nelson A. Miles* (Chicago: The Werner Company, 1897), 290.

made no plan of ambush. Had there been any such foresight, women and children would not have been left in danger in the camp, which caused great consternation among the warriors. Custer mistook the women and children stampeding in a northerly direction down the valley for the main body of Indians. The warriors merely divided into two groups, one going between the noncombatants and Custer and the other circling his rear.[460]

There is no reason to countenance the interpretation that places Crazy Horse on a far northern sweep through the valley and around the battlefield. It did not happen. The Indian accounts are clear concerning his whereabouts. Only after the collapse of the Calhoun-Keogh position did Crazy Horse continue north where he may have, finally, confronted the last of Custer's men making their stand on the far knob of the ridge. Even this is far from certain. Flying Hawk indicated (see 6:10(a) segment) that during the final phase of the battle, the great Oglala leader jumped on his pony and chased off after one of the last fleeing troopers. Crazy Horse may have had nothing at all to do with the final fight on Last Stand Hill.

Some early descriptions of the fight might be excused simply because they did not make use of Indian accounts. Yet, as more Indian accounts became available, Crazy Horse's prowess multiplied in Malthusian bounds. Where did the initial story of the northern sweep originate? Indian accounts that appeared within a few years of the battle, stories from men such as Kill Eagle, Red Horse, Afraid of Eagles, Low Dog, Crow King, Hump, Iron Thunder, and Sitting Bull, made no mention of such a maneuver. Gall appears to have been the first to start the snowball rolling. In 1886, enjoying favored status with the authorities, he attended the battlefield's ten-year anniversary and, being the most renowned ex-warrior present, quickly ingratiated himself to several influential whites. Edward S. Godfrey, a lieutenant at the battle, and David F. Barry, note-taker and photographer, both succumbed to Gall's apparent sincerity and freely used his statements in their own writings. "Crazy Horse went to the extreme north end of the camp," Gall said. He turned right and went up a very deep ravine and "he came very close to the soldiers on their north side." Crow King fired at Custer's men from the south, Gall said, "and Crazy Horse from the north."[461]

This is fine storytelling, but Gall did not ride with Crazy Horse that day and did not see where he went. What we may have, however, is a pretty fair rendition of actual events as passed down through Indian oral tradition. Gall may only have been repeating the story as he heard it. Unfortunately, the story that Gall told was not the story that the white recorders understood. First, Gall, like Antelope, most likely perceived Battle Ridge in an east-west orientation, and when he said Crazy Horse was north of the ridge, he meant he was in the Keogh area, the side of the ridge opposite that of the river. Since the white recorders perceived the ridge in north-south terms, they drew their maps showing Crazy Horse approaching from north of the Last Stand Hill end of the ridge. Second, the white exaggeration of the village size greatly distorted Crazy Horse's movements. Gall said he rode down the

---

460. Carroll, *Ricker Tablets*, 49; Robert M. Utley, *Custer and the Great Controversy*, 92; Graham, *The Custer Myth*, 63.
461. Marquis, *Custer on the Little Big Horn*, 104–14; Graham, *The Custer Myth*, 47–79, 89–96; Burdick, *Barry's Notes*, 13.

valley to cross at a ford beyond the northern end of the village. True, but the northern end was at Medicine Tail Ford. Since the white recorders believed the village stretched three or four miles along the valley, they drew their maps showing Crazy Horse crossing the Little Bighorn at a ford downstream of the northern end of Battle Ridge.

White recorders attached themselves wholeheartedly to Gall's narration and read what they wanted into it from their own preconceptions. From that point on, Crazy Horse's movements go off on a tangent, and are built upon by subsequent historians until the present day, in which we find a story far removed from reality. This lamentable condition developed from a number of factors: different terrain perceptions between Indian and white, white exaggeration of the village size, poor critical examination of the accounts, and a reluctance to take the time to research the primary sources again, when so many others had already done the groundwork and concurred with the consensus explanation. If scores of writers concluded that Crazy Horse circled to the far north to attack Custer, there seemed little reason to challenge the accepted wisdom. An incorrect premise was accepted, perpetuated, and distorted with each telling. Thus we have the paradox faced by all historians: rely on prior scholarship or go through the painstaking task of rebuilding every story from the ground up. By exercising the latter option, little time is left to pursue new theories. Yet, if we rely too heavily on others we risk perpetuating a story such as Crazy Horse's sweep to the north, which has drifted out of the realm of history and into the land of fantasy.

In the final analysis we must return to the primary sources for historical accuracy. Crazy Horse was an extraordinary warrior, courageous, daring, and a stellar example for his followers. But he was no figure from Homeric legend, touched and guided by the gods.[462]

By six o'clock, Crazy Horse had been fighting on the landward side of Battle Ridge (label it the north side or east side at your preference) for over one hour. As the battle shifted north, Crazy Horse and his followers moved with the flow, pushing along the Keogh escapees, and finally confronting Yates's battalion already engaged in its stand on the north end of the ridge. Custer and Crazy Horse never knew of each other's presence on the field. They probably never saw each other, but if they did, they certainly did not know who they saw. In any case, it did not matter one iota by this time.

---

462. For a more detailed account, see Gregory F. Michno, "Crazy Horse, Custer, and the Sweep to the North," *Montana The Magazine of Western History* 43, no. 3 (summer 1993): 42–53.

V

Victory

C 6:00 - 6:10
Last Stand

0   1/8   1/4 Mile
1/4 Mile - 440 Yards

N

TM
TE
WL
L
G
IH
RH
Cemetery Ravine
LB
BB
Deep Ravine
YT
SB
Battle Ridge
LH
LH
YN
FB
Finley Ridge
Greasy Grass Ridge
Calhoun Hill
Little Bighorn River
Deep Coulee

LAST STAND, 6:00–6:10

WL 6:00–6:10, **Wooden Leg** [last 5:50, next 6:10(a)]. Remaining mounted most of the time, Wooden Leg rode from place to place north of the ridge. While his older brother, Yellow Hair, crept in closer with the other warriors, Wooden Leg stayed farther back, as his father had asked.

From a gulch just north of the west end of the ridge, he could see that all the soldiers were killed except for a band that remained hidden behind their dead horses. He could see along the north slope of the ridge, where hundreds of Indians crept in closer. The soldiers, however, could not see the warriors, except on occasion when one might jump up quickly to shoot and duck back down again. Wooden Leg could not see the soldiers either, but he knew where they were as they fired from behind their horses.

Wooden Leg dismounted and let out his long lariat for leading his horse while he, too, crept a little closer up the slope. During this portion of the battle, Wooden Leg fired several shots with his captured rifle and about twelve shots with his six-shooter. It was much easier to shoot while crawling up the slope than it had been on horseback. Still, he could not see any particular soldiers to shoot at, so he just sent his bullets in their direction.

Wooden Leg crawled to a slope a short distance north of the hill where the stone monument now stands. About half a lariat length in front of Wooden Leg, a Lakota wearing a warbonnet was lying down behind a clump of sagebrush. Other Indians, boys included, mingled nearby, crowding in to try to strike a blow on any dead soldiers they might find. A Cheyenne boy was lying down right next to the warbonneted Lakota. As the man peeped up to fire, a soldier bullet hit him exactly in the middle of the forehead. His arms and legs jumped spasmodically for a few moments, then he died. The boy quickly slid back downhill into the gully and ran away.[463]

FB 6:00–6:10, **Flying By** [last 5:50, next 6:10(a)]. As Flying By rode the ridge to the north, he saw bodies of the soldiers who had been killed all the way along his path. As far as he could see there had only been one stand, and it was made in the place where Custer would be killed, down at the end of the long ridge.[464]

LB 6:00–6:10, **Lone Bear** [last 5:40, next 6:10(a)]. The soldiers were pushed along the ridge to the far end, where they turned for another fight. Though the battle there "was not so long or as firm as the one made" in Keogh's sector, the fight on Custer Hill was at close quarters, and "there was a good stand made."[465]

G 6:00–6:10, **Gall** [last 5:50, next 6:10(b)]. Gall neared the end of the ridge where the last soldiers were making a stand. "They were fighting good," he

---

463. Marquis, *Wooden Leg*, 234–36.
464. Hammer, *Custer in '76*, 210.
465. Hardorff, *Lakota Recollections*, 157, 162.

said. "The men were loading and firing, but they could not hit the warriors in the gulley and in the ravine. The dust and smoke was as black as evening."[466]

L 6:00–6:10, **Lights** [last 5:50, next 6:10(a)]. Lights had moved away from the hot fight going on around Custer Hill. Looking back, he could see the soldiers who had fled the Keogh fight joining those making the stand on the hill. Most of them were on foot. They settled in to make a longer stand there than anywhere else on the field. But by this time the warriors had captured plenty of guns and ammunition and were better equipped to fight. Subsequently, many soldiers were killed on the hilltop where the monument now stands.[467]

TE 6:00–6:10, **Two Eagles** [last 5:40, next 6:10(a)]. The soldiers had scattered during the fighting along the ridge. A number of them headed from the Keogh area toward Custer Hill and, while they went north, the warriors moved in. All the way from Calhoun Hill to Custer Hill, the "soldiers and Indians were very close to each other," said Two Eagles.

The most stubborn stand the soldiers made was on Custer Hill. From his position a short way north and west of that point, Two Eagles noticed the hilltop was very level and the soldiers took the spot to continue their defense. It mattered little. "They were killed on top of the ridge," Two Eagles declared.[468]

RH 6:00–6:10, **Red Hawk** [last 5:40, next 6:10(a)]. The Indians put their captured weapons to use against the retreating soldiers. The bluecoats were "falling back steadily to Custer Hill where another stand was made," said Red Hawk. "Here the soldiers made a desperate fight."[469]

TM 6:00–6:10, **Two Moon** [last 5:50, next 6:10(a)]. After Two Moon's second failed charge against the Gray Horse troop, he rode up on a ridge (Cemetery) to assess the action. There he met the Cheyenne council chief, Black Bear, replete with a large warbonnet. They saw a wounded soldier lying on the ground. Two Moon jumped off his horse and took the man's scalp.

After mounting up, he rode along the ridge and came to a group of four dead soldiers. They all were wearing good clothes; one had on a red flannel shirt, and the others wore shirts with red stripes on the arms. "I jumped off my horse and took their clothes and their guns," Two Moon said.

Thus temporarily satisfied with his prizes, Two Moon turned back to watch the fight. The combat was so close he could hardly distinguish the Indians from the soldiers. Nevertheless, the "grey bunch" was still fighting. "Custer was a brave man," Two Moon said. "I give him credit for attacking a people that vastly outnumbered his." However, Two Moon thought something was the matter with Custer's men. "They did not run nor seek shelter, but stayed right out in the open where it was easy to shoot them down. Any ordinary bunch of men would have dropped into a

466. Burdick, *Barry's Notes*, 13.
467. Hardorff, *Lakota Recollections*, 167, 170, 173.
468. Ibid., 148, 149.
469. Ibid., 44.

watercourse, or a draw, where they could have fought for a long time."Two Moon thought that maybe the soldiers had too much whiskey to drink.[470]

LH 6:00–6:10, **Left Hand.** Born in the Powder River country, the son of a man known as Cherry, Left Hand was actually part Blackfoot and part Cheyenne. For most of his life, however, he had been affiliated with the Arapahos and had joined four of them scouting for Shoshones when fate led them to the battleground.

When Reno attacked, Left Hand dressed for the fight wearing only a breechcloth and shirt. His medicine was a piece of buffalo hide made into a cross with two feathers in it, which he wore in his hair. During the battle with Reno, Left Hand got separated from the other Arapahos and continued to fight on his own.

Later in the day up on the ridge, the soldiers were nearly surrounded when Left Hand rode into the battle. There was much shooting, bullets whizzed all around, Indians yelled, and the scene was one of utter chaos. Left Hand, mounted and carrying a lance with a point sharpened like an arrow, saw a wounded Indian on foot. He looked like one of the army's Crow or Arikara scouts. Left Hand rode him down and struck him in the chest. The lance went clear through the Indian and he fell over a pile of dead soldiers.

The thrill of this conquest, however, did not last long. Left Hand found out that he had killed a Lakota, and the dead man's friends were threatening to kill him in revenge. One Lakota tried to take Left Hand's horse away from him, but he refused to give him up. In a classic understatement, Left Hand commented, "Everyone was excited."[471]

YN 6:00–6:10, **Yellow Nose** [last 5:40, next 6:10(a)]. Running down the fleeing soldiers, Yellow Nose moved along the ridge toward the northern end. It was mayhem. "The running horses filled the air with blinding dust," he said, "which, together with the smoke of the firing, caused great confusion."Yellow Nose dashed into the maelstrom. Two Indian horses collided, and both riders and mounts fell and rolled in the dirt. Yellow Nose barely avoided them. Turning about, he again used his captured flag to count coup on a soldier. The Indian yells, the rattle of gunfire, and the tramp of the horses' feet were deafening. In the turmoil, Indians killed some of their own warriors by mistake.

One of those killed was Lame White Man. Yellow Nose heard that the Cheyenne chief had put on a soldier's coat that he had found. A Lakota, thinking he was a soldier, shot him, only to be killed in turn by an Arapaho who thought the Lakota was one of Custer's scouts.[472] The fight had truly escalated into a frenzy of killing.

SB 6:00–6:10, **Standing Bear** [last 5:50, next 6:10(a)]. Moving north along the ridge to where he could see better, Standing Bear noticed dismounted soldiers holding their horses by the bridles. "They were ready for us," he said, and when they began to shoot, "the bullets were just raining." Yet, even then, many

470. Hardorff, *Lakota Recollections*, 138; Dixon, *Vanishing Race*, 182.
471. Graham, *The Custer Myth*, 111.
472. "Yellow Nose Tells," 16; Rankin, ed., *Legacy*, 135.

Indians kept in the ravines while creeping up, and most of the bullets passed harm-lessly overhead.

Custer was now on the ridge, his soldiers sitting on the hill with their hats off. Standing Bear finally overcame his reluctance to get into the thick of the fight. "Hokahey!" he yelled, as he joined in with a band of warriors charging up the hill. One of them, Bear Horn, rode up too close to shoot at a soldier and was himself shot down.

Standing Bear's group started back downhill when a man named Burst Thunder came up and said that a little farther down was a dead Ree they could scalp. They rode over to the dead Indian. One of the party had just finished pulling the hair off the "Ree" when two Cheyennes rode up. Although he had suggested lifting the scalp in the first place, Burst Thunder had second thoughts. When he asked the Cheyennes if they could identify the man, one of them dismounted and turned the dead Indian over. To everyone's surprise and consternation, he was a Cheyenne. "This shows how crazy everyone was at this time," Standing Bear said.[473]

Next, three riders appeared carrying another dead Cheyenne across their horses. Standing Bear watched them trail off down the hill. When he next looked up at the soldiers, there were fewer of them left alive. Just then, he heard some of the men say, "They have gone!" Standing Bear looked over to see most of the remaining cavalry horses on Custer Hill breaking loose and running away.[474]

IH 6:00–6:10, **Iron Hawk** [last 5:40, next 6:10(a)]. After watching the "bullet-proof" Cheyenne make several bravery runs at the soldiers on the ridge, the fight again settled into another long-distance shooting match. On Last Stand Hill, Iron Hawk saw about twenty men on horseback and about thirty men on foot. "The Indians pressed and crowded right in around them on Custer Hill." But the soldiers were not yet ready to die. Said Iron Hawk, "We stood here a long time." Finally, he heard a voice call out, "Now they are going, they are going." Iron Hawk "looked up and saw the cavalry horses stampeding. They were all gray horses."[475]

LH 6:00–6:10, **Little Hawk** [last 5:50, next 6:10(a)]. The soldiers that had run along the ridge now gathered with the remainder on the round knoll where the monument stands. Little Hawk saw them first tie their horses in fours, but soon after, they set them loose. The horses scattered, but most of them ran down to the Little Bighorn.[476]

YT 6:00–6:10, **Young Two Moon** [last 5:50, next 6:10(a)]. The Indians fought dismounted against the men of the Gray Horse Company on the hill. With no quick resolution, however, they decided to mount up and charge. At this point, Young Two Moon saw the soldiers turn their gray horses loose. Some of them ran right through the Indians and down to the river.

473. DeMallie, *Sixth Grandfather*, 185–86; Powell, *Sacred Mountain*, 1028, 1371; Vestal, *Warpath*, 199. The Indian thought responsible for doing the actual scalping of Lame White Man was the Minneconjou Little Crow, brother of Hump and Iron Thunder.
474. DeMallie, *Sixth Grandfather*, 186
475. Hardorff, *Lakota Recollections*, 66; DeMallie, *Sixth Grandfather*, 191.
476. Greene, *Lakota and Cheyenne*, 64.

The divide above Cemetery Ravine where Iron Hawk and others witnessed the last gray horses stampeding from Custer Hill.

As the warriors charged to the top of a hill, they could see other companies fighting nearer to the river. Then all of the soldiers turned their horses loose. The fighting became furious and the Gray Horse Company was destroyed on the hill near where they had driven the Indians (Two Moon's second charge) out of sight.[477]

BB 6:00–6:10, **Big Beaver** [last 5:50, next 6:10(a)]. After the warbonneted Lakota had been shot right in front of him, Big Beaver crawled back down the coulee to put a bit more distance between himself and the deadly soldier bullets. About that time, a soldier mounted a sorrel horse and began to ride as fast as he could toward the east. Two Cheyennes cut him off and killed him along the eastern side of the coulee where Keogh had once held his position.

Big Beaver moved closer as the Cheyennes scalped the man. Before they moved on, he saw them hang the bloody hair on a branch of sagebrush like a grisly trophy. Big Beaver went over and searched through the dead soldier's pockets, finding a few useful items. Then he took the man's gun. He held it up proudly and admired it, for it was the first one he had ever had.

477. Ibid., 70.

*The knoll northeast of Custer Hill where Big Beaver may
have witnessed the shooting of the warbonneted Lakota.*

Making his way back down the coulee, Big Beaver noticed there was some new commotion at the end of the ridge. The Indians were all rushing toward the hill where the soldiers were making their last desperate fight.[478]

DISCUSSION. By this point, you may have noted other discrepancies in the Indian accounts, but this time they are not from the pen of D. H. Miller. In the 5:50 segment, Wooden Leg described a trooper running away to the north. He was chased by Indians but eventually he stopped and killed himself, after which Big Beaver took the soldier's gun. In that same segment, however, Big Beaver said he was crawling up on the north slope of Custer Hill. In front of him, a warbonneted Lakota was shot in the head and Big Beaver quickly crawled away. The 6:00 segment brings us similar stories, but in reversed order. Wooden Leg said he saw a warbonneted Lakota shot in the head, and a Cheyenne boy running away. Big Beaver said he saw a soldier riding away to the east. Two Cheyennes killed the man and Big Beaver took his gun. Which is the correct story and sequence?

---

478. "Big Beaver's Story," Blummer Ms., 53.

Wooden Leg told Dr. Marquis his story in the late 1920s. He visited with him and occasionally accompanied the doctor to the battlefield. In 1928, Big Beaver visited both Marquis and Joseph A. Blummer at the latter's store in the little community of Garryowen, located near Reno's first skirmish line in the valley. Joe Blummer wrote of the visit in a manuscript in which he hoped to compile what he had learned directly from the battle participants so that future students could follow up on his findings.

For three days, Big Beaver, Marquis, and Blummer walked the battlefield and talked each night in Joe's store. Big Beaver's story comes from Blummer's manuscript. The incidents described by Big Beaver, such as the shooting of the Lakota with the warbonnet, the fleeing trooper killed and scalped by two Cheyennes, and the capture of the gun, are events that he personally saw or participated in. His chronology is also more consistent with the flow of events: after the killing of the escapee, Big Beaver got his gun and returned in time to see the Indians rushing up on the last defenders on the hill. In Wooden Leg's rendition, the trooper escapes, then the Indians settle down for more long-range firing that results in the warbonneted Lakota being shot in the head.

Gravemarker 174, where Big Beaver found the scalped trooper and captured his first rifle.

Author Richard G. Hardorff made note of the inconsistencies. Marquis credited Wooden Leg with witnessing the shooting of the warbonneted Lakota when it was Big Beaver's observation, and he credited Wooden Leg with witnessing the death of the fleeing trooper as a suicide victim when it was Big Beaver's observation that the trooper was a homicide victim. Hardorff intimates that Marquis may have altered the Big Beaver–Wooden Leg testimony to better fit his mass suicide theory.[479]

Sadly, this appears to be the case. Marquis had many Cheyenne informants, including Wooden Leg, Big Beaver, Red Bird (Little Wolf), Turkey Leg, and Antelope (Kate Bighead). Although Wooden Leg supplied the bulk of the story, Marquis may have "fleshed out" parts with the testimony of the other Indians and lumped it all together as if it was all seen by Wooden Leg.[480] Marquis's methods may also cause consternation concerning the reliability of the Antelope account. Many of her phrases closely resemble those attributed to Wooden Leg. How much of that is due to Indian oral tradition and how much is due to Marquis will be difficult to determine.

Back on the far end of the ridge, time was running out for the remnants of Custer's battalion. Companies E and F still put up a stiff resistance. They were augmented by perhaps ten survivors of the Keogh debacle, but these late additions did little to postpone the inevitable. As shown by the positions of the bodies of both men and horses below the crest, the defenders of Custer Hill were still mainly concerned about the threat to the south and west. They had already been making their own stand prior to the collapse of the Calhoun-Keogh groups.[481]

As the warriors closed in on the hilltop, the defenders still made a forlorn attempt to salvage the situation. If it worked, they had the very slightest possibility that some might survive. If it failed, they had thrown away all hope of salvation. After the battle, the soldier of fortune, 5th U.S. cavalryman, and later U.S. marshal Chris Madsen received information from Sitting Bull concerning the soldiers' last stratagem. "The troops turned the horses loose in the hope that the Indians would follow them, thereby giving Custer a chance to escape. The Indians, however, paid no attention to the horses, but bore steadily down upon the knoll, and the horseless soldiers, unable to take flight, were slain to a man."[482]

The soldiers' plan had failed. It is likely they set most of their remaining horses loose with the intention that they run north and east. If the Indians chased the horses toward the hills, perhaps the soldiers would have a better chance of reaching the cutbanks along the river. Standing Bear said that some horses did go north, where they were caught by the Indian boys in the hills. But most of the mounts, hungry and thirsty, turned to head for the river. Even if they had not, there were still too many fish for the available bait.

Bearing in mind Iron Hawk's comment that the stampeding mounts "were all gray horses," one might wonder just how many grays could have been released at

479. Hardorff, *Hokahey!*, 67, 73.
480. George B. Grinnell faced a similar situation with numerous Cheyenne informants. He chose not to tell the story of the battle as if it were from one individual, but acknowledged that it was a composite gleaned from many voices. See Grinnell, *Fighting Cheyennes*, 346.
481. Trinque, "Defense of Custer Hill," 30.
482. Homer Croy, *Trigger Marshall: The Story of Chris Madsen* (New York: Duell, Sloan and Pearce, 1958), 15.

this time. We have nearly come to the end of the fight and once again we meet more of those ubiquitous gray horses. Their conspicuous gray-white color, when compared with the more nondescript bays and sorrels, make them prominent in many accounts. However, the forty or so men of Company E in Custer's battalion were not the only ones with gray-white mounts. Traditionally, the trumpeters also rode gray horses, as did the regimental band. The band did not accompany the regiment on its final sortie, but its fittest horses were distributed among the companies when left behind at the Powder River camp. Adj. William W. Cooke also rode a white horse. Thus, there may have been upwards of fifty-five grays riding with Custer's battalion.

The first losses apparently occurred when Runs The Enemy and about thirty Indians cut a number of the horses out from below the present monument area and ran them to the river, where Waterman witnessed their arrival and Bobtail Horse captured two. Although other Indians assuredly kept some, Runs The Enemy released his when he returned to the fight. Shortly after these grays were cut out, Lame White Man and the suicide boys hit the same area and more grays were lost, either stampeded or shot. Yet, there were still enough to gather again at Custer Hill for Two Moon and others to recognize them there as a distinct group. Another portion must have been subsequently shot by the Indians or felled by troopers as breastworks as the situation deteriorated.[483] Iron Hawk and Young Two Moon then described gray horses running from Last Stand Hill. In the next segment we will find Black Elk sighting grays coming to the river and Feather Earring catching five of them. After all was said and done, Soldier Wolf estimated a total of about eighty or ninety head of government horses had been captured alive.[484]

The explanation for this seemingly large number of gray horses galloping through so many Indian accounts must stem in part from the likelihood that the Indians kept seeing, capturing, and releasing a number of the same horses over and over again. Perhaps a dozen or more were taken in the Runs The Enemy episode, and maybe another dozen were killed or captured in the Lame White Man–suicide boys attack. This leaves twenty or more grays to gather on the hill, remnants of Company E, the trumpeters, and headquarters staff—still a recognizable group for Two Moon to comment about. Of the grays taken to the river, some were released because of wounds, exhaustion, or because their captors had to return unhindered to the fight. The thirsty horses stayed at the Deep Ravine Ford, drinking their fill. Subsequently, they were recaptured and re-released a number of times. On the hill, more grays were killed, run off, or destroyed for breastworks. Near the end, the horses Iron Hawk saw stampeding from Last Stand Hill may have been all grays, but they had to be only a small handful.

Of late there have been some fine archaeological studies that have provided new light on some of the mysteries of the battle. One of them, by Richard A. Fox Jr., has taken the stance that the Custer battle had "no famous last stand"—that the last stand is a myth.[485] Certainly there was no last stand a la Errol Flynn in the 1941

483. Trinque, "Defense of Custer Hill," 23, 27.
484. Greene, *Lakota and Cheyenne*, 52.
485. Fox, *Archaeology, History*, 17, 201, 216, 330.

movie *They Died with Their Boots On,* where Custer remains on his feet until the end, standing next to the guidon flapping in the breeze and facing hundreds of circling warriors with his sabre drawn and six-gun blazing while scores of his men lie dead at his feet until, finally, he takes the last bullet and clutches his chest as he dies, the last of the last.

Perhaps the conjured image of a last stand is more a matter of semantics and nuance. Because Sergeant Butler may have died after the fight, or because a trooper may have been stabbed while feigning death in the aftermath, does not mean there was no last stand. Was there no last stand at the Alamo because a few remaining defenders ran to take sanctuary in the mission chapel? Of course not. Granted, there was no Hollywood-style last stand on the Little Bighorn. Yet, it is also clear from numerous Indian accounts that portions of Companies E and F had been fighting from their position on or near the end of the ridge for more than an hour. The Indians—including Flying By, Gall, Wooden Leg, Lights, Two Eagles, Red Hawk, Flying Hawk, Lone Bear, Yellow Nose, Yellow Horse, Tall Bull, and Two Moon—told us the soldiers made a stand. Good Voiced Elk also said, "No stand was made until they got to the end of the long ridge."[486] Other Indians will make similar comments in the next segment.

Although the individual observers' recollection of the stand's duration and intensity varied, the fact that it took place cannot be dismissed. Most of the Indian casualties on Custer's field were inflicted by soldiers defending the northern portion of the battleground (see 6:10(b) Discussion). The troopers made several "stands," and one of them was "last." The time spent in their fight and the results of their shooting are all the proof we need to show that they defended their ground tenaciously. A revisionist interpretation using archaeological evidence and claiming an apparent paucity of government cartridges on Custer Hill cannot change this, and neither can political correctness. Although the next time segment tells of the remaining troopers running from Custer Hill, they held their ground and fought from their position as long as they humanly could. Because they all eventually died does not mean they did not desperately try to live. I call this a "last stand." So did the Indians.[487]

---

486. Good Voiced Elk interview, Ellison Collection.
487. I do not believe Fox generated his conclusions with politically correct considerations in mind. His is a scholarly work and it is much more involved than will meet the eye of the casual reader. What I am concerned about are "popularizers" who might happily pick up on some of Fox's statements and run with them for their own purposes. "It is difficult to argue with Fox's conclusion," reads one. Indeed. It is doubly difficult when you never even try. See Welch, *Killing Custer,* 45–46, 57, 64, 77–80, 145–46, 166, 169–70, 279, for commentary about genocide, greed, and injustice. I submit that Fox's writing about panicked troopers and no "last stand" plays right into the hands of those more concerned with officious moralizing than with finding historical truths.

RUN TO THE RIVER, 6:10–6:20(A)

WL 6:10–6:20(a) **Wooden Leg** [last 6:00, next 6:10(b)]. Just after the warbonneted Lakota had been shot in the forehead, Wooden Leg saw a mounted soldier suddenly appear behind the Indians who were coming from the east along the ridge. The soldier was galloping through them, back to the east, as fast as he could make his horse run.

Wooden Leg thought he had hidden somewhere until most of the Indians passed by. A band of warriors chased after him, but Wooden Leg lost sight of them as they rode beyond a curve in the hilltop. He guessed that they must have caught and killed him.

More soldiers would run. Although Wooden Leg was on the opposite side of the ridge and could not see them directly, he learned afterwards that seven bluecoats broke away and ran down the coulee toward the river. He also learned that they did not get very far.[488]

A 6:10–6:20(a) **Antelope** [last 5:50]. After she saw the Lakota boy shot, there was a time of waiting as the older men urged caution. Soon, however, the shots quit coming from the places where the soldiers were lying behind their dead horses. The Indians jumped up and ran toward them. Leaving her spot of relative safety north of the soldier hilltop, Antelope moved closer. Although she could not see them, Antelope heard that seven white men sprang to their feet and tried to run to the river.[489]

HD 6:10–6:20(a) **He Dog** [last 5:40]. After participating in the run that broke the soldier lines, He Dog helped drive the fleeing troopers along the ridge. At the far end, Custer's men were putting up a good fight. They did not run out of ammunition, for He Dog found cartridges on the dead soldiers.

Custer was fighting on the hill where the monument now stands, and he never got much closer to the river than that hilltop. At last, a number of bluecoats jumped up to run. "When the men rushed from Custer's last stand toward the river," He Dog said, "the dismounted ones took to the gully, and the mounted ones tried to get away to [the] south toward Finley [Ridge]." One mounted trooper (perhaps Foley or Butler) rode out of the fight beyond the deep gully before being overtaken. However, He Dog maintained, "Only a few soldiers who broke away were killed below toward the river."[490]

TM 6:10–6:20(a) **Two Moon** [last 6:00]. Two Moon rode closer to the hill where Custer's men were still fighting. He saw one soldier running away, trying to get to the high hills beyond the battlefield. The Indians chased after him and killed him.

The whole valley in front of Two Moon was filled with smoke, and the bullets flew around him like buzzing bees. Individual voices could not be heard because of

488. Marquis, *Wooden Leg*, 236–37.
489. Marquis, *Custer on the Little Big Horn*, 90.
490. Hammer, *Custer in '76*, 207; Hardorff, *Lakota Recollections*, 77.

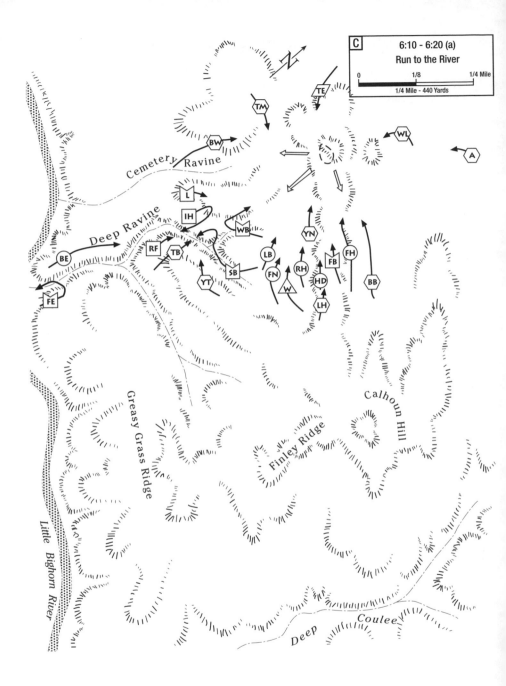

the war cries, the galloping horses, the blowing of the bugles, and the constant firing of the guns. One brave man rode along the soldier lines, trying to shout out orders above the noise. He rode a sorrel horse, with white face and white forelegs.

The Indians swirled around, but the soldiers killed only a few. At last, about five men on horseback and forty soldiers on foot started for the river. They were led by the man on the sorrel horse. He wore a buckskin shirt, carried a big knife, and had long black hair and a mustache. With his men, he moved from the hill down toward the deep gully before he staggered and fell. The soldiers were all covered with dust and Two Moon could not distinguish the officers from the men. The soldiers fought hard but were all killed. One man with braids on his arm ran alone down toward the river, then around and over a hill. Two Moon thought he might escape, but a Lakota fired at him and hit him in the head. He was the last escapee.[491]

LH 6:10–6:20(a) **Little Hawk** [last 6:00, next 6:10(b)]. After the horses were turned loose, one company, all dismounted but one man, went down toward the Little Bighorn. Little Hawk saw the lone mounted soldier, riding a sorrel, try to make his escape. The Indians shot at him but could neither hit nor overtake him. However, when he was almost out of range, one lucky ball hit him and knocked him off his horse. He is the only man, Little Hawk thought, who does not have a stone gravemarker today.[492]

RH 6:10–6:20(a) **Red Hawk** [last 6:00]. After making a desperate fight on Custer Hill, Red Hawk saw the remaining soldiers retreat downhill to where they made a third stand. There the bluecoats were surrounded again and the Indians rushed them. "Some of the soldiers broke through the Indians and ran for the ravine, but all were killed without getting into it," Red Hawk explained.

From the third stand, one soldier did succeed in getting away. When he had gone quite a distance, and the Indians had all but given up on catching him, they saw him fall from his horse. The pursuing warriors went up to him and found a bullet wound in his right temple. Since no one was near him, they believed he must have shot himself.[493]

L 6:10–6:20(a) **Lights** [last 6:00]. From his position near Deep Ravine, Lights saw the soldiers make their move downhill. They were still well armed. Some had rifles and all carried revolvers. They did not panic or shoot themselves, but fought their way down from Custer Hill toward the Deep Ravine. The Indians killed them along the line. A few tried to get away by jumping over the high banks at places between the hill and gully, but Lights did not know of any soldiers who escaped to the river.[494]

---

491. Dixon, *Vanishing Race*, 183; Hunt, *I Fought With Custer*, 213–14; "Two Moons Recalls," 13; Hardorff, *Memories*, 111. In the last, in a 1901 interview with J. M. Thralls, Two Moon said only nineteen men broke away from Custer's group, and that a circle of seventeen stone monuments show which way they ran. This is likely the same group of seventeen stones described by Big Beaver (6:10A), which shows that none of these men made it into the Deep Ravine.
492. Greene, *Lakota and Cheyenne*, 64.
493. Hardorff, *Lakota Recollections*, 44–45.
494. Ibid., 167, 168, 170, 174.

BW 6:10–6:20(a) **Brave Wolf** [last 4:20]. Brave Wolf had been following the retreating soldiers since they were near the ford. They held their line of battle all the way, he said, "fighting and falling all the way up, nearly to where the monument now stands."

Brave Wolf thought most of the horses were killed on the way, and those soldiers that got to the hilltop were on foot. "A part" of the troopers who reached the hill continued over and tried to get to the stream, but the Indians "killed them all going down the hill, before any of them got to the creek. It was hard fighting," Brave Wolf added, "very hard all the time. I have been in many hard fights, but I never saw such brave men."[495]

RF 6:10–6:20(a) **Rain In The Face** [last 5:30]. Rain In The Face noticed that most of the Indians had kept back, continually moving in a circle around the soldiers, while others made bravery runs directly through them. The bluecoats could not counter the Indian tactics forever.

Presently, the soldiers began to mount up. They appeared to be fleeing back along the ridge in the direction of Reno's position far to the south. The warriors followed them, Rain In The Face said, "like hundreds of blackbirds after a hawk." While some soldiers fled, however, "a larger body remained together at the upper end of a little ravine, and fought bravely until they were cut to pieces." Rain In The Face had always thought the white men were cowards, but this fight changed his mind. "I had a great respect for them after this day," he said.[496]

YN 6:10–6:20(a) **Yellow Nose** [last 6:00, next 6:10(b)]. As the Indians moved in on the remaining soldiers, the battle became frenzied, with the scalping of Lame White Man a prime example. The soldiers moved to a small mound at the end of the ridge. On the hilltop, Yellow Nose thought he could recognize the soldier chief, Custer, by the fringed buckskin suit he wore.

Yellow Nose estimated that there were about thirty men fighting with Custer at the last stand, all on foot. The man he thought to be the soldier chief stood conspicuously among his men, hatless, his auburn hair flying in the wind. As the Indians pressed in upon him, Yellow Nose thought that "several soldiers lost courage and ran to lower ground, close to the base of the mound." Custer, however, shouted loudly to them, and they drew nearer to him when they heard his voice.[497]

FH 6:10–6:20(a) **Flying Hawk** [last 5:50]. Flying Hawk had kept after the fleeing soldiers until they got to where Custer was making a stand at the end of the ridge. There "the living remnant of his command were now surrounded."

The Indians rode around the troopers, yelling the war whoop. There was so much dust that none were able to see very well, but the Indians continued to circle and pump shots into the soldiers as fast as they could. One soldier was seen to run away to the east, but Crazy Horse jumped on his pony and went after him. The

495. Greene, *Lakota and Cheyenne*, 46–48.
496. Eastman, "Rain-In-The-Face," 18.
497. "Yellow Nose Tells," 16–17.

man got about a half mile from the hill where the other soldiers died before Crazy Horse brought him down.

Flying Hawk moved closer in a tightening ring around the soldiers. The men on the hill were dismounted but still had some horses with them. Whenever a soldier was killed and a horse escaped, an Indian was sure to catch him. Suddenly all the living men on Custer Hill jumped up and ran toward the river. The Indians matched their move, and quickly "were on both sides of the retreating men, killing them with arrows, guns and clubs." Flying Hawk surmised that all the men on Custer Hill must have been killed before the rest made their run for the river.[498]

FN 6:10–6:20(a) **Fears Nothing** [last 5:40]. As Fears Nothing moved north, the soldiers went to the point of the ridge where the last defenders were killed. Before they all died, however, Fears Nothing said that a number of soldiers "made a break through a narrow gap in the Indian line and ran toward the river trying to escape." As they ran, the warriors followed them and killed them with stone war clubs or wooden war clubs, some of the latter having spear points on them. In the pursuit, one Indian stumbled into a gully right among the soldiers and was killed by them.[499]

TE 6:10–6:20(a) **Two Eagles** [last 6:00]. Although Two Eagles thought the troopers made the most stubborn fight on Custer's Hill, they were eventually forced to make a desperate move. The last of the surviving soldiers suddenly ran toward the Deep Ravine. Their horses had been killed or stampeded by then, and the last men were all dismounted. The escaping soldiers were all killed in their flight downhill. Two Eagles never saw or heard of any of them reaching the river.[500]

LB 6:10–6:20(a) **Lone Bear** [last 6:00]. The soldiers had been fighting hard and making a good stand on Custer Hill, and the end the battle was at very close quarters, Lone Bear said. The soldiers fought for a short time on the top of the hill, but were forced over to the side. Lone Bear said that Custer Hill "was the first and only place where the soldiers tried to get away, and only a few from there." No soldier ever made it as far as the river.[501]

W 6:10–6:20(a) **Waterman** [last 5:30, next 6:10(b)]. The soldiers at the end of the ridge were entirely surrounded, and the whole country was alive with thousands of Indians. Waterman saw some of these troopers make a break for freedom. "A few soldiers tried to get away and reach the river," he said, "but they were all killed. A few did get down to the river, but were killed by some Indians there. The Indians were running all around shooting and yelling, and we were all very excited." [502]

---

498. Hardorff, *Lakota Recollections*, 50–51; McCreight, *Firewater*, 114.
499. Hardorff, *Lakota Recollections*, 32.
500. Ibid., 147, 149.
501. Ibid., 157, 159.
502. Graham, *The Custer Myth*, 110.

FB 6:10–6:20(a) **Flying By** [last 6:00]. The stand the soldiers made at the end of the long ridge finally came to an end, after a battle that Flying By said lasted half the afternoon. Although the soldiers were still firing and seemed to have plenty of ammunition, the pressure of the Indians closing in on them forced their hand. At the last part of the battle, said Flying By, "soldiers were running through [the] Indian lines trying to get away." However, "only four soldiers got into [the] gully toward [the] river."[503]

YT 6:10–6:20(a) **Young Two Moon** [last 6:00]. Young Two Moon saw what the Gray Horse Company did and how it was destroyed on the hillside. Another company "retreated down toward a little gulch where they tried to fight under cover." He believed the last of the soldiers were slain in the little creek where they took refuge, although "those in the creek were all killed before he got there."[504]

SB 6:10–6:20(a) **Standing Bear** [last 6:00]. Shortly after Standing Bear saw the remaining cavalry horses stampeding off the hill, he heard another alarm given: "They are gone!" From the hilltop, the soldiers began retreating down toward the Little Bighorn. The warriors all around him hollered, "Hokahey! Hurry, hurry!" Standing Bear joined them as they ran directly at the soldiers.

He was in the middle of the charge. The soldiers and Indians were all mixed together, maybe four or five Indians to every white man, and there were so many guns going off that they combined into a continuous rumble. He could hear no individual voices, but they all seemed to blend together and float on top of the clouds.

Standing Bear did not consciously know what he was doing, but he fought almost by instinct. Coming upon a soldier, Standing Bear swung his pistol at the man's head. The gun crashed into him and he fell down. Standing Bear killed him. Staring at the motionless white man for a moment, Standing Bear came back to his senses. He must get out of this place. He knew that in the heat of battle the Indians sometimes killed their own men. As he retreated he witnessed another hand-to-hand combat. A Lakota grabbed a soldier's bridle and the soldier jumped off his horse in great fear. Immediately, several more Indians overwhelmed and killed the white man. They all counted coup on him and went on.

The soldiers who had gotten past the Indians went along the hill and into a draw where tall grass grew. But the Indians were right on top of the soldiers and it was no use trying to hide. One warrior rushed in on them, then others, and soon the Indians killed every last soldier. Again, the Indians mistakenly killed some of their own men who had gone too far ahead of the rest. It was quite a sight, with dead men and horses mixed and piled together.[505]

IH 6:10–6:20(a) **Iron Hawk** [last 6:00]. The last gray cavalry horses had broken away from the hill. Little Bear, who had ridden with Iron Hawk for the past two hours, adjusted his saddle blanket and got ready, giving out more of his familiar advice: "Take courage, the earth is all that lasts."

503. Hammer, *Custer in '76*, 210.
504. Greene, *Lakota and Cheyenne*, 70.
505. DeMallie, *Sixth Grandfather*, 186–87.

Iron Hawk watched Little Bear's horse rear up and start toward Custer Hill. As he went up the slope, his little gray pinto was shot out from under him. Little Bear jumped clear and began to run back. Then he took a bullet in the leg and began to hobble back downhill. His friend Elk Nation rode out to save him. The soldier bullets kicked up dust all around them, but Little Bear succeeded in mounting up behind Elk Nation.

Just as they returned, another cry went out: "Now they have gone!" Iron Hawk looked up to see that the soldiers were all running down toward the Hunkpapas. They yelled, "Hokahey," and rushed up to meet them. On the right, a man named Red Horn Buffalo rode directly into them. They circled the soldiers on all sides. Then Iron Hawk saw Red Horn Buffalo's horse gallop past—empty saddled. It was the last he saw of the man.

It was time to fight. Iron Hawk had been staying behind the front lines most of the day, and he was armed with nothing but his bow and arrows, but the time for watching had passed. He was right among the soldiers. They had come to fight and Iron Hawk finally accepted the fait accompli—they had forced his hand. He, too, was there to fight.

The level ground in the middle distance just above Deep Ravine, where Iron Hawk, Standing Bear, White Bull, and others fought the fleeing troopers.

A soldier was running directly at Iron Hawk. He whipped out his bow, nocked an arrow and stretched it to its fullest. The arrow tore straight through the man's ribs and Iron Hawk heard his piercing scream. Quickly turning, Iron Hawk saw two more fleeing soldiers and he joined in the chase. They were down by a little creek when a brave named Brings Plenty killed one of them. Iron Hawk caught up to the second soldier. "These white men wanted it," Iron Hawk rationalized, "they called for it and I let them have it."

Iron Hawk swung his bow like a club and hit the soldier crosswise over the shoulders. He staggered. Iron Hawk swung again and again—once, twice, three times—grunting like a bear, "Hownh!" every time the bow connected with the back of the white man's head. Even after he fell to the ground, Iron Hawk continued to beat him. "I was very mad," he said, "because the women and children had run away scared and I was thinking about this when I did this killing."

As he came out of his frenzy, Iron Hawk took note of his position on the field. The headstones that today stretch down from Custer's Hill delineate the run these soldiers made. The farthest one along the line is the very spot where Iron Hawk killed his second man. He might have killed almost the last of Custer's men to die that day.

Iron Hawk saw an Indian riding along the upper banks of the little creek. He was hollering a warning that one soldier was sneaking along the gulch. The warrior shouted, pulled out a shiny knife, and charged down at him. He cut the soldier up in pieces. Iron Hawk was suddenly exhausted from the excitement and the fighting. He turned his back on the hill and began to make his way back down toward the river.[506]

TB 6:10–6:20(a) **Tall Bull** [last 5:00, next 6:10(b)]. Tall Bull had kept out of the thickest fighting, but when his brother-in-law Lame White Man led the charge against the troopers who had come down from the ridge, Tall Bull followed along. When the soldiers got close to where the monument now is, they turned and rushed to the hilltop.

On a hill near the deep gully, Tall Bull heard more volley firing coming from the hill where the soldiers were making their last stand. It was the first volley firing he had heard since the beginning of the fight at Finley Ridge. Up on the hill, where the remnants of the troops congregated, the gray horses were mixed with the bays. Then a good many of the soldier horses ran to the northwest, down toward the stream where the Indians caught them.

Following this, Tall Bull heard a big war whoop announcing that the bluecoats were coming. "A few soldiers started to run directly down toward Little Sheep Creek, but the Indians killed them all before they got there." Down the hill from the edge of the ridge they ran, firing their guns at random. "Soldiers came on foot and ran right through us into [the] deep gully," Tall Bull said, "and this was the last of the fight, and the men were killed in this gully."[507]

506. Ibid., 191–92.
507. Greene, *Lakota and Cheyenne*, 53; Hammer, *Custer in '76*, 213.

WB 6:10–6:20(a) **White Bull** [last 5:50]. White Bull was thankful to have overcome the strong white soldier. He felt his nose and smiled, glad that the soldier was not able to get his teeth on it. He took the man's pistol and cartridge belt. White Bull rested awhile before starting again for the enemy.

He was between the river and the soldiers on the hill when about ten of them made their last run. White Bull and his group blocked them. Two soldiers veered off and the Indians got down in the draw and waited for them. White Bull drew a bead on one and pulled the trigger. He went down. At the same time a Cheyenne shot the other bluecoat. They both rushed forward and White Bull was able to get first coup on one and second coup on the other. It was his sixth and seventh of the day.

Now the rest of the soldiers came running toward them. White Bull got one of the soldier's guns and he and the Cheyenne rolled out of the draw to make their escape. There were not many white men left by this time. White Bull started uphill toward the last of the fight, when suddenly something thudded into his ankle and he stumbled and fell. He felt his leg. It was numb, and the ankle was swollen, but the skin was not broken. He thought he must have been hit by a spent bullet. White Bull crawled into a ditch and lay there. Soon all the soldiers would surely die and he could safely get out of the line of fire.[508]

BB 6:10–6:20(a) **Big Beaver** [last 6:00]. Big Beaver carried off his new gun and went to join the other Indians farther down the coulee. As he approached, he saw them all rushing up toward the hill where the monument now stands.

Following along, Big Beaver reached the crest and looked over. No soldiers were standing, but some were still firing prone, from behind horses, or sitting up. The Indians rushed forward, when, according to Big Beaver, "some men, about fifteen, got up over to the west or on the E Troop position and run [sic] for the river, right down the coulee."

The soldiers looked frightened. They must have had little or no ammunition because they did not shoot as the Indians ran them down. Big Beaver thought they were trying to save themselves by running to the river to hide in the brush by the riverbank. The last seventeen gravemarkers down the coulee below the monument represent the escaping soldiers. Big Beaver could see nothing else of the battlefield from that point, because the smoke and dust were so very thick.[509]

BE 6:10–6:20(a) **Black Elk** [last 4:20]. After showing his mother the scalp he had taken in the valley, Black Elk sat and listened to the women singing. For quite awhile he tried to watch the battle across the river, but could not see much because of the dust. Yet, even across the valley he could hear the shooting and the buzzing of the bullets.

Many other young boys were nearby with their mothers and sisters. About six of them were preparing their ponies to go to the fight, and they asked Black Elk to join them.

---

508. White Bull, Box 105, Notebook 24, Campbell Collection; Hardorff, *Lakota Recollections*, 117, 126; Vestal, "Man Who Killed Custer," 9.
509. "Big Beaver's Story," Blummer Ms., 54.

While riding downhill and across the valley, they could see gray horses coming toward them, running down the opposite bank to the river. The boys rode across the Greasy Grass at a ford that led up through the bluff and up a gulch toward the battlefield. Partway up, Black Elk could hear men hollering and see the soldiers coming down the hill. Their arms swung in such a manner that they appeared to be running, but they were only walking. Indians whirled around them and it seemed that they could have trampled them down even without weapons. Before Black Elk got up there, the white men had been wiped out.[510]

FE 6:10–6:20(a) **Feather Earring** [last 4:50]. The death and burial of his brother had taken much of the fight out of Feather Earring. He saw some of the action on the bluffs across the river, but by the time he got down to the end where Custer was fighting, the battle was almost over.

Near the river, Feather Earring came upon five gray horses. They were all wounded and trembling, but he drove them across to the west bank. Perhaps he could salvage some prizes out of this battle.[511]

← DISCUSSION. The hilltop was surrounded by a constricting circle of Indians. Most of the soldiers had been there for an hour or more, while some had just arrived from the Keogh-Calhoun debacle. They were still firing, but their ammunition supply rapidly dwindled. Some horses had been killed for breastworks while others were released in the hope that the Indians would chase after them. Had anyone on Custer Hill, desperately peering through field glasses, seen traces of Reno's or Benteen's men on Weir Point three miles away? John Gray's time-motion study of that episode indicates that troops may have occupied that high point from about 5:35 P.M. to after 6:00 P.M.[512] Perhaps the sight of troops to the south was the factor that caused the men to ultimately attempt the breakout. Even if Reno's and Benteen's men had already vacated Weir Point, they knew that potential succor might lie in that direction. Custer's men—once on the attack, then forced to defend, and finally reduced to a last stand—now found themselves in a run for their lives.

As in much of the testimony we have examined, the number of men said to have run for the river varies per individual account. Although Wooden Leg and Antelope did not see the incident directly, they heard that seven men ran. He Dog said that some men ran, but only a few were killed toward the river. Lights said men fought their way down and a few were killed jumping over the banks between the hill and gully. Yellow Nose said thirty men fought on the hill, but only several ran to lower ground. Flying Hawk said men ran toward the river, but he did not give a number. Fears Nothing said a number of soldiers tried to break through. Two Eagles said the last survivors ran toward the river. Lone Bear and Waterman both said only a few soldiers tried to get away. Flying By said some soldiers tried to get away, but only four got into the gully. Standing Bear said soldiers retreated and some got into

---

510. Neihardt, *Black Elk*, 125; DeMallie, *Sixth Grandfather*, 193.
511. Graham, *The Custer Myth*, 97.
512. Gray, *Custer's Last Campaign,* 310, 320.

the draw. Iron Hawk said soldiers ran downhill, and that he killed the last one near the deep gully. Only one got into the ravine, but he was then killed by an Indian with a knife. Tall Bull said soldiers ran through the Indians into the deep gully. White Bull said about ten soldiers made the escape run. The Hunkpapa Good Voiced Elk told Walter Camp that about twenty-five or thirty men ran to the deep gully.[513]

On a slightly different tack, Big Beaver said about fifteen men ran down the coulee, but their point of origin appears to have been from a defensive position farther west down from Custer Hill, where E Troop had first been positioned. A few other Indians also indicated that there may have been a secondary "last stand," not on Custer Hill, but down on the divide between Cemetery Ravine and Deep Ravine, where a cluster of about a dozen gravemarkers is located today. Two Moon said about forty-five men came downhill fighting well, led by a man in buckskin wielding a big knife. Red Hawk said after the fight on Custer Hill, the remaining soldiers retreated to a third stand where they were again surrounded and killed before any of them reached Deep Ravine. Rain In The Face said some soldiers fled, but a larger body remained together at the end of a little ravine where they fought bravely before being cut to pieces.

Lt. Oscar F. Long of the 5th U.S. Infantry was on the battlefield in 1878 with a party under Col. Nelson A. Miles. A number of warriors who had been in the battle accompanied them. Long reported the Indians telling him that, during the last stand, forty of Custer's men let their horses loose, broke from the hill, and tried to reach the river, but all were killed. The specific Indians Long named as informants were White Bull (Ice), Hump, and Brave Wolf.[514] This may be so, but we must remember that Ice remained in camp and Hump had been badly wounded during the assault on Calhoun Hill. Neither was in a position to see the final moments on Custer Hill. Apparently Brave Wolf was there, but he told Grinnell that "all their horses had been killed before they got quite to the top of the hill," and "a part of those who had reached the top of the hill, went over and tried to go to the stream."[515] The number "forty" appears tentative and conditional.

The estimates of fleeing soldiers range from a few to 45, with the majority tending toward the lower end. Statistically, we might justify throwing out the high and low extremes and working with the mid-ranges to form generalizations, but, for curiosity's sake, Two Moon's high of 45 might be investigated further. He estimated not only the largest number of soldiers moving downhill at the end of the battle but also the largest number (105) fighting on Custer Hill before the move. These estimates could be compared with his body count after the battle, when he indicated 488 willow sticks were gathered, one for each dead trooper.

Is this a propensity for exaggeration or just a plain ignorance of numbers, similar to problems the Indians had with mileage estimates? I prefer not to take the extreme view of Dr. Charles Kuhlman, who called Two Moon "the Cheyennes' prize liar."[516] What if Two Moon simply used a different system of reckoning? Proportionally, if

---

513. Good Voiced Elk interview, Ellison Collection.
514. Brust, "Oscar Long," 6–7.
515. Brave Wolf, Notebook 325, Grinnell Collection.
516. Kuhlman, *Legend Into History*, 204.

488 sticks represented about 200 bodies, perhaps his estimate of 105 men defending the hill translates into about 43 men in reality. This number of defenders now
falls between Iron Hawk's estimate of 50 and Yellow Nose's estimate of 30. Apply-
ing the same proportion to the men moving to the river means that Two Moon's
45 now becomes 18, which falls between White Bull's 10 and Good Voiced Elk's
25, and matches very well with Big Beaver's 15.

Another concern with Two Moon's estimate of forty-five men moving down
from the hill is that this incident is not mentioned in any of his other interviews.
The "five horsemen" and "may be so forty" men on foot only appears in Hamlin
Garland's 1898 *McClure's Magazine* account. In the 1901 interview by J. M. Thralls,
Two Moon said nineteen men broke away. In a *Harness Gazette* account published
in 1908, the story is trimmed to state that "some" men tried to get away toward the
river, but they were all killed. In 1907 and 1909 interviews by Richard Throssel, in
the 1909 council as recorded by Joseph Dixon, and in three 1913 talks with interviewers and interpreters Eli S. Ricker, Henry Leeds, and Willis T. Rowland, there
are no mentions of any large number of men leaving Custer Hill late in the battle.
In fact, in the last 1913 interview, the large number becomes only "a man in buckskin," who is shot a bit north of Custer Hill and finally staggers and falls a little
south of the same hill (see fig. 6).[517]

Was Garland's account flawed by poor interpretation? Were the "may be so
forty" men really Two Moon's rendition of Company E's move downhill earlier in
the fight? The improbability of a large, late flight of men has been amply demonstrated by Custer student Bruce Trinque. He concluded that there were simply not
enough bodies found along the Cemetery Ravine–Deep Ravine lines to account
for thirty or forty fleeing soldiers at the end of the battle, and thus, the Indian
narratives that point toward a late, large-scale escape attempt from Custer Hill must
be rejected as inaccurate.[518] A theory insisting that almost all of the soldier deaths
came late in the fight as a result of panic, and occurred at the bottom of the Deep
Ravine, does not follow from the data and will not pass examination.[519]

Given the logic of the situation, the limitation of the actual number of soldiers
involved, and the more frequent estimates of "few," "some," or "several," the true
number of soldiers fleeing Custer Hill at the end of the fight must have amounted
to about a dozen. Those men may have even managed to make an abbreviated
"stand" on the divide below Custer Hill before the last of them continued their
abortive flight. Like the number of gray horses that ran from Custer Hill just before
this episode, the number of men actually leaving Custer Hill was not large. Those
that reached the Deep Ravine to die were only a handful.[520]

---

517. "Two Moons Recalls," 12–13; Hardorff, *Memories*, 111, 118, 127.
518. Trinque, "Defense of Custer Hill," 28–30.
519. Hardorff, *Memories*, 16–17.
520. The fact that very few soldiers were killed in Deep Ravine was an argument made in Michno, *E Troop*.
     Although I did not have access to the Blummer manuscript at that time, Big Beaver's indication that the
     last fifteen to seventeen memorial markers along the lower south skirmish line represented the death

Was this the end of the fight? As a follow-up to the argument that there was no last stand, anthropologist Richard Fox stated that the last fighting "petered out in and around Deep Ravine."[521] Certainly, those Indians who remained in and around Deep Ravine, who did not have a line of sight back to Custer Hill, must have thought that the action there constituted the battle's finale. But no two people will see a battle in the same light, especially those viewing separate events on opposite sides of a hill. White Bull fought the soldiers during their flight, yet he was on his way uphill when hit in the leg. He rolled into a ditch to sit out the battle. Obviously, there was still something going on up the slope. The Indians told us there was a last stand. They also told us there were survivors on Custer Hill *after* the run to the river. The troopers had shot their bolt. Now the warriors converged on Custer's Hill to finish off the last of the last.

---

sites of the last fleeing troopers is further evidence that few of them made it to Deep Ravine, and the present markers are a good representation of where the men actually fell. More supporting evidence (from Box 1, Walter Camp Collection, Brigham Young University) is in a letter written by Charles F. Roe to Walter Camp, 11 November 1909: "I put up the markers near the deep ravine you speak of," said Roe. "There never was twenty-eight dead men in the ravine, but near the head of said ravine, and only two or three in it."

521. Fox, *Archaeology, History*, 216, 330.

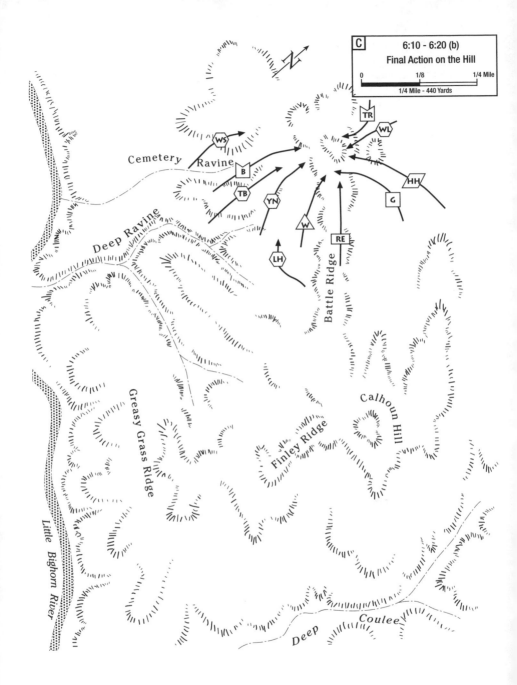

C | 6:10 - 6:20 (b)
Final Action on the Hill

0   1/8   1/4 Mile
1/4 Mile - 440 Yards

N

Cemetery Ravine

Deep Ravine

Greasy Grass Ridge

Little Bighorn River

Finley Ridge

Battle Ridge

Calhoun Hill

Deep Coulee

WS
B
TB
YN
W
LH
RE
TR
WL
HH
G

FINAL ACTION ON THE HILL, 6:10–6:20(B)

YN 6:10–6:20(b) **Yellow Nose** [last 6:10(a)]. The hatless man with the auburn hair had caught Yellow Nose's attention. Earlier, Yellow Nose had shot a soldier and was attempting to count coup on him when the soldier called for help. Several troopers rushed to his rescue. One fired at Yellow Nose at such close range that his face and eyes were blasted with powder, the near miss leaving a gash across his forehead and wounding his pony in the head.

Now, Yellow Nose again saw the man who had shot at him. He was on the hilltop, one of the last still fighting. Yellow Nose had lost his gun, but he still had an old saber, captured in a previous encounter. He rode at the white man. The man fired his pistol and Yellow Nose's pony bolted and ran beyond him. Getting his mount under control, he turned for another run. The soldier must have been out of ammunition, for he did not fire, but instead bent his knees as if to ward off the saber blow. Yellow Nose struck him on the back of his head with the flat of the blade. Stunned, the soldier sank to the ground. Yellow Nose rode off in pursuit of the few remaining fugitives. He later came to believe his adversary was the soldier chief, Custer.[522]

LH 6:10–6:20(b) **Little Hawk** [last 6:10(a)]. After the soldiers ran to the river and the lone rider tried to escape, the Indians again turned their attention to the hilltop. The last place Little Hawk saw the soldiers was on the knoll where the monument stands. "From there," he said, "most of them were killed by Indians hidden behind the little ridge, but there was some charging in to these troops by Indians."

Little Hawk noticed Yellow Nose still in the forefront of the battle and commented on his capture of the flagstaff with a gilt lance head. He thought about fifteen flags were captured altogether.[523]

B 6:10–6:20(b) **Beard** [last 4:40]. It had been over an hour since Beard had crossed at the ford. The battle was a turmoil of dust and warriors and soldiers, with bullets and arrows hissing all around. Beard heard bugles blow and saw the flash of war clubs and knives glinting in the sun. He rode to and fro, calling out the traditional cry, "It's a good day to die!"

A Lakota named Spotted Rabbit rode up and challenged the warriors to join him in trying to capture the white leader alive. Beard had no idea what they might do after they caught him, but it was a daring feat and would require more skill and courage than simply killing him. He followed the warriors as they charged the hill.

A tall white man in buckskins who shouted at the soldiers appeared to be the leader. Beard charged at him, right behind Spotted Rabbit. Just before they were about to ride him down, Spotted Rabbit's horse was shot from under him. Beard's pony, Zi Chischila, shied away to one side, and in a few seconds it was too late. A

522. "Yellow Nose Tells," 16–17.
523. Greene, *Lakota and Cheyenne*, 64.

Minneconjou named Charging Hawk rushed in and shot the buckskin-clad leader. Shortly thereafter, the rest of the soldiers were dead. The battle was over.[524]

HH 6:10–6:20(b) **Hollow Horn Bear** [last 5:40]. Having seen the destruction of Keogh's men, Hollow Horn Bear moved north, always keeping on the opposite side of the ridge from the river. In the last stand the soldiers fought as hard as they did at any other point. They did not appear to run out of ammunition and he did not see any of them make a rush to get away. "They were all brave men," Hollow Horn Bear said.

If the soldiers ran at all from the hill toward the river, Hollow Horn Bear did not see them. When the Indians finally made a rush to the hill, he could see there were still a few of the Gray Horse men in the fight. Now the fighting was at close quarters. Hollow Horn Bear was finally able to wield his war club.[525]

RE 6:10–6:20(b) **Runs The Enemy** [last 5:50]. Runs The Enemy and his Two Kettles chased the soldiers north along the ridge. The soldiers that were scattered across the field now converged on the far end. "The others came back to where the final stand was made on the hill," he said, "but they were few in number then."

Runs The Enemy participated in the last fight. "The soldiers then gathered in a group where the monument now stands," he said, "and then the soldiers and Indians were all mixed up. You could not tell one from the other. In this final charge I took part and when the last soldier was killed the smoke rolled up like a mountain above our heads, and the soldiers were piled one on top of another, dead, and here and there an Indian among the soldiers."[526]

TR 6:10–6:20(b) **Turtle Rib** [last 5:40]. Turtle Rib had been closing in on the end of the ridge when a soldier mounted up and raced away across a hollow. He was the third Indian to chase after him. The soldier rode like the wind, and it appeared that he would get away when suddenly he killed himself.

Turtle Rib rode back to the fight, but it was almost over. No stand had been made except at the end of the long ridge, where the bay and gray horses were all mixed together. "The Indians were up close, and the soldiers were shooting with pistols," Turtle Rib said. The Indians dashed among them, shooting arrows, and, in the smoke and dust, accidentally hit some of their own men. The soldier bullets were also deadly, for Turtle Rib's nephew was killed on the hilltop.

In the end, many Indians had been killed and wounded, but not one soldier came off the battlefield alive. They were all killed where they lay.[527]

G 6:10–6:20(b) **Gall** [last 6:00]. Around the hill the soldiers had been fighting well, Gall said, but they could not hit the Indians in the ravines. Once in awhile he could catch a glimpse of the soldiers through the dust. Finally, the time was ripe to put an end to it. "We charged through them with our ponies," Gall said.

524. Miller, "Echoes," 38.
525. Hardorff, *Lakota Recollections*, 183–84.
526. Dixon, *Vanishing Race*, 176–77.
527. Hammer, *Custer in '76*, 201–2.

They cut across Custer Hill just a few rods south of where the monument stands. "When we had done this," Gall declared, "the fight was over."[528]

TB 6:10–6:20(b) **Tall Bull** [last 6:10(a)]. After the few escaping soldiers were killed in the gully, Tall Bull rode toward the ridge. His horse had been wounded many times throughout the long day. Nearing the hilltop, and perhaps pierced again by one of the final deadly missiles, the poor brute collapsed. Tall Bull slid off the dying horse and counted seven bullet holes in the animal. He finished the last few yards to the hilltop on foot.[529]

WS 6:10–6:20(b) **White Shield** [last 5:50]. The Gray Horse Company held their horses to the last, and then almost all of them were killed. White Shield did see one man escape on a sorrel, but Old Bear and Kills In The Night chased him. The latter fired and missed, but Old Bear fired and the soldier fell. When they got up to him, they found a bullet had hit him in the back between the shoulders.

Back on the hill, when the last of the surviving companies got together, they did not last long. "When about the last man dropped in the G[ray] H[orse] Co[mpany]," White Shield said, "the Ind[ian]s made a charge and killed the wounded with hatchets, arrows, knives, etc."[530]

W 6:10–6:20(b) **Waterman** [last 6:10(a)]. After the few soldiers tried to escape to the river, the rest of the Indians rushed to the top of the hill to finish off those still alive. When Waterman got to the top he saw a man he identified as Custer. He was dressed in buckskin and was down on his hands and knees. He had been shot in the side and blood was coming from his mouth. Four other soldiers sat nearby, and they were also badly wounded.

The Indians closed in. Waterman killed his only soldier. He rushed up to him and shot him with his gun. He did not scalp him, he said, "because the Arapahoes do not scalp a man with short hair, only long hair."

Waterman stopped to catch his breath. All the soldiers were down, their bodies filled with arrows. He had lost sight of the man he thought was Custer. It was over.[531]

WL 6:10–6:20(b) **Wooden Leg** [last 6:10(a)]. The shots quit coming from the hilltop about the time the seven soldiers broke away running down the coulee. Warriors around Wooden Leg were calling out that the white men must all be dead. They rushed forward.

Through the dust and smoke on the hilltop it looked like a thousand dogs might look if they were all mixed together in a fight. In a short while it was over. The white men all appeared to be dead when, suddenly, one raised himself up on his elbow. Wooden Leg got a good look at the wild expression on his face. He was big, with plump cheeks, a stubby black beard, and a long mustache curled up at the ends. He was lying just above where the middle of the group of white stone markers stands today, on the southwest slope of the hill. He held a six-shooter in his

528. Burdick, *Barry's Notes*, 13, 15.
529. Greene, *Lakota and Cheyenne*, 53; Powell, *Sacred Mountain*, 1028.
530. White Shield, Notebook 348, Grinnell Collection.
531. Graham, *The Custer Myth*, 110.

Last Stand Hill, site of the final desperate action.

right hand. The nearby Indians were frightened by what seemed to have been a man returning from the dead. However, a Lakota warrior jumped forward and grabbed the man's gun. He shot the soldier through the head and other Indians struck and stabbed him. "I think he must have been the last man killed in this great battle," said Wooden Leg.[532]

◆ DISCUSSION. It should not take much insight to divine the fact that, since dead men cannot get up and run, the fugitives that died near Deep Ravine had to have left Custer Hill before the Indians converged on the hill and killed them. Obviously, there still were men fighting on Custer Hill after the run for the river, all the archaeology in the world notwithstanding. Likely they were the wounded, the exhausted, or some able-bodied die-hards who refused to abandon the wounded. For the most part, it may have been only a mopping-up operation; yet Waterman, Runs The Enemy, and Turtle Rib indicated a sharp struggle was still necessary to put an end to it. Turtle Rib even lost his nephew in the last swirl of chaos. Gall rode through them, Hollow Horn Bear used his war club, and Beard and Yellow Nose even indicated that a man they thought was the soldier leader was one of the last white men to remain standing. Little Hawk and White Shield said a final charge was necessary to finish off the soldiers. In addition, the young Oglala Jack Red Cloud said Custer's men dismounted and gathered in a bunch, kneeling and shooting from behind their dead horses while the Indians circled around and fired until the last of the soldiers were killed. Lights also said the final fight on the end of the

532. Marquis, *Wooden Leg*, 237–39.

ridge was at close quarters, "near enough to look into each others eyes."[533] After the Indians drew the curtain on the final act, there were no soldiers left to attempt an escape. Last Stand Hill is aptly named.

About 210 soldiers died in Custer's battalion. How many Indian casualties were suffered in annihilating those five companies, and where on the field were they hit? A 1993 compilation by Richard G. Hardorff indicates 16 warriors died or were mortally wounded. Bear With Horns was killed along Custer Ridge, and Black White Man (Black Wasichu) went down on the west slope of Custer Hill. Black Bear (Closed Hand or Fist) and Limber Bones (Limber Hand) were killed on the north slope of Custer Hill. Open (Cut) Belly was killed near the present cemetery grounds. Noisy Walking went down near Deep Ravine, and Lame White Man was hit a few hundred yards down Custer Ridge from Last Stand Hill. Hardorff lists nine more deaths, location unknown: Guts, Red Face, Cloud Man, Lone Dog, Elk Bear, Kills Him, Bad Light Hair, Many Lice, and Young Skunk.[534]

From the Indian accounts examined heretofore, we have also noted additional woundings and possible deaths. Iron Hawk saw that Little Bear was hit and that Red Horn Buffalo was knocked off his horse while charging the soldiers on Custer Hill. Wooden Leg said two Lakotas were killed in the ravine near Noisy Walking during Lame White Man's charge.[535] A Hunkpapa named Lone Man corroborated one of the Lakota deaths, as did the wife of the Hunkpapa Little Assiniboine.[536] Iron Hawk claimed to have been shot below the ribs during the battle.[537] Turtle Rib said his nephew was killed right on top of Custer Hill. Antelope saw a Lakota boy shot on the north slope of Custer Hill. Wooden Leg saw a Lakota with a shot jaw in the gully on the north slope. Wooden Leg or Big Beaver saw the warbonneted Lakota shot in the head on the north side of the hill. Black Elk saw two dead Lakotas near Custer Hill, in addition to seeing Black Wasichu dead. Feather Earring found a dead Lakota a few hundred yards up Deep Ravine from the river. Hump was wounded in the charge south of Calhoun Hill. Nearby, Eagle Elk saw one Indian shot through the head, and both he and Standing Bear saw another man who was shot in the jaw, whom Standing Bear identified as Long Elk.

About ten of the above casualties are unnamed, which match up rather nicely with the nine "unknowns" from Hardorff's above list. But more important for this discussion than the exact names of these Indian casualties is the field location where they were hit. By dividing the field into two similar northern and southern rectangles (see fig. 13), it becomes clear that all seven of Hardorff's known deaths occurred in the northern sector; none received mortal wounds in the south. If the nine names with unknown locations on Hardorff's list can be matched up with nine nameless Indians with known locations on my list, then a very striking point is evident: fifteen out of sixteen deaths on Custer field occurred in the north, and only one, the unnamed Indian Eagle Elk saw shot in the head, occurred in the south! If we include nonfatal woundings with the deaths, nineteen out of twenty-two casualties occurred in the north. Contrary to popular conceptions, this contra-

533. Dixon, *Vanishing Race*, 169; Hardorff, *Lakota Recollections*, 169.
534. Hardorff, *Hokahey!*, 82.
535. Marquis, *Wooden Leg*, 243.
536. Camp Mss., IU, Box 5, Folder 1.
537. Hardorff, *Lakota Recollections*, 67.

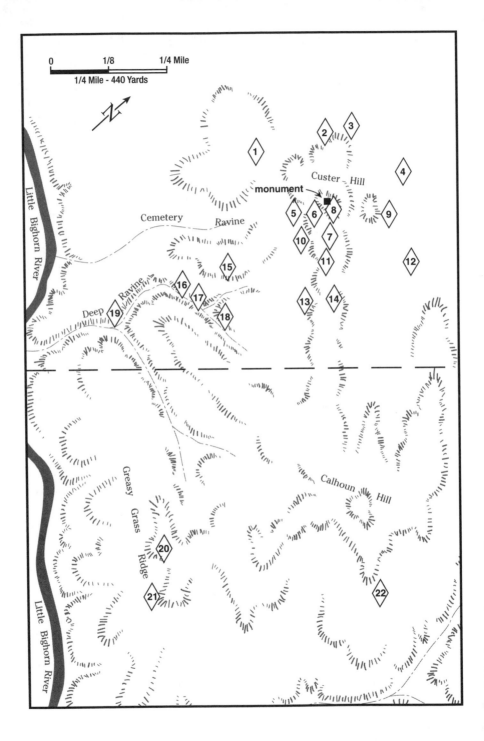

Figure 13. Indian Casualties

1. Cut Belly (Open Belly) killed near present cemetery grounds, per Wooden Leg.

2. Black Bear (Closed Hand, Fist) killed on north slope of Custer Hill, per Wooden Leg.

3. Limber Bones (Limber Hand) killed on north slope of Custer Hill, per Wooden Leg.

4. Lakota boy killed, witnessed by Antelope.

5. Black Wasichu (Black White Man) mortally wounded on west slope of Custer Hill, seen by Black Elk.

6. Lakota warrior killed near Custer Hill, per Black Elk.

7. Lakota warrior killed near Custer Hill, per Black Elk.

8. Turtle Rib's nephew killed on Custer Hill, witnessed by Turtle Rib.

9. Warbonneted Lakota killed on north side of Custer Hill, seen by Wooden Leg and/or Big Beaver.

10. Little Bear wounded while charging Custer Hill, seen by Iron Hawk.

11. Red Horn Buffalo wounded, possibly mortally, while charging Custer Hill, seen by Iron Hawk.

12. Lakota warrior wounded in jaw, seen by Wooden Leg.

13. Lame White Man killed, identified by Wooden Leg, Tall Bull, and others.

14. Bear Horn (Bear With Horns) killed while chasing soldiers on Battle Ridge, witnessed by Standing Bear.

15. Iron Hawk wounded in ribs (site is uncertain), per his own statement.

16. Lakota warrior killed in Lame White Man charge, seen by Wooden Leg.

17. Lakota warrior killed in Lame White Man charge, noted by Wooden Leg, Lone Man, and wife of Little Assiniboine.

18. Noisy Walking mortally wounded in upper Deep Ravine, found by Wooden Leg, Antelope, and others.

19. Lakota warrior killed, found by Feather Earring a few hundred yards up Deep Ravine from the river.

20. Lakota warrior wearing bird on his head killed, seen by Eagle Elk.

21. Long Elk wounded in mouth, seen by Standing Bear.

22. Hump wounded in leg during charge on Calhoun Hill, per his own statement.

dicts the conception of a great number of kills being made by Calhoun Hill's stout defenders.

Historically, there has been support for the idea that Calhoun Hill was the best defended position on the field. Douglas Scott et al., Richard Fox Jr., and Richard Hardorff ascribed to the idea, particularly in light of the great number of army cartridges discovered on that part of the field.[538] Hardorff devoted an entire book to the study of the Indian casualties at the Little Bighorn. Yet, even after two books and compiling numerous lists, Hardorff somehow still concluded that the resistance was fierce on Calhoun Hill, the fighting was furious on the southern slopes of Calhoun Ridge, and that eleven Indian casualties occurred in that area.[539]

How? In the first place, some of the Indian testimony Hardorff used to show a stout Calhoun Hill defense is open to question. He cited Eagle Elk to show there was a furious fight on the south slope of Calhoun Hill and included the Yellow Nose–flag incident. Yet, when placed in context with the events before and after, we find some of this action took place just after the crossing of the river at Medicine Tail Ford and the remainder, particularly when Long Elk was shot in the jaw, probably occurred near Greasy Grass Ridge or Finley Ridge. Standing Bear also saw Long Elk—in fact, he said it was the first thing he saw when crossing the river—and that he was west of Custer at the time. None of these events occurred on the south slopes of Calhoun Hill.[540]

Hardorff said the Blackfoot Lakota Kill Eagle told of seeing a Cheyenne kill a Lakota on Calhoun Hill. He also said the incident was corroborated by Wooden Leg. Yet Wooden Leg could hardly have seen any such thing on Calhoun Hill. He clearly said the fight was over by the time he got there.[541]

Hardorff placed the Standing Bear charge episode on Calhoun Hill. Yet Standing Bear rode in front of Bear Horn (Bear With Horns), and Hardorff deduced that Bear Horn must have charged from the head of Deep Ravine against a soldier on Custer's ridge. Immediately following this, Standing Bear rode downhill to find Indians scalping an already dead Lame White Man. If all this supposedly took place early on the south slopes of Calhoun Hill, Lame White Man would not yet have even entered the fight, let alone be lying dead and scalped. Right after this incident, Standing Bear saw the soldiers run from Custer Hill at the end of the battle. Obviously, what Standing Bear described happened too late and too far north to be associated with the Calhoun Hill defense.[542]

Hardorff infers that the Waterman account showed Lame White Man was killed in the fight at Calhoun Hill, but Waterman never said such was the case. In fact, the reconstruction in this work shows the likelihood that the incident occurred in the north instead.[543] Using Gall's statements, Hardorff argued that eleven Indians died

---

538. Scott et al., *Archaeological Perspectives*, 126; Fox, *Archaeology, History,* 130–31, 331; Hardorff, *Markers*, 46; Wayne Wells, "The Fight on Calhoun Hill," 2nd Annual Symposium, Custer Battlefield Historical & Museum Association (Hardin, MT: CBH&MA, 1988): 22.
539. Hardorff, *Hokahey!*, 61–62; Hardorff, *Markers*, 46.
540. Hardorff, *Hokahey!*, 61–63. For a comparison see the Eagle Elk 4:20 and 4:50 segments and the 5:00 segment for Standing Bear.
541. Hardorff, *Hokahey!*, 63–64. See also the 5:40 Wooden Leg segment.
542. Hardorff, *Hokahey!*, 64–65. See also the 6:00 Standing Bear segment.
543. Hardorff, *Hokahey!*, 67. See also the 5:20 and 5:30 Waterman segments.

in Deep Coulee during the "fierce fight at Calhoun Ridge." He also said that Gall was "standing at this very location in 1886" when he made the observation. This is not true. Gall made the statement about the number of Indians killed, "Eleven down in that creek . . . four over there . . . two in that coulee," while he was standing *on Custer Hill*. He made the statement to a number of people, including the St. Paul *Pioneer Press* reporter that Hardorff cited as the source of this information. Another witness, Edward S. Godfrey, lieutenant of Company K at the time of the battle, substantiates the fact that Gall presented the information while sitting near the monument. When the Hunkpapa became convinced that the interpreter was not telling the story correctly, he motioned for Godfrey to come along with him. The two of them, accompanied by Godfrey's old trumpeter, George B. Penwell, then rode over to Calhoun Hill, where Gall told and acted out the story once again. In Godfrey's recapitulation, there is not one reference to any Indians being killed in the ravine (Deep Coulee) below Calhoun Hill. In fact, Godfrey said that Gall indicated no Indians were hit because they hid too well, jumping up only for a second to fire, then ducking down again. When the warriors finally rose to attack, they bowled Calhoun over with ease. Never was there mention of an Indian casualty to Godfrey while they were on Calhoun Hill. Gall's "Eleven down in that creek" statement to the *Pioneer Press* reporter came while he was sitting by the monument on Custer Hill, not at Calhoun Hill, thus his "two in that coulee" was probably a reference to the Deep Coulee–Calhoun Hill location—which substantiates the poverty of casualties in the south.[544]

In another instance, Hardorff cited a letter by John W. Pope, who visited the battlefield as a 5th Infantry lieutenant in 1878. Hardorff said Pope learned from the Indians who accompanied him to the field that nearly all the Indian casualties in the fight occurred around Calhoun Ridge. Again, Pope said nothing of the kind. The Indians told Pope that "one troop was formed well forward, making an angle forward with the other troops along the Custer Ridge." This troop made a considerable fight and nearly all of the Indians killed fell at this fight. The troop was then driven back to where it was overwhelmed along with the rest of the command, and when the fight was nearly over, a few soldiers ran downhill to try and get shelter in the timber. Certainly these Indians could very well have been talking about the Custer Hill end of the field, for the situation mirrors the movements of Companies E and F as well or better than it does Companies C and L. In fact, since we have deduced that the great majority of deaths (15 out of 16, or 93 percent), or killed and wounded (19 out of 22, or 86 percent), occurred in the north, we must realize that Pope's letter absolutely has to be speaking of the Custer Hill part of the fight. That is where almost all the Indian casualties occurred.[545] As we have seen, Wooden Leg said most of the Indians were hit during the Lame White Man attack, more than on any other section of the field. Gall and Pope were both telling us the same thing: the greater number of casualties were suffered in the north.

544. Hardorff, *Hokahey!*, 61; Mangum, "Gall," 36; Graham, *The Custer Myth*, 89, 91, 93, 95.
545. Hardorff, *Hokahey!*, 61; Graham, *The Custer Myth*, 115.

Hardorff faulted Charles Kuhlman for using the Pope letter to argue for the existence of a south skirmish line. He said of Kuhlman, among other things, that his imagination was greater than his ability to adhere to facts, that he ignored contrary evidence, and that he considered only the data that supported his hypothesis.[546] There must be some sort of poetic justice involved here, for if Kuhlman is rightly accused of the above sins, then Hardorff reciprocated, quid pro quo, in his own methodology.

Granted, much of the Indian testimony is ambiguous upon first glance, but it is only with a long stretch of the imagination that one could cite the above events as proof of a tough battle around Calhoun Hill. More likely, Red Hawk (5:00) told us the true situation: the soldiers delivered many volleys, but the firing did not have any perceptible effect. Even so, Hardorff appeared to be puzzled as to why there were so few accounts of casualties around Calhoun Hill. Besides Gall (whose words Hardorff misapplied), he said, "Most other informants are silent on this point." Exactly—and that should have been a clue. The Indians were silent for a reason: there were few, if any, Indian casualties below Calhoun Hill.[547]

Hardorff did not believe any troop made a hearty defense below Custer Hill. He does not believe the Lame White Man attack took place against E Troop in the upper reaches of Deep Ravine. He stated that Company E was never deployed as a unit anywhere near Deep Ravine, and it was an absolute fact that a south line never existed because the command had been destroyed while moving north to Custer Hill![548] Such statements deny almost every Indian account we have examined, and operating from that frame of reference will inevitably skew any subsequent thinking on the matter.

That mind-set has detracted from Hardorff's study, *Hokahey!* Undoubtedly he spent much time and research on the book, yet his analysis of the Calhoun Hill episode reaches conclusions that do not follow from the data. The distribution of the Indian casualties tells a different story.

The men on Calhoun Hill probably were defending their position adequately— volleying sharply but hitting little. The Indians at this time were still seeking safety in distance, protected by the terrain, and exposing themselves rarely. They had not yet gone into a close-range mode as they would following the Crazy Horse–White Bull breakthrough. On Calhoun Hill, the defenders suppressed one desultory charge, and the Indians were at that time content to harass the soldiers with long-distance fire. It is not surprising they suffered so few casualties.

The fact that a relatively large number (thirty-four) of army cartridges were found in the Calhoun Hill–Finley Ridge area proves little, other than that the soldiers had some time to stand around and pop long-range shots at distant Indians. Unfortunately for the troopers, they hit few Indians and they did not succeed in deterring them from a subsequent offensive. Fewer expended army cartridges (only

546. Hardorff, *Markers*, 62; Michno, *E Troop*, 259.
547. Hardorff, *Hokahey!*, 61; Utley, "Sitting Bull," 5. In the latter article, Utley inadvertently touches on a similar conundrum: if Gall was prominent in the fighting around Calhoun Hill, why did no warriors remember seeing him there?
548. Hardorff, *Markers*, 58, 63; Hardorff, *Hokahey!*, 65–68.

fifteen) were found on Custer Hill and along the south skirmish line,[549] yet the northern defenders, with one less company, accounted for 93 percent of the Indian deaths.

Richard Fox indicated that relic collecting can compromise the material record left on a battlefield, but he argued that there was no selective collecting on the Custer battlefield. He said indiscriminate collecting over the long run is always random and thought it unlikely that collectors would have picked over other troop positions and left Calhoun Hill relatively untouched.[550] Yet thirty-four cartridges were found in the Calhoun Hill–Finley Ridge positions, in the center of an area where possibly one Indian died, while fifteen cartridges were found in the South Line–Custer Hill area, around which fifteen Indian deaths occurred. For Fox's argument to hold water, the soldiers from Companies E and F would have to have been inestimably superb marksmen compared to the men of Companies C, I, and L. Remnant cases show that while those soldiers in the south killed one Indian with thirty-four shots, those in the north killed fifteen Indians with fifteen shots, hitting 100 percent of their targets.

What makes altogether better sense is that the action probably was much more furious around Custer Hill, with Lame White Man, the suicide boys, and other pursuing Indians forsaking long-range sniping and finally moving into harm's way at close range, thus easing the soldier's task of hitting a target. In addition, it is obvious that many more cartridges were indeed removed from the Custer Hill end than have been removed from Calhoun Hill. Therefore, the battlefield contains a skewed relic sample and we cannot reconstruct Indian or troop movements based on their patterns. Custer Hill has been the focal point of visitors from day one to the present. It has been picked cleaner than Calhoun Hill.

The deceiving patterns of relics found on the battlefield should not lead us astray. Calhoun Hill was not the best defended position. Clearly, there was a stubborn last stand on Custer Hill and the soldiers there sold their lives dearly. That they did so is supported by the greatly disproportionate number of Indian casualties surrounding that position. Drawing on a great Calvin Coolidge aphorism, "when people are out of work, unemployment results," we must also conclude that when people are killed, dead bodies result. Where were the bodies? They were on and around Custer Hill. It is there we find the last stand. We should rely less on relic patterns, while building our conclusions on a primary base of historical documents combined with some common sense.

Although archaeological discoveries may be counted as a positive contribution to our understanding of the battle, unintended consequences are already in evidence. In addition to those who use the physical record for their own moral agendas, some authors attempt to integrate archaeological evidence with the written record when they have but a superficial understanding of the battle's temporal and spatial features, resulting in even more confusion. Charles Robinson somehow placed Keogh's wing waiting for Custer on the ridge between Calhoun Coulee and Deep

---

549. Fox, *Archaeology, History*, 85, 102, 108, 123. The scale of the mapped cartridges leads to some overlapping and distortion, making exact numbers difficult to determine. In any event, cartridges in the south outnumber those in the north by about two to one.
550. Ibid., 127–28.

Ravine. Subscribing to the revisionist sequence of events, Robinson said Keogh sent Calhoun down Calhoun Coulee, where he scattered the encroaching Indians and occupied a low ridge commanding the depression. Robinson asserted that Calhoun had the only unit that deployed or fought in an organized manner. In fact, what Robinson was probably trying to describe was Company C's move down to Finley Ridge. Apparently not knowing where this terrain is, he then said that the bodies on Finley Ridge were scattered enough to suggest a rout—which, in reality, was on the same terrain where he described Calhoun making a firm stand.[551] Jumping on the bandwagon of current revision without a full knowledge of the original source material and the terrain will lead to the same problems as in the false "Crazy Horse out of the north" scenario. Battle students must stop following popular footprints and use the primary sources to form their own trails.

By 6:10 P.M., back on the Little Bighorn battleground, the rattle of the bullets had subsided to an occasional scattered popping. The fighting around Cemetery Ravine and Deep Ravine was over, and the last survivors on Custer Hill had been ridden down. The Indians, perhaps themselves surprised at the abrupt termination of the clatter, looked around for their foe. But there were none to be seen still standing or firing. If any soldiers were left alive, they were badly wounded or playing dead.

---

551. Robinson, *A Good Day to Die*, 191, 193.

Aftermath, 6:20 and Later

The eddies of dust and smoke curled off up the valley, drifting toward the bluffs still occupied by Reno's and Benteen's battalions. Most of the warriors had belatedly gone back to deal with them. The soldier sortie to the high ground later known as Weir Point was too little, too late. They returned, hesitant and confused, back to the bluffs where they had idled away the past two hours of valuable time.

On Custer's field, some Lakota and Cheyenne warriors lingered, to be joined by many inquisitive women and children crossing over to see the aftermath of the great battle. Feather Earring returned to the east bank of the river, near the mouth of Deep Ravine. He had tried to drive home the five wounded, trembling gray horses but decided they were hurt too badly. He set them free, either to recover or to die, and went back toward the main ridge.

About two hundred yards from the river, Feather Earring went to look at two bodies. One was a dead Indian, the other a dead white man. He saw movement. The white man's heart was still beating. He called out to a nearby Lakota, "Your grandfather has been killed by that man. . . . I don't think he is dead; you had better shoot him." The Lakota came up and put an arrow through him. The soldier jumped up, for he had only been playing dead. The Indian put another arrow into him. Now, said Feather Earring, he was truly dead.[552]

Iron Hawk witnessed a similar incident. After he had killed two soldiers on the slopes above the upper Deep Ravine and the battle appeared over, he began to go toward the river when he saw the women and children approaching. Iron Hawk heard some playful hollering and went over for a closer look. Some women had removed the clothes of a "dead" soldier when, suddenly, the naked man hopped up and began to fight with them. He was swinging two women around while they were trying to stab him. A third woman came up and used her knife on the white man to put an end to the struggle. Iron Hawk was anxious to leave this place. He decided to go south where the other soldiers were still putting up a fight.[553]

In the meantime, Black Elk made his way toward the top of the ridge, and walked among the soldiers. "When we got there, some of them were still alive, kicking," he said. He and the other boys shot arrows into the wounded soldiers. Sometimes they pushed the protruding arrows in further by hand.

Black Elk tried to take one man's coat, but another Indian pushed him away and took the coat for himself. Then he saw something bright and yellow hanging from a chain on the soldier's belt. He did not know what it was, but it was beautiful and engraved, like an ornament. He used it as a necklace and only later learned that it was a watch.

About this time, the women arrived on the hilltop where the gray horses were lying about. Most of the Indian dead had already been removed by then, and only a few were left. Black Elk saw another wounded white man who was raising his

552. Graham, *The Custer Myth*, 98.
553. DeMallie, *Sixth Grandfather*, 192.

arms and groaning. He took out his last blunt arrow and shot the man right in the forehead. His arms and legs began to quiver.

From there, Black Elk saw Indians cradling a wounded comrade. He went closer and found it was Chase In The Morning's brother, Black Wasichu (Black White Man). He had been shot through the right shoulder, and the bullet had traveled downward and lodged in his left hip, because he was leaning over the side of his horse when he was shot. Black Elk's father and Black Wasichu's father were so angry about the terrible wounding that they went and butchered a white man. They cut him open. He was fat and his meat looked good enough to eat.

Black Elk rode all around the northern battlefield. Another boy asked him to scalp a man. Black Elk was becoming an old hand at this. He cut off the man's hair and gave it to the boy. The Indians were then gathering up the last of their dead and Black Elk tired of the affair. He could smell nothing but blood and gunpowder, and he was becoming sick of it. Yet he wasn't sorry. He was a happy boy. He knew beforehand what was going to happen. He had seen it all in his visions. His people were relatives to the Thunder-beings and he had known the soldiers were going to be wiped out. Contented, Black Elk returned to his tipi.[554]

On the hilltop, several warriors saw, or thought they saw, the white leader. Fears Nothing said he saw Custer's horse, a chestnut sorrel with stocking legs, and Custer's body clothed in buckskin. Standing Bear took a buckskin shirt from one of the dead white men and gave it to his mother. She kept it for many years. He later heard that Custer was supposed to have worn a buckskin shirt and came to believe that it had been his, until he learned that several other buckskin shirts were found among the dead. At the time of the battle, Standing Bear said, no one recognized Custer's body or even knew it was Custer they had been fighting. Young Little Wolf echoed the fact. "We did not know it was Custer," he said. "After [the] fight we discussed the identity of [the] soldiers & [we] all thought it [was] Crook."[555]

White Shield saw a soldier that he later came to believe might have been Custer, lying on the outer edge of where the Gray Horse troopers died, near where the monument now stands. The man was stripped of his buckskin shirt and his trousers. He had a big red handkerchief and fine, high boots with a knife stuck into a boot scabbard. The man had a long mustache, but no other hair on his face. He had marks pricked into his skin (tattoos) on the arms above the wrists. Lying beside him was a six-shooter and a saber. "They had sabers with them," White Shield affirmed. There were few Indians dead on the ridges, he added, because, for the most part, "they did not charge in to [the] soldiers, but shot them from behind the hills." There were at least three exceptions that White Shield knew of. "White Bull's son [Noisy Walking], Mad Wolf [Lame White Man] and Limber Lance [Limber Hand or Limber Bones] charged among the sold[iers] and were killed."[556]

White Cow Bull and other warriors were on the hill shouting victory yells when the women heard them and came up to strip the bodies of the soldiers. Those who had lost husbands, brothers, or sons began to butcher the soldiers.

---

554. Ibid., 193–94.
555. Hardorff, *Lakota Recollections*, 28; Hammer, *Custer in '76*, 215; Camp Mss., IU, Box 7, Folder 5.
556. White Shield, Notebook 348, Grinnell Collection.

White Cow Bull looked for bullets and weapons among the dead. He turned over a naked body and recognized the white man who had worn the buckskin jacket at the ford—the one he had shot off of his horse and into the water. White Cow Bull remembered how close some of his bullets had come, so he decided to cut off the man's trigger finger for medicine to make him an even better shot.

Just then he heard a woman's voice. He turned to see Meotzi, her son Yellow Bird, and an older Shahiyela woman standing behind him. The older woman pointed to the body and said, "He is our relative." They signed for him to go away. White Cow Bull looked at Meotzi and smiled, but she did not return the gesture. He wondered if she thought it was wrong for him to try to cut off the finger of an enemy. He had spent the entire battle hoping Meotzi would hear of his brave deeds, and now she had found him attempting to take a dead man's finger. Somewhat chastened, White Cow Bull moved away.

As he pretended to look for other bullets, he glanced back to see Meotzi looking down at the body. The older woman poked her bone sewing awl into the white man's ears. "So Long Hair will hear better in the Spirit Land," she said. It was the first White Cow Bull had heard that Long Hair was the soldier chief they had been fighting.[557]

Other warriors had various impressions of the aftermath. Flying Hawk said that most of Reno's men were mutilated, but few of Custer's men were. Two Eagles saw a Cheyenne woman with short hair who was in mourning for her son who was killed at the Rosebud battle. She carried an ax to the field. One wounded private had just lifted himself up, but was quickly caught and held down by two warriors. She dispatched him with her ax. Antelope witnessed a similar incident. She saw a wounded, dazed soldier sitting on the ground and rubbing his head. Three Lakotas seized him and stretched him out on his back. Two held his arms down while the third cut off his head with a sheath knife.[558]

After the final onslaught, Runs The Enemy saw the body of one Indian that had been hit across the head with a war ax. As he was leaving to check on his family, he saw Indians piling up the white men's clothes, and there was still shooting all over the hill wherever wounded soldiers were found. He did not see any soldiers scalped. Lone Bear thought that many soldiers were wounded but alive after the fight, and that they were killed and stripped by the women. Foolish Elk said many women came to the field to strip the dead. He did not remain to see if any of the wounded were scalped and killed, but he thought most of them were killed before the general firing stopped. Turtle Rib said the Indians were too busy caring for their own killed and wounded to scalp and mutilate the soldiers. They went off to fight Reno

---

557. Miller, "Echoes," 34. This incident supposedly developed out of the March 1869 conference in the Southern Cheyenne Medicine Arrow Lodge, in which Custer negotiated for the release of captive white women, but failed to live up to the bargain by not releasing three Indian hostages he had taken. The Cheyenne Stone Forehead had poured ashes over Custer's boot to give him bad luck if he ever broke his promise not to fight the Cheyennes again—thus, the story of the old woman poking his ears to make him hear the Cheyenne warnings better in the next life. Later, Antelope also heard this story, but she understood that a Lakota warrior did cut off one joint of Custer's finger before leaving. See Marquis, *Custer on the Little Big Horn*, 96.
558. Hardorff, *Lakota Recollections*, 50, 150; Marquis, *Custer on the Little Big Horn*, 91.

and did not remain to scalp the dead. However, he added, what the women did afterwards he did not know. Pretty White Buffalo said the women crossed the river behind the braves. When they came to the hill, Long Hair and two hundred of his men were already dead. The village boys shot many of the dead soldiers again, "for the blood of the people was hot and their hearts bad, and they took no prisoners that day."[559]

When the battle on the hill had ended, White Bull raised himself up, testing his sore leg. His friend With Horns found him, helped him up on a horse, and led it back across the river. Back in his father's lodge, he rested, ate, and had his wound dressed, while Sitting Bull himself wrapped the leg in buffalo fur. The great Hunkpapa gently chided him for his recklessness. "My nephew, you must be careful, sometime you may be killed." White Bull smiled, for it had been a great battle and he liked it very much.

After he had regained his strength, White Bull went back to the battlefield to try and find the saddle and leggings that he had thrown off. The soldiers were all stripped, but he saw no one mutilating the dead. On the hilltop where the fighting had been at close range he met his cousin Bad Soup. He had been around Fort Abraham Lincoln for a time and knew the white leader by sight, the one they called "Long Hair." Now Bad Soup pointed the man out to White Bull. Later, while watering his horse at the river, he noted one Indian with a fine looking sorrel. "Is that a good horse?" White Bull asked. The Indian, Sounds The Ground As He Walks, son of the Santee Inkpaduta, answered, "I know it is [a] good horse, as it was Long Hair's." White Bull was able to find his saddle and leggings, plus he got two pairs of soldier's pants, which he washed in the river and took home to his father.[560]

After the fight, Beard searched among the bodies on the hill. The soldier chief he had tried to capture lay on the ground with the reins of his horse's bridle still tied to his wrist. It was a fine, blaze-faced sorrel with white stockings. A Santee named Walks Under The Ground took the horse and announced that this was the white leader, Long Hair. It was the first that Beard knew who they had been fighting. He thought it was a strange name for a soldier chief who had short hair.[561]

Wooden Leg poked around the dead soldiers on the hill, noticing one man with blue and red paint colorings (tattoos) on his skin. Nearby he found a dead man (Lt. William W. Cooke) with enormous side whiskers. "Here is a new kind of scalp," he said, as he skinned off one half of the man's long, light yellow beard.

When he heard that Noisy Walking was badly wounded, Wooden Leg went down in the deep gulch where he was said to be lying. A youth about the same age

---

559. Dixon, *Vanishing Race*, 177; Hardorff, *Lakota Recollections*, 160; Hammer, *Custer in '76*, 199, 202; McLaughlin, *My Friend the Indian*, 46.
560. White Bull, Box 105, Notebooks 23 & 24, Campbell Collection; Vestal, "Man Who Killed Custer," 9–10. It was not until 1957 that Campbell (Vestal) bestowed the "honor" of killing Custer on White Bull, stating that after Bad Soup pointed the soldier chief out to him, White Bull was reported to have said, "If that is Long Hair, I am the man who killed him." This statement is not in any of Campbell's original notes on White Bull.
561. Miller, "Echoes," 38. The incongruity of the scene, where the reins of a live horse are still tied to the wrist of the dead Custer, is another one of Miller's gems.

as Wooden Leg, Noisy Walking had three bullet wounds and had been stabbed in the side. "How are you?" Wooden Leg asked him. "Good," Noisy Walking managed to say, but Wooden Leg could see that this was not the case. Word had been sent to his relatives and they would soon be arriving to help him off the field. Wooden Leg continued back up the ravine toward the ridge.

There he came upon the body of a scalped Indian who looked familiar. He went to find his brother Yellow Hair, and they returned and rolled the body over. It was Lame White Man. Several other Cheyennes came over and confirmed the identification. They assumed he had been killed by some Lakotas, mistaking him for a Crow or Shoshone scout. They knew he had accompanied the young men in their charge and apparently had been killed on his way back down from the ridge. A bullet had gone through his right breast and exited out his back, and he also had many stab wounds. Yellow Hair took a blanket from his horse and covered the body while a young man hurried across the river to tell his people.[562]

Little Hawk also heard about what had happened to Mad Heart Wolf (Lame White Man), whom he called "one of the bravest of men of modern times." He was always in the front of the fighting, Little Hawk said. He was killed and was found in the very midst of the dead soldiers. Some Lakotas thought he was a scout in the service of the troops. They scalped him, "taking one side of the head with the long hair. When they found he was a Chey[enne] chief, they brought back the scalp and put it on the head again."[563]

Tall Bull received word of Lame White Man's death. He rode west to the hill where Twin Woman and her children had been watching the battle. "My brother-in-law is one of those killed," he told his sister quietly. "Prepare a travois for him." They fixed up two poles and a flat surface upon which the body could be lashed. When they reached him he was still stripped, as when he had come from the sweat lodge. He was coated with dust and a portion of his scalp was missing. Wooden Leg returned and helped them roll the body onto the buffalo-hide travois.

The mourning family members took Lame White Man's body back to the village. They dressed him in a fringed buckskin shirt and leggings and wrapped him in a fine robe, burial clothing fit for a great fighting man. Then they bore him across to the north side of the river and hid him well in the sandy rock bluffs.[564]

Antelope had ridden around the battlefield, seeing Indians cutting off the arms and legs of more soldiers. Finally a Cheyenne told her that her nephew was down in the deep gulch, halfway to the river, where many of the Cheyennes and Oglalas had been in the first part of the battle. Antelope's two-hour search was over. She found Noisy Walking, shot and stabbed several times. She waited with him while word was taken to his family.

Soon, Noisy Walking's mother and her sister came to get him. Wooden Leg also returned after helping with Lame White Man. They put Noisy Walking on the travois bed and took him across the river to the camp. At sundown he lay on a bed of buffalo robes shaded by a willow dome erected by the women. His father, White

562. Marquis, *Wooden Leg*, 240–42.
563. Little Hawk, Notebook 346, Grinnell Collection.
564. Powell, *Sacred Mountain*, 1033; Marquis, *Wooden Leg*, 242.

Bull (Ice), was there, while his mother sat just outside the entrance. Wooden Leg came to visit, inquiring of his condition. Again Noisy Walking tried to put up a brave front. He was good, he said, but he was terribly thirsty. After a short silence, Wooden Leg said, "You were very brave." Noisy Walking trembled every time he tried to move, and his words came hard. Finally he said to his father, "I wish I could have some water—just a little of it."

"No," said Ice. "Water will kill you." So powerful as a holy man and as a doctor, so strong in blessing and saving others, Ice could do nothing to save the boy. He choked on his words as he quietly talked to his only son. Late that night, Noisy Walking died.[565]

Understandably, there was a mixture of emotions in the village that night. There was joy, explained Pretty White Buffalo, for a great victory had been won at comparatively little cost. Yet there was grief, too, for what wife, mother, or sister gives thought to victory when she finds her relative dead on the field? "So it was," said Pretty White Buffalo, "that in the midst of the rejoicing, there was sorrowing among the women, who would not be comforted in knowing that their dead had gone to join the ghosts of the brave."[566]

Too many men had gone to the spirit land, never again to see the lush grasses of the valley, the flash of lightning over the plains, never to cry or laugh again around the campfire with friends and family. To Moving Robe, as she slowly rode back to the village, thinking at times about her dead little brother, the contest was not a massacre but a hotly fought battle. Brave men who came to punish the Indians were met by equally brave warriors, and the soldiers were defeated. But it was all to no avail. In the end, Moving Robe mused, the Indians still lost.[567]

◄ DISCUSSION. For the last time, we come up against some of the questionable D. H. Miller Indian accounts. Several Indians mentioned the soldier chief fighting at the end, either with pistols or carbine. Several Indians mentioned the stampeding of the soldier horses or their killing for use as breastworks. Beard, however, found the soldier chief that he had tried to capture lying dead on the ground, with the reins of his horse still looped around his wrist. Somehow, the horse calmly stood by his side on the hilltop, untouched by the death and destruction.

In 1932, White Bull told Walter Campbell that the Santee son of Inkpaduta had taken Long Hair's horse. In 1971, Miller wrote that Beard had a similar meeting with Inkpaduta's son, who announced to him that the sorrel he had found was Custer's.

In "Echoes of the Little Bighorn," Miller did not even write of White Bull's wounding. He indicated the apparently unhurt Indian was around to see the end of the fight, including incidents such as Iron Hawk's description of the woman fighting with the naked *wasichu*. In addition, Miller said it was Bad Soup who stripped and identified Custer while White Bull stood at his side.[568] White Bull told Campbell

---

565. Powell, *Sacred Mountain*, 1033; Marquis, *Custer on the Little Big Horn*, 91.
566. McLaughlin, *My Friend the Indian*, 46.
567. Hardorff, *Lakota Recollections*, 95–96.
568. Miller, "Echoes," 36.

that he went back to the field only after resting, eating, and getting his wound patched up. Custer had been stripped long before.

Beard's description of his and Spotted Rabbit's attempt to capture the white leader alive may have to be relegated to the realm of Miller's imagination. The Minneconjou's inclination to get into the thick of the fighting is certainly at variance with Miller's renditions. In a taped conversation with Dewey Beard shortly before his death, the old Indian had little to say about participating in the actual fighting. In fact, his concerns seemed to be worlds away: "I found some dry bread and some pork while everyone was fighting," he recalled. "It was good, so I ate it."[569]

In fact, it seems fairly certain that no Indian recognized Custer during or after the battle. Shave Elk said, "We did not suspect that we were fighting Custer and did not recognize him either alive or dead." Wooden Leg said no one could recognize any enemy during the fight, for they were all too far away. The Cheyennes did not even know a man called Custer was in the fight until weeks later. Antelope said none knew of Custer being at the fight until they later learned of it at the agencies. Thomas Marquis learned from his interviews that no Indian knew Custer was at the Little Bighorn fight until months later. Many Cheyennes were not even aware that other members of the Custer family had been at the fight until 1922, when, Marquis said, he himself first informed them of that fact.[570]

Nevertheless, in *Custer's Fall,* Miller drew the scene of an old woman who poked a sewing awl into Custer's ear. She was identified as Mahwissa, the sister of Chief Black Kettle, who died in Custer's 1868 attack on the Washita, and the aunt of Meotzi (Monahsetah). White Cow Bull was the unnamed Lakota who succeeded in cutting off Custer's finger. With the light-haired Yellow Bird standing nearby, who had been fathered by Custer, Meotzi was said to have "gazed in silence at the naked pale-skinned body she had once loved."[571] It is all painted as a just, fitting end for one who would satisfy his lust for a captive Indian woman and who would defy the odds and his orders in a personal quest for glory.

Was a woman named Mahwissa on the field and poking an awl into the ears of a man that she identified as Custer? Could Meotzi have been standing alongside to see the naked body of a dead lover? The scene smacks more of a teenage pulp romance than of history. Did White Cow Bull fail at cutting off Custer's finger? Walking on Custer Hill two days after the battle, Capt. Henry B. Freeman of the 7th Infantry wrote in his journal: "Yates' finger had been cut off to get his ring."[572] As with so many other incidents, these are tantalizing tidbits that straddle the line between truth and fiction. We will probably never know for sure.

Although I have tried to limit this story to the "who," "where," and "when" aspects from the Indian narratives, it is almost impossible to leave the battle without

---

569. This quote comes from a cassette tape sent to the author by Custer scholar Tom Bookwalter. It contains a 1955 conversation with Dewey Beard that was translated by one of his relatives, Frances Twin.

570. Liddic, *Camp on Custer,* 123; Marquis, *Wooden Leg,* 378; Marquis, *Custer on the Little Big Horn,* 96; Marquis, *Cheyennes of Montana,* 243.

571. Miller, *Custer's Fall,* 168–70.

572. George A. Schneider, ed., *The Freeman Journal: The Infantry in the Sioux Campaign of 1876* (San Rafael, CA: Presidio Press, 1977), 59.

a brief shot at the "why" behind the outcome. After all is said and done, why did Custer lose, or rather, why did the Indians win? First, we must eliminate some of the factors that did not affect the final outcome. A concise overview entitled "What Did Not Happen at the Little Big Horn" has been presented by Jay Smith: the village was not too large and there were not too many Indians; Custer did not violate any principles of war; there was no ambush; the Indians did not have better guns; the army's guns were not defective; the command was not too tired to fight, nor did they have too many new recruits.[573] Others have added a potpourri of reasons, including a lack of intelligence, failure to reconnoiter, attacking too early, disobeying orders, glory seeking, regimental discord, psychological disorders, and so on, ad infinitum.

Of these, a huge village and an immense number of warriors traditionally have been the idée fixe of past chroniclers, running the gamut among historians, journalists, reporters, novelists, and cartoonists. A vain, glory-hunting Custer was overwhelmed by swarming savages. These are erroneous impressions that need to be permanently set aside. If one had to choose any of the above arguments as having any modicum of validity, a logical choice might be a facet of the "principles of war" argument: that of dividing one's force in the face of the enemy. This bears further explanation.

Whereas it may be best to avoid dividing up a command in the proximity of an enemy during large-scale maneuvers with army-sized units (although Napoleon seemed to have success with it), such is not the case during small-scale tactical cavalry maneuvers. Custer Battle student Bruce Trinque has very ably pointed out Custer's adherence to the principles for a successful engagement in fighting a small, guerilla-type, mobile enemy. Citing the successful tactics used by the British army in scores of their "Small Wars," Trinque showed that Custer did nearly everything necessary to defeat his foe. For example, proven tactics called for individual initiative, mobility, maintaining the offensive, acting without delay, playing not for safety but to win, and fighting whenever the opportunity arose. It was accepted that regular soldiers would never shirk an encounter even with a superior irregular force of enemies, and that division of force for an enveloping attack combined with a frontal attack was most preferable. On a small scale, and up to a certain point, Custer acted appropriately.[574]

Problems arose, however, when tactics broke down from small-scale to micro-scale. According to then-Bvt. Maj. Edward S. Godfrey, fire discipline—the ability to control and direct deliberate, accurate, aimed fire—will decide every battle. No attack force, however strong, could reach a defensive line of steady soldiers putting out a disciplined fire.[575] The British army knew such was the case, as did Napoleon, who commented that two irregular Mameluke warriors could defeat three French cavalrymen. However, 1,000 Frenchmen could beat 1,500 Mamelukes.[576] The deciding factor was strength in unity—fire discipline.

---

573. Smith, "What Did Not Happen at the Little Big Horn," 8–13.
574. Bruce A. Trinque, "Small Wars and the Little Big Horn," TMs photocopy, 1994, 1–22.
575. E. S. Godfrey, "Cavalry Fire Discipline," *By Valor & Arms: The Journal of American Military History* 2, no. 4 (1976): 31–36.
576. Trinque, "Small Wars," 16.

Theoretically, on the Little Bighorn, with a *small*-scale defense in suitable terrain and an open field of fire of a few hundred yards, several companies of cavalrymen in close proximity, under strict fire control, could have easily held off two or
three times their number of Indian warriors. In reality, on the Little Bighorn, with
a *micro*-scale defense in unsuitable, broken terrain, several companies of cavalrymen
not in close proximity, with little fire control, could not hold off two or three times
their number of Indian warriors.

The breakdown stems from an attitude factor, but this must not be understood
in pejorative terms. Custer exhibited an arrogance, not necessarily of personal nature but rather as a part of his racial makeup. Again, this is not *racist,* but *racial.* It was
endemic in red versus white modes of warfare and implies nothing derogatory to
either side. Historically, Indians fled from large bodies of soldiers. It was Custer's
experience that it was much harder to find and catch an Indian than to actually
fight him.[577] Successfully following small-unit tactics and naturally influenced by
past experience, Custer attacked. He was on the offensive. He knew he must remain on the offensive to be successful. Even after Reno had been repulsed and the
hammer-and-anvil tactic would no longer work as first envisioned, he was maneuvering, looking for another opportunity to attack. The positions of Calhoun on his
hill, or of Yates on his hill, or of Keogh as a reserve in his vale, were not defensive
positions. They were temporary operational pauses for one whose mind was still on
"attack." Even after the Indians had taken away the initiative, Custer's mind-set
would not allow him to shift into another frame of reference. He did not take his
final position with defense in mind. Although a rough, boxlike perimeter was formed,
it appeared more as a matter of circumstance than intent. Custer probably never
realized that his men's very survival was on the line, at least not until it was too late
to do anything about it. They were not in good defensible terrain. They were not
within mutual supporting distance. They were not under the tight fire control of
their officers. When the critical point was reached, the soldiers found themselves
stretched beyond the physical and psychological line that would dictate "fight or
flight." The "bunkie" was not close enough. The first sergeant was far away. The
lieutenant was nowhere to be seen. Seemingly out of supporting distance of his
comrades, the individual trooper found himself desperately alone. Some stands were
made, particularly on and within a radius of a few hundred yards of the knoll that
became known as Custer Hill, where almost all of the Indian casualties occurred.
However, when it came down to one on one, warrior versus soldier, the warrior
was the better fighter.[578]

It was the judgment of Robert Utley, with no attempt at being facetious, that
perhaps the best way to understand the battle's outcome was to realize "that the

---

577. Gary M. Thomas, *The Custer Scout of April, 1867* (Kansas City, MO: Westport Printing, 1987), 1–2; Brian
   W. Dippie, ed., *Nomad: George A. Custer in Turf, Field and Farm* (Austin: University of Texas Press, 1980),
   123.
578. In a previous study, Michno, *E Troop,* 278–79, I argued that the area below Custer Hill, known as the
   south skirmish line, was a viable defensive position. I reserved judgment on the remaining portions of
   the field. Upon this examination, I would reiterate that the south line and Custer Hill positions both
   witnessed the staunchest defense, if only for the fact that the soldiers in those positions inflicted the
   most Indian casualties. In contrast, the soldiers on the southern half of the field, Keogh's battalion,
   offered little effective defense.

Army lost largely because the Indians won." To represent the result only in terms of
military failings devalues Indian strengths. The Lakotas and Cheyennes were strong,
well led, well armed, united, confident, and ready to fight if forced to do so.[579]

Custer may have done almost everything as prescribed, but it was insufficient to
overcome the combination of particular circumstances, some of his own making,
which confronted him that day.

It has been said that all historical interpretation is relative, that every change in
the present revises our perspectives of the past, that every age writes its history
anew, and that some of the "new" western history has become less optimistic and
"darker," as our old heroes and traditions die or are forced out of favor.[580] The fact
that every generation rewrites its history is particularly true in the case of the Little
Bighorn battle, where Custer and his men have gone from heroes to villains in the
last half century.[581] In fact, at the Little Bighorn there were neither heroes nor
villains in a classic sense. Where we Americans seem to enjoy painting conflicts in
black and white, reality proves our answers are found in shades of gray.

Some interpretations of the Little Bighorn fight will stand up to scrutiny and
some will not. Several changes to standard stories have been suggested here. For
example, there was no clash between Indians and cavalry on the river at Medicine
Tail Ford; Yates's battalion rode back to meet Custer on Nye-Cartwright Ridge;
Gall was late to the fight and did not lead any major assault; Lame White Man did
not attack any troop in the Calhoun Coulee–Calhoun Ridge area; and the fight
around Calhoun Hill produced very few Indian casualties.

These conclusions were not manufactured because there was any particular ax
to grind. I did not particularly care which coulee Crazy Horse rode in, but I
definitely wanted to know which one he chose. The underlying driving force behind this study was incontrovertibly to find out *what happened* at the battle by using
the testimony of the only ones who could tell it. It was a learning experience.
Although we all knew the ending, I had no foreknowledge of how the details of
the story would develop until I engaged in assembling them, minute by minute. In
fact, some preconceptions were discarded in the building process.

The first bias I had to overcome was the time factor. A number of assessments
gave me the idea that the last stand was over by five o'clock or shortly thereafter.[582]
It proved impossible to squeeze all the events described by the Indians into such a
constricted temporal framework. A narrator might tell of riding against Reno in

579. Utley, *Cavalier in Buckskin*, 194.
580. For examples of shifting historical interpretations over the years, see Ernst Breisach, *Historiography:
     Ancient, Medieval, and Modern* (Chicago: University of Chicago Press, 1983); Patricia N. Limerick, Clyde
     A. Milner II, Carles Rankin, eds., *Trails: Toward a New Western History* (Lawrence: University of Kansas
     Press, 1991); Gerald D. Nash, Richard W. Etulain, eds., *The 20th Century West: Historical Interpretations*
     (Albuquerque: University of New Mexico Press, 1989); Gerald D. Nash, *Creating the West: Historical
     Interpretations 1890–1990* (Albuquerque: University of New Mexico Press, 1991); John Lukacs, "Revis-
     ing the Twentieth Century," *American Heritage* 45, no. 5 (September 1994): 83–89; Slotkin, *Gunfighter
     Nation*.
581. Dippie, *Custer's Last Stand*, 122–23; Hutton, "Custer in Hollywood," 29–56; Hutton, "Little Big Horn to
     Little Big Man," 19–45.
582. D. A. Kinsley, *Custer Favor the Bold: A Soldier's Story* (New York: Promontory Press, 1992), 535; Wells,
     "Fight on Calhoun Hill," 25; Gray, *Custer's Last Campaign*, 320, 372; Darling, *Custer's Final Hours*, 23–24;

one sentence and describe shooting at a trooper on Custer Hill in the next, obviously compressing events we know were separated by considerable time. As noted of Crazy Horse's movements, these warriors did not ride winged steeds. In addition, the Reno-Benteen survivors had a stake in perpetuating the idea that the Custer fight was over quickly. It was not in the best interests of the army, or to a number of officers' careers, if it could be shown that they dawdled for two hours during Custer's death struggle.[583]

Prior to this exercise it could also be argued that, among other things, the Indian village was very large and contained massive numbers of warriors, that Yates had gone directly from Medicine Tail Ford to Calhoun Hill, and that Crazy Horse went down the valley to attack Custer Hill from the north. None of these contentions stood up to examination. On the other hand, some preconceptions could not be altered, in spite of trying to view the evidence from varying angles. For instance, there is not sufficient proof to alter the contention that Lame White Man made his attack against a troop on the northern half of the field. In addition, although the idea of a tough defense on Calhoun Hill had to be discarded, the fact that a last stand still occurred on Custer Hill remains a certifiable part of our history. Author Michael Kammen pointed out that serious history does not have to be anathema to myth, and that Americans want their collective memories to be sanguine and supportive, yet at the same time unwarped and true.[584] This is just what we have on the Little Bighorn. The knowledge that a last stand truly occurred, that it exists in fact as well as through a "mystic chord of memory," should preserve it in spite of revisionist interpretations and political correctness.

If we have found some previous explanations of battle events unsatisfactory, so be it. The Indians told us what happened. We have only to listen to them. But their story is not quite finished.

William Hedley, "'We've Caught Them Napping!' The Little Bighorn Time Warp," 3rd Annual Symposium, Custer Battlefield Historical & Museum Association (Hardin, MT: CBH&MA, 1989): 64–65; Kuhlman, *Legend Into History*, 190. Many accounts indicate the battle ended between 5:00 and 5:30, while Kuhlman thought the fight might have died out as late as 7:00.

583. King, *Massacre*, passim.

584. Michael Kammen, *Mystic Chords of Memory: The Transformation of Tradition in American Culture* (New York: Vintage Books, 1993), 482, 627.

VI

Vagabonds

The old ways quickly drew to a close. After the fight, the combined camps moved up the Little Bighorn to the base of the Bighorn Mountains, but inexorably families broke off to go their own ways, scattering to look for game or returning to the reservations. Through the month of July, the villages moved over to the Rosebud, crossed to the Tongue, moved downstream, crossed to the Mizpah and Powder, and neared the Yellowstone. In August, more groups split off, some going south up the Powder, some crossing the Yellowstone to head north to the Missouri River, others going east to the badlands of the Little Missouri. Some bands, including the followers of Crazy Horse, headed south up the Little Missouri toward Slim Buttes, while others, including Sitting Bull's band, headed north down the Little Missouri toward Killdeer Mountain.[585] The great village of June 1876 was no more.

On September 9, 1876, General Crook's men hit the Indian camp at Slim Buttes. Red Horse was again surprised in camp, much as he had been at the Little Bighorn. Later in the day, Crazy Horse, He Dog, and Tall Bull came from nearby camps to help fight.[586]

Meanwhile, Gen. Philip H. Sheridan had authorized that all agency Indians be stripped of their horses and weapons. A government commission arrived to demand the sale of the Black Hills. Threatened with loss of rations, the chiefs at Red Cloud, Spotted Tail, and the Missouri River agencies "touched the pen" and gave up the Black Hills and all hunting rights outside the newly defined Great Sioux Reservation.[587]

With the approaching winter, Crook and Colonel Miles prepared for new expeditions. In October, Miles, traipsing across much of eastern and northern Montana, hounded and persuaded a coalition of almost 2,000 Minneconjous and Sans Arcs into surrendering. The Hunkpapa contingent under Sitting Bull and Gall headed north toward Canada. In November, units of Crook's command, under Col. Ranald S. Mackenzie, scattered the Cheyenne village of Little Wolf and Dull Knife on the Red Fork of the Powder. The Cheyennes lost about forty people, plus much of their winter shelter, food, and clothing.[588]

The pressure did not let up. In January 1877, Miles found Crazy Horse's village on the Tongue River, captured a small party of women and children, including Wooden Leg's sister, Crooked Nose, and held off the counterattack. It was another demoralizing episode for the distraught Indians. By April, almost all of the hostile bands had come in to the agencies, where the comparative safety and free rations began to look attractive. In May, Crazy Horse led in his Oglalas to Red Cloud Agency, accompanied by He Dog, Little Hawk, Big Road, Little Big Man, and nearly 1,500 people.

Also in May, Miles led his soldiers after a recalcitrant band of Minneconjous under Lame Deer, father of Flying By. Accompanying his units as scouts were the Minneconjou Hump, recovered from his Little Bighorn wound, the Oglala Short Bull, and the Cheyennes Brave Wolf and Ice (White Bull). Ice had apparently

585. Gray, *Centennial Campaign*, 380.
586. Jerome A. Greene, *Slim Buttes, 1876: An Episode of the Great Sioux War* (Norman: University of Oklahoma Press, 1982), 74, 117.
587. Utley, *Frontier Regulars*, 280–81; Sarf, *Little Bighorn Campaign*, 293.
588. Utley, *Frontier Regulars*, 283–84.

overcome his grief over the death of Noisy Walking and saw the folly of continued resistance, for he volunteered to remain with Miles as a "hostage" to show the good faith of his people and was the first to enlist as a scout. In a battle at Muddy Creek, a tributary of the Rosebud, Lame Deer and fourteen of his followers were left dead on the battlefield, and Ice may have been instrumental in saving Miles's life. He also took the scalps of Lame Deer and his nephew, Big Ankle.

After the fight, Ice was summoned to Miles's tent. For his good service he was given the horses they had captured and told always to keep the soldier gun he had used to fight the hostile Lakotas. Ice offered Big Ankle's scalp to Miles, who declined the gift.

Ice kept his gun until 1905, when it was destroyed in the fire that burned down his house. Miles had also asked what else he could do for Ice, but the Cheyenne answered that he wished for nothing except to be allowed to live in the country where he belonged. At first, Ice resisted attempts to introduce the Indians to farming, believing it a threat to traditional Cheyenne culture. Those who would tear up the earth would become "crazy" like the white man. However, in 1882 he eventually chose some farmland on the Tongue River near the mouth of Otter Creek. When Ice became familiar with the white man's agriculture, he said he wanted to plant a garden of raisins. He said that it was the best food the white man had, so far as he could find out, and he wanted to fill his garden with them. Ice died in 1921.[589]

By September, the last of Lame Deer's survivors straggled into the agencies. Except for Sitting Bull's bands in Canada, the free life of unfettered wandering was almost over.

The summer of 1877 was a time of tension on the Spotted Tail and Red Cloud agencies, due mainly to the presence of Crazy Horse. He was angry because he thought he had been promised an agency of his own on the Powder River and because Lakotas had been recruited to scout for the soldiers. Both sides thought he might lead an outbreak at any time. Lt. Col. Luther P. Bradley, the commander at Camp Robinson, asked for reinforcements. General Crook ordered Bradley to arrest Crazy Horse.

On September 7, the Oglala was being taken through the camp by Little Big Man, Turning Bear, Wooden Sword, and Leaper, when he noticed bars on the windows of the building they were entering. Jail! A scuffle broke out. Little Big Man tried to pinion Crazy Horse's arms from behind. Knives flashed. A soldier ran forward with his bayonet.

"They have stabbed me," Crazy Horse cried out. He staggered backwards and fell on the parade ground. In the gathering crowd were Red Feather and He Dog, and the latter was allowed to go to Crazy Horse. He saw a red knife on the ground beside him. He Dog used his blanket to cover the wounded leader. He was gasping for breath. "See where I am hurt," he said. "I can feel the blood flowing."

589. Ibid., 285–88; Gray, *Centennial Campaign*, 351; Robert M. Utley, *The Last Days of the Sioux Nation* (New Haven: Yale University Press, 1963), 18–19; Thomas W. Dunlay, *Wolves for the Blue Soldiers: Indian Scouts and Auxiliaries with the United States Army, 1860–90* (Lincoln: University of Nebraska Press, 1987), 143; Grinnell, *Fighting Cheyennes*, 387, 390–93; Marquis, *Cheyennes of Montana*, 11–12; Miles, *Personal Recollections*, 244, 247; Orlan J. Svingen, *The Northern Cheyenne Indian Reservation 1877–1900* (Niwot, CO: University of Colorado Press, 1993), 16, 31.

He Dog pulled back his shirt and saw two wounds. One thrust went in between his ribs in the back and very nearly came through in front. There was a rising lump just under the skin where the thrust ended. The second wound had entered the small of his back and hit a kidney. Crazy Horse was taken inside and died later that evening. His father, Worm, came for the body of the boy that he had given his original name to. That night, Worm placed the corpse in a wagon and spirited it off to a bluff above Beaver Creek in northwest Nebraska. There the grieving father and mother hid the body of Crazy Horse in a crevice in the rocks, where it remains, unmarked and undisturbed, to this day.[590]

In the 1930s, He Dog was the last surviving representative of the Oglala grand councilors, the appointed chiefs of highest rank, better known as the "shirt-wearers," a title Crazy Horse had once held. He was a judge on the Court of Indian Offenses at Pine Ridge from the 1890s until advanced age and failing sight made further service impossible. Although later blind and crippled with arthritis, he passed on much information to white interviewers concerning the life of Crazy Horse. Eleanor Hinman called him "the living depository of Oglala tribal history and old-time customs." He died in 1936 at the age of ninety-six.[591]

In November 1877, Congress authorized the creation of an Indian police force, and one of the first to enroll was Hump. He became the chief of police on the Cheyenne River Reservation, yet was one of the reactionaries opposing any further surrender of Indian lands. As late as 1889, Hump still ran a soldier lodge and, along with Kicking Bear and Big Foot (previously known as Spotted Elk), was a zealot in the Ghost Dance craze of 1890. Perhaps intuiting the future, his last-minute defection from the hard-core dancers in December of that year meant he would miss the Wounded Knee debacle. Hump, old and blind, died in 1908.[592]

The 1880s witnessed a new drive to solve the "Indian problem." Congressional arguments had been made to make the Indians a happy and prosperous people, according to white lifestyles, by granting them individual homesteads. In 1883, courts of Indian offenses were established and became tribunals for handling minor crimes on the reservations. The Major Crimes Act of 1885 declared that certain offenses, including murder, committed by Indians on reservations, would fall under the jurisdiction of the United States courts, which was a major encroachment on tribal autonomy. In 1887 the Dawes Act attempted to break up tribal relations by granting land allotments in severalty to individual Indians—one-quarter section to each head of family—and to make every Indian receiving an allotment a citizen of the United States. In the same year the Indian commissioner argued for the exclusive use of English in Indian schools, and in 1888 a new law regulated marriages between white men and Indian women. In 1889 the commissioner argued for the great need to Americanize the Indians and absorb them into white society.[593]

590. Carroll, ed., *Hinman Interviews*, 14–15, 30, 35; Sandoz, *Crazy Horse*, 412–13; Kadlacek, *Kill an Eagle*, 53–54, 70, 79–80, 89, 106, 125, 155. There appear to be as many versions of Crazy Horse's death as there were witnesses.
591. Carroll, ed., *Hinman Interviews*, 7, 17–18.
592. Utley, *Last Days*, 81–82, 96–97, 132, 173; Vestal, *Warpath*, 272; Hyde, *Sioux Chronicle*, 221, 285.
593. Francis Paul Prucha, *Documents of United States Indian Policy* (Lincoln: University of Nebraska Press, 1990), 151, 155, 160, 167, 171, 174, 176, 177.

The Indians reacted diversely to the efforts to change their lifestyle. Some acquiesced and made the conversion. Others resisted by turning to the Ghost Dance religion, which promised a new world for the Indians. The whites would be pushed back across the ocean from where they had come, and all the Indians who had ever lived would come back to live lives unmarred by pain, sickness, or death.

Beard became an avid believer. He was convinced the buffalo would return and his departed ancestors would come back from beyond the grave to share in the great revival of Lakota culture. The dancers, however, appeared to be a threat to the whites, and the soldiers soon moved nearer the reservations. In December 1890, Beard and his family were camped with Big Foot's Minneconjous at Wounded Knee Creek. The soldiers surrounded the camp and ordered the Indians to give up their weapons. A gun was fired, possibly by Sitting Bull's deaf-mute stepson, Blue Mountain, who did not understand the order, or by Black Coyote, "a crazy man" of bad influence. Immediately, chaos reigned. Some soldiers let loose with carbines and Hotchkiss guns while others galloped after the fleeing Indians to cut them down. Beard ran for a gully, but was struck by bullets in the arm, chest, and leg. He waited there in the snow-filled cutbank and prayed for death. In the camp, Beard's wife, child, mother, father, sister, and two younger brothers lay dead.[594]

One man who did not live to witness the end at Wounded Knee was Sitting Bull. He had been steadily losing followers since the breakup of the great camp of 1876. In 1877, Two Moon's Cheyennes surrendered. By 1880, Spotted Tail, Rain In The Face, and Big Road came in. In early 1881, Gall and Crow King followed suit. In April, Low Dog's band surrendered at Fort Buford, leaving Sitting Bull, One Bull, and a few others still holding out against the inevitable. They finally straggled in during July 1881.[595]

Sitting Bull remained a prisoner for a time at Fort Randall. In 1882, he consented to enroll his stepson, Little Soldier, in the white man's mission school, and in 1883 Sitting Bull and his family were transferred to Standing Rock Agency. In the mid-1880s, Sitting Bull traveled with Buffalo Bill's Wild West show, participating in reenactments of the Last Stand and making money selling his autograph. Accompanying him with Cody's troupe were Gray Eagle, Flying By, and Pretty White Buffalo's husband, Spotted Horn Bull. The next season Sitting Bull was not allowed to travel with Cody's show, "for the good of the other Indians," agent James McLaughlin explained. By 1890, the Lakota tribes verged on cultural breakdown.[596]

In December 1890, the Ghost Dancers had everyone on edge. It was believed that Sitting Bull was about to leave Standing Rock to join the high priests of the dance, Kicking Bear and the Brulé Short Bull, at Pine Ridge Agency. Agent McLaughlin issued orders for the Indian police to arrest Sitting Bull. Early on the morning of December 15, they burst into Sitting Bull's cabin and announced that he was to come with them. Pretty White Buffalo was nearby, pacing outside the circle of men. With perhaps more untimely bravado than discretion, she called out

594. Miller, "Echoes," 38–39; Dee Brown, *Bury My Heart at Wounded Knee: An Indian History of the American West* (New York: Holt, Rinehart & Winston, 1970), 442, 444.
595. Utley, *Lance and Shield*, 216, 222, 231.
596. Ibid., 244, 263, 266, 281.

in derision, "Here are a multitude of jealous men!" The situation deteriorated and soon the nearby households were aroused, and an angry crowd of Sitting Bull's supporters gathered around the police.

Sitting Bull was being led to his horse as threats were shouted between the factions. Shots were fired. Within a few minutes, five policemen, including Bull Head, a Hunkpapa who had fought with Sitting Bull at the Little Bighorn, took fatal rounds. Of Sitting Bull's family and friends, Catch-the-Bear, Black Bird, Spotted Horn Bull, and Brave Thunder died, as did Sitting Bull's adopted brother Jumping Bull (Little Assiniboine) and his son, Chase Them Wounded. Sitting Bull's fourteen-year-old son, Crow Foot, was killed. Sitting Bull himself went down with bullets in his chest and head. The remaining police threw Sitting Bull's body into a wagon with the bodies of the dead policemen on top of him. They hauled him back to the agency as they had been ordered to do.[597]

Sitting Bull's cabin was shipped to Chicago for the 1893 World's Fair. Less is known about what happened to his peripatetic remains. His body may have been buried in a box at Fort Yates, North Dakota, or it may have been secreted away to an unknown site by his followers. In the early 1900s the Fort Yates grave was exhumed, but a femur taken from it proved to be that of a young woman. The monument and grave were moved several times. In the 1960s the Army Corps of Engineers came across the possible grave while building a dike in the former cemetery. Today, one monument for Sitting Bull stands at Fort Yates, yet a group from Mobridge, South Dakota, maintains the chief rests near their city, at a site high above man-made Lake Oahe.[598]

In January 1891, the last of the Ghost Dance apostles laid down their weapons. General Miles wished to send twenty-five of the leaders, including Kicking Bear and Short Bull, east to Fort Sheridan, Illinois. However, Buffalo Bill Cody wanted to take the prisoners with his Wild West show. Although the commissioner of Indian Affairs thought circus life demoralizing, Cody pressured enough people to get the okay. The ringleaders of the movement that had caused so much suffering, death, and disillusionment were not placed in a stockade but were allowed to help Cody's troupe make a profitable visit to Europe.[599]

One by one, the Indians began to succumb to unknown maladies or old age. In the early 1880s, Gall and Crow King had been Agent McLaughlin's lieutenants in the crusade against the old way of life. When Crow King died suddenly in 1884, his last rites administered by a Black Robe of the Catholic Church, Gall became the agent's favorite Hunkpapa. Also in 1884, Sitting Bull's mother, Her Holy Door, died, and in 1888, Old Black Moon passed away at the age of seventy-three.[600]

Gall had apparently been the unwitting puppet of McLaughlin, the agent using him, granting him favors, and cajoling him into favoring policies that would ease the transition of the Indians from a wild, free people into model farmers and Christians. McLaughlin encouraged Gall's suggestions of Sitting Bull's cowardice at the

597. Ibid., 297, 300–305; One Bull, Box 104, Folder 11, Campbell Collection.
598. Dayton Duncan, *Out West: American Journey Along the Lewis and Clark Trail* (New York: Penguin Books, 1988), 171–74.
599. Utley, *Last Days*, 271–72.
600. Utley, *Lance and Shield*, 251–52.

Little Bighorn. He made him a chief and influenced his appointment as an Indian judge. Gall, in turn, was instrumental in persuading the Indians to open up more of the Dakota reservations to white settlement.

In 1888, Gall and a number of other Lakotas visited Washington, D.C. He was described as "a big, stout, bully fellow," weighing about 250 pounds. Invited to dinner by Capt. Edward S. Godfrey, Gall was observed to put away oysters in the shell like a practiced old fisherman.

It was almost guaranteed that if Sitting Bull was tolerant of the Ghost Dance, Gall would work against it. Holding councils with anyone who would listen from his camp on the Missouri River, Gall worked with the agent to guide the Hunkpapas along the white man's road, pleading with them to abandon the dance and return to the white man's church and school. In his last years he became more sedentary and overweight. He died at Oak Creek, South Dakota, on December 5, 1894, from either anti-fat medicine, a fall from a wagon, or complications from old stab wounds.[601] Perhaps he had simply lost the will to live.

Two Moon surrendered to Colonel Miles at Fort Keogh in April 1877 and later enlisted as a scout. He was the first to contact Little Wolf when that leader brought his Cheyennes north after the flight from their reservation in Oklahoma Territory. Once surrendered, Two Moon lived in peace the rest of his life and remained interested in the progress of the Cheyennes in learning the intricacies of white civilization. In 1882, he moved from Fort Keogh to the Northern Cheyenne Reservation in Montana, living most of his remaining days in a cabin near the banks of Rosebud Creek.

He told his story to reporter Hamlin Garland in 1898. "That was a long time ago," he said. "I am now old, and my mind has changed. I would rather see my people living in houses and singing and dancing. You have talked to me about fighting, and I have told you of the time long ago. All that is past." Garland described Two Moon as placid yet powerful, with a broad brow, and as he spoke he used his extended arms for gestures both dramatic and noble. There was no anger in his voice. He was thoughtful, patient, and courteous, even to his enemies.

Two Moon went to Washington with Wooden Leg and others in 1913 and met President Woodrow Wilson on another trip in 1914. Old and almost blind, Two Moon ceased to wander in his last years, roaming the prairie now only in his thoughts. He died in 1917.[602]

The Arapahos who fought at the Little Bighorn managed to get away during darkness the second night after the battle. They crawled out of their wickiup, quietly mounted their ponies, and slipped away, riding around the foot of the Black Hills to Fort Robinson.

It had been many moons since that day. Yellow Eagle, Yellow Fly, and Well-Knowing One were dead. By 1920, only Waterman and Left Hand remained. Waterman remembered how his face was painted yellow and red at the battle, and

---

601. Marquis, *Custer on the Little Big Horn*, 104–11; Utley, *Lance and Shield*, 275; Utley, *Last Days*, 151; Vestal, *Warpath*, 271.
602. Graham, *The Custer Myth*, 101, 103; Marquis, *Wooden Leg*, 360; Dan L. Thrapp, *Encyclopedia of Frontier Biography*, vol. 3 (Lincoln: University of Nebraska Press, 1988), 1455; Svingen, *Cheyenne Indian Reservation*, 31.

how he carried his medicine around his neck. He still carried the same medicine root in a deerskin bag. But now, many changes had occurred. The buffalo were gone, and the Indians who once roamed free were wards of the government. Waterman's people were poor and did not have much to eat. He was an old man and believed that he, too, must soon pass over to the great mystery.

Left Hand remained active as long as his old body would let him. Hooking up with Tim McCoy, an ex-soldier turned movie actor, Left Hand had a part in the movie *The Covered Wagon* and appeared with McCoy for the grand opening of Sid Grauman's Egyptian Theater in Hollywood in 1923. But within a few years, Left Hand could no longer play the movie role of a "wild" Indian. He began to think of the past days when he was a young man, when there were plenty of free Indians, and when the white men used to trade them guns for buffalo robes. Thinking back to the Ghost Dance, Left Hand remembered it as a day when they were told that if they danced for a long time the buffalo would return and the Indians would again be free and happy. It did not work. The Indians, he thought, were prisoners on their own reservations. The buffalo were gone and the antelope were gone. Now Left Hand, along with the other old men, could only sit by the fire, sing old war songs, and dream of the past.[603]

Wooden Leg continued to wander for a time after the Battle of the Little Big-horn. His sister, Crooked Nose, was captured by Miles in the January 1877 attack, as was Twin Woman, Lame White Man's wife. In the spring, as the tribes talked of surrender, some chiefs went to Fort Keogh to see what the terms might be. It was here that Ice decided to remain as a hostage to ensure the good faith of the other Cheyennes, and then decided to become a scout for the soldiers, earning the enmity of some in Wooden Leg's band. The other chiefs returned to the Indian camp. Crooked Nose had been very distraught as a captive, thinking she would never see her people again. When the chiefs came to council, her hopes grew, but because her husband did not come in with them, and when they departed without her, she was again thrown into deep grief. She got out the hidden pistol that Wooden Leg had once given her and shot herself dead. Wooden Leg's heart almost stopped when he heard what had happened. She had been a very good, kind sister.

The Cheyennes took different paths. Little Wolf decided to go to the agency. Smaller groups under Two Moon, as well as Ice's people, went to Fort Keogh. Wooden Leg, after staying out a while longer, finally turned himself in at Fort Robinson, where he joined the Cheyenne exodus to Oklahoma Territory. His brother, Yellow Hair, did not come in. He was killed by whites on the upper Tongue after Wooden Leg reached his new southern home.

The Northern Cheyennes lived in the territory for one year before intolerable conditions forced many of them to want to return. Little Wolf and Dull Knife led their breakout with half of the tribe. Wooden Leg, his father, and their family decided not to go, resolving to make a living there and stay out of trouble.

---

603. Graham, *The Custer Myth*, 110–12; Tim McCoy with Ronald McCoy, *Tim McCoy Remembers the West* (Lincoln: University of Nebraska Press, 1988), 151–52, 181–84. It is interesting to note that much of Left Hand's and Waterman's stories came from conversations with Tim McCoy, who later passed them along to be publicized by Gen. Hugh Scott.

After six years the Northern Cheyennes were allowed to return to their old country. Wooden Leg's father, Many Bullet Wounds, had died, so the trip was made by Wooden Leg, his mother, his remaining brother and sister, and his new Southern Cheyenne wife.

Wooden Leg's family settled on the Tongue River. In 1889 he joined other Cheyennes in a new scouting unit out of Fort Keogh. He learned to drink whiskey and spent most of his scout's pay on it. During the Wounded Knee fight, his scout unit was held behind a hill while the white soldiers did the killing. Afterwards he helped track down some of the fleeing Lakotas.

While some Indians were still afraid of retribution for the killing of Custer and would not attend the thirtieth battle anniversary, Wooden Leg had no such qualms. After all, he was paid $3 per day for each of the four days of the affair. Also attending were young Little Wolf, White Elk, Bobtail Horse, Brave Bear, and Two Moon. Two Moon filled the ears of the white interviewer Dr. Joseph K. Dixon with many lies, Wooden Leg said. The other Indians could only laugh at his stories.

In 1908, at fifty years of age, Wooden Leg was baptized. In 1913 he went to the capital with Two Moon, young Little Wolf, and others. He went to the top of the Washington Monument and sailed out on the "great water," where all the Cheyennes took sick and vomited. "It is the same as whiskey," they said.

Back on the Tongue, the Indians were allowed to have their Great Medicine dances from 1927 to 1929. Wooden Leg was appointed an Indian judge at $10 per month. One of the toughest rules he had to enforce was the order that called for all Indian men to send away all of their wives but one. However, if the men were discreet, Wooden Leg tried not to be too strict an enforcer.

Wooden Leg held his position as a judge for ten years. During that time his youngest brother, Twin, passed away. By 1930, Wooden Leg thought there were about twenty Cheyenne battle participants still alive. Bobtail Horse, he knew, lived over on the Rosebud side of the reservation. Wooden Leg kept his farm near the little town of Lame Deer. He had about twenty-one acres of land back from the valley on a little creek flowing into the Tongue River. He grew alfalfa, oats, wheat, and corn, and had a vegetable garden. The crops, along with his scout's pension and judge's pay, provided enough money for food and clothing for his wife and son. He didn't really need to farm, he decided, but he liked to have more so he could help his friends.

As the years passed, Wooden Leg found he could not farm as much and was unable to be as generous as he had been. He liked to think of the old times, when every man had to be brave, and he longed to relive some of the past days when old friends would get together and share their coffee, sugar, and tobacco. But he could not get around as he did in the nimbleness of his youth. "I become tired more quickly than I did in past times," he said. "It appears my legs are not now made of wood, as they used to be."[604] Wooden Leg, perhaps walking free again, went to join his departed friends in 1940.

---

604. Marquis, *Wooden Leg*, 283–84, 294–97, 303, 316, 320–21, 324, 333–36, 348–50, 355, 360, 364–66, 369, 373, 381–84; Jerome A. Greene, *Yellowstone Command: Colonel Nelson A. Miles and the Great Sioux War 1876–1877* (Lincoln: University of Nebraska Press, 1991), 164, 195.

Antelope, who witnessed much of the Battle of the Little Bighorn while searching for Noisy Walking because she had no offspring of her own, finally had a boy-child, William Big Head, who grew up to be a Cheyenne policeman in the 1920s. In 1928, Marquis was driving on the battlefield with Black Bird and his wife, Antelope's niece. Black Bird was a Cheyenne who had been eleven years old at the time of the battle. His wife was then a nine-year-old girl. Marquis noticed the old woman in the rear seat, her blanket drawn over her, weeping uncontrollably. Black Bird explained: she was mourning for her cousin, Noisy Walking, who had been killed somewhere downslope of them, fifty-two years earlier.[605]

After the tribes split up following their 1876 victory, White Cow Bull never saw Meotzi again. Perhaps still in love with her, or haunted by her as a symbol of the golden memories of youth, White Cow Bull never married. He lived many years on the Pine Ridge Reservation in South Dakota. Author-artist David H. Miller talked to him several times and made three portraits of him before his death in 1942.[606]

A few months after the Little Bighorn battle, about the time of the Slim Buttes fight, One Bull and White Bull had gone on a horse-stealing raid to the Black Hills. They joined with another small group of Indians who had brought along their very pretty wives. The raid went badly. As the selected white victims turned to chase and shoot at the fleeing Indians, White Bull called out to his brother that he would make a stand while the others got away. One Bull yelled back a rather pragmatic and characteristic response: it was fine with him, but then again, "if these other Indians get killed, you and I can marry their women." In the midst of the flying bullets and pounding hooves, the brothers laughed. They were having the time of their lives.

One Bull remained for a long while with Sitting Bull in Canada, being one of the last to surrender in 1881. In October of that year, One Bull sat for a painting. The artist noted that "because of his beautifully moulded features, his flashing eyes, and his superb form," One Bull was the secretly beloved darling of all the officers' wives and daughters at Fort Randall.

One Bull tried to follow the white man's way, placing his children in the agency Congregational day school, and joining the Indian police. He still lived near Sitting Bull and his extended family on the banks of the Grand River in the late 1880s.

Although still venerating his uncle as a policeman and signer of the land agreement giving up portions of the Lakota reservation, One Bull felt he must report the Ghost Dance activities to Agent McLaughlin. The agent dispatched One Bull and other police to remove Kicking Bear from the reservation. The fever had spread too far, however, and although Kicking Bear and his acolytes left, the dance soon spread to Sitting Bull's people. Possibly because he saw the likelihood of a conflict, One Bull asked to be excused from any police duty aimed at Sitting Bull. He was told to do his job or give up his uniform. One Bull resigned. He was no longer a *ceska maza*, "metal breast."

605. Marquis, *Cheyennes of Montana*, 38, 225.
606. Miller, "Echoes," 34.

One Bull got a job hauling freight to the agency from Mandan. After one trip he returned home early on the morning of Sitting Bull's death. His wife, Red Whirlwind, had been staying in Sitting Bull's cabin during his absence. When the police burst in, she had managed to slip away and hide in a nearby chicken coop. One Bull had just fallen asleep when he heard the guns. When he ran to Sitting Bull's cabin, he was warned away by the surviving police. What about his wife, One Bull demanded? The women had taken refuge in the chicken coop, he was told. Pointing their rifles, they told him to get his wife, go home, and stay there. One Bull complied. He later remembered the affair with a great sadness.[607]

In his later years, One Bull remained active in tribal affairs and participated in many public gatherings. He and his wife would win all the tipi-pitching races that were popular at tribal fairs until about 1915. They "adopted" authors Reginald and Gladys Laubin and taught them much of the old crafts, enabling them to write their book on the history, construction, and use of the tipi.

In 1937, One Bull went with another of his adopted sons, Walter Campbell, to visit Mount Rushmore. One Bull, still with much feeling for the one he had lived with and protected for so many years, thought that the head of Sitting Bull should join the presidents' heads on the mountain. On June 23, 1947, at the age of ninety-four, One Bull died. He was buried next to his wife, Red Whirlwind, in the mission cemetery on Little Oak Creek, near Little Eagle, South Dakota.[608]

Unlike his brother, White Bull roamed only for a short time after the Little Bighorn fight. In October 1876, up to his old tricks of charging up close to soldiers looking for coups, White Bull was wounded in the upper left arm. The bullet went clear through, broke the bone, and knocked him out. Sitting Bull asked Makes Room to keep an eye on his reckless son—and told him he should fight no more. White Bull, followed by about fifty warriors, gave himself up later that month.

In 1881, White Bull was made a "shirt-wearer," and took up the burden of leading and providing for the Minneconjou. He pushed along the white man's road with the same vigor he had shown on the warpath. He lived in a log cabin, got a wagon, and eventually owned more than one hundred horses. He joined the Congregational Church and, from the missionary, learned to read and write in his own language in order to record the story of his people. White Bull was an Indian policeman for a time and a judge at the Indian Court. He claimed never to have been drunk in his life and tried to keep whiskey off the reservation. White Bull never participated in the Ghost Dance, because he had dreamed that those who took part in it would be killed, as actually happened at Wounded Knee.

Life on the reservation was boring. It seemed to be a punishment to an old rover like White Bull. Perhaps to spice things up a bit, he managed to take fifteen wives during his long life. He was a man and a chief, yet he sometimes felt that he was treated like a child. In 1901 cattlemen wished to lease some of the Indian lands, but they offered a very low price. Although some Indians agreed to it, White Bull held out for a better deal. In a fit of rage, the agent threw him in the guardhouse, where

---

607. Vestal, *Warpath*, 208–9; Utley, *Lance and Shield*, 242, 255, 270, 283, 295–96, 299, 300, 303, 394.
608. Laubin, *Tipi*, 17, 57–61, 108, 140; Vestal, *Warpath*, viii, xix; Hardorff, *Lakota Recollections*, 109.

he was kept in solitary confinement for three months. White Bull still would not sign, and the agent had no alternative but to free him.

Makes Room, White Bull's father, died in 1905 at the age of eighty. The next year, White Bull, at fifty-seven years of age, was called upon to help the government control about four hundred Utes that had fled their reservation. He met them near the Powder River and listened to their grievances. Because he was Sitting Bull's nephew and a famous warrior, they listened to his words. They caused no trouble as he led them first to Fort Meade, then to his Cheyenne River Reservation, where they lived peacefully for another five years before returning to Utah.

White Bull attended the fiftieth anniversary of the Little Bighorn battle in 1926. He was chosen to lead hundreds of Indians, including eighty Lakota and Cheyenne battle participants, to Last Stand Hill, where they met the 7th Cavalry, with seven surviving troopers. When the parties met, White Bull and General Godfrey rode out in front and clasped hands. White Bull gave Godfrey a blanket, and in return received a large American flag.

In his last years, White Bull kept the flag as one of his most treasured mementos. Thinking back, White Bull believed the saddest day of his life was when his eldest son died of a hemorrhage at age thirteen. But the happiest day, he thought, as a smile broke over his face, was when he was honored above all the other Indians by leading the procession to the hilltop on the great battlefield where he had fought so long ago. Then again, the deaf old man said as he held an ear trumpet up while talking to his biographer, Walter Campbell, perhaps his happiest day was yet to come. Perhaps it would be when White Bull's story would come out in a book and be there always, for all men to read and remember. White Bull died at ninety-eight years of age, about one month after his brother, on July 21, 1947.[609]

When Crazy Horse was killed in September 1877, Black Elk's Oglalas fled to Canada for the next three years. Just after their return to the United States, at age sixteen, Black Elk had more visions of the Thunder-beings. He revealed them to the tribe elders and, by 1881, at age eighteen, he began his career as a medicine man.

In 1886, in order to learn more about the white man's way of life, he signed two one-year contracts at $25 per month to travel with Buffalo Bill's Wild West show. The next year the troupe went to England, but when it sailed back, Black Elk and two other Indians missed the boat. They joined another show and traveled with it through France, Germany, and Italy. He returned to Pine Ridge in 1889.

Black Elk, exposed to English and Christianity, was baptized as an Episcopalian. His trip had given him a more realistic perspective of the world. He took a job as a store clerk at Pine Ridge, and if the Ghost Dance had not come along his life may have taken a different path. Black Elk saw parallels between the dance and his own visions, and it gave his life renewed meaning. When the battle broke out at Wounded Knee, Black Elk tried to ride in front of the soldiers, to draw their bullets and save his people. Although he received a wound, he cried because he could do nothing

---

609. Vestal, *Warpath*, viii, ix, xviii, 220, 223, 226, 230–32, 271, 243–49, 251–56.

to help them. The movement in which he had invested high psychic expenditures had proved a cruel disappointment. Many Lakotas were left with an indifference toward religion in general. Black Elk kept a dichotomous affinity for both Christianity and his old spiritual beliefs.

In 1892, Black Elk married Katie War Bonnet, who bore him three sons. Katie was a member of the Catholic Church and, after the turn of the century, Black Elk curbed his shamanic healing practice and also joined the Roman Catholic Church. Katie died in 1903. The next year, while Black Elk was treating a seriously ill boy, a priest burst into the ceremony and threw away Black Elk's drum and rattle, calling him Satan and expelling him. Black Elk sat dejected nearby, sensing that the priest's powers were greater than his. Black Elk decided he would never practice Lakota religious ceremonies again. He took instruction and shortly thereafter was baptized into the Catholic Church as Nicholas Black Elk.

In 1906 Black Elk married Anna Brings White and had two more children. In 1912 he developed tuberculosis, which he suffered from throughout the rest of his life. When Black Elk met author John Neihardt in 1930, it gave him a new sense of purpose, for he finally found someone to whom he could pass on all the old ways of life. At age sixty-seven, Black Elk could at last disclose his visions. Although he felt a need to teach Neihardt Lakota history, it brought back many memories. Black Elk sat with Neihardt in the Pine Ridge badlands and looked toward Harney Peak on the western horizon in the Black Hills, the center of the world where he had been taken in his vision. "The more I talk about these things the more I think of old times," the old man said, "and it makes me feel sad." Black Elk had given away his great vision to Neihardt, and when it was done he believed he had also transferred the spiritual abilities lying dormant within him. "I have given you my power," he said, "and now I am just a poor old man."

Niehardt and Black Elk later climbed Harney Peak. On the way up, Black Elk felt that if he really had any power left, there would surely be some thunder and rain on the summit. On top, Black Elk donned long red underwear (a substitute for body paint), a breechcloth, moccasins, and a headdress of buffalo hide with eagle feathers. He carried a simple pipe with colored ribbons symbolizing the four world directions. Black Elk offered his prayers to the Six Grandfathers, the Great Spirit. The day, which had been bright and clear, was soon darkened with clouds, low thunder, and a scant, chill rain. "O make my people live!" Black Elk called out, only to be answered by a low rumble of thunder. After the ceremony, Neihardt said, he seemed broken and very sad.

Black Elk's tuberculosis grew progressively worse in the 1940s. His second wife died in 1941, and he spent some time in a sanitarium. He could not participate in church activities and lived his last years with his son Ben and his family in Manderson, South Dakota. There, on August 19, 1950, Black Elk died.[610]

Beard's prayer for death was not answered as he lay wounded in the snowy gulch at Wounded Knee. While recovering, he thought of nothing but revenge.

---

610. DeMallie, *Sixth Grandfather*, 6–17, 23, 31, 35–36, 44, 48, 55, 68, 74.

He knew places in the Badlands where he might hide and wage a one-man war against the soldiers. Fortunately, Beard's lone vendetta against the U.S. Army never materialized.

Nelson Miles took command of the military and sought justice through prosecution of the 7th Cavalry officers responsible for the Wounded Knee tragedy. As a survivor of the fight, Beard's testimony was vital to the War Department's prosecution. Although little resulted from the investigation, Beard and Miles became fast friends, and through the general Beard was able to meet other high officials. After the turn of the century, Beard came to Washington and was introduced to Adm. George Dewey, fresh from his victory at Manila Bay in the Spanish-American War. Beard took the naval hero's surname as his own. Known to the Minneconjou as Iron Hail, nicknamed Beard, he now came to be called Dewey Beard.

While in Washington, Beard was asked by sculptor James Earle Fraser to pose for a bas-relief profile to be used for a new coin. The buffalo nickel, issued in 1913, was a composite of Beard's features and those of an Oglala and a Piegan Indian. As a similar "honor," Hollow Horn Bear's photograph was selected to appear on the fourteen-cent stamp issued in 1922. It was a gesture the Brulé would not live to appreciate. After visiting President Wilson in Washington, D.C., in 1913, Hollow Horn Bear took sick and died.[611]

Dewey Beard returned to the Dakotas and remarried. He and Alice Beard remained together for fifty more years, harmonious fixtures of the community. As old resentments faded, Beard's prominence grew as one of the last survivors of the Custer fight. David H. Miller met Beard in 1936. Even at the age of seventy-eight, Beard was described by Miller as tall and lodgepole straight. His jutting jaw housed a full set of his own even, white teeth, which remained until his dying day. His long black hair was arranged in two loose hanks. While some Lakotas wore it that way for spiritual power, Beard had different reasons. He explained in Lakota, for he never learned English, that he grew his hair as it was, "because our Saviour, Jesus Christ, is always pictured with long hair."

When Beard's only offspring, his son Tommy, died of tuberculosis, Miller tried to help him through his heartbreak. Beard responded by naming Miller as his newly adopted son. When Miller was married in Rapid City in 1954, Dewey and Alice appeared at the ceremony. They presented the new couple with a brilliant red and green old-time courting blanket that Alice had painstakingly made. Beard placed the blanket over the shoulders of Miller and his wife, encircling them in the Lakota fashion of marriage, and told them they were "one, now and always."

The last white survivor of the Battle of the Little Bighorn, Charles Windolph, had died in 1950. By November of 1955, Dewey Beard, too, was gone, and in the pulsing of a historical heartbeat, the great number of those who fought that day in 1876 seemed to suddenly fall silent.[612]

It appears almost a universal characteristic of old friends gathered around a checkerboard or a campfire that their talk will inevitably drift to visions of the past.

611. Kadlacek, *Kill an Eagle,* 113; Hardorff, *Lakota Recollections,* 176.
612. Miller, "Echoes," 39.

For every generation there is a uniting event around which a common identity can be built, around which bonds of camaraderie can be formed. To have lived the times, faced the danger, and fought the good fight will unify the participants as in no other manner. The Indians of the Plains, who had once been vagabonds of choice, freely roaming prairie and mountain, faced a tremendous lifestyle shock when confined to the reservations. The vagabonds who once moved literally like the wind, could now roam only in their thoughts. They did not grow old and, as a matter of course, find their thoughts turning toward the past. Their thoughts necessarily turned toward the past, and in fact and in deed, with little or no future on the reservation, they became old. The event that united the participants, that drew their thoughts to the old days, was the great fight on the Little Bighorn, the year Long Hair was killed, according to the Minneconjou calendar. Although it may not have been the epitome of Lakota culture, independence, or lifestyle, it was a turning point that all subsequent years came to be measured against. The sun, hot and bright on June 25, 1876, during the middle moon in the month of Cherries Ripening, would prove to be the high point of the day, the high point of the summer, and the high point of the old men's lives. It truly was the Lakota Noon.

INDIAN TIME APPEARANCES

OGLALA

Black Elk — 3:00, 3:10, 3:30, 3:40, 3:50, 4:00, 4:20, 6:10A
Eagle Elk — 3:00, 3:30, 3:50, 4:00, 4:20, 4:50, 5:10
Fears Nothing — 3:00, 3:30, 4:00, 4:30, 5:00, 5:10, 5:40, 6:10A
Flying Hawk — 3:10, 3:50, 4:00, 4:10, 4:30, 4:50, 5:00, 5:40, 5:50, 6:10A
Foolish Elk — 4:10, 4:50, 5:50
He Dog — 3:10, 3:40, 3:50, 4:20, 5:30, 5:40, 6:10A
Lone Bear — 4:10, 5:30, 5:40, 6:00, 6:10A
Low Dog — 3:00, 4:50
Red Feather — 3:10, 3:20, 3:30, 3:40, 3:50, 4:00, 4:10, 4:40, 4:50, 5:00, 5:30, 5:40, 5:50
Red Hawk — 4:10, 4:20, 4:30, 5:00, 5:40, 6:00, 6:10A
Shave Elk — 4:00, 4:10
Short Bull — 4:00, 4:30
White Cow Bull — 3:00, 3:10, 4:00, 4:10, 4:20, 5:10, 5:40

BRULÉ

Two Eagles — 4:00, 4:20, 5:00, 5:40, 6:00, 6:10A
Hollow Horn Bear — 4:20, 5:00, 5:40, 6:10B

ARAPAHO

Left Hand — 6:00
Waterman — 4:20, 5:00, 5:20, 5:30, 6:10A, 6:10B

TWO KETTLE

Runs The Enemy — 3:10, 3:20, 3:50, 4:00, 4:10, 4:20, 4:40, 4:50, 5:00, 5:10, 5:20, 5:30, 5:40, 5:50, 6:10B

MINNECONJOU

Beard — 3:00, 3:10, 3:20, 3:40, 4:10, 4:40, 6:10B
Feather Earring — 3:30, 4:50, 6:10A
Flying By — 3:50, 4:10, 4:40, 5:10, 5:50, 6:00, 6:10A
Hump — 4:10, 4:20, 4:50
Iron Thunder — 4:00, 4:10, 4:20
Lights — 3:20, 4:10, 5:10, 5:40, 5:50, 6:00, 6:10A
One Bull — 3:00, 3:10, 3:30, 3:40, 3:50, 4:00, 4:20, 4:30
Red Horse — 5:10, 5:20, 5:30
Standing Bear — 3:00. 3:10, 3:40, 4:30, 5:00, 5:10, 5:40, 5:50, 6:00, 6:10A
Turtle Rib — 3:10, 4:30, 5:40, 6:10B

White Bull — 3:00, 3:10, 3:20, 3:30, 3:50, 4:00, 4:10, 4:20, 4:30, 4:40, 4:50,
5:00, 5:10, 5:20, 5:30, 5:40, 5:50, 6:10A

HUNKPAPA

Crow King — 5:00
Gall — 3:10, 3:20, 3:30, 3:50, 4:00, 4:10, 4:30, 4:40, 5:00, 5:30, 5:40, 5:50, 6:00,
6:10B
Iron Hawk — 3:00, 3:10, 3:20, 3:40, 4:00, 4:20, 5:30, 5:40, 6:00, 6:10A
Moving Robe — 3:00, 3:10, 3:40, 3:50, 5:00
Pretty White Buffalo — 3:00, 3:10, 3:20, 4:00, 4:10, 4:30, 4:50
Rain In The Face — 3:10, 5:00, 5:30, 6:10A

CHEYENNE

American Horse — 3:00, 3:50, 4:00, 4:20
Antelope — 3:00, 3:10, 3:50, 4:00, 4:30, 5:00, 5:10, 5:20, 5:30, 5:40, 5:50,
6:10A
Big Beaver — 5:50, 6:00, 6:10A
Bobtail Horse — 4:00, 4:10, 5:20
Brave Wolf — 4:20, 6:10A
Ice — 4:20
Little Hawk — 3:30, 5:40, 5:50, 6:00, 6:10A, 6:10B
Soldier Wolf — 4:20
Tall Bull — 3:50, 4:20, 5:00, 6:10A, 6:10B
Two Moon — 3:10, 3:40, 3:50, 4:00, 4:10, 4:20, 4:40, 4:50, 5:00, 5:10, 5:30,
5:40, 5:50, 6:00, 6:10A
White Shield — 4:00, 4:10, 4:20, 5:50, 6:10B
Wolf Tooth — 4:20, 4:30, 4:40, 4:50, 5:10, 5:20, 5:30
Wooden Leg — 3:10, 3:40, 3:50, 4:00, 4:10, 4:30, 4:40, 4:50, 5:10, 5:20, 5:30,
5:40, 5:50. 6:00, 6:10A, 6:10B
Yellow Nose — 4:00, 4:10, 4:20, 5:40, 6:00, 6:10A, 6:10B
Young Two Moon — 4:40, 4:50, 5:40, 5:50, 6:00, 6:10A

Selected Bibliography

Adjutant General's Office. *Chronological List of Actions, &c., with Indians from January 15, 1837 to January, 1891.* Ft. Collins, CO: Old Army Press, 1979.

Ambrose, Stephen E. *Crazy Horse and Custer: The Parallel Lives of Two American Warriors.* New York: Doubleday & Company, 1975.

American Psychiatric Association, eds. *Diagnostic and Statistical Manual of Mental Disorders DSM III-R.* Washington, D.C.: American Psychiatric Association, 1987.

Barnard, Sandy. *Digging Into Custer's Last Stand.* Terre Haute, IN: AST Press, 1986.

———. *Shovels and Speculation: Archaeology Hunts Custer.* Terre Haute, IN: AST Press, 1990.

Barzun, Jacques, and Henry F. Graff. *The Modern Researcher.* New York: Harcourt, Brace and World, 1957.

Benham, D. J. "The Sioux Warrior's Revenge." *Canadian Magazine* 43 (September 1914): 455–63.

Bloch, Marc. *The Historian's Craft.* New York: Random House, 1953.

Bradley, James H. *The March of the Montana Column: A Prelude to the Custer Disaster.* Edited by Edgar I. Stewart. Norman: University of Oklahoma Press, 1961.

Brady, Cyrus T. *Indian Fights and Fighters.* McClure, Philips & Company, 1904. Reprint, Lincoln: University of Nebraska Press, 1971.

Breisach, Ernst. *Historiography: Ancient, Medieval, and Modern.* Chicago: University of Chicago Press, 1983.

Brininstool, E. A. *Troopers With Custer: Historic Incidents of the Battle of the Little Big Horn.* Harrisburg, PA: Stackpole, 1952. Reprint, Lincoln: University of Nebraska Press, 1989.

Brown, Dee. *Bury My Heart at Wounded Knee: An Indian History of the American West.* New York: Holt, Rinehart & Winston, 1970.

———. *The Year of the Century: 1876.* New York: Scribners, 1966.

Brust, James. "Fouch Photo May Be First." *Greasy Grass* 7 (May 1991): 2–9.

———. "Into the Face of History." *American Heritage* 43, no. 7 (November 1992): 104–113.

———. "Lt. Oscar Long's Early Map Details Terrain, Battle Positions." *Greasy Grass* 11 (May 1995): 5–13.

Buecker, Thomas R. "A Surgeon at the Little Big Horn: The Letters of Dr. Holmes O. Paulding." In *The Great Sioux War 1876–1877: The Best From Montana The*

Magazine of Western History. Edited by Paul L. Hedren. Helena: Montana Historical Society Press, 1991.

Burdick, Usher L., ed. *David F. Barry's Indian Notes on the Custer Battle*. Baltimore: Proof Press, 1937.

Carland, John. "The Massacre of Custer." *Bighorn Yellowstone Journal* 1, no. 4 (autumn 1992): 2–5.

Carroll, John M., ed. *The Benteen-Goldin Letters on Custer and His Last Battle*. Lincoln: University of Nebraska Press, 1991.

———, ed. *A Bit of 7th Cavalry History with All Its Warts*. Bryan, TX: J. M. Carroll & Company, 1987.

———, ed. *Custer's Chief of Scouts: The Reminiscences of Charles A. Varnum*. Lincoln: University of Nebraska Press, 1987.

———, ed. *The Eleanor H. Hinman Interviews on the Life and Death of Crazy Horse*. Nebraska Historical Association: Garryowen Press, 1976.

———, ed. *A Seventh Cavalry Scrapbook*. Vols. 1–13. Bryan, TX: J. M. Carroll & Company, 1978–79.

———, ed. *Ten Years with General Custer Among the Indians (and other writings by John Ryan)*. Bryan, TX: J. M. Carroll & Company, 1980.

———, ed. *They Rode With Custer*. Mattituck, NY: J. M. Carroll & Company, 1987.

———, ed. *The Two Battles of the Little Big Horn*. New York: Liveright, 1974.

———, ed. *A Very Real Salmagundi; Or, Look What I Found This Summer*. Bryan, TX: J. M. Carroll & Company, n.d.

———, ed. *Who Was This Man Ricker and What Are His Tablets That Everyone Is Talking About?* Bryan, TX: J. M. Carroll & Company, 1979.

Chandler, Melbourne C. *Of Garryowen in Glory: The History of the 7th U.S. Cavalry*. Annandale, VA: Turnpike Press, 1960.

Clark, George M. *Scalp Dance: The Edgerly Papers on the Battle of the Little Big Horn*. Oswego, NY: Heritage Press, 1985.

Coffeen, Herbert. *The Custer Battle Book*. New York: Carlton Press, 1964.

Connell, Evan S. *Son of the Morning Star*. New York: Harper & Row, 1984.

Croy, Homer. *Trigger Marshall: The Story of Chris Madsen*. New York: Duell, Sloan & Pearce, 1958.

Custer, George Armstrong. *My Life on the Plains or, Personal Experiences with Indians*. Norman: University of Oklahoma Press, 1962.

Darling, Roger. *General Custer's Final Hours: Correcting a Century of Misconceived History*. Vienna, VA: Potomac-Western Press, 1992.

———. *A Sad and Terrible Blunder: Generals Terry and Custer at the Little Bighorn: New Discoveries.* Vienna, VA: Potomac-Western Press, 1990.

Dawkins, Richard. *The Blind Watchmaker.* New York: W. W. Norton & Company, 1986.

DeMallie, Raymond J., ed. *The Sixth Grandfather: Black Elk's Teachings Given to John G. Neihardt.* Lincoln: University of Nebraska Press, 1985.

Dippie, Brian W. "Brush, Palette and the Custer Battle: A Second Look." *Montana The Magazine of Western History* 24, no. 1 (winter 1974): 64–66.

———. "Of Bullets, Blunders, and Custer Buffs." *Montana The Magazine of Western History* 41, no. 1 (winter 1991): 76–80.

———. *Custer's Last Stand: The Anatomy of an American Myth.* Lincoln: University of Nebraska Press, 1976.

———, ed. *Nomad: George A. Custer in Turf, Field and Farm.* Austin: University of Texas Press, 1980.

Dixon, Joseph K. *The Vanishing Race: The Last Great Indian Council.* Garden City, NY: Doubleday, Page & Company, 1913.

Dolan, John. "That Fatal Day: An Interview with Private John Dolan." In *That Fatal Day: Eight More with Custer,* 7–9. Howell, MI: Powder River Press, 1992.

Doran, Robert E. "Battalion Formation and the Custer Trail." 3rd Annual Symposium. Custer Battlefield Historical & Museum Association, Hardin, MT, 1989.

Dowd, James Patrick. *Custer Lives!* Fairfield, WA: Ye Galleon Press, 1982.

DuMont, John S. *Custer Battle Guns.* Canaan, NH: Phoenix Publishing, 1988.

Duncan, Dayton. *Out West: American Journey Along the Lewis and Clark Trail.* New York: Penguin Books, 1988.

Dunlay, Thomas W. *Wolves for the Blue Soldiers: Indian Scouts and Auxiliaries with the United States Army, 1860–90.* Lincoln: University of Nebraska Press, 1987.

Dupuy, Trevor N. *Understanding War: History and Theory of Combat.* New York: Paragon House Publishers, 1987.

Dustin, Fred. *The Custer Tragedy. Events Leading up to and Following the Little Big Horn Campaign of 1876.* Ann Arbor, MI: Edwards Brothers, 1939. Reprint, El Segundo, CA: Upton & Sons, 1987.

Eastman, Charles A. *Indian Heroes and Great Chieftains.* Boston: Little, Brown, 1918.

———. "Rain-In-The-Face: The Story of a Sioux Warrior." *Bighorn Yellowstone Journal* 2, no. 3 (summer 1993): 12–19.

Erdos, Richard, and Alphonso Ortiz, eds. *American Indian Myths and Legends.* New York: Pantheon Books, 1984.

Farwell, Byron. *Ball's Bluff: A Small Battle and Its Long Shadow*. McLean, VA: EPM Publications, 1990.

Fehrenbach, T. R. *Comanches: The Destruction of a People*. New York: Da Capo Press, 1994.

Finerty, John F. *War-Path and Bivouac*. Norman: University of Oklahoma Press, 1961.

Fischer, David Hackett. *Historians' Fallacies: Toward a Logic of Historical Thought*. New York: Harper & Row, 1970.

Foote, Shelby. *The Civil War: A Narrative Fredericksburg to Meridian*. New York: Random House, 1963.

Forrest, Earle R. *Witnesses at the Battle of the Little Big Horn*. Monroe, MI: Monroe County Library System, 1986.

Fougera, Katherine Gibson. *With Custer's Cavalry*. Lincoln: University of Nebraska Press, 1986.

Fox, Richard A., Jr. *Archaeology, History, and Custer's Last Battle: The Little Big Horn Reexamined*. Norman: University of Oklahoma Press, 1993.

Frost, Lawrence A. *The Court Martial of General George Armstrong Custer*. Norman: University of Oklahoma Press, 1968.

———. *Custer Legends*. Bowling Green, OH: Bowling Green University Popular Press, 1981.

———. "Two Sides of a General." In *Custer and His Times, Book Three*. Edited by Gregory J. W. Urwin and Roberta E. Fagan. El Paso, TX, and Conway, AR: Little Big Horn Associates and University of Central Arkansas Press, 1987.

Fussell, Paul. *Wartime: Understanding and Behavior in the Second World War*. Oxford: Oxford University Press, 1989.

Gabriel, Richard A. *No More Heroes: Madness and Psychiatry in War*. New York: Hill & Wang, 1987.

———. *The Painful Field: The Psychiatric Dimension of Modern War*. Westport, CT: Greenwood Press, 1988.

Gibbon, John. "Arms to Fight Indians." *Bighorn Yellowstone Journal* 3, no. 2 (spring 1994): 9–16.

———. *Gibbon on the Sioux Campaign of 1876*. Edited by Michael J. Koury. Reprinted from *The American Catholic Quarterly Review* (April–October 1877), Bellevue, NE: Old Army Press, 1970.

———. Gifford, Don. *The Farther Shore: A Natural History of Perception 1798–1984*. New York: Vintage Books, 1991.

Godfrey, Edward S. "Cavalry Fire Discipline." *By Valor and Arms: The Journal of American Military History* 2, no. 4 (1976): 30–36.

———. "Custer's Last Battle 1876." *Century Magazine* (January 1892). Reprint, Golden, CO: Outbooks, 1986.

Graham, William A. *The Custer Myth: A Source Book of Custeriana*. Lincoln: University of Nebraska Press, 1953.

———. *The Story of the Little Big Horn: Custer's Last Fight*. New York: Century, 1926. Reprint, Lincoln: University of Nebraska Press, 1988.

Gray, John S. *Centennial Campaign: The Sioux War of 1876*. Ft. Collins, CO: Old Army Press, 1976.

———. "Couriers of Disaster." *Research Review: The Journal of the Little Big Horn Associates* 17 (December 1983): 3–17.

———. *Custer's Last Campaign. Mitch Boyer and the Little Big Horn Reconstructed*. Lincoln: University of Nebraska Press, 1991.

———. "Last Rites for Lonesome Charley Reynolds." *Montana The Magazine of Western History* 13, no. 3 (summer 1963): 40–51.

———. "Nightmares to Daydreams." *By Valor and Arms: Journal of American Military History* 1 (summer 1975): 31–39.

———."A Vindication of Curly." 4th Annual Symposium. Custer Battlefield Historical & Museum Association, Hardin, MT, 1990.

Greene, Jerome A. *Evidence and the Custer Enigma: A Reconstruction of Indian-Military History*. Golden, CO: Outbooks, 1986.

———. *Lakota and Cheyenne: Indian Views of the Great Sioux War, 1876–1877*. Norman: University of Oklahoma Press, 1994.

———. *Slim Buttes, 1876: An Episode of the Great Sioux War*. Norman: University of Oklahoma Press, 1982.

———. *Yellowstone Command: Colonel Nelson A. Miles and the Great Sioux War 1876–1877*. Lincoln: University of Nebraska Press, 1991.

Griffith, Paddy. *Rally Once Again: Battle Tactics of the American Civil War*. Wiltshire, England: Crowood Press, 1987.

Grinker, Roy R., and John P. Spiegel. *Men Under Stress*. New York: McGraw-Hill, 1945.

Grinnell, George Bird. *The Cheyenne Indians: Their History and Ways of Life*. Vol. 1. Lincoln: University of Nebraska Press, 1972.

———. *The Fighting Cheyennes*. New York: Scribner's, 1915. Reprint, Norman: University of Oklahoma Press, 1956.

Hammer, Kenneth M. *Custer in '76. Walter Camp's Notes on the Custer Fight*. Provo, UT: Brigham Young University Press, 1976. Reprint, Norman: University of Oklahoma Press, 1990.

———. *The Glory March*. Monroe, MI: Monroe County Library System, 1980.

———. *Men With Custer: Biographies of the 7th Cavalry, June 25, 1876*. Ft. Collins, CO: Old Army Press, 1972.

Hardorff, Richard G. *Cheyenne Memories of the Custer Fight: A Sourcebook*. Spokane, WA: Arthur H. Clark, 1995.

———. *The Custer Battle Casualties: Burials, Exhumations and Reinterments*. El Segundo, CA: Upton & Sons, 1989.

———. *Hokahey! A Good Day to Die! The Indian Casualties of the Custer Fight*. Spokane, WA: Arthur H. Clark, 1993.

———. *Lakota Recollections of the Custer Fight: New Sources of Indian-Military History*. Spokane, WA: Arthur H. Clark, 1991.

———. *Markers, Artifacts and Indian Testimony: Preliminary Findings on the Custer Battle*. Short Hills, NJ: Don Horn Publications, 1985.

Hassrick, Royal B. *The Sioux: Life and Customs of a Warrior Society*. Norman: University of Oklahoma Press, 1964.

Hedley, William. "'ps Bring Pacs:' The Order That Trapped the Custer Battalion." 4th Annual Symposium. Custer Battlefield Historical & Museum Association, Hardin, MT, 1990.

———. "'We've Caught Them Napping!': The Little Big Horn Time Warp." 3rd Annual Symposium. Custer Battlefield Historical & Museum Association, Hardin, MT, 1989.

Hodder, Ian. *Reading the Past: Current Approaches to Interpretation in Archaeology*. Cambridge: Cambridge University Press, 1986.

Hofling, Charles K. *Custer and the Little Big Horn. A Psychobiographical Inquiry*. Detroit: Wayne State University Press, 1981.

Hughes, Robert P. "The Campaign Against the Sioux in 1876." *Journal of the Military Service Institution of the United States* 18, no. 79 (January 1896).

Hunt, Frazier, and Robert Hunt. *I Fought With Custer: The Story of Sergeant Windolph, Last Survivor of the Battle of the Little Big Horn*. New York: Scribner's, 1954. Reprint, Lincoln: University of Nebraska Press, 1987.

Hutton, Paul A. "'Correct in Every Detail': General Custer in Hollywood." *Montana The Magazine of Western History* 41, no. 1 (winter 1991): 29–56.

———. "From Little Big Horn to Little Big Man: The Changing Image of a Western Hero in Popular Culture." *Western Historical Quarterly* 7, no. 1 (January 1976): 19–45.

———. "Hollywood's General Custer: The Changing Image of a Military Hero in Film." *Greasy Grass* 2 (May 1986): 15–21.

Hyde, George E. *Life of George Bent Written From His Letters*. Norman: University of Oklahoma Press, 1968.

———. *Red Cloud's Folk: A History of the Oglala Sioux Indians*. Norman: University of Oklahoma Press, 1937.

———. *A Sioux Chronicle*. Norman: University of Oklahoma Press, 1993.

Hynds, A. A. "Sergeant Hynd's Reminiscences." *Research Review: The Journal of the Little Big Horn Associates* 6, no. 4 (winter 1972): 62–69.

Jamieson, Kathleen Hall. *Dirty Politics: Deception, Distraction, and Democracy*. New York: Oxford Press, 1993.

Johnson, Alfred B. "Custer's Battlefield." *Bighorn Yellowstone Journal* 2, no. 4 (autumn 1993): 17–20.

Jordan, Robert Paul. "Ghosts of the Little Big Horn." *National Geographic* 170, no. 6 (December 1986): 787–813.

Kadlacek, Edward and Mabell. *To Kill an Eagle: Indian Views on the Last Days of Crazy Horse*. Boulder, CO: Johnson Publishing, 1981.

Kammen, Michael. *Mystic Chords of Memory: The Transformation of Tradition in American Culture*. New York: Vintage Books, 1993.

Kammen, Robert, Joe Marshall, and Frederick Lefthand. *Soldiers Falling Into Camp: The Battles at the Rosebud and the Little Big Horn*. Encampment, WY: Affiliated Writers of America, 1992.

Keegan, John. *The Face of Battle*. Middlesex, England: Penguin Books, 1976.

Keegan, John, and Richard Holmes. *Soldiers: A History of Men in Battle*. New York: Elisabeth Sifton Books, Viking Penguin, 1986.

Keim, DeB[enneville] Randolph. *Sheridan's Troopers on the Border: A Winter Campaign on the Plains*. Philadelphia: 1870. Reprint, Lincoln: University of Nebraska Press, 1985.

Keller, Doug. "Myths of the Little Big Horn." 2nd Annual Symposium. Custer Battlefield Historical & Museum Association, Hardin, MT, 1988.

King, W. Kent. *Massacre: The Custer Cover-Up*. El Segundo, CA: Upton & Sons, 1989.

———. *Tombstones for Bluecoats: New Insights Into the Custer Mystery*. Vols. 1–4. Marion Station, MD: Author, 1980–81.

Kinsley, D. A. *Custer Favor the Bold: A Soldier's Story*. New York: Promontory Press, 1992.

Knight, Oliver. *Following the Indian Wars: The Story of the Newspaper Correspondents Among the Indian Campaigners*. Norman: University of Oklahoma Press, 1960.

Krause, Wesley. "Guns of '76." 6th Annual Symposium. Custer Battlefield Historical & Museum Association, Hardin, MT, 1992.

Kuhlman, Charles. *Legend Into History*. Harrisburg, PA: Stackpole, 1951.

Laubin, Reginald and Gladys. *The Indian Tipi: Its History, Construction, and Use*. Norman: University of Oklahoma Press, 1957.

Libby, Orin G., ed. *The Arikara Narrative of the Campaign Against the Hostile Dakotas—June, 1876*. Glorieta, NM: Rio Grande Press, 1976.

Liberty, Margot. "Oral and Written Indian Perspectives on the Indian Wars." In *Legacy: New Perspectives on the Battle of the Little Bighorn*. Edited by Charles E. Rankin. Helena: Montana Historical Society Press, 1996.

Limerick, Patricia Nelson. *The Legacy of Conquest: The Unbroken Past of the American West*. New York: W. W. Norton & Company, 1987.

Limerick, Patricia Nelson, Clyde A. Milner II, and Charles E. Rankin, eds. *Trails: Toward a New Western History*. Lawrence: University of Kansas Press, 1991.

Linderman, Frank B. *Red Mother*. New York: John Day, 1932.

Lukacs, John. *Historical Consciousness or the Remembered Past*. New York: Schocken Books, 1985.

———. "Revising the Twentieth Century." *American Heritage* 45, no. 5 (September 1994): 83–89.

Mangum, Neil C. "Destruction, Examination, and Reconstruction: A Review of the Archaeological Survey Conducted on Custer Battlefield, 1983–85." In *Custer and His Times, Book Three*. Edited by Gregory J. W. Urwin and Roberta E. Fagan. El Paso, TX, and Conway, AR: Little Big Horn Associates and University of Central Arkansas Press, 1987.

———. "Gall: Sioux Gladiator or White Man's Pawn?" 5th Annual Symposium. Custer Battlefield Historical & Museum Association, Hardin, MT, 1991.

Marquis, Thomas B. *The Cheyennes of Montana*. Algonac, MI: Reference Publications, 1978.

———. *Custer on the Little Big Horn*. Algonac, MI: Reference Publications, 1967.

———. *Keep the Last Bullet for Yourself*. Algonac, MI: Reference Publications, 1976.

———, narr. *Memoirs of a White Crow Indian*, by Thomas H. LeForge (1928). Lincoln: University of Nebraska Press, 1974.

———. *Wooden Leg: A Warrior Who Fought Custer*. Lincoln: University of Nebraska Press, 1931.

Marshall, Robert A. "How Many Indians Were There?" In *Custer and His Times, Book Two*. Edited by John M. Carroll. Little Big Horn Associates, 1984.

Marshall, S. L. A. *Men Against Fire: The Problem of Battle Command in Future War.* Gloucester, MA: Peter Smith, 1978.

McClernand, Edward J. *On Time for Disaster: The Rescue of Custer's Command.* Lincoln: University of Nebraska Press, 1989.

McCoy, Tim, with Ronald McCoy. *Tim McCoy Remembers the West.* Lincoln: University of Nebraska Press, 1988.

McCreight, M. I. *Firewater and Forked Tongues: A Sioux Chief Interprets U.S. History.* Pasadena, CA: Trail's End Publishing, 1947.

McCrone, John. *The Ape That Spoke: Language and the Evolution of the Human Mind.* New York: William Morrow & Company, 1991.

McDonough, James Lee. *Stones River: Bloody Winter in Tennessee.* Knoxville: University of Tennessee Press, 1980.

McLaughlin, James. *My Friend the Indian.* Seattle: Superior Publishing, 1970.

Merington, Marguerite, ed. *The Custer Story: The Life and Intimate Letters of George A. Custer and His Wife Elizabeth.* Lincoln: University of Nebraska Press, 1987.

Michno, Gregory F. "Crazy Horse, Custer, and the Sweep to the North." *Montana The Magazine of Western History* 43, no. 3 (summer 1993): 42–53.

———. *The Mystery of E Troop: Custer's Gray Horse Company at the Little Bighorn.* Missoula, MT: Mountain Press Publishing, 1994.

———. "Space Warp: The Effects of Combat Stress at the Little Bighorn." *Research Review: The Journal of the Little Big Horn Associates* 8, no. 1 (January 1994): 22–30.

Miles, Nelson A. *Personal Recollections and Observations of General Nelson A. Miles.* Chicago: Werner, 1897.

Miller, David Humphreys. *Custer's Fall: The Indian Side of the Story.* New York: Duell, Sloan & Pearce, 1957. Reprint, Lincoln: University of Nebraska Press, 1985.

———. "Echoes of the Little Bighorn." *American Heritage* 22, no. 4 (June 1971): 28–39.

Mulligan, Tim. "Custer and the Little Big Horn: A Needed Perspective." *Research Review: The Journal of the Little Big Horn Associates* 8, no. 1 (spring 1974): 10–14.

Myers, Steven W. "Roster of Known Hostile Indians at the Battle of the Little Bighorn." *Research Review: The Journal of the Little Big Horn Associates* 5, no. 2 (June 1991): 2–20.

Nash, Gerald D. *Creating the West: Historical Interpretations 1890–1990.* Albuquerque: University of New Mexico Press, 1991.

Nash, Gerald D., and Richard W. Etulain, eds. *The Twentieth Century West: Historical Interpretations.* Albuquerque: University of New Mexico Press, 1989.

Neihardt, John G. *Black Elk Speaks: Being the Life Story of a Holy Man of the Oglala Sioux*. Lincoln: University of Nebraska Press, 1979.

Nichols, Ronald H., ed. *Reno Court of Inquiry: Proceedings of a Court of Inquiry in the Case of Major Marcus A. Reno*. Crow Agency, MT: Custer Battlefield Historical & Museum Association, 1992.

————. "The Springfield Carbine at the Little Big Horn." 2nd Annual Symposium. Custer Battlefield Historical & Museum Association, Hardin, MT, 1988.

Nightengale, Robert. *Little Big Horn*. Edina, MN: DocuPro Services, 1996.

Overfield, Loyd J., II. *The Little Big Horn, 1876: The Official Communications, Documents and Reports*. Lincoln: University of Nebraska Press, 1990.

Pennington, Jack. "The Reno Court: The Second Cover-Up." *Research Review: The Journal of the Little Big Horn Associates* 9, no. 1 (January 1995): 18–23.

Powell, Peter John. *People of the Sacred Mountain: A History of the Northern Cheyenne Chiefs and Warrior Societies 1830–1879*. Vol 2. San Francisco: Harper & Row, 1981.

————. *Sweet Medicine: The Continuing Role of the Sacred Arrows, the Sun Dance, and the Buffalo Hat in Northern Cheyenne History*. Vol. 1. Norman: University of Oklahoma Press, 1969.

Pratkanis, Anthony R., and Elliot Aronson. *Age of Propaganda: The Everyday Use and Abuse of Persuasion*. New York: W. H. Freeman & Company, 1992.

Prucha, Francis Paul. *Documents of United States Indian Policy*. Lincoln: University of Nebraska Press, 1990.

Rickey, Don Jr. *Forty Miles a Day on Beans and Hay*. Norman: University of Oklahoma Press, 1963.

————. *History of Custer Battlefield*. Billings, MT: Custer Battlefield Historical & Museum Association, 1967.

Robinson, Charles M., III. *A Good Year to Die: The Story of the Great Sioux War*. New York: Random House, 1995.

Roe, Charles Francis. "Custer's Last Battle." In *Custer Engages the Hostiles*. Ft. Collins, CO: Old Army Press, 1973.

————. Report to Assistant Adjutant General, Department of Dakota, August 6, 1881. Little Bighorn Battlefield National Monument Files.

————, to W. M. Camp, Chicago, 6 October 1908. TL photocopy. Little Bighorn Battlefield National Monument Files.

Rosenberg, Bruce A. *Custer and the Epic of Defeat*. University Park: Pennsylvania State University Press, 1974.

Sandoz, Mari. *The Battle of the Little Bighorn*. Philadelphia: J. B. Lippincott, 1966.

————. *Crazy Horse: The Strange Man of the Oglalas*. Lincoln: University of Nebraska Press, 1961.

Sarf, Wayne M. *The Little Bighorn Campaign: March–September 1876*. Conshohocken, PA: Combined Books, 1993.

Savage, William W. Jr. "A Manifesto." *Journal of the West* 33, no. 4 (October 1994): 3–4.

Schneider, George, ed. *The Freeman Journal: The Infantry in the Sioux Campaign of 1876*. San Rafael, CA: Presidio Press, 1977.

Schoenberger, Dale T. *The End of Custer: The Death of an American Military Legend*. British Columbia, Canada: Hancock House Publishers, 1995.

Scott, Douglas D., and Richard A. Fox Jr. *Archaeological Insights into the Custer Battle: An Assessment of the 1984 Field Season*. Norman: University of Oklahoma Press, 1987.

Scott, Douglas D., Richard A. Fox Jr., Melissa A. Connor, and Dick Harmon. *Archaeological Perspectives on the Battle of the Little Big Horn*. Norman: University of Oklahoma Press, 1989.

Scott, Douglas D., ed. *Papers on Little Big Horn Battlefield Archaeology: The Equipment Dump, Marker 7, and the Reno Crossing*. Lincoln: J & L Reprint, 1991.

Scott, Hugh Lenox. *Some Memories of a Soldier*. New York: Century, 1928.

Sills, Joe Jr. "The Recruits Controversy: Another Look." *Greasy Grass* 5 (May 1989): 2–8.

————. "Weir Point, Another Perspective." *Research Review: The Journal of the Little Big Horn Associates* 3, no. 2 (June 1986): 25–28.

————. "Were There Two Last Stands?" 2nd Annual Symposium. Custer Battlefield Historical & Museum Association, Hardin, MT, 1988.

Slotkin, Richard. *Fatal Environment: The Myth of the Frontier in the Age of Industrialization 1800–1890*. New York: HarperCollins, 1994.

————. *Gunfighter Nation: The Myth of the Frontier in Twentieth-Century America*. New York: HarperCollins, 1993.

Smith, Jay. "What Did Not Happen at the Battle of the Little Big Horn." *Research Review: The Journal of the Little Big Horn Associates* 6, no. 2 (June 1992): 6–13.

Stands In Timber, John, and Margot Liberty. *Cheyenne Memories*. Lincoln: University of Nebraska Press, 1967.

Stewart, Edgar I. *Custer's Luck*. Norman: University of Oklahoma Press, 1955.

Svingen, Orlan J. *The Northern Cheyenne Indian Reservation 1877–1900.* Niwot, CO: University of Colorado Press, 1993.

Sweet, Owen J., to W. M. Camp, Chicago, 24 November 1912 and 13 January 1913. TL photocopy. Little Bighorn Battlefield National Monument.

Sykes, Charles J. *A Nation of Victims: The Decay of the American Character.* New York: St. Martin's Press, 1992.

Thomas, Gary M. *The Custer Scout of April, 1867.* Kansas City, MO: Westport Printing, 1987.

Thrapp, Dan L. *Encyclopedia of Frontier Biography.* Vols. 1–3. Lincoln: University of Nebraska Press, 1988.

Trinque, Bruce A. "The Cartridge-Case Evidence on Custer Field: An Analysis and Reinterpretation." 5th Annual Symposium. Custer Battlefield Historical & Museum Association, Hardin, MT, 1991.

———. "The Defense of Custer Hill." *Research Review: The Journal of the Little Big Horn Associates* 8, no. 2 (June 1994): 21–31.

———. "Elusive Ridge." *Research Review: The Journal of the Little Big Horn Associates* 9, no. 1 (January 1995): 2–8.

———. "Small Wars and the Little Bighorn." TMs photocopy, 1994: 1–22.

"Two Moons Recalls the Battle of the Little Big Horn." *Bighorn Yellowstone Journal* 2, no. 1 (winter 1993): 9–13.

Urwin, Gregory J. W. "'Custar Had Not Waited for Us': One of Gibbon's Doughboys on the Custer Battle." In *Custer and His Times, Book Three.* Edited by Gregory J. W. Urwin and Roberta E. Fagan. El Paso, TX, and Conway, AR: Little Big Horn Associates and University of Central Arkansas Press, 1987.

———. *Custer Victorious: The Civil War Battles of General George Armstrong Custer.* Rutherford, NJ: Fairleigh Dickinson University Press, 1983.

———. "Was the Past Prologue?: Meditations on Custer's Tactics at the Little Bighorn." 7th Annual Symposium. Custer Battlefield Historical & Museum Association, Hardin, MT, 1993.

Utley, Robert M. "The Battle of the Little Bighorn." In *Great Western Indian Fights.* Edited by B. W. Allred. Lincoln: University of Nebraska Press, 1960.

———. *Cavalier in Buckskin: George Armstrong Custer and the Western Military Frontier.* Norman: University of Oklahoma Press, 1988.

———. *Custer and the Great Controversy: The Origin and Development of a Legend.* Pasadena, CA: Westernlore Press, 1960.

———. *Custer Battlefield: A History and Guide to the Battle of the Little Big Horn.* Handbook 132. Washington, D.C.: National Park Service, 1988.

————. *Frontier Regulars: The United States Army and the Indian 1866–1891.* New York: Macmillan Publishing, 1973.

————. *The Lance and the Shield: The Life and Times of Sitting Bull.* New York: Henry Holt & Company, 1993.

————. *The Last Days of the Sioux Nation.* New Haven, CT: Yale University Press, 1963.

————. "Sitting Bull." *Greasy Grass* 10, no. 4 (May 1994): 2–7.

————, ed. *The Reno Court: The Chicago Times Account.* Ft. Collins, CO: Old Army Press, 1983.

Van de Water, Frederic. *Glory Hunter: A Life of General Custer.* Indianapolis: Bobbs-Merrill, 1934. Reprint, Lincoln: University of Nebraska Press, 1988.

Vaughn, J. W. *Indian Fights: New Facts on Seven Encounters.* Norman: University of Oklahoma Press, 1966.

Vestal, Stanley. "The Man Who Killed Custer." *American Heritage* 8 (February 1957): 6–9, 90–91.

————. *Warpath: The True Story of the Fighting Sioux Told in a Biography of Chief White Bull.* Boston: Houghton-Mifflin, 1934. Reprint, Lincoln: University of Nebraska Press, 1984.

Walker, Judson Elliott. *Campaigns of General Custer in the Northwest, and the Final Surrender of Sitting Bull.* New York: Promontory Press, 1881.

Ward, Andrew. "The Little Bighorn." *American Heritage* 43, no. 2 (April 1992): 76–86.

Weibert, Don. *Custer, Cases and Cartridges: The Weibert Collection Analyzed.* Billings, MT: Author, 1989.

Weibert, Henry, and Don Weibert. *Sixty-Six Years in Custer's Shadow.* Billings, MT: Falcon Press Publishing, 1985.

Welch, James, with Paul Stekler. *Killing Custer: The Battle of the Little Bighorn and the Fate of the Plains Indians.* New York: W. W. Norton, 1994.

Wells, Wayne. "The Fight on Calhoun Hill." 2nd Annual Symposium. Custer Battlefield Historical & Museum Association, Hardin, MT, 1988.

————. "Little Big Horn Notes: Stanley Vestal's Indian Insights." *Greasy Grass* 5 (May 1989): 9–19.

Wilke, Lynn H. "A Sight Picture: Paint and Feathers." *Newsletter.* Little Bighorn Associates 28, no. 5 (July 1994): 4–6.

Willert, James. *Bourke's Diary from Journals of 1st Lt. John Gregory Bourke June 27–September 15, 1876.* La Mirada, CA: Author, 1986.

Yellow Nose. "Yellow Nose Tells of Custer's Last Stand." *Bighorn Yellowstone Journal* 1, no. 3 (summer 1992): 14–17.

Zimmerman, Barbara. "Mo-nah-se-tah: Fact or Fiction?" 4th Annual Symposium. Custer Battlefield Historical & Museum Association, Hardin, MT, 1990.

Unpublished Sources

Cartwright, R. G., to E. S. Luce, Crow Agency, MT., July 25, 1946. TL photocopy. Civil Reference, National Park Service, Record Group 79. National Archives, Washington, D.C.

Correspondence of Edward S. Luce, R. G. Cartwright, Elwood Nye, Charles F. Roe, and Owen J. Sweet, Little Bighorn Battlefield National Monument. Hardin, MT.

George Bird Grinnell Manuscript Collection, Braun Research Library, Southwest Museum. Los Angeles, California.

J. A. Blummer Manuscript. Little Bighorn Battlefield National Monument. Civil Reference Branch, National Park Service, Record Group 79. National Archives, Washington, D.C.

Luce, E. S., Crow Agency, MT, to Regional Director, National Park Service, August 14, 1946. TL, photocopy. Civil Reference, National Park Service, Record Group 79. National Archives, Washington, D.C.

Walter Mason Camp Collection, Harold B. Lee Library, Brigham Young University. Provo, Utah.

Walter M. Camp Manuscripts, Lilly Library, Indiana University. Bloomington, Indiana.

Walter M. Camp Notes, Ellison Collection, Denver Public Library. Denver, Colorado.

Walter S. Campbell Collection, University of Oklahoma Library. Norman, Oklahoma.

INDEX